Foundations
of Critical Thinking

Foundations
of Critical Thinking

Royce P. Jones
Illinois College

HARCOURT COLLEGE PUBLISHERS

Fort Worth   Philadelphia   San Diego   New York   Austin   Orlando
San Antonio   Toronto   Montreal   London   Sydney   Tokyo

Publisher	Earl McPeek
Executive Editor	David Tatom
Market Strategist	Adrienne Krysiuk
Developmental Editor	Cathlynn Richard
Project Editor	Rebecca Dodson
Art Director	Susan Journey
Production Manager	Serena Sipho

Cover credit Copyright © 2001 PhotoDisc

ISBN: 0-15-507275-7
Library of Congress Catalog Card Number: 99-85936

Address for Domestic Orders
Harcourt, Inc., 6277 Sea Harbor Drive, Orlando, FL 32887-6777
800-782-4479

Address for International Orders
International Customer Service
Harcourt, Inc., 6277 Sea Harbor Drive, Orlando, FL 32887-6777
407-345-3800
(fax) 407-345-4060
(e-mail) hbintl@harcourtbrace.com

Address for Editorial Correspondence
Harcourt College Publishers, 301 Commerce Street, Suite 3700, Fort Worth, TX 76102

Web Site Address
http://www.harcourtcollege.com

Printed in the United States of America

0 1 2 3 4 5 6 7 8 9 039 9 8 7 6 5 4 3 2 1

Harcourt College Publishers

Preface

This text provides an introduction to critical thinking, or the systematic attempt to make the best judgment possible on available evidence. While people have thought critically for centuries, critical thinking as an area of inquiry is a relatively recent phenomenon, and not one that is limited to a single discipline within the academy. For this reason, it is important that a writer of a critical thinking text explain his or her approach to the subject.

I treat the subject of critical thinking as a development of informal logic, or that branch of the science of logic that is concerned with the content and context of arguments rather than their form. This branch of logic has existed for a long time as a miscellaneous assortment of important insights concerning (1) the relevance of premises to conclusions, (2) the adequacy of certain kinds of support for conclusions, (3) errors arising from a misuse of language, and (4) the distinction between factual disputes and those arising from verbal misunderstandings. In this text, I examine these topics from the perspective of practical everyday reasoning.

It is a commonplace of logic that every argument has one or more premises and a conclusion, and that the conclusions of good arguments are tied securely to their premisses, like parachutists attached to the umbrella of protection above them. The conclusions of good arguments have a real connection to their premises and are supported by them. As an aid to understanding this, Chapter 1 introduces the terms and distinctions of formal and informal logic which are essential to an examination of arguments. Argument evaluation, with special reference to the relevance and adequacy of premises to conclusions, is examined in Chapter 2. Problems of language that impede critical thinking are considered in Chapter 3. The traditional informal fallacies are introduced in several chapters rather than one, in order to present them in contexts in which they typically emerge and enable students to practice recognizing them. See Chapters 3, 4, 5, 7, and 11 for discussions of the informal fallacies. Also, see Appendix III for extra exercises on the fallacies.

Since much thinking, critical and otherwise, is prompted by disputes, Chapter 9 presents a classification of disputes, and extended exercises in dispute analysis and resolution can be found in Chapters 10 and 11. The basics of traditional and modern formal logic are covered in Chapters 12, 13, and 14. I assume the Boolean interpretation of existential import in Chapter 12, which makes it possible to present Venn diagrams without the emendations required to make them work on the traditional Aristotelian interpretation. Predicate logic falls beyond the scope of the text, but Chapters 13 and 14 introduce proofs of validity and invalidity in propositional logic.

A table of writing exercises is found at the end of Appendix I, as well as in the Instructors Manual. Appendix II is included for instructors who wish to examine definitions. In my classes, I sometimes introduce the material in this appendix after the material in Chapter 3.

This text is supported both by an Instructor's Manual and a Web site. The Instructor's Manual contains solutions to text exercises and class presentation suggestions, and the Web site contains student exercises for every chapter in the text as well as information of interest to instructors. The Web site can be accessed at http://www.harcourtcollege. com. Instructors should contact their local Harcourt sales representative for instructions on accessing the instructors' portion of the Web site. Those who do not know the name of their local representative should visit the Rep Locator service on the Web at http://www. harcourtcollege.com/eservice/salesrep/index.html or call the Harcourt Customer Services department at 800-544-6678.

ACKNOWLEDGMENTS

I am very much indebted to Albert B. Randall, Peter Wenz, and Holly Martin for helpful and encouraging written comments. Expressions of appreciation are also due to George Agich, Harry Berman, Gershon Grunfeld, Richard Palmer, and Eric Springsted, participants in a philosophy discussion group from which I draw great inspiration. For her informed and insightful comments, I thank Victoria Graves. For his help with research, I thank W. Michael Westbrook. For continuing encouragement in my work, I thank James E. Davis. These students in my introductory logic and critical thinking class kindly offered me comments on the text: Brittany Cronister, Kim Koehne, Seth Richards, and Scott Stewart. Shannon M. Irlam, Cassandra E. O'Connor, Debra J. Neathery, and Lois J. Taylor assisted me in reading the page proofs of the manuscript, but are not to blame for any remaining errors.

At Harcourt College Publishers, I express my appreciation to David Tatom for his kindness and clear vision for the text. I am indebted to Cathy Richard, who brought both her good spirit and her skills as a writer to the process of development and revision. I am also indebted to Brenda Whitfield, whose professional and technical skills are evident in the Web page she developed for the text. For her diligent efforts in guiding the manuscript through the production process, I thank Rebecca Dodson.

The following reviewers of various drafts of the manuscript are offered sincere appreciation: Craig Bach, Drexel University; Dasiea Cavers-Huff, Riverside Community College; Mario Morelli, Western Illinois University; Albert Randall, Austin Peay State University; John E. Sallstrom, Georgia College and State University; and Ted Zenziger, Regis University.

Last, I particularly thank my wife, Rebecca Carnow Jones, who has seen portions of every draft of the text and whose ability in conversation to go straight to the heart of an issue has been an immeasurable help in making the narrative clearer than it otherwise would have been.

Brief Contents

Contents

CHAPTER 3

Terms   35

CHAPTER 4

Grounds of Inference I: Facts and Hypotheses   47

CHAPTER 5

Grounds of Inference II: Facts, Generalizations, and Principles   66

CHAPTER 9

The Subjects and Kinds of Disputes   134

CHAPTER 10

Negotiations and Resolutions   157

CHAPTER 14

Propositional Logic II: Determining Validity in Propositional Logic   249

APPENDIX I

Spotting Arguments and Writing Argumentative Essays   274

APPENDIX II

Achieving Clarity through Definitions   286

Introduction

CRITICAL THINKING AND AN OVERVIEW OF WHAT'S TO COME

Critical thinking is the attempt to make sound judgments without being distracted by irrelevant considerations. Unfortunately, we are not always at our best when called on to make decisions or evaluate evidence, and in some cases our own wishes and desires interfere with our better judgment. In other cases, there is nothing wrong with our judgment, but we are forced to deal with individuals who are more interested in getting their own way than in finding out what is fair, right, or true. The following cases illustrate these points.

THE CASE OF THE MISSING MONEY

Doris, a third-year law school student, lives in an old, frame, multifamily apartment house with several other tenants. Since bathroom and kitchen facilities are communal, she has become accustomed to meeting her fellow tenants in the hallway and seeing them at mealtimes. However, following several reports of money stolen from tenants' billfolds and purses, the meals have become occasions for angry and suspicious interchanges. As a result, Doris has decided to prepare her meals in the kitchen and eat in her room.

On Friday evening, Doris enters the kitchen to brew a pot of tea and finds Rick, a tenant who shares a room with his brother Vick, eating a frozen dinner. They exchange pleasantries, with Doris saying that she's just seen Vick down the hallway, and Rick saying that Vick is going out for the evening. As Doris fills her teapot, George, another tenant, storms into the kitchen, saying, "I've been robbed! I can't believe it! I'm sure my door was locked, but when I returned from the shower, fifty dollars was missing from my billfold!"

Doris wheels around from the stove to face George, who is still clad in his bathrobe. "Just now?" she asks. "You were robbed just now?"

"Yes," says George, running his hand through his hair in frustration and disappointment. "I wasn't out of my room for more than ten minutes, but when I got back, my money was gone."

"Oh, my goodness," says Doris, placing her hand to her chin and looking at Rick, her black eyes large with nervous wonder. "I told you I just saw Vick. It was not five minutes ago, and he was standing outside George's door, stuffing bills into his pocket. I didn't think anything about it at the time. I thought that he was just . . . "

Rick's reaction to these words is instantaneous. He springs to his feet, throws his fork into his frozen dinner, and screams, "You're accusing my brother of being a thief? Why, you little twit! If you had a life of your own, you wouldn't go around sticking your nose into other people's business. I've a good mind to . . . "

At this, George holds up his hand and says, "Hold on, Rick. I'm the one who lost some money, not you, and I appreciate Doris saying what she knows." His tone is noticeably firm.

In response, Rick glances back and forth between George and Doris, his face contorted with anger. Finally, with an obvious effort at self-control, he shakes a finger at Doris, says "I warn you," and storms out of the room.

When Rick is gone, George says "Rick forgot his fork" in an attempt to make light of the situation, but Doris, who is shaken by Rick's response, doesn't hear him.

In this case, Rick is not thinking clearly or critically. Although his strong feelings for his brother are understandable, perhaps he will realize in a cooler moment that he overreacted. Doris's disclosure was prompted not by malice, but by her realization that she had been in the hallway within moments of the time the crime was committed. Perhaps Rick will also realize that due to the circumstances that exist in the house, any lead—even those involving his brother and himself—must be pursued. **In thinking critically, we do not struggle to become unfeeling or emotionless persons, but rather to make judgments in which our feelings and emotions are directed to their proper objects and are consequently aids rather than impediments to our judgment.**

THE CASE OF THE CONTRACT NEGOTIATION

Shortly after graduating from law school and passing the bar exam in her state, Doris is hired by AJZ, a corporation located in a major southern city in the United States. She is one of two attorneys in the corporation. The other attorney is a seasoned veteran of many contract negotiations, but the day before he is to begin negotiations on an important contract with the city he has a heart attack and is hospitalized. Doris is assigned to take his place in the negotiations. She has been on the job for only one week.

The contract sent by the city for AJZ to examine and approve is for the renovation of the interior of several older city-owned buildings. The buildings are to be rebuilt from the inside out, with provisions made for handicapped access, elevators, and conduits for the installation of modern communication devices, such as computers and in-house television. Doris studies the contract late into the night and discovers clauses which state that AJZ warrants that the exterior surfaces of the buildings in question are in no need of repair and that, in addition, AJZ waives its right to sue the city. Doris is shocked by these clauses.

The next day Doris calls the office of Sam Abrams, an experienced attorney who is handling negotiations on the contract for the city. Abrams is in the inner circle of the mayor's political associates and is very powerful. Doris is referred to the secretary of one of Abrams's assistants. She asks that Abrams call her concerning the contract. He doesn't. She calls back repeatedly over the next five days but gets no response. With only twenty-four hours to go before the deadline for signing the contract, she finally gets through to Abrams. She explains that AJZ was not asked to examine the exterior of the buildings and therefore cannot warrant that they are in no need of repair. When she adds that she cannot allow her corporation to sign away its right to sue the city, Abrams says, "What do you mean? No one's ever questioned these clauses before. Who are you, anyway? Those clauses are standard in city contracts. Either AJZ signs the contract or we find someone else to do the work."

Doris sits alone at her desk for some moments after Abrams slams down the receiver. "It's going to be a long week," she mutters to herself with a sigh.

In this case, Doris is forced to negotiate with Sam Abrams, an individual who cites an irrelevant consideration in favor of the clause in the contract that he has sent to her. The fact that the clause has appeared in previous contracts is no indication that it should be in the present contract. It is even possible that the clause was out of place or inappropriate in the previous contracts in which it appeared. Abrams is not thinking critically and probably has no interest in doing so. What, however, is critical thinking?

Critical thinking **is the activity in which you attempt to form or evaluate judgments with the aid of relevant and reliable considerations.** It's sometimes not easy to know what's relevant and reliable, so figuring that out is a part of critical thinking, too. In critical thinking you also apply criteria and principles to particular cases, and when someone offers a judgment out of the blue without any support for it, you have to be able to look through the clouds for unidentified criteria or principles that might be flown in to defend it. In addition, critical thinking requires an ability to determine the implications of facts and assertions.

A critical thinker is a person who does his or her best to make sound judgments and occasionally succeeds. You don't have to be a genius to do this, but **to be a critical thinker you should develop some specific practices:**

- Gather and sift through the information that seems to be needed to make the judgment.
- Be patient when the information doesn't make sense or seems to be absurd or stupid.
- Reexamine previous judgments and revise them when new information becomes available or when you find that you've begun to look at the old information in a new way. Persistence in continuing to hold to a judgment is a virtue only so long as a preponderance of evidence continues to indicate that it is true or wise.
- Be aware of your own fallibility. Even people who exercise due care in coming to judgments sometimes make mistakes.

It is helpful in contemplating this last point to remember that even if we as critical thinkers were infallible, or nearly so, in our power to make judgments, we would still discover, on later inspection, that some of our judgments were either false or unwise. This would be the case since many, if not most, of our judgments are unavoidably based on evidence that is incomplete. Sometimes, it is simply impossible for us to get all of the information that we would like to have or that would be helpful to us to have in coming to a decision. Remembering this, **our goals in critical thinking should simply be to make the best judgment possible on available evidence and to recognize when we lack the evidence we need to make a decision.**

When our judgments turn out to have been incorrect or unwise, we go through a period of reflection in which we evaluate ourselves. Especially if our error or foolish judgment affects us personally, we may find that we are upset with ourselves. If we made our judgment without considering all the available evidence—a "snap" judgment, as it's called—perhaps we *should* be upset with ourselves. But if we considered all relevant available evidence in coming to our judgment, we have no reason to be angry at ourselves for the conclusion we drew. However, even though we have no reason to berate ourselves for our previous judgment, in evaluating our judgment-making ability we are likely to end up thinking of ourselves as being more inept than we actually are if we do not carefully distinguish what we know now from what we knew at the time we made the judgment. If our judgment was based on the relevant evidence available at the time, then the evidence we have now that clearly indicates that our judgment was incorrect or unwise could not have been a factor in making it. In evaluating our judgments and our judgment-making capacity, we should accordingly make every attempt to separate what we know now from what we did not know and could not have known when we made our judgment, even though it may not always be simple to recapture the conditions under which our judgment was originally made.

As a critical thinker, you must be ready to stand your ground when you've considered an issue and come to a judgment that seems correct to you. Many people hold to their beliefs just because other people believe them, but **critical thinkers do their own thinking. They're willing to risk the disapproval of others if the judgments they come to are unpopular.**

In **the first stage of the development of critical thinking,** people often assume that their judgments are always right on the mark and that their critical thinking skills don't need to be improved. This is among the greatest dangers to critical thinking. People in **the second stage** recognize that they sometimes make poor choices and often assume as a result that when they don't think what someone else thinks that they must be wrong and the other person right. Those who have passed this stage and entered **the third stage** direct their attention to the considerations that would be relevant to making a sound judgment and consider that it is these—rather than the personalities, fame, reputations, or power of those deliberating—that are of primary concern.

There are no simple recipes for becoming a critical thinker, but making the attempt is well worth the effort. No one *knowingly* thinks in an uncritical manner or makes unfounded and misguided judgments any more than one *knowingly* buys a carton of rotten eggs. If you want to improve your judgment, this text can probably help you.

AN OVERVIEW OF WHAT'S TO COME

You may be wondering whether you'll get along well with this text. I can't answer that question, since I don't know who you are, but I *can* tell you that my students' comments on previous drafts of this text pointed me to those passages where I flew off too far into the ozone, and that that enabled me to eliminate the pain-causing sections. So be comforted by that.

You may also be wondering whether you have a talent for critical thinking. That's something worth thinking about. After one of my students came to me and said, "I'm just not logical," I found myself wondering if critical thinking is like other things: Do some people have a natural talent for it while others have to struggle to learn it? As a guitar player, I've noticed that some musicians have an uncanny ear for a melody and an unerring sense of rhythm and time, while others don't. Do some people have an uncanny ear for making and defending judgments, while others don't? I don't know, but I'm convinced that **critical thinking can be learned** and that even people with talent can improve their thinking through practice. I'll say something more about the matter of practice later, but first let me tell you how I came to write this text, and lay its overall plan before you.

You're familiar with the term *grounds,* no doubt. We hear attorneys, for example, speak of *grounds for divorce.* These grounds are the foundation, or support, for the divorce action. When we defend our judgments—either in court or out, and either to ourselves or to someone else—we rely on grounds. One cool autumn day I decided to catalog all the grounds I found people using, just to find out how many kinds there are.

That's how this text got started. After several years of observing the way people defend their inferences or judgments, I concluded that there are at least five grounds:

- Facts
- Generalizations
- Principles
- Analogies
- Criteria

You'll come to have a good understanding of these grounds after reading Chapters 4, 5, 6, 7, and 8.

The rest of the text grew from reflections prompted by my analysis of these grounds. After cataloging the grounds, I asked myself where we usually go wrong in using them. The answer I eventually got is that we take one or the other of them to be true in a particular case when it isn't, or to be relevant when it isn't, or to be adequate to support our case when it isn't. I am convinced that **the majority of our difficulties in critical thinking can be traced back to problems of truth, relevance, and adequacy.** Accordingly, Chapter 2 focuses on truth, relevance, and adequacy in connection with the process of distinguishing between good and bad arguments. Like people you meet your first day on campus and run into again the rest of the school year, you'll encounter the problems of truth, relevance, and adequacy throughout this text. Look for them. Just as the people you meet dress in different clothes from day to day, the problems of truth, relevance, and adequacy appear in different guises from one kind of argument to another, so you'll need to learn to recognize them despite their different appearances.

After considering the ways in which we go wrong in using the grounds of inference, we'll see that much of our critical thinking occurs in response to perplexing or problematic situations. Chapter 4 discusses the process of forming hypotheses in attempting to solve problems.

When I reached this stage, I realized that I'd been thinking all along about the solitary individual attempting to come to correct judgments in particular situations, but that in many cases, we find ourselves in opposition to others in disputes. This circumstance raises so many important considerations for critical thinking that three chapters—Chapters 9, 10, and 11—are needed to distinguish different kinds of disputes, separate negotiable from nonnegotiable issues, and identify tactical maneuvers.

Finally, as I thought back over all I'd done, I realized that throughout the process I'd been using and relying on the terms and technical distinctions of the science of logic without thinking too much about it. This made me realize that none of us think alone. We rely on a long history of work in logic. We can't avoid words like *true, false, argument, conclusion, valid,* and many other terms of logic, and we can't avoid the distinctions hammered out by logicians over many years. This being the case, I decided that logic would have to provide the shell of my text. Chapter 1, therefore, provides an introduction to arguments. That gives us a common vocabulary that we will use throughout the text. Chapter 3 follows up on this concept with a consideration of terms, since these are the bricks with which we build our houses of thought. Last, in Chapters 12, 13, and 14, we put the roof on the house by examining traditional and modern techniques for determining the validity of arguments.

If critical thinking is anything like playing a musical instrument, it has to be practiced. No one ever becomes a great guitarist without picking up a guitar and playing it hour after hour, and no one ever becomes a critical thinker without working at it long and hard. In the following chapters, we consider many kinds of situations that require critical thinking. As you work your way through each chapter, attempt to apply the material to situations in which you find yourself or to those that you witness. In that way, you can form habits of critical thinking that will serve you in good stead.

A LOOK AHEAD

In this Introduction, we have explained what we mean by *critical thinking* and provided a brief overview of the text. Chapter 1 concentrates on the elements and kinds of arguments and introduces these key terms which are used throughout the remainder of the text: *proposition, premiss, conclusion, implication,* and *inference.*

Exercises

Answer the following questions.

1. How is critical thinking defined?
2. What does an individual have to be willing to do in order to be a critical thinker?
3. Should critical thinkers be unfeeling or emotionless persons?
4. What is the chief obstacle to becoming a critical thinker?
5. What three stages in the development of critical thinking skills are outlined in this introduction?
6. The majority of our difficulties in critical thinking can be traced to what three problems?
7. Case questions.

    A. In "The Case of the Missing Money," Doris tells Rick and George that she has seen Rick's brother Vick outside George's door stuffing money into his pocket, and Rick becomes enraged, refusing to believe that Doris is telling the truth. As a critical thinker attempting to make the best judgment possible on available evidence, what would you advise Doris to do following this incident?

    B. In "The Case of the Contract Negotiation," Doris must decide how to deal with Sam Abrams's demand. Critical thinkers should be willing to risk the disapproval of others if their judgments are unpopular, but should Doris insist on changes in the contract even if this means losing it? What would you do if you were in her situation?

Chapter 1

———●———

INTRODUCTION TO ARGUMENTS

In this chapter, we define *logic* and investigate the elements of arguments. We also distinguish arguments from explanations and justifications. This prepares us for a discussion of the evaluation of arguments in Chapter 2.

———●———

ARTHUR'S OLD-FASHIONED REGISTRATION

The central computer system broke down the night before Arthur was to register as a first-semester freshman. Acting quickly to prevent a delay in the registration process, the dean had long tables set up in the gym and commandeered secretaries from all over campus to fill out forms and collect fees.

Arthur was in line by 8 A.M., but still the line of students ahead of him stretched half way around the gym. By 9:30, the temperature had risen to eighty degrees. Without thinking much about it, Arthur fanned himself with his registration packet and looked around aimlessly. His mind had wandered off, so he started slightly when the young woman in front of him turned around and said, "Excuse me, but do you have a pen I could borrow? I left mine in the dorm."

"Sure," said Arthur. He pulled out a pen and passed it to the young woman.

"Thanks. I'm going to fill out my schedule of classes. Might as well do something while I'm waiting."

"Right," said Arthur. "What are you taking?"

"English literature, American history, biology, communications, and logic."

"Logic? I wouldn't do very well in that. I'm not very logical."

"You might be surprised. My roommate thought the same thing, but she took the course last year and got an A in it."

"Well, what's it all about? By the way, my name's Arthur."

"I'm Gail, and my roomie says it's about arguments."

"I don't like arguments; I'm a peace-loving sort of guy."

"No, not arguments like fighting with someone; arguments like proving something."

"Hm. That's interesting. Could you give me an example?"

"Yes, I can," Gail replied after some thought. "Last night my roomie and I went out for a hamburger. I ordered lettuce, tomato, pickle, and mustard on mine, but they left off the tomato, so I went back to the cashier and told her about it. 'We're out of tomatoes,' she said. 'Well, give me onions,' I said. 'All right, but that'll be forty-five cents extra,' she said. 'No, it won't,' I said. 'Those onions aren't extra; they're to replace the tomato I've already paid for.' Well, the cashier shook her head no to that, but the manager, who'd overheard us, came over and told the cashier to give me some onions; so I got onions."

Arthur scratched his head. "I thought you said the arguments weren't like fights with someone."

"Oh, I wasn't thinking about that. I guess I did have a fight with the cashier, but what I was getting at was that I gave her a reason to give me some onions. In arguments you give reasons for something."

"Well, you didn't convince the cashier."

"No, but still I gave her a reason. An argument doesn't cease to be an argument just because someone doesn't accept it."

Arthur became reflective. "I suppose some arguments would be better than others at that. What I mean is, some reasons someone might give you might not be good enough to make you accept what they say."

"That's the idea," said Gail, who a moment before had absent-mindedly slipped Arthur's pen into her purse. "In fact, separating good arguments from bad ones is a huge part of what logic is all about."

"Say, you seem to know a lot about logic, not to have had the course," Arthur observed.

"My roomie talked about it all the time, and I even read a part of her text," Gail explained.

It had never occurred to Arthur to read a text for a course he wasn't taking. He didn't dwell on the point, however, for he and Gail had reached the registration table, and she was about to turn away. "Say," he said, "I've enjoyed talking to you. How about going out to dinner tonight? We could maybe take in a movie afterward."

"No," Gail said.

"No?" Arthur responded with some surprise.

"That's right; no."

"But why?" Arthur asked.

"I don't have to have a reason for saying no," Gail said, turning away. "There are some things you don't have to have a reason for."

That didn't sound very logical to Arthur, but he signed up for logic anyway—after borrowing a pen from the student behind him.

THE ELEMENTS OF ARGUMENTS

Logic is the science that consists in the description and evaluation of arguments. Though we may not always focus our attention on them, we encounter arguments in almost every circumstance of our daily lives. They are present in our casual conversations, the books and magazines we read, and the videos we watch. They occur in bedrooms, boardrooms, and courtrooms, and in the halls of universities as well as the corridors of power. Arguments are as pervasive as the music in shopping malls, but unlike such music, we ignore them to our own detriment; for they are instruments that assist us in determining whether proposals for our beliefs are likely to be true.

In an **argument,** something is set forth as unproblematic, or at least as something that can be taken for granted for the present, and that in turn is said to lead to something else that ought to be accepted. In her example of an argument, Gail took it for granted that she had paid for tomatoes on her hamburger and that a person ought to receive whatever he or she has paid for. On these assumptions, it seemed to her that she ought to be given some tomatoes. The connection between what she took for granted and what she took to follow from what she took for granted seemed to her to be very strong. Her assumptions seemed to support her demand for tomatoes. The purpose of logic is to distinguish between those arguments in which there is a strong connection between what is taken for granted, and what is supposed to follow from that, and those in which the connection is weak or nonexistent. Those arguments in which there is a strong connection are good; those in which the connection is weak or nonexistent are bad.

Before we can set forth criteria for distinguishing good arguments from bad ones, we must set forth the elements that all arguments, good or bad, will have. **Every argument is made up of assertions that have truth value or, in other words, of assertions that are either true or false.** These assertions are referred to either as *statements* or as **propositions,** though in this text we use the second term more than the first. Propositions are not the declarative sentences in which they are found; rather they are the meanings of those sentences. This suggests that a particular proposition may be expressed in more than one formulation in a language or in more than one language. In addition, propositions can contain propositions as component parts. "Alice is elected president and Zelda is elected secretary" is an example. "Alice is elected president" and "Zelda is elected secretary" are component parts in the example. They are called *simple propositions,* since they contain no other propositions as parts. The example proposition taken as a whole is a *compound proposition,* or one that contains two or more simple propositions as parts.

Propositions differ from nonsense utterances, and from questions, commands, requests, and exclamations. Observe the following sentences:

1. No human infants are able to walk without assistance before the age of six months.
2. Will you accompany me to the concert?
3. Shut that window!
4. I wish that I could paint and draw like the great masters.

The first of the preceding sentences is a proposition. The claim made in the sentence is either true or false. A question is found in the second sentence. A proper response to it is yes, no, or maybe. It would probably never occur to someone to tell the person who asked the question that his or her question was false or true. Such a response, if it did occur, would betray a lack of understanding as to the job that questions perform in communication. Similarly, commands, such as that found in the third sentence, would not be thought of as being true or false. Commands can be appropriate or inappropriate, or convenient or inconvenient, but they have no truth value.

Some sentences contain expressions of wish or desire. The fourth sentence is an example. Is it a proposition? Hopes, fears, desires, and so forth are in themselves neither true nor false. A hope may be either capable of realization or vain, a fear well founded or groundless, and a desire wise or foolish, innocent or licentious. However, the fourth sentence is a proposition, since it is either true or false that the person making the statement has the expressed wish.

PREMISSES AND CONCLUSIONS

Let us examine the way in which propositions can enter into arguments. If a proposition expresses something that is taken for granted or assumed to be true in the argument, it functions as a **premiss.** If a proposition expresses that to which the assumption, or premiss, is supposed to lead, it functions as the **conclusion. The premisses of an argument lend support to, or provide evidence for, the conclusion. The conclusion is that which is asserted to be proved by the premisses. Arguments can, and often do, have more than one premiss, but for any particular argument there is only one conclusion.**

Unless it can be determined whether a proposition in an argument is the one that is being proved (the conclusion) or one that is supposed to do the proving (a premiss), it is impossible to know what the argument is. In some cases, the argument that is intended can only be determined from the context in which it is expressed.

BRANDON SWEENEY HEARS A COMPLAINT

There was a knock at the door of Brandon Sweeney, dorm counselor. "Come in!" he shouted in a gruff voice. In a moment the door slowly opened, and a young man of medium build entered. His shoulders were slightly stooped. "Oh, hello, Arthur. What's up?"

"Oh, er, nothing. I just thought I'd stop by."

"Well, that's nice, but I was just about to go out; so if you don't mind, maybe . . ."

"Actually, there is something. It's Mike."

"Mike?" There was an element of surprise in Brandon's voice, but it was due not to the fact that Arthur had referred to Mike but rather to the fact that Arthur had cut him off in mid-sentence. Brandon expected the men in his wing of the dorm to listen to him when he spoke, and his expectations were usually realized. "What about Mike?" he asked. His voice betrayed his annoyance.

"Well, Mike's all right, I guess, but . . . " Arthur's voice trailed off.

"But what?" Brandon demanded.

"But, well, Mike's a smoker, and I'd hoped to be placed with a nonsmoker. I don't smoke myself, and I'm somewhat allergic to cigarette smoke. My room application did state a preference for a nonsmoker."

"Yeah, I know, but we didn't have enough nonsmokers to go around. Maybe next semester we can do better."

"There's also his messiness," Arthur went on. "Mike throws his clothes on the floor and even piles them on my desk."

"Then tell him not to do that."

"I have, but it doesn't do any good."

"Things are rough all over. You'll have to learn to adapt if you expect to make it in college."

"I understand that, but I'm very unhappy. Perhaps I could put up with the smoke and the mess, but there are times when I'm even a little uncomfortable about going into the room."

"Why would you be uncomfortable? It's your room."

"It's my room, but Mike's girl is usually there, and I get the feeling they'd rather be alone."

"Mike's girl. You mean Gail?"

"Yes."

"Well, look, there's nothing wrong with guys having girlfriends."

"Of course not, but that's not the point. The point is that your room is supposed to be a place where you can go anytime you want to and be left alone if you want to be left alone."

"Well, the dorm rules allow the men to have women in their rooms during specified hours. Are you asking to be moved to another room when one is available?"

"No."

"What, then? Do you want me to kick Mike out of the dorm? I can't, you know."

"No, I don't want you to kick Mike out of the dorm."

"Well, what on earth do you want?"

"I came to tell you that I'm moving out of the dorm and that I want my room deposit back."

"Oh," said Brandon. "Well, there are problems with that, too."

"I expect you to solve those problems and get my deposit," said Arthur, walking to the door.

"Hey, where do you think you're going?"

"I'm going to pack," said Arthur over his shoulder.

Brandon stared at the door for some moments after Arthur closed it behind him.

There is an argument in this dialogue, though it might be described as incipient since Arthur leaves much of the work of piecing it together to Brandon. At first, Brandon has to determine what Arthur wants, or what he is getting at. He does this by asking him whether he wants to be moved or to have Mike kicked out of the dorm. Finally, Arthur tells him that he is moving out of the dorm and that he wants his room deposit returned. That is the twofold conclusion to which Arthur's remarks were leading.

As Brandon stares at his door following Arthur's departure, he is able to recall the premisses, or supporting considerations, which Arthur deftly presented. Those premisses are as follows:

- Arthur's request to be placed with a nonsmoker had not been honored.
- Arthur was allergic to cigarette smoke.
- Mike would not cooperate with Arthur in keeping the room clean.
- Mike made the atmosphere in the room uncomfortable by leaving his clothes on Arthur's desk and by bringing his girlfriend to the room.

Premiss Indicators

Since, as, inasmuch as, because, for, for the reason that, having established that, in the light of this evidence, in view of the fact that, given that

Conclusion Indicators

Therefore, accordingly, ergo, hence, it follows that, it may be inferred that, so, the inescapable conclusion is that, thus, thus is it proved that, thus we have no alternative but to conclude that

Indicators That Introduce Both a Premiss and a Conclusion

From this it follows that, from this it may be inferred that, this implies that, this entails that, this strongly suggests that

These four premisses provided the supporting evidence for Arthur's conclusion that he was justified in moving out of the dorm and demanding a return of his room deposit.

As the dialogue illustrates, in some cases the nature and content of an argument cannot be determined apart from the situation in which it is expressed. In other cases, however, arguments contain indicator words, which make it possible to identify the premiss, or premisses, and the conclusion with some degree of accuracy.

Several of the premiss and conclusion indicators end with the word *that*. Although there are exceptions, the word *that* usually introduces a proposition. In each of the indicators that introduce both a premiss and a conclusion, *this* refers back to the premiss, whereas *that* refers forward to the conclusion.

Premiss and conclusion indicators are not infallible guides. *Because,* for example, might introduce not a premiss to an argument but an explanation for a statement or action. However, when an argument is stated apart from any particular context, it might not be possible to identify premisses and conclusion without indicators.

IMPLICATION AND INFERENCE

We've observed that arguments are made up of propositions. However, they are not simply lists or inventories of propositions. Were we to open the drawer of a secretary's desk, we might find glue, pencils, pens, paper clips, scissors, stamps, and string. Other than their being located in the drawer, these items would bear no special relationship to one another. They would simply be so many items. Similarly, propositions listed one after another would not be an argument, but only so many propositions. For them to be an argument, they would have to be related to one another in a particular way. How would they have to be related?

We have said that the propositions that function as premises in an argument provide evidence, or support, for the truth of the proposition that serves as the conclusion. The conclusion is said to be supported by, or proved by, the premises. **When premisses do in fact have some bearing on the truth of a conclusion, they are said to *imply* the conclusion. When the conclusion is in fact supported by the premisses, it is said to be *implied by* the premisses. The relationship between premisses and conclusion in an argument, then, is one of *implication.***

Conclusions are implied by premisses, and premisses imply conclusions, but human beings *infer* that propositions imply, or are implied by, other propositions. When an individual draws an inference, that individual is reasoning. If human beings could not reason, the science of logic would never have been developed, but logicians do not describe the reasoning process as it actually occurs in human beings. Instead, they examine the outward evidence of reasoning, as indicated in the spoken or written word. The chief purpose of logic is to establish criteria by which it can be determined whether one proposition implies another.

ARGUMENTS, EXPLANATIONS, AND JUSTIFICATIONS

There is an important difference between arguments and explanations. Arguments function to prove their conclusions, but **explanations** function to clarify some obscure meaning or to show how some puzzling occurrence fits in with or follows from some preceding events. Meanings can often be explained through the use of illustrations or examples, which are kinds of explanations. It is sometimes said that one picture is worth a thousand words, but one can also explain by doing. Andres Segovia, the great classic guitarist, would play a passage of music in a particular way to show his students how it should be played. In this mode of instruction, the student could hear what Segovia wished to communicate regarding the desired technique or approach. The performance constituted an explanation by demonstration. The following case provides an example of another sort of explanation.

THE CASE OF THE FROZEN WATER

"I put two trays of water in the freezer at the same time," said George. "When I returned an hour later, the water in one of the trays was frozen, but the water in the other was not. Why was that?"

"Oh, that's easy," said Kathleen. "The freezing point of water is relative. Contrary to what you might think, the warmer the water the faster it will freeze. In the case you mention the water in one tray must have been warmer than the water in the other."

"Hm," said George with a reflective tug at his chin. "Come to think of it, I did fill one tray from the hot water faucet, the other from the cold."

Kathleen's response in this case is an attempt at explaining the matter that interests George. If it is correct, it is an explanation.

In some cases, explanations are intended not only to explain something but to justify it as well. This is particularly the case with human actions, as is illustrated by the following case.

THE GOOD SAMARITAN GOES HOME[1]

"Samuel, where have you been?" asked the Good Samaritan's wife. "I expected you yesterday."

"I'm sorry, Sarah. Let me wash the road dust off my feet and I'll explain."

Sarah watched her husband wash his feet, then handed him a towel. "Well?" she said when his feet were dry.

Samuel smiled and put his hand on his wife's shoulders. "I would have been here yesterday, but for the fact that I stopped to help a man on the road to Jericho."

"You thought that was more important than coming home?" asked Sarah. "Yesterday was our son Micah's birthday, and yesterday evening we were supposed to have dinner with the Bermans."

"I know, but the man had been attacked by robbers and beaten pretty badly. He was half dead. I just couldn't walk on by and leave him to suffer and maybe die, so I bound up his wounds as best I could and took him to an inn for the night."

"Oh," said Sarah. "I had no idea."

"Do you forgive me, then?"

"Of course, Samuel. You're a good Samaritan, you know. That's one reason I love you."

---

[1] The following dialogue is inspired by the Parable of the Good Samaritan, which is found in the New Testament in Luke 10:30–35, but it is entirely fanciful.

The case of the Good Samaritan differs in an important way from the frozen water case. We may need to explain why water freezes at a particular rate, but we don't need to *justify* its freezing. Water just freezes, that's all. By contrast, human actions need to be justified on occasion. When the Good Samaritan's wife asks him to explain his failure to return at the expected time, he tells her of the pressing need of the individual he found by the side of the road, and that not only explains his failure to return but justifies it as well, since it is an accepted moral principle that one individual should come to the aid of another who is in need.

The case of the Good Samaritan shows us that an explanation can also be a justification if it demonstrates that an individual is not blameworthy in his or her conduct and that the individual acted properly, sometimes despite initial appearances to the contrary. In offering justifications, however, individuals are not always attempting to demonstrate that they are not blameworthy. A judge, parent, or friend may justify a decision or action when there is no question of his or her having acted in a blameworthy manner. In general, **justifications** are simply considerations, facts, or reasons that are sufficient to establish the correctness of a judgment, decision, or action.

Summary

Arguments, which are described and evaluated in the science of logic, are made up of propositions. Unlike questions, commands, requests, and exclamations, propositions have **truth value.** In other words, they are either true or false.

Simple propositions contain no other propositions as component parts, but *compound* propositions do contain other propositions as component parts. This sentence contains one proposition and is therefore a simple proposition:

Geneva Bolen plays the piano.

This sentence contains two propositions and is therefore a compound proposition:

The author of this text has a dog and a cat.

The first proposition in this sentence is "The author of this text has a dog," and the second is "The author of this text has a cat." The two propositions are simple in that they contain no other propositions as component parts, but the proposition in which they are expressed is a compound proposition in that it contains them both. Some compound propositions contain more than two simple propositions, as we'll discover later.

Until a proposition forms a part of an argument, it is simply a freestanding assertion that is either true or false. When it appears in an argument, however, it serves either as a premiss or a conclusion. The function of the premiss is to provide evidence for the conclusion. The conclusion is the proposition that is asserted to be proved by the premiss(es). As it appeared earlier, "Geneva Bolen plays the piano" served as a freestanding proposition. In the following argument, however, it functions as a premiss:

Geneva Bolen plays the piano.
Therefore, she reads music.

The conclusion to this argument, as we see from the conclusion indicator word *therefore,* is "she reads music." A moment's reflection convinces us that we can't safely infer from the fact that Geneva Bolen plays the piano that she reads music, since a considerable number of people play musical instruments without being able to read music. However, even though it's not a very good one, the argument is still an argument, since it contains a proposition that functions as a premiss and one that functions as a conclusion.

In the second sentence of the preceding paragraph, we use the word *infer.* Inferring is a mental activity performed by human beings. *We* infer one proposition from another, but *premisses* "imply" conclusions, and conclusions are "implied by" premisses.

In an argument, an attempt is made to prove a conclusion. In an explanation, by contrast, an attempt is made to clarify a meaning or show how a puzzling event follows from other events. It is not necessary to prove that the puzzling phenomenon exists. That is apparent. It is in fact the existence of the puzzling phenomenon that spurs the quest for an explanation. Upon entering my kitchen, I discover a pool of water near one wall. How do I account for its presence? Is there a leak in the roof or the pipes leading to the sink? Has my dog splashed water from her water bowl or, worse, had an accident? I have an explanation for the presence of the pool of water if I can answer any of these questions affirmatively.

In human affairs, we sometimes distinguish between explanations and justifications. As George is waiting at a stoplight, a motorist strikes him from the rear, breaking his left taillight and bending his bumper. The motorist apologizes to George, saying, "I wouldn't have hit you, but there's a leak in my brake line and all I have is my hand brake." The leaky brake line explains why the motorist couldn't stop, but it doesn't show that the motorist is not blameworthy for knowingly driving with faulty brakes. In short, his explanation is not also a justification.

A LOOK AHEAD

In this chapter we have presented the elements of arguments but have said nothing about argument evaluation. The purpose of premisses is to provide supporting evidence for the conclusions of arguments, but how do we determine whether premisses, in fact, fulfill their purpose? How do we determine whether an argument is a good one? We take up these questions in Chapter 2.

Exercises

Answers to questions marked with an asterisk may be found in the back of the text.

I. Answer the following questions.

1. How many premisses can an argument have?
2. How many conclusions can an argument have?
3. Which of these words would not ordinarily be used to introduce a conclusion: *therefore, hence, because, it follows that.*
*4. Which of these words would not ordinarily be used to introduce a premiss: *since, inasmuch as, for these reasons, thus.*
5. What distinguishes arguments from lists or inventories of propositions?
6. What does it mean to say that a conclusion is "implied" by a premiss?
7. Explain the distinction between *implication* and *inference.*
8. What is the chief purpose of logic?
9. How do arguments and explanations differ from one another?
10. Can you provide an example of an explanation that is also a justification (or an attempted justification)?

II. Classify each of the following as a proposition, a question, a command, a request, or an exclamation. If a sentence contains an expression of a wish or desire, indicate that. If a sentence contains more than one proposition, indicate that.

1. Don't let your left hand know what your right hand is doing.
2. If you have not paid your library fines, your transcript will not be forwarded to you.
3. To know him is to love him.
*4. Let's get married.
5. I would like to visit another country.
6. Twin Oaks is neither a town nor a city.
7. What a place Twin Oaks is!
8. Your trunk is large, but mine is larger.
*9. How big is your trunk?
10. I must read Kant's collected works.

III. Each of the following passages contains at least one argument. Rewrite the passages, with the premiss (or premisses) coming first and the conclusion coming last. Draw a line under the conclusion in each argument.

1. Human beings lack the physical strength of some of the other animal species. However, Homo sapiens will always be the dominant species, since the level of intelligence of its members is greater than that of any other species.
2. Taxation consists in taking money from the rich to give to the poor, but if the poor are simply given money without having to work for it, they will have no incentive to seek employment. From this it follows that if we were to eliminate taxes we would eliminate both unemployment and poverty.
3. The right to property includes, among other things, the right to acquire and dispose of material possessions. For this reason, to eliminate the right to property would be to eliminate freedom.
*4. Federal environmental regulations would be unnecessary if everyone were willing to work for the common good. However, people, or most people, act in their own self-interest. That is quite all right, so long as the interest of one person is not the disadvantage of another. When it is, most people go ahead and act in their own interest anyway. That is why we have a polluted environment. One

group finds it can make money by manufacturing goods that pollute the streams and rivers, and members of this group go ahead and pollute without regard to the environment. Those people who didn't make money off the pollution suffer from the pollution, but they won't step in and clean it up. Why? Because it costs money, and they're not going to spend their money for someone else. That means that the federal government has to step in to see that it is done.

5. Karl Marx argued somewhat as follows: The goal of the political process is justice, but injustice exists wherever there are class distinctions. In a capitalist society, the class that owns the means of production is the dominant class and always acts in its own interest. The result is that the members of the other class, which is the working class, are slaves to their paychecks and are always at a disadvantage. This is unjust, for injustice consists in the domination of one class by another. To overcome this injustice, all class distinctions must be eliminated.

6. Pavlov surgically inserted a tube into the salivary gland of a dog. The tube drained into a jar, which collected the dog's saliva. When the dog was placed in a harness in a closed room and presented with food through a small door, with Pavlov and his assistants standing outside unseen, the dog salivated. This being no dog food commercial, but rather a serious scientific experiment, the salivation was called the *unconditioned response*.

   On several successive occasions, Pavlov turned on a light at the same time as he presented the dog with food. Of course the dog salivated. Finally, Pavlov turned on the light without presenting the dog with food, and it still salivated. This salivation was the *conditioned response*.

   This experiment suggests that the behavior of a canine can be changed or modified by changes in its environment. The experiment also suggests that changes in a canine's behavior can occur without the canine having done anything on its own to bring about the change, for it is highly unlikely that the dog made a conscious decision to salivate whenever the light came on. It is ludicrous to suppose that it reflected on its rather dull experience with the food and light and decided to take action on its own saying, "I don't need food to salivate; why, I can do that with just the light, and henceforth I will!" The most likely supposition is that the change in the dog's behavior took place without the dog even being aware of it.

IV. State the conclusion, or conclusions, defended in the following passages.

   1. If you pay for something, you ought to receive it. Gail paid for tomatoes on her hamburger. Therefore, she ought to receive tomatoes.
   2. I should be able to have a little peace and quiet in my dorm room, at least part of the time. It has been said that a person's home is his or her castle. That means that the home is a refuge for people. That is to say, it is a place where they can be alone or enjoy the company of family and friends. It is a place where they ought to be able to engage in pursuits that give them pleasure. What holds for the home holds for the dorm, I say.
   3. Whenever her husband is drinking, Mrs. Malthus is blue, and whenever he's sober, she's happy. Her husband must be sober now, because she's happy.

*4. These boards, which were glued together, have fallen apart. There is no evidence that force was applied to them, so their separation must be due to some other cause.

5. Under extreme heat, glue softens and gives way. These boards, which were glued together, have fallen apart. I find no evidence that force was applied to them. They must have been subjected to extreme heat at some time.

6. The American Indians roamed the area that is now the United States long before the arrival of Europeans, but they were gradually displaced from their land and overwhelmed by European technology. What was theirs by right of occupation was taken from them by force without provocation. Because of this, American Indians today deserve to be treated with respect.

7. The handwriting of medical doctors is nearly always illegible, but medical doctors make a lot of money. I don't see any need to practice penmanship.

8. As the twig is bent, so grows the tree. As the puppy is trained, so grows the dog. As the child is trained, so becomes the woman or man. This young man has been in trouble with the law on several occasions. The fault lies not with him, but with his parents.

*9. It is said that philosophy bakes no bread, so you shouldn't waste any time on it. By that reasoning, since you could never win a war with Congress fighting for you, you shouldn't waste your time on Congress.

10. The religion of the ancient Greeks and Romans consisted of extravagant fables and groundless superstitions, credited by the vulgar and weak, and maintained by the more enlightened, from selfish or political views; the same was clearly the case with the religion of the Egyptians; the same may be said of the Brahminical worship of India and the religion of Fo, professed by the Chinese; the same, of the mythological systems of the Peruvians, of the stern and bloody rites of the Mexicans, and those of the Britons and Saxons; hence we may conclude that all systems of religion, however varied in circumstances, agree in being superstitions kept up among the vulgar from interested or political views of the more enlightened classes. (Richard Whately)

V. Several students at an undergraduate institution were asked whether they believed in miracles. Their answers follow. Which, if any, contain arguments, and which, if any, contain explanations?

Question: Do you believe in miracles? Why or why not?

1. Yes, because I believe everybody has a guardian angel and they watch out for you.

2. Yes. I really don't know why. I guess it's kind of comforting to believe in them.

3. Yes. I'm really not sure why. I just believe.

4. Yes, because I've read many books on miracles and they seem believable.

5. Yes. I don't know why. It just kind of makes you feel better. It gives you some kind of hope.

6. No. I believe in luck.

7. Yes. Anything is possible because of God.

8. Yes, because I think anything out of our normal sphere of experience makes our lives more interesting and I believe we live in an interesting world.

9. Yeah. I guess most of it is from my faith. Miracles are from God.

Chapter 2

SEPARATING GOOD ARGUMENTS FROM BAD

The concern of this chapter is **the evaluation of arguments. This consists in determining whether the premisses are true and examining the connection that is asserted to hold between the premisses and the conclusion.**

ARE THE PREMISSES TRUE?

The question of whether the premisses of an argument are in fact true is not answered within the argument itself. This is because premisses do not serve to provide evidence for their own truth but rather to provide evidence for another proposition, which is the conclusion. Occasionally, premisses are known on independent grounds to be true, or false, as the case may be. In these cases, there is no need to investigate them further. In other cases, their truth value is not known, and it is necessary to seek evidence that confirms or disconfirms them. If it is determined that the premisses of an argument are false, then they do not establish the truth of the conclusion. Just as dead batteries cannot light a flashlight bulb, so false premisses cannot prove a conclusion. This holds for all arguments.

HOW ARE THE PREMISSES
CONNECTED TO THE
CONCLUSION?

When it is established that the premisses of arguments are false, there is no need to examine them further. For arguments with true premisses, however, it is necessary to examine the connection that is asserted to hold between the premisses and the conclusion. Two kinds of connection between premisses and conclusions are asserted in arguments. These correspond to the distinction between deductive and inductive arguments, so let's examine this distinction.

DEDUCTIVE ARGUMENTS

In *deductive arguments,* **it is asserted that the premisses provide conclusive evidence for the conclusion. If this assertion is correct, the argument is *valid,* which means that it is impossible for the conclusion to be false if the premisses are true as asserted. If the assertion is incorrect, the argument is *invalid* and it is possible for the conclusion to be false even though the premisses are true.** Therefore, **deduction** is a form of inference in which it is claimed that the conclusion, which is the proposition inferred, is conclusively established by the premisses.

It is the forms of deductive arguments, rather than their content, which determines their validity. Consider this argument:

> If William Jefferson Clinton is from Hope, Arkansas, then he is from the United States.
> William Jefferson Clinton is from Hope, Arkansas.
> Therefore, William Jefferson Clinton is from the United States.

This argument is valid. Substituting "F" for "William Jefferson Clinton is from Hope, Arkansas," and "G" for "William Jefferson Clinton is from the United States," we expose this form:

> If F then G.
> F.
> Therefore, G.

All arguments with this form are valid.

Compare this valid argument with this following invalid form that uses the same propositions:

> If William Jefferson Clinton is from Hope, Arkansas, then he is from the United States.
> William Jefferson Clinton is from the United States.
> Therefore, William Jefferson Clinton is from Hope, Arkansas.

Here's the form of this invalid argument:

> If F then G
> G.
> Therefore, F.

It can be difficult to convince someone of the invalidity of this argument, since it has true premisses and a true conclusion, but the very fact of its invalidity means that it is possible to construct another argument that has the same form, but that has true premisses and a false conclusion. This technique is known as the technique of *refutation by logical analogy.* This response to the argument illustrates the technique:

> If William Jefferson Clinton is a Catholic priest, then he is a man.
> William Jefferson Clinton is a man.
> Therefore, William Jefferson Clinton is a Catholic priest.

The premisses in this argument are true, but the conclusion is false, which indicates that its form is invalid.

On the spur of the moment, it may not be possible to think of an argument of the form you need in which it is evident that the premisses are true and the conclusion false. In this case, the technique of *refutation by alternate conclusion,* which is similar to the previous technique, can be used to advantage. In this technique, you point to one or more alternate conclusions that are not ruled out, or made impossible, by the premisses of the argument to be refuted. Suppose this argument is defended:

> If Tong has a Ph.D., then she may be addressed as "Doctor."
> Tong may be addressed as Doctor. Therefore, she has a Ph.D.

A refutation by alternate conclusion to this argument would consist in the observation that the premisses of the argument do not rule out the possibility that Tong might have an M.D. or a Doctor of Education. In either of these cases, the conclusion would be false even though the premisses were true.

For another example, suppose someone presents this argument:

> If this building contains asbestos, then it fails to meet current safety standards.
> This building fails to meet current safety standards.
> Therefore, this building contains asbestos.

To respond to this argument, one need only point out that the conclusion does not follow necessarily from the premisses since the building may fail to meet current safety standards for any number of reasons that have nothing to do with asbestos content. For example, the building may be asbestos-free but fail to meet current safety standards because its walls are painted with lead-based paint or because it does not have a fire escape.

Our examination of deductive arguments reveals that if their premisses are true, and their forms valid, their conclusions are necessarily true. Valid arguments with true premisses are described as **sound.** With this understood, we can consider the connection between premisses and conclusions in inductive arguments.

INDUCTIVE ARGUMENTS

By contrast with deductive arguments, ***inductive arguments* are marked by the assertion that the premisses, if true, provide evidence short of conclusive evidence for the truth of the conclusion.**

The following is an inductive argument, since the conclusion is not claimed to follow with absolute certainty from the premisses.

> Jerry's car is in the garage, but he plans to go to Georgene's party. In all
>   likelihood, he will attempt to catch a ride with someone else, since he's short
>   on money.

The conclusions of inductive arguments are often introduced by phrases like *in all likelihood, it is probable that,* or *it is likely that.* The word *that* introduces the conclusion itself, while the preceding part of the phrase indicates the likelihood with which the conclusion is asserted to be true. The strength of the claims made in inductive arguments can be arranged on a crude scale that runs from strong to weak. Phrases that are on the same level indicate approximately the same degree of strength. Consider the following arrangement:

STRONG CLAIM

It is

    highly probable   nearly certain

    probable   likely

    possible   possible, but not likely

    unlikely

    highly unlikely

WEAK CLAIM

    This scale, which is meant to be suggestive only, makes it easier for us to explain how inductive arguments can be evaluated as better or worse. One inductive argument asserts that its conclusion follows from its premisses with a high degree of probability. If this is the case, and its premisses are true, the argument is excellent. Another inductive argument asserts that its conclusion is possibly, though not likely, true, given its premisses. If this is the case, and its premisses are true, the argument is excellent. But what are we to say of an inductive argument with true premisses that asserts that the conclusion follows with a high degree of probability when in fact it follows with only a medium degree of probability? Are we to say that the argument is fairly good, but not excellent? We might, but it would be better to say that the claim made is simply too strong for its premisses. A stronger and better argument can be built on the original premisses in cases like this by substituting a conclusion that claims less for the original conclusion. Where *P* stands for premiss, and *C* for conclusion, suppose the original argument looked like this:

    P1, P2, and P3 are true.

    Therefore, it is highly probable that C is true.

Investigation shows that the conclusion is too strong for the premisses, even though the premisses are true. The original conclusion is then dropped, and another substituted, with this result:

    P1, P2, and P3 are true.

    Therefore, it is possible that C is true.

This argument is stronger than the first because the claim made in the conclusion does not exceed the evidence presented in the premisses. The goals of inductive arguments, as this account of their evaluation suggests, are to begin with true premisses and to assert the conclusion with a degree of probability that neither exceeds nor falls short of that which is justified by the premisses. It is not always easy to do this.

THE CONTENT OF ARGUMENTS

It is often expedient for us to examine the content of deductive arguments to determine whether the asserted connection between premises and conclusions in fact holds. Although the forms of such arguments determine their validity, it can be difficult to expose complicated forms on short notice. This is especially true if one or more propositions in the argument are taken for granted and not explicitly stated, for this requires a restatement of the argument in which we tease out the points that the arguer has taken for granted. For inductive arguments, which are not valid or invalid but simply stronger or weaker, it is not simply expedient but essential to examine content to determine whether the asserted connection holds.

In the following discussion we delve into the content of propositions by considering the relevance and adequacy of premises. For arguments with clear and unambiguous premises, all problems of content can be traced to these two considerations. For simplicity, we assume that the premisses we are considering are true.

RELEVANCE

The problem of relevance is that of determining what kind of evidence is suitable for grounding, or supporting, a conclusion. Remembering that the premisses of arguments provide the supporting evidence for their conclusions, **we define *relevant evidence* as evidence that, if true, increases the likelihood that a proposition being defended is true.** The following case provides an example of relevant evidence.

THE THERMOSTAT COVER

On walking through the dining room, Pat noticed that the metal cover of the thermostat was lying on the floor. The thermostat itself was mounted on the inside wall of the dining room, about five and a half feet above the floor. Her two boys, Rick and Pete, aged six and two, had been playing in the dining room, so Pat called them in.

"All right, you two," she asked, "which one of you took the cover off the thermostat?"

"It wasn't me, Mama," said Rick, the older boy. "It was Pete. I saw him do it."

Pat looked first at one boy and then the other, and shook her head sadly. "You're not telling the truth," she said, "and you'll have to be punished for that."

"But Mama, I didn't do it!"

"Yes, you did. You're tall enough to reach the thermostat, but your two-year-old brother isn't."

In this case, the relevant facts are (1) the two boys' heights and (2) their recently playing in the dining room. The second fact, taken by itself, would implicate either boy. The first fact is decisive, however, since it shows that only one boy was of a height sufficient to reach the thermostat. Other facts besides these are irrelevant. It is irrelevant, for example, that Pat is the mother of both boys and that the thermostat is located in the dining room.

The facts that are irrelevant to the identification of the boy who removed the thermostat cover may not be irrelevant to some other question. For example, the fact that Pat is the mother of the boys may be relevant to the question "Does Pat have the authority to discipline the boy who lied?" As his mother, Pat has that authority, but if she were not his mother, she might not. This shows us that **relevance is relational. Facts by themselves are not relevant to anything whatsoever; they are relevant, when they are, only to particular questions that arise in particular contexts.** In Chapters 4 through 7, we will be led again and again to questions of relevance.

ADEQUACY

The *problem of adequacy* **is that of determining whether the evidence that is considered to be relevant is sufficient to establish the truth of the conclusion. In general, evidence is adequate if it is (1) true, and (2) relevant, and (3) no more is claimed in the conclusion than is warranted by the premisses.** We will concentrate on the third of these conditions.

The first point to observe is that the adequacy of some premisses to establish their conclusions is a function of the context in which they are presented. The standard of proof required by scientists operating within the carefully regulated environment of the laboratory may differ from the standards dictated by rules of evidence in the law or the customs of a deliberative body such as the board of directors of a corporation. Standards operative within the law or some deliberative body may in turn differ from the level of proof expected within the setting of a family or between friends.

The standard of proof also varies in accordance with the kind of case being considered. Just as the height of the hurdles in a race may be lower for children than for adults, so the standard of proof might be lower in one kind of case than it is in another. In the law, for example, the standard required in civil cases is lower than that in criminal cases. Proof by a preponderance of the evidence is generally the standard in civil cases, while the standard in criminal cases is proof beyond a reasonable doubt. Context determines what counts as adequate.

In our analysis of inductive arguments, we discovered that we should not assert conclusions with a degree of probability not warranted by the premisses. If we do so, the premisses are not adequate in relation to the conclusion. We can strengthen our arguments by reducing the force with which we assert our conclusion, but we can also strengthen our arguments for some conclusions by **piling fact upon fact.** The following two versions of "The Case of Mrs. Clark" illustrate this point.

THE CASE OF MRS. CLARK: VERSION I

"I don't think Mrs. Clark likes me," says Alice.

"Why do you say that?" asks Tom.

"She brushed by me in the grocery store this morning without saying a word."

"Perhaps she didn't see you."

"She saw me, all right. Not only that, I said 'Hello, Mrs. Clark,' but she didn't even turn her head."

"You mustn't think that Mrs. Clark doesn't like you. At times she can be very friendly, but most of the time she acts like a crab to everyone."

"You don't think it's just me, then?"

"No, I don't." Saying this, Tom gives Alice a reassuring pat on the shoulder, but she remains unconvinced.

"I think it's me. I don't believe she's ever liked me," she says.

"Look," says Tom. "One night I called Mr. Clark about the Businessman's Auction. Mrs. Clark answered in a nasty tone and said, 'Is this important? Carl is very busy, you know.' So you see, she's just a crab, that's all."

"Oh, I don't know," Alice replies with a shake of her head. "Maybe she was in a bad mood that night. I just don't think she likes me."

In this version of the case, Tom offers one piece of supporting evidence, and it is perhaps not surprising that Alice is not convinced. Let's revisit the case.

THE CASE OF MRS. CLARK: VERSION II

Just as before, Alice says that she doesn't think Mrs. Clark likes her, but this time Tom responds like this:

"Look, one night I called Mr. Clark about the Businessman's Auction. Mrs. Clark answered in a nasty tone and said, 'Is this important? Carl is very busy, you know.' On another occasion—it was before we got married—I was invited to the Clarks' for dinner. I got there seven minutes late and Mrs. Clark said, 'Perhaps you should set your clock ahead. No one else had any trouble getting here on time.' On still another occasion, I saw the Clarks out for a walk and waved their way. Mr. Clark waved back, but Mrs. Clark stared straight through me as if she didn't see me. Moreover, Marge Henderson told me that at the Ladies' Club Mrs. Smith, the hostess, served tea and snacks and Mrs. Clark told her that her tea would have been fine if it hadn't been for the faint odor of silver polish from the silver service. You see? You shouldn't think she's singled you out. She's just a crab, that's all."

"Well, maybe you're right," replies Alice meditatively. "I didn't know all those things."

The two versions of "The Case of Mrs. Clark" illustrate the fact that **a number of facts taken together with one another can sometimes make a case that no one of them could have done by itself.** Just as the weight of a stack of dinner plates is increased by each plate added to the stack, so the weight of arguments can be increased by piling fact upon fact. The material in Chapters 4 through 7 provides us with several opportunities to elaborate upon this point.

Summary

In evaluating arguments, we examine the connection that is asserted to hold between premises and conclusion, and we determine the truth values of the premises and conclusions. Arguments can be defective in one or more of these ways:

- One or more of the premises of the argument can be false.
- In deductive arguments, the premises can be true, but the argument invalid.
- The claim made in the conclusion can be disproportionate to the evidence provided in the premises.
- The premises, even though true, can be irrelevant to the conclusion.
- The premises, even though true, can be inadequate to prove the conclusion.

A LOOK AHEAD

The arguments we have examined thus far have presented no problems of interpretation. Their premises and conclusions have been clear, and we have had no difficulty in understanding what they assert. This is not the case with all arguments. In the next chapter, we discover that unclear and misused terms can undermine arguments and that it is as difficult to think clearly with ambiguous terms and propositions as it is to run a footrace on fishing nets.

Exercises

Answers to questions marked with an asterisk may be found in the back of the text.

I. Respond to the following statements. Answer 3 through 9 with "true" or "false."

   1. What is the twofold process of examining inductive and deductive arguments?
   *2. There are two goals for inductive arguments. What are they?
   3. Validity is a function of the subject matter or content of deductive arguments.
   4. The validity of an argument is not determined by the truth of its premises.
   5. The validity of an argument is determined by the truth of its conclusion.
   6. It is logically possible for the conclusion of a valid argument to be false when its premises are true.

7. It is logically possible for the conclusion of a valid argument to be false when one or more of its premises are false.
8. The invalidity of invalid arguments can be exposed by constructing counterarguments with the same form but with true premises and a false conclusion.
9. The invalidity of invalid arguments can be exposed by pointing to one or more alternate conclusions that are not ruled out, or made impossible, by the premisses of the argument to be refuted.

II. The following argument forms are valid. Identify the valid arguments in this exercise by matching them up with these forms. State the commonly accepted name for each valid form (*Modus Ponens,* for example). For arguments that do not have one or the other of the valid forms and are consequently invalid, construct either a refutation by logical analogy or a refutation by alternate conclusion.

MODUS PONENS	MODUS TOLLENS	DISJUNCTIVE SYLLOGISM (FIRST FORM)	DISJUNCTIVE SYLLOGISM (SECOND FORM)	HYPOTHETHICAL SYLLOGISM
If F then G.	If F then G	Either F or G.	Either F or G.	If F then G
F.	Not G.	Not F.	Not G.	If G then H.
Therefore, G.	Therefore, not F.	Therefore G.	Therefore, F.	Therefore, if F then H.

Note: As you study these forms, please observe that only Disjunctive Syllogism has two forms. In a valid Disjunctive Syllogism, it doesn't matter whether the "F" or the "G" proposition is denied in the second premiss. In Modus Tollens, by contrast, the second premiss can only deny the "G" proposition.

EXAMPLE Lois is either a freshman or a sophomore. She's not a sophomore. Therefore, she's a freshman.

This argument corresponds to the second form of disjunctive syllogism and is therefore valid. To expose the form, replace "Lois is a freshman" by *F* and "Lois is a sophomore" by *G*. The second premiss denies the *G* proposition in the first premiss, which makes it possible to affirm the *F* proposition in the conclusion.

1. If the messenger brings bad news, then Atilla has him put to death. The messenger brings bad news. Therefore, Atilla has him put to death.
2. If Sheila is correct, then the pass is intercepted by the quarterback. The pass is intercepted by the quarterback. Therefore, Sheila is correct.
3. If he has gained weight, then he is not exercising as much as before. He is exercising as much as before. Therefore, it must not be true that he has gained weight.
*4. If Shelby purchases a ticket, then he is admitted to the theater. He does not purchase a ticket. Therefore, he is not admitted to the theater.
5. If she completed the dance course, then she studied the fox trot. She did not complete the dance course. Therefore, she did not study the fox trot.
6. Either she completed the dance course, or she failed to study the fox trot. She did not complete the dance course. Therefore, she did not study the fox trot.

7. If Rosemary was sick this morning, then she had too much to drink last night. Rosemary is a teetotaler. Therefore, she was not sick this morning.

8. If the snow melts, the rivers swell with water. If the rivers swell with water, the fields are flooded. Therefore, if the snow melts, the fields are flooded.

*9. If the election is rigged, then the people protest. If the people protest, then concessions are made. Therefore, if the election is rigged, then concessions are made.

10. It is 8 o'clock if the traffic is heavy; but the traffic is not heavy. Therefore, it is not 8 o'clock.

11. If it is 8 o'clock, the traffic is heavy; but it is not 8 o'clock. Therefore, the traffic is not heavy.

12. The traffic is heavy, if it is 8 o'clock. The traffic is heavy. Therefore, it is 8 o'clock.

III. The following exercises are intended to give you practice in determining the strength of inductive arguments. Follow the instructions in each case.

   *1. Review the dialogue entitled "Brandon Sweeney Hears a Complaint" in Chapter 1. State the strengths and weaknesses of Arthur's argument in that dialogue. Is Arthur's case sufficiently strong to warrant his conclusion?

   2. Read the facts of the following cases and answer the questions at the end of each.

THE CASE OF MARIE ROGET[1]

The mangled body of a young woman was found floating near the shore of the river Seine. The face was swollen with dark blood. Beauvais, a man who viewed the body, identified it after some hesitation as that of Marie Roget, a young woman who had disappeared some days before. As reported in the Paris newspapers, his identification was based on the following observations:

   a. The hair on the deceased's arm.

   b. The feet of the deceased were small, as were those of Marie Roget.

   c. A hat found near the river was similar to the one Marie Roget was wearing when last seen.

   d. There were flowers in the hat. Marie Roget had placed flowers in her hat.

   e. The hose worn by the deceased were like those customarily worn by Marie Roget.

   f. The general size and appearance of the body of the deceased was like that of Marie Roget.

---

[1] This case is adapted from "The Mystery of Marie Roget," by Edgar Allan Poe.

Questions

1. The meaning of one of the facts above is not as clear as that of the others. Identify that fact, and state what it might possibly mean.
2. Is any one of the above facts sufficient taken by itself to justify the conclusion that the mangled body is possibly that of Marie Roget? If you answer this question affirmatively, identify the fact and state why it is sufficient. If you answer negatively, take each fact in turn and explain why it is insufficient, taken by itself, to justify the conclusion that the mangled body is possibly that of Marie Roget.
3. Are the facts, taken in conjunction with one another, sufficient to justify the conclusion that the mangled body is most likely that of Marie Roget? Why?
4. Are the facts, taken in conjunction with one another, sufficient to justify the conclusion that the mangled body is definitely that of Marie Roget? Why?
5. Suppose that facts *a* through *e* are as stated, but that fact *f* had been this: The general size of the body of the deceased seemed to be somewhat larger than that of Marie Roget. In that case, would the combined facts have led you to the conclusion that the body was not likely to have been that of Marie Roget? Why?

THE CASE OF BASIL AND THE DIAMOND NECKLACE

Basil stands accused of having stolen a diamond necklace from the apartment of Sabina, the well-known singer. With Inspector Marvel on vacation, Faraday, his assistant, gathers the facts listed below. Your task is to assist Faraday by dividing the facts into these three groups:

Group I: Relevant facts that increase the probability that Basil stole the necklace.

Group II: Relevant facts that decrease the probability that Basil stole the necklace.

Group III: Irrelevant facts—that is, facts that have no bearing on the question of whether Basil stole the necklace.

On criteria for determining relevance: In this particular case, a relevant fact that increases the probability that Basil stole the necklace is one that suggests that he had (1) a motive for stealing the necklace or (2) the opportunity to steal it. (A motive is a reason of a special sort; it is something that prompts, or might prompt, a person to act. Opportunity, in this case, means "the person had a chance to put his hands on the diamond necklace.") If you can establish both of these, and there are no significant facts in Group II, you will have built a strong case for Basil's being the thief. If you cannot establish these, your case is weak.

A relevant fact that decreases the probability that Basil stole the necklace is one which suggests either that someone else stole the necklace or that the necklace was not in fact stolen. Facts of this sort—Group II Facts—must be balanced against those in Group I in determining the overall probability of Basil's having stolen the necklace.

The Facts of the Case

a. Basil is Sabina's former lover.

b. Sabina's apartment is located on the twentieth floor of a downtown high-rise.

c. Those who gain access to the elevators in Sabina's apartment building must be identified by a security guard.

d. Sabina threw a party for her agent and the members of her band three nights before the theft was discovered.

e. Basil, who wasn't invited, crashed Sabina's party.

f. One day after the party, Sabina fired Kalinka, her backup singer who was dating Lenny, the lead guitarist.

g. Sabina had inherited the diamond necklace from her grandfather.

h. The diamond necklace was kept in a jewelry box in Sabina's bedroom.

i. Basil knew the location of the diamond necklace.

j. Earrings that match the diamond necklace were kept with it in the same jewelry box. The earrings were not taken.

k. Basil filed for bankruptcy two weeks before the diamond necklace was reported stolen.

l. The day after the party, Basil was seen leaving a pawn shop.

m. The diamond necklace and the earrings were insured for a quarter of a million dollars.

n. The insurance on the diamond necklace and the earrings was taken out two days before the party.

o. The security guard on duty the night of the party is Basil's second cousin.

p. Basil's and Sabina's fingerprints were found on the box containing the diamond necklace, along with those of an unidentified person.

q. Basil wrote the arrangements for the songs on Sabina's last album, but since his breakup with Sabina has been blacklisted by artists who record in Los Angeles.

r. At age 14, Basil was arrested for shoplifting, but he has had no arrests since.

s. Sabina reported her diamond necklace missing on her last European tour, but it was subsequently discovered in the pocket of her guitar case.

t. Sabina, who is dieting, was reportedly in a bad mood the night of her party.

u. Sabina has openly accused Basil of having stolen the diamond necklace.

v. The *Skipping Pebble,* a gossip magazine, has published a photo of Basil with Mildred, his new girlfriend. In the photo, Mildred is wearing a diamond necklace like the one stolen.

w. The day after Sabina reported the theft of her necklace, Mildred reported that her necklace had been stolen.

x. Lenny claims to have seen Basil alone in Sabina's bedroom on the night of the party. He says that Basil hurriedly left the bedroom when he saw Lenny.

Questions

You have now placed the facts of "The Case of Basil and the Diamond Necklace" in the groups indicated. Your next task is to answer the following questions. In answering them, you may want to review the paragraph in the preceding box that begins with "On criteria for determining relevance."

1. Are the facts which you placed in Group I sufficient by themselves to make it possible that Basil stole the necklace? Why?

2. When the facts that you placed in Group I are balanced against the facts that you placed in Group II, is it probable that Basil stole the necklace? Why?

Chapter 3

TERMS

One obstacle to critical thinking is a simple lack of words suited to the problem at hand. The necessity of suitable words is suggested by reflection upon the related trades of carpentry and cabinet making. A carpenter who constructs houses is acquainted with braced frames, platform frames, and balloon frames. He or she can identify foundation walls, beams, bearing posts, bridges, gables, girders, headers, joists, lintels, rafters, studs, and other parts of a house. The differences between back saws, handsaws, jig saws, compass saws, and coping saws are clear to the carpenter, as are the differences between tang and socket chisels and jack planes, smooth planes, jointer planes, fore planes, and block planes. Carpenters are also acquainted with the differences between common nails, box nails, barbed box nails, casing nails, finishing nails, brads, cuts, tacks, and corrugated fasteners. And joints? A carpenter or cabinet maker is familiar with butt joints, miter joints, dado joints, lap joints, and mortise and tenon joints. Persons who do not know the meaning of these words for forms of construction, parts of houses, tools, and methods of joining wood are novices in carpentry and cabinet making. Moreover, no novice can become an expert in these areas without learning these words. Similarly, in any area which becomes the focus of reasoning there are words which must be known if thinking is to proceed. Without those words, a person cannot name objects, form abstract concepts, identify patterns, make distinctions, form hypotheses, envision possibilities, or, in short, think critically. Words, in an image suggested by carpentry, are the lumber of thought. For this reason, the first order of business in critical thinking is to master the words which are relevant to the matter at hand.

A second obstacle to critical thinking is the misuse of available words. Our task in the remainder of this chapter is to introduce distinctions and procedures which are of use in clarifying the meaning of words and reducing the likelihood that they will be misused. We begin by observing that words can be classified according to their function or their part of speech. **To describe a word as a "term" is to indicate its function. *Terms* refer to objects or classes of objects, as well as actions, circumstances, qualities, and thoughts.** Thus they are distinguished from verbs like *are* and adjectives like *all,* which do not refer to objects. **A term can be one word alone or several words taken together.** Thus, *diamond* and *The Star of India* are both terms.

SINGULAR AND GENERAL TERMS

Some terms are singular, while others are general. **Singular terms refer to individual objects.** Examples are *the man who wrote* <u>Hamlet</u>*, the Eiffel Tower,* and *Charles Dickens.* As the last example indicates, singular terms include proper names, which can refer to more than one individual. *Charles,* for example, is the name of many men, but the term is classified as singular since in particular uses it refers to specific individuals.

 General terms do not name individuals but instead can be applied equally to any of an indefinite number of objects. Examples are *motorcycle* and *clothing. Language* is general in that it can be applied indifferently to any number of particular languages, such as Sanskrit, German, English, Greek, and Latin.

 The distinction between singular and general terms differs from the distinction between singular and plural words. The latter distinction is one of number. Singular words denote one object, while plural words denote more than one. *Calf* is singular. Its plural form is *calves.* Notice the difference between the two distinctions. *Calf* can be used to refer to an individual, and so is singular, but it is also general in that it can be used indifferently of the young of Guernseys, Holsteins, and other breeds of cows, as well as other animals, such as elephants.

COLLECTIVE TERMS

A third class of terms, in addition to the singular and the general, is the **collective. These terms refer to a group of objects taken together as a whole.** Examples are *army, committee, faculty, jury,* and *team.* **Unlike general terms, collective terms cannot be used to denote individuals taken separately, or distributively.** *Motorcycle* and *calf,* which are general terms, denote individual objects, but no individual object is a *committee, faculty, jury,* or *team.*

 Collective terms are singular, but are sometimes incorrectly used as if they were plural. These sentences illustrate this:

1. St. Alphonse's ABC Church recently honored their pastor and first lady for twenty-five years of loyal service to the church and the community.
2. XYZ Corporation invites you to join them in supporting local law enforcement.

Since *St. Alphonse's ABC Church* and *XYZ Corporation* are collective terms and are singular (as opposed to plural), Sentences 1 and 2 should have been written in this way:

- St. Alphonse's ABC Church recently honored its pastor and first lady for twenty-five years of loyal service to the church and the community.
- XYZ Corporation invites you to join it in supporting local law enforcement.

 Sentences 1 and 2 illustrate the error of using a form of a plural pronoun with a singular noun. One can understand why the error is attractive to some people. *Their* and *them* have connotations of human warmth which *it* does not have. Ministers of churches often emphasize that their church is nothing more than its members, and the CEOs of corporations want their corporations to have a friendly image. Nevertheless, for *their* and *them* to be used correctly, the examples need to be rewritten as follows:

- The members of St. Alphonse's ABC Church recently honored their pastor and first lady for twenty-five years of loyal service to the church and the community.
- The employees of XYZ Corporation invite you to join them in supporting local law enforcement.

On this rewriting, reference is made to a number of individuals rather than to a collectivity.

The following sentence illustrates the error we are discussing, but with reference not to a collective term, but to a term which refers to individuals taken one by one, or distributively.

Every camper should bring their own flashlight.

The referent in this sentence is each individual camper, so, for a camp which admits both males and females, the sentence should read like this:

Every camper should bring his or her own flashlight.

The error of shifting from the singular to the plural is *grammatical*.[1] **A common logical error consists in shifting from the distributive to the collective in the course of an argument.** The error is illustrated in this argument:

The men who live in our little town are pleasant enough.
Last Saturday's lynch mob was composed of the men who live in our little town.
Therefore, last Saturday's lynch mob was pleasant enough.

In the premisses, the indicated men are taken one by one as individuals, but in the conclusion they are referred to as a group or collectivity (i.e., as the lynch mob). The problem is that individual members of a group or class can have characteristics which the class itself does not have. A particular member of a lynch mob can be quite pleasant taken by himself, but a lynch mob is an ugly phenomenon. A race car driver might run into another car on the track, but an association of race car drivers cannot do that. A priest might practice pederasty, but pederasty certainly cannot be practiced by a priesthood.[2] **When a term is used distributively in a premiss but collectively in the corresponding conclusion, the fallacy which results is called *composition*.**

---

[1] The error we have been discussing occurs so often these days that it is worth observing, with regard to our examples of plural pronouns used as singular pronouns, that languages develop in being used. Usage which is considered incorrect at one time may come to be accepted at a later time. Early in the twentieth century, for example, *contact* was used only as a noun, but today is used both as a noun and a verb. Similarly, "their" and "them" may come in time to be accepted as both singular and plural pronouns.

[2] In ethical reflection we often draw a distinction between individual and collective responsibility. An individual member of a group can be responsible for a particular action, but the group itself may not be responsible. Thus, the chief executive officer of a major corporation can commit murder, but the corporation itself may not be responsible for murder. In the public mind, however, there may be a psychological association between the individual and the group so that the group shares in the negative appraisal of the individual. If the CEO was closely identified with the corporation as a result of having acted as its spokesperson, the public might express its disapproval by failing to buy the corporation's products for awhile. Such is the force of what is commonly called "guilt by association."

The opposite error, or *division*, consists in shifting from a collective to a distributive use of a term. Here is an example of such a shift:

> The Supreme Court cannot misinterpret the law.
> Justice Zeno sits on the Supreme Court.
> Therefore, Justice Zeno cannot misinterpret the law.[3]

The Supreme Court by definition cannot misinterpret the law since it is the final court of appeal[4] but when the Supreme Court interprets a law, or hands down a decision, it does so as a body. Members of the Court may write opinions on the decision, but the decision is the decision of the whole. A particular justice, on the other hand, can err in speaking as a member of the Court. He or she errs by definition if his or her judgment does not coincide with that handed down by the Court itself.

By permission of Johnny Hart and Creators Syndicate, Inc.
Fallacy of Division

> Buffalo are a vanishing species.
> This animal is a buffalo.
> Therefore, this animal is vanishing.[5]

Here, a characteristic of a class is attributed to a member of a class. The shift here is so obvious that the argument is no more than a joke, though in other cases the shift can be more difficult to detect.

The distinction between the collective and the distributive, which we have been discussing with reference to terms, has important applications in the law. Several individuals can assume obligations both as a group (collectively) and separately (distributively). Individuals who issue a *joint and several* note, for example, bind themselves both as a group and as individuals to pay the specified amount of money to the payee. The individuals issuing the note, who are referred to as *obligors* or *makers,* are jointly and severally liable to

---

[3] Adapted from W. S Jevons, *Elementary Lessons in Logic: Deductive and Inductive.*
[4] There are other senses in which supreme courts might be said to err, but they are not germane to our example.
[5] Source unknown.

pay the money. This means that if the obligors fail to pay the money, the payee can sue them all as a group, or sue one or more of the obligors, but not all of them. If the obligors had issued a joint note, as opposed to a joint and several note, they could be sued as a group but not as individuals. When sued as a group, the obligors are codefendants.

HELPFUL HINT

Of all the mistakes associated with the distinctions we have examined thus far, the most common in everyday speech is the use of collective terms as if they were plural. The following is adapted from an actual letter. Can you find a mistake in either the opening or concluding sentences?

(Letter from the Wildlife Coordinator)
Opening sentence: The investigative group on the plight of the dolphin has met to plan its activities.
Concluding sentence: As Wildlife Coordinator, I hope that the investigative group will hear from many people, and I look forward to receiving their report.

In the opening sentence, *it* is correctly used. *Investigative group* is singular. In the concluding sentence, *their* is incorrectly used. *Their* is the possessive form of *they*, which is a plural pronoun. Instead of their, *its* should be used. Given that *their* is plural, *their* could refer to the *many people* from whom the study group is expected to hear.

AMBIGUITY OF TERMS

Terms are clear, ambiguous, or vague as determined by the context in which they are used. As used:

Clear terms are those whose meaning is understood.
Ambiguous terms have more than one possible meaning.
Vague terms are those with a range of applications, some of which are problematic or indefinite. Examples are *beard, wealthy, thick,* and *scientific.*

In Chapter 8, we treat relative terms, which are one kind of vague term,[6] but in what follows we concentrate on the ambiguity of terms.

In some cases, it is not immediately clear that a term has more than one meaning. This is true both for written and for spoken words. In elementary school, I competed in

---

[6] See the section headed "Standards in Rankings." Also, see the entry for *vague* in the Glossary.

a friendly way with the girl who sat to my left. On one occasion, our teacher returned a test in mathematics. "I made 90," I said to the girl. "What did you make?"

"I made 90, too," she said.

"That's very good," I replied, thinking that she had said *92,* and earned a better grade than I.

If an individual uses a term in one sense in one connection, and a second sense in another, the individual is said to **equivocate** upon the term. **If a term is used with one meaning in the premises of an argument and another in the conclusion, the result is a fallacy of *equivocation.***

Some equivocations are no more than puns or plays upon words: Some believe that constructing puns is merely a way of punishing people (pun, *pun*ishing—get it?) And there is no doubt that some fallacies of equivocation are no more than jokes:

> Some dogs are brave.
> My dog is brave.
> Therefore, my dog is some dog.

(In its first occurrence in this argument, *some* means at least one. In its second occurrence, it is used in an honorific sense to mean *very special,* or *very commendable.*) Nevertheless, when the equivocation is not as obvious as it is in these examples, the resulting confusion can be serious. While *too* and *two* have the same pronunciation, they are spelled differently and their meanings are unrelated. However, the meanings of other terms *are* related, and in those cases confusion is possible.

I know of no better example of this than one provided by Wesley Newcomb Hohfeld, who observes with regard to *right,* taken in a legal sense, that the term " . . . tends to be used indiscriminately to cover what in a given case may be a privilege, a power, or an immunity, rather than a right in the strictest sense. . . ."[7] Given this, it is possible for an attorney to use the term *right* as a synonym for *privilege* in the premise of an argument and then conclude—still using the term *right*—that his or her client has an immunity. Privileges, however, do not carry immunities with them, so the conclusion is fallacious. Whether the fallacy in the argument is detected by the opposing counsel or the judge, however, is an open question.

Hohfeld quotes an important text in jurisprudence as follows:

> If the expression of widely different ideas by one and the same term resulted only in the necessity for . . . clumsy paraphrases, or obviously inaccurate paraphrases, no great harm would be done; but unfortunately the identity of terms seems irresistibly to suggest an identity between the ideas expressed by them.[8]

The observation in this passage is well worth remembering. Where an identity of terms does not denote an identity of ideas, but instead denotes a plurality of ideas, thinking can be confused rather than clear. Correct reasoning requires that every word be used with a single meaning throughout the course of an argument. When this requirement of

---

[7] Wesley Newcomb Hohfeld, *Fundamental Legal Conceptions as Applied in Judicial Reasoning* (Westport, CT: Greenwood Press, Publishers, 1964), p. 36. Cited hereafter as Hohfeld.

[8] Ibid., p. 40. Hohfeld is quoting Holland, *Elements of Jurisprudence,* tenth ed., p. 139. No further bibliographical details are given.

correct reasoning is not met, two distinct ideas can be blended, and thus confused, like two shirts whose different colors fade into one another in the wash. Clear thinking requires that such confusions be avoided.

Our discussion indicates that confusions and misunderstandings are possible due to ambiguities in the words we use, but entire sentences can also be ambiguous. One kind of ambiguous sentence is the **amphiboly. In these sentences, the ambiguity arises from the grammatical structure of the sentence.** One classic example is this prophecy in Shakespeare's *Henry VI:*

The Duke yet lives that Henry shall depose.

It is impossible to determine whether the meaning of the sentence is that the Duke shall depose Henry, or Henry the Duke. A more recent example is

I've whipped better men than Joe Louis.[9]

Does this statement mean that the individual has whipped men who are better than Joe Louis or that the individual has whipped better men than Joe Louis has whipped? It is impossible to decide between these two meanings. I was told, years ago, of a sign on a seedy tavern in southern Oklahoma which read

Clean and decent dancing every night except Sunday.

You can undoubtedly find two interpretations of this amphiboly. **The fallacy of amphiboly consists in choosing the wrong interpretation of an amphibolous statement.**

It is difficult on occasion to determine whether the ambiguity in a sentence is occasioned by a word within the sentence—which indicates an equivocation—or by the structure of the sentence—which indicates an amphiboly. The ambiguity in a sentence containing an equivocation can be eliminated, in some cases, by substituting a word for the one which causes the ambiguity. Consider this sentence:

Tanya leaped from the boat then ran to the bank and picked up the money.[10]

Does *bank* mean shore, or does it mean a building with a vault? If the former, the ambiguity is eliminated by substituting *shore* for *bank;* if the latter, by adding other words, such as *First National.* The ambiguity in amphibolies cannot be eliminated by word substitution, since in these cases the ambiguity lies in the structure of the sentence itself.

THE EMOTIVE FORCE
OF WORDS

Lexical, or dictionary, definitions of words provide us with the meanings which words have in current usage. Words, however, convey feelings and emotions which dictionaries are ill equipped to convey. This ability of words to express emotions arises in part

[9] Joe Louis was a heavyweight boxing champion. I owe this example to Kenneth R. Merrill.
[10] Source unknown.

from their sounds. Some words are relatively cold or hard, while others are soft or warm. For example, compare *core* with *wine,* and *chest* with *breast.* The emotional content of words also arises from the manner in which they are put together in writing and speech. In addition, words have connotations which cause emotive responses in individuals. In the United States, some years ago, the word *communist* elicited emotional responses in some uses. The connotation of *propaganda* continues to be negative. Advertisers, at least, much prefer *advertising* to *propaganda. New* and *improved* have such positive connotations that their use in advertising is persistent, inevitable, and nearly inescapable. The connotation of *home* is so warm and favorable by comparison with that of *house* that realtors persist in saying that they sell homes, when it is clearly the case that, as the old saying has it, "a house is not a home."

The emotional connotations of words are of great interest to us as critical thinkers, since it is possible for individuals to persuade others that their opinion is true simply by their clever use. Some years ago, I introduced a motion in a committee meeting at the school where I teach. The Chair of the meeting, knowing that one of my colleagues opposed the motion, immediately turned to him and said, "Well, how do you respond to that?" My colleague responded quickly and loudly, and in a voice filled with contempt. "To *that?*" he asked rhetorically. "I have no response to *that.*" Those words as they appear on the page before you can scarcely convey the feeling with which they were spoken. To my colleagues, they were like a blast of fire from an enormous coal-fired furnace which scorches everything in its path. After they were spoken, my proposal stood no chance of consideration on its merits. It went down to defeat solely on the force of my colleague's scorn.

When an attempt is made to secure a conclusion by means of emotion rather than by reason and fact, a critical thinker should point that out. In some cases, responses like the following may be appropriate:

- You are using words which are prejudicial to my case, and favorable to yours.
- You are more interested in exciting emotion than in listening to my reasons for what I say.
- By your very tone of voice, you are attempting to slant the issue in your favor.
- Let us consider the matter together impartially.

Responses like this are not always possible or effective in discussions with others, since feelings on an issue can run so high that it is impossible to offer any comment which will not make the other party to the conversation even more angry than he or she already is. Nevertheless, it is still better to be able to recognize an attempt to secure agreement by emotional expression, and not be fooled by it, than not to be able to recognize it. The opinions of those who cannot distinguish between passion and proof are likely to be determined by emotional appeals rather than by relevant and adequate evidence. Opinions determined in this way shift, like loose straws, with the winds of public opinion.

Emotional words and phrases are sometimes illegitimately used to secure assent to propositions which lack the support of relevant and adequate evidence, but emotion itself is not the enemy of good argument. Emotion directed to the proper object is entirely appropriate and desirable, as the words of Abraham Lincoln, delivered upon a Civil War battlefield, amply demonstrate.

THE GETTYSBURG ADDRESS

ABRAHAM LINCOLN

Fourscore and seven years ago our fathers brought forth on this continent a new nation, conceived in liberty, and dedicated to the proposition that all men are created equal. Now we are engaged in a great civil war, testing whether that nation, or any nation so conceived and so dedicated, can long endure. We are met on a great battlefield of that war. We have come to dedicate a portion of that field, as a final resting place for those who here gave their lives that that nation might live. It is altogether fitting and proper that we should do this. But, in a larger sense, we cannot dedicate—we cannot consecrate—we cannot hallow—this ground. The brave men, living and dead, who struggled here, have consecrated it, far above our poor power to add or detract. The world will little note, nor long remember, what we say here, but it can never forget what they did here. It is for us the living, rather, to be dedicated here to the unfinished work which they who fought here have thus far so nobly advanced. It is rather for us to be here dedicated to the great task remaining before us,—that from these honored dead we take increased devotion to that cause for which they gave the last full measure of devotion—that we here highly resolve that these dead shall not have died in vain—that this nation, under God, shall have a new birth of freedom—and that government of the people, by the people, for the people, shall not perish from the earth.

This noble speech evokes powerful emotions, but ones which are appropriate to the occasion on which it was delivered. If you can appreciate the contrast between the emotions which this speech inspires and some of the emotion-filled utterances which you hear in the parking lots of shopping malls or on television, then little more need be said about the emotive force of words. Neither need arguments be constructed in defense of the proposition that emotion, directed to its proper object, is entirely appropriate in human communication.

Summary

- *Terms* are words which refer to objects or classes of objects, as well as actions, circumstances, qualities, and thoughts.
- *Singular terms* refer to individual objects, but *general terms,* which do not name individuals, can be applied equally to an indefinite number of objects.
- *Collective terms* refer to a group taken together as a whole, but terms used *distributively* denote individuals taken separately, or one by one.
- The fallacy of composition occurs when a term is used distributively in a premiss but collectively in the conclusion which is supposed to follow from it.

- In the fallacy of division, a term is used collectively in a premiss, but distributively in the conclusion which is supposed to follow from it.
- A *vague* term is one which has a range of applications, some of which are problematic or indefinite.
- A *clear* term is one which is understood in the context in which it is used.
- An *ambiguous* term is one which has more than one possible meaning in the context in which it is used.
- *Amphiboly.* A sentence whose grammatical structure renders it ambiguous. "I have lived here twice two and four years" is an example. It is impossible to state whether the meaning of the sentence is intended to be "I have lived here eight years" or "I have lived here twelve years," since it is impossible to know whether "twice" refers to *two and four* or only to *two*.
- Emotion directed to the proper object is not the enemy of good argument. However, critical thinkers should be aware of attempts to secure conclusions by means of emotional words and phrases rather than by reason and fact.

A Good Exercise and a Look Ahead

If you're like me, you're often affected by emotion-filled words without directly being aware of it, or without being aware of it until after they've done their work. While emotion is not necessarily the enemy of clear thinking, it's important to be aware of its use. One good exercise in developing your awareness of emotion-filled words is to rewrite number 7 in Appendix IV, "Extended Exercises in the Examination of Reasoning," eliminating its emotional content so far as possible. Another good exercise is to rewrite number 5, *adding* emotion-filled words and phrases to make it tug at your heartstrings. In addition to drawing your attention to emotion-filled words, these suggested exercises provide good practice in writing.

In the next chapter, we examine the use of emotion in arguments in connection with the fallacious "Argument to the People" and "Argument from Pity." This occurs in the context of our consideration of facts as a ground of inference. (Facts, you recall, are one of the five grounds of inference identified in the Introduction.)

Exercises

Answers to questions marked with an asterisk may be found in the back of the text.

I. Identify the fallacies of composition or division in the following arguments.

1. All times when our country's automobile manufacturers benefit are times when the import duties on foreign automobiles are increased. Our country's automo-

bile manufacturers are a part of the national economy, so the national economy would benefit from an increase in import duties on foreign automobiles.

2. Athens waged war upon Sparta. Xanthippe was a citizen of Athens. Therefore, Xanthippe waged war upon Sparta.

3. Work Is Us is an inefficient company. Bill is employed there, so he won't answer your e-mail message for months.

*4. Rome wasn't built in a day. This salad dressing is Roman. Therefore, it cannot be mixed in a day.

5. It only takes a few minutes to read The Book of Ruth. The Book of Ruth is a book of the Holy Bible. The Holy Bible can therefore be read in a few minutes.

6. The program committee failed to secure a speaker for the evening. Patricia and Hans are members of the program committee. Therefore, Patricia and Hans failed to secure a speaker for the evening.

7. Neither Patricia nor Hans did anything to secure a speaker for the evening, but as members of the program committee they were charged with that responsibility. Therefore, the program committee did nothing to secure a speaker for the evening.

II. Which of the following passages contain equivocations on key terms?

1. In the teahouse the relative numbers of the sexes were being discussed when the baker said that there were an equal number of men and women in the world. Nasrudin contradicted the baker, saying that there were only about ten percent men. When someone asked for an explanation Nasrudin said this: "Ninety percent do what their wives tell them to do."[11]

2. All braces are supports, but some supports are not braces.

3. Nothing is worse than death, and nothing is what I have in my pocket. Therefore, what I have in my pocket is worse than death.

*4. He lowered himself into the lifeboat and rowed to the bank for some money.

5. Politicians and eyes have one thing in common: each can be nearsighted.

6. St. Anselm defined *God* as that which none greater than can be conceived.

7. "Which shoe do you put on first?" asked a playful Peutrell.

After a moment's reflection, Carlotta replied, "My left shoe."

"That's incorrect," said Peutrell.

"How can you say that?" asked a bewildered Carlotta. "Surely I know which shoe I put on first."

"No matter which shoe you put on first," replied a smug Peutrell, "the other one's left. Therefore, you put on your right shoe first."

"In this moment," said Carlotta sadly, "I realize that it would be impossible to overestimate your capacity for silliness."

8. Cowardly people are said to be *yellow*. Look at this man with hepatitis; he's yellow. He must be a coward.

9. It was Monday in kindergarten, and all the students were sharing a period of show and tell about something interesting that happened at home over the

---

[11] Idries Shah, *The Pleasantries of the Incredible Mulla Nasrudin* (New York: E. P. Dutton, 1971), 185.

weekend. When Johnnie's turn came, he went to the board, put a dot on it, and sat down. The teacher said, "Johnnie, what is so interesting about a dot?"

Johnnie replied, "Teacher, it is not a dot; it is a period."

This caused the teacher to ask, "But what is so important about a period?"

Johnnie responded, "I don't know, but my big sister missed one, and I have never seen so much excitement around our house."[12]

III. Read articles 7 and 8 on flag burning in Appendix IV, "Extended Exercises in the Examination of Reasoning." Write the emotion-filled words and phrases which you find in these articles on a separate sheet of paper. Is the use of emotion in these articles appropriate? Is one article more filled with emotion than the other? State which article and why.

---

[12] From Albert B. Randall, "The Ontological Significance of Laughter: A Phenomenological Exploration." Unpublished manuscript. Used by permission.

Chapter 4

GROUNDS OF INFERENCE I
FACTS AND HYPOTHESES

The purpose of this chapter is to investigate facts as a ground of inference. We consider the process of forming hypotheses to explain facts, and common difficulties encountered in determining which facts are relevant to particular cases. This enables us to identify the following fallacies of reasoning:

- Accent
- Argument to the people
- Complex question
- Argument from force
- Argument from authority
- Argument from pity
- Ad hominem argument

FACTS AND HYPOTHESES

By a **fact** we mean **a circumstance or state of affairs which is not in doubt, or which has been verified in some way.** In the following case, an attempt is made to reconstruct events from particular facts.

"THE SWEDISH MATCH"

In "The Swedish Match," a short story by Anton Chekhov, a police superintendent is approached by a young man who states that his employer, a man named Klyauzov, has been murdered. At Klyauzov's lodge, the police superintendent learns that Klyauzov has not been seen for more than a week. Upon attempting to enter

the man's bedroom, the superintendent discovers that the door is locked, with the key on the inside.

Tchubikov, the examining magistrate, and Dyukovsky, his assistant, take over the investigation. The bedroom door is battered open and they enter. By the solitary window they see a big wooden bed. On it lies a quilt, which is much creased and crumpled. A pillow lies upon the floor. Beside the bed there is a small table, which holds a silver watch, silver coins worth twenty kopecks, and sulphur matches. In addition to the bed and the table there is a chair, but no other furniture. Under the bed there are two dozen empty bottles, an old straw hat, and a jar of vodka, while under the table there is one dust-covered boot.

Further inspection of the room reveals a trace of a knee upon the windowsill and, upon the floor, a Swedish match of the sort used to light fires. Both the floor and the bed are free of stains, but the latter shows signs of a struggle. The quilt smells of beer, and the pillow, which is found six feet from the bed, shows marks of teeth.

From these facts, combined with the knowledge that Klyauzov was a strong man, Dyukovsky concludes that the deceased was attacked by three individuals. Two held him upon his bed while a third smothered him with the pillow—thus the signs of a struggle upon the bed. When the deed was done, the pillow, having no further use, was tossed across the room. Klyauzov's body was then dragged through the window and taken to a place of hiding. Theft was not the motive for the murder, since Klyauzov's watch and money were left behind.

We see that Dyukovsky observes the facts, which are stated in the second and third paragraphs, and then forms the hypothesis stated in the fourth paragraph. **Hypotheses are prospective reconstructions, reformulations, or representations of the situation or matter at hand in which the factor or element which is found to be problematic has been eliminated.** The formation of a hypothesis can be likened to the process of rewriting a script with a view to reaching the final curtain without one of the characters who appeared in the original script. The character in this analogy is the problem, and the final curtain is that condition or state of affairs in which our perplexity or frustration has been overcome.

Dyukovsky's reconstruction of the events in the bedroom fits the observed facts, but do his conclusions follow from those facts with necessity? They do not, as is seen from the fact that it is possible to imagine alternative reconstructions which fit the facts as well as Dyukovsky's. Here is one such reconstruction:

"THE SWEDISH MATCH": AN ALTERNATIVE HYPOTHESIS

There are two criminals. One stands guard outside, while the other slips in through the window. Klyauzov is in bed asleep, but the criminal brushes against the chair, waking him up. A struggle ensues, during which the criminal attempts to smother Klyauzov with the pillow. Klyauzov throws him off. The criminal then flees through the window, with Klyauzov following him in hot pursuit. When Klyauzov drops to the ground, the criminal who has waited outside strikes him on the head, killing him. The criminals then drag the body away to a place of hiding. Theft was the motive for the entry into the bedroom, but the criminals are too frightened by their murder to return to Klyauzov's bedroom for his valuables.

The point is not that this reconstruction is better than Dyukovsky's, but rather that it is no more nor less likely than his. Moreover, neither of these reconstructions might be the correct one. The best that can be said, given the available facts, is that each reconstruction sets forth a series of events which might have taken place. When the argument is inductive, the conclusion follows from the premiss with a degree of probability, but not with necessity. As guides to choosing the best hypothesis in the circumstances, the following criteria are helpful.

CRITERIA FOR HYPOTHESES

- The hypothesis should account for the facts it is intended to explain. (*Criterion of relevance*)
- The hypothesis should explain all of the relevant facts. (*Criterion of explanatory adequacy*)
- The hypothesis should assume no more than is necessary to explain the facts. (*Criterion of simplicity*)

- The hypothesis should not contradict well-established facts. *(Criterion of consistency with known facts)*
- It must be possible to verify or falsify the hypothesis. *(Criterion of verifiability)*

MANIPULATING FACTS AND PEOPLE

Let us put thoughts of hypotheses to the side and think again of facts, relying once more upon "The Swedish Match." We observe that the facts which are open to Inspector Dyukovsky's inspection are simply there. No one has attempted to manipulate or change them. No one, that is, has rearranged the room in a manner calculated to mislead him. (If you wonder how I know that, it's because I've read the story.) That means that all Inspector Dyukovsky has to do is piece the facts together and reconstruct the events which took place. In many of the cases we encounter, however, others attempt to distort the facts in order to lead us to conclusions which serve their own purposes. This is sometimes done by **drawing attention to certain points while directing attention away from certain other points. The fallacy associated with this technique is known as** *accent.* In a sales letter or advertisement, certain lines may be printed in larger letters than others and in bold type while other lines containing relevant choice-affecting information might be reproduced in very small letters or in fine type. In cases like these, all the relevant information may be provided, but some of it is presented in a manner calculated to make it easy to overlook.

Accent

The fallacy of accent includes the practice of quoting out of context. Imagine an advertisement for a film containing this quotation from a famous film critic: ". . . best movie of the year. . . ." The three dots, or "ellipses," indicate that a part of the original statement by the critic has been omitted. If that statement in its entirety had been "This could have been the best movie of the year with competent directing and experienced acting" the portion quoted would clearly have misrepresented the critic's view and conveyed the wrong impression to the reader. In this technique, information is distorted and the reader provided with misinformation. The critic's actual words are quoted, but taken out of their original context.

Reprinted with special permission of King Features Syndicate.

Quoting out of context

Accent is a form of manipulation. So is **the fallacious *argument to the people*, which consists either in using emotional language designed to drive people to particular conclusions or in using phrases like "everybody knows" or "no one these days thinks"** to create the illusion that the majority opinion is necessarily the correct one. In appealing to popular opinion, the argument to the people suggests that the true opinion is the one held by most people. This certainly sounds democratic, but it's a poor way to distinguish fact from fiction. According to the argument to the people, if most people believe that toads cause warts, then it must be true that they do. Of course it's also true on this reasoning that if the majority cease to believe that toads cause warts, then it's no longer true that they do.

THE ARGUMENT TO THE PEOPLE: EMOTIONAL FORM

No right-thinking person could fail to appreciate the corrosive effects which sex-sodden rock music has upon the impressionable minds of our cherished youth. Arise, my friends! Put on the armor of musical taste and take up the sword of righteous combat against those who would profit from the pounding misery which assaults us from our great nation's airways!

Argument from Force
By permission of Johnny Hart and Creators Syndicate, Inc.

Another way to manipulate individuals is to assume an attitude and use words and phrases appropriate to a situation which does not exist. Suppose a man were to telephone a woman who was a casual acquaintance and say, "Would you rather me take you to dinner at Rafferty's tonight, or would you prefer Arturo's?" This question would be appropriate if the woman had previously agreed to have dinner with the man, but if the question were the opening question in their conversation, with no prior mention of dinner, the man would be assuming, perhaps without good reason, that the woman wanted him to take her to dinner.

Questions like the one in the last example are known as **complex questions.** The name should not lead you to suppose, however, that complex questions will always be expressed in question form. A helpful synonym for the word *question* is *issue*. **The fallacy of complex question or complex issue consists in asking a question or presenting an issue which is complex as if it were a simple matter.** An issue is complex if it requires that a variety of dissimilar considerations be weighed in the balance or if it must be handled in stages or steps. In the typical complex question, one bypasses the first stage of the discussion and asks for a response or commitment which is appropriate only at a second or later stage. If Patricia says to her boy friend, "Oh, George, let's have a large wedding," the statement is a form of complex question if George has not previously made a commitment to marry Patricia.

Techniques of *manipulation* such as those we have been discussing **are distinguished from techniques of *coercion* in that the latter involve the use of force. Force includes physical force, threats, and intimidation. In the *argument from force*,**[1] **force is (fallaciously) used to determine the truth value of a proposition or the rightness or wrongness of a circumstance or state of affairs. The use of force is fallacious in that it is irrelevant to the question of fact.** Suppose you were playing softball with a person who claimed that it was his turn to bat when he had just struck out and another team member was waiting in line. Suppose further that the person who had just struck out owned the bat and ball being used for the game. If that person were to say, "It's my turn to bat again; I own the bat and ball," his threat would be clear. He would be saying that he would leave the field with his equipment and end the game if not given his way. His threat might have great psychological force and be successful, but his argument would be fallacious since it had no bearing on the question whether it was his turn to bat.

INDIRECT EVIDENCE: WHOSE OPINION DO YOU TRUST?

Another point of interest in "The Swedish Match" is that the facts, as found in the condition of the room, were open to Inspector Dyukovsky's direct inspection. He didn't have to rely upon anyone else to get them for him. There are many cases, however, in which

---

[1] The Latin name for this Fallacy is *Argumentum ad Baculum.*

we are called upon to rely upon the testimony of others in deciding what is fact or what we ought to believe. When we become ill, for instance, if we are not trained physicians ourselves, we go to a doctor and ask his or her advice. There's nothing wrong with that. In fact, it makes good sense to consult with doctors when we're ill. However, in the solitary fact that a person like a doctor is an authority in one area, and ought to be trusted in that area, we have no good reason to think that he or she ought to be trusted in some other area. A physician surely knows much more about medicine than the lay person, but that doesn't mean that he or she knows more about cars, lawn mowers, or quilting. A lay person, in fact, may know a lot more about these things than the doctor. **The fallacy of taking a person to be a trustworthy authority outside his or her own field of expertise is the *argument from authority.*** Compare:

My Aunt Bertha, who has bunions, says I have don't have a broken bone in my foot.

with

My family physician, who took an X ray, says I have a broken bone in my foot.

Whose opinion are you going to trust?

In the argument from authority, the arguer is distracted by authority.

IRRELEVANCE

Let's return to "The Swedish Match" once more. As Dyukovsky surveyed the room, he saw one dust-covered boot under the table, which, for him, fit in with his hypothesis of a struggle. How reasonable to think Klyauzov dropped his boots beside his bed when he retired for the evening and that the boot was kicked under the table during his struggle with the three men who attacked him! But you and I as critical thinkers must examine this fact again. If the boot was kicked under the table from beside the bed, how do we account for the layer of dust upon it? Boots which have been recently worn are not caked with dust. The more reasonable hypothesis is that the boot had lain unused under the table for some time.

This line of reasoning leads us to recognize that Dyukovsky took the dust-covered boot to be a relevant fact when it wasn't. It had nothing to do with the events which took place in the room. The roads to irrelevance are many, but we conclude this chapter with an examination of only two of them.

THE ARGUMENT FROM PITY

People are sometimes misled as to what's relevant in a particular case by their feelings of sympathy or pity for someone. There's nothing wrong with sympathy or pity, but it's a fallacy known as the **argument from pity** to reason from the fact that a person ought to be pitied to conclusions of fact unrelated to that. Suppose that a young man has been charged with armed robbery and that his attorney states in his defense that the young man is not guilty of the crime and points out to judge and jury that the young man was raised in poverty and cruelly mistreated by his parents. Those who heard the account of the young man's unfortunate past might appropriately be moved to pity him, but their pity should not blind them to the fact that the young man's misfortunes have no bearing upon the factual question whether he committed the act of armed robbery with which he has been charged.

By permission of Mel Lazarus and Creators Syndicate, Inc.

The argument from pity.

AD HOMINEM ARGUMENTS

In the argument from pity, people substitute their feelings for relevant facts and draw a conclusion based on those feelings. In the **ad hominem** argument, which is also fallacious, people argue that a person ought to accept a conclusion given his or her situation, or they simply abuse the person instead of attempting to disprove what the person says. **In arguments of this sort, reference is made to an individual who has made a claim rather than to the claim the individual has made.**

In the **situational ad hominem** one points to a person's circumstances. Someone says, for example, "You ought to approve of Israeli policy. After all, you're Jewish." To this, the Jewish person can reply, "My being Jewish has nothing to do with it. If I approve of the policy, it's because it encourages peace and strengthens the Israeli economy."

The relevant argument is directed at what the person says.

The ad hominem argument is directed against the person rather than what he or she says.

Perhaps the most common form of ad hominem argument is the abusive ad hominem. In this form, one individual simply attacks or abuses another. The person rather than the proposition or question at issue is made the focus of attention. Two men were discussing the philosopher Bertrand Russell's defense of pacifism. A person who had overheard snatches of their conversation asked them whose views they were discussing. When one of them told her, the person said, "Oh, I wouldn't pay any attention to him. He was an atheist." This move from the issue (whether Russell's pacifism was defensible) to the person (Russell) is characteristic of the ad hominem. The move is fallacious because the point mentioned is irrelevant.

THE CASE OF THE CONGRESSMAN'S AFFAIR

A male congressman who has introduced an important piece of health care legislation is subsequently discovered to have been having an affair with Ms. Z___, one of his assistants. At the congressman's next press conference, the matter of the affair is introduced by a reporter in this manner: "Sir, it has been reported that you are having an affair with Ms. Z___. Is this true, and if so, how long have you been having the affair?"

The congressman responds to this question, saying, "You're raising this question because you want the health care legislation which I have introduced to fail. As you surely know, this legislation is absolutely vital to the American people. I would have hoped that a reporter in your position would exercise more judgment in the questions he asked."

In ad hominem arguments, personal attacks or abuse often include references to an individual's motives, interests, or special relationships. An individual might propose a course of action only to be told that the proposal is self-serving in that he or she, as well as others, would benefit from adoption of the proposal. Alternately, an individual might attack the motives of someone who has put him or her in a difficult position. In "The Case of the Congressman's Affair," the congressman attempts to shift attention from the question whether he is having an affair to the irrelevant issue of the reporter's motives in asking him whether he is. In the process, he commits the ad hominem fallacy. While he may succeed in shifting attention to other matters, it is still the case that the congressman makes a logical error.

A FINAL WORD ON THE FALLACIES

Accent, complex question, and arguments to the people are fallacies of manipulation. Ad hominem arguments and the arguments from authority, force, and pity share in common the fact that the information in the premiss which is supposed to support the conclusion is irrelevant to its truth. The form of the argument to the people which emphasizes popular or majority opinion is also fallacious due to irrelevance. Remember, however, as we argue in Chapter 2, that relevance is contextual. In considering whether the evidence found in the premisses of arguments is relevant, and consequently worthy of consideration, it is always necessary to bear in mind the conclusion which is being defended. The threat of force by the thug on the street is presumably irrelevant to the question whether he has a right to your money, but presumably quite relevant to the question whether you give him your money. Your plumber's opinion as to the best player in the NFL may not be as well informed as that of a sports commentator, but his or her opinion on your pipes is probably more authoritative than the commentator's would be.

Summary

In this Chapter we have discovered that facts, which are one of the five grounds of inference examined in the text, are circumstances or states of affairs which are not in doubt, or which have been verified in some way. We begin with facts in attempting to reconstruct events. Upon opening our refrigerator door, for example, we discover that the food inside is warm. That the food is warm is a fact. But why is it warm? In seeking to answer this question we form hypotheses, or reconstructions of events which would have led to the food being warm. Some possible hypotheses are these:

- The refrigerator has been switched off.
- Its thermostat has been turned up.
- The refrigerator has malfunctioned.
- The power supply to the wall socket has been interrupted.

If any one of our hypotheses corresponds to what actually took place, it accounts for the fact that our food is warm. However, without further investigation, we do not know whether one of our hypotheses is correct.

These criteria serve as aids to forming hypotheses: relevance, explanatory adequacy, simplicity, consistency with known facts, and verifiability.

In addition to examining facts and hypotheses, we have considered some informal fallacies which occur as the result of manipulation, coercion, and our need to rely upon others for information. Also, we have examined fallacies which occur when we are distracted by irrelevant considerations. You'll find a brief sketch of these fallacies in the following paragraphs.

Let's think again of our simple but riveting refrigerator example. Upon discovering the warm food, there is no reason for us to doubt our senses. It is a fact that the food is warm. Moreover, it is highly unlikely in this case that someone is attempting to play a joke on us or otherwise deceive us, for instance, by replacing our cold carton of milk with a warm one. In other cases, however, people attempt to manipulate facts in order to deceive others. This is done by drawing attention to some points while directing attention away from others, or by quoting statements out of context. When we are led by such tactics to reason erroneously, the fallacy is called *accent*.

Others may also attempt to lead us to ignore relevant facts or points which ought to be investigated by using emotional language or phrases like "everybody knows." Such attempts are typical of *arguments to the people*. Through *complex questions,* people attempt to get us to assume a state of affairs which doesn't exist. "When are you going to drop out of school and get a job?" is a complex question. The person asking it wants a simple answer, like "At the end of this semester," but the person who's been asked the question may not in fact be planning to drop out of school. In that case, the question invokes a state of affairs contrary to fact.

People can also attempt to coerce us into accepting particular conclusions through the use of physical force, threats, or intimidation. An angry customer speaking to a store manager says, "Unless you agree that this tricycle I bought for my daughter is defective, and return my money, I'll take my business elsewhere." The threat may lead the manager to return the customer's money, but it does not settle the factual question whether the tricycle is defective. The customer's threat is an example of an *argument from force.*

When we are not in a position to get the facts we need, and find it necessary to rely upon the statements of other people, we can fall into error by assuming that a person is trustworthy outside his or her own field of expertise. This is the error we call the *argument from authority.* We would commit this error if we were to reason that our endodontist's views on U.S.-China relations is correct because he or she is highly skilled in performing such procedures as root canals.

In our deliberations we can also be distracted by irrelevant considerations. In the *argument from pity,* we reason from the fact that a person deserves our sympathy to an unrelated conclusion. A professor who concludes that a student deserves an A on his history exam because he sprained his ankle on an icy sidewalk reasons in this fallacious manner. In the *ad hominem argument,* we focus upon the person who makes a statement rather than what he or she says. The Chaplain of a college was teaching a Bible course. One of his students missed an exam for no good reason, but asked to make up the exam. The Chaplain refused, whereupon the student said, "You're supposed to be merciful. You're the Chaplain." In saying this, the student focused upon the person rather than the issue, which was whether she ought to be allowed to make up her exam.

A Look Ahead

In the next chapter, we consider inferences from facts to generalizations, as well as the application of generalizations and principles to particular cases. This gives us a further opportunity to explore the issues of the relevance of premisses to conclusions and the adequacy of premisses to establish their conclusions.

Exercises

Answers to questions marked with an asterisk may be found in the back of the text.

I. The following exercises require you to form hypotheses or construct imaginative situations which will account for the indicated facts. Follow the instructions in each exercise.

1. Read the following case, then complete the two exercises described at the end.

On Thursday afternoon, Samantha, George, and Rufus join Carl at his lakeside cabin. The four plan to spend a long weekend together, their sole objective being to relax and enjoy themselves. Samantha and George are married to one another. Although Samantha dated Carl for two years, the two are now nothing more than friends. George and Rufus served in the army together. Rufus and Carl were once business partners, but the business went into bankruptcy. Carl could have kept the business afloat by mortgaging his lakeside cabin, but chose not to do so.

Samantha and Carl cook dinner for the group on Thursday evening. They obviously enjoy each other's company. George, who is not completely convinced that they are nothing more than friends, watches them with a careful eye. The four friends share a bottle of wine at dinner.

On Friday morning at seven, George and Carl go fishing. Samantha tells them that she plans to take a sun bath, then drive into town for groceries. Rufus, who has opened an accounting service and does not get much exercise, states that he plans to go hiking. At ten, however, according to a statement he later gives the police, Rufus receives a call from his most important client and reluctantly drives back to town. He tells Samantha, who is sunning herself at the time, that he probably will not be able to return until the next day. Samantha estimates the time of Rufus's departure as ten fifteen. She tells the police that she showered shortly thereafter and left for town no later than eleven o'clock. She remembers hearing a news broadcast on the local radio station as she drove into town, and these are always given at the beginning of the hour.

At noon, according to the statement he later gives the police, George remains behind to watch Carl's fishing pole for him while Carl returns to the cabin for a package of cigarettes. At twelve thirty, George, who wonders why Carl has not returned, sees flames coming from the direction of the cabin. Running to the scene, he finds the cabin ablaze. The flames are too intense for him to go inside, so he runs to the nearest phone, which is a quarter of a mile away, to call the fire department.

The cabin is utterly destroyed by the fire. The remains of a human body are found inside. Although it is burned beyond recognition, a wristwatch lying by its left hand is identified as Carl's. A broken kerosene lantern is also found in the charred remains. Authorities conclude that the cabin caught fire when the lantern was broken but are puzzled as to why the lantern would have been lit in the middle of the day.

a. Given these facts, and acting upon the hypothesis that Carl was murdered, outline one possible series of events leading to his death. Name the murderer or murderers in your account.

b. Given these facts, and acting upon the hypothesis that Carl's death was accidental, outline one possible series of events leading to his death.

2. The characters in the following story, which is based upon "The Age of Miracles," by Melville Davisson Post,[2] are these:

Uncle Abner. A detective.

Randolph. An attorney and friend of Abner's.

Julia. A young friend of Abner's.

Adam Wolf. Deceased brother of Benton Wolf. In life, a boisterous man who hunted all the time. He and his brother Benton seized Julia's inheritance, which consisted in the house and land on which they live, by means of a weakness in the deed to the property.

Benton Wolf. A quiet man who was hardly ever seen outside the house. He seems eccentric, since he keeps his own coffin.

---

[2] See Melville Davisson Post, "The Age of Miracles," in *Uncle Abner: Master of Mysteries*. This collection of stories, which was originally published in 1918, has been reprinted by several publishers.

The story is set in Virginia in the mid-nineteenth century. Abner and Randolph meet Julia on the grounds of the estate which Julia's parents, now deceased, had previously owned. Adam Wolf has died as a result of a hunting accident and his body is lying in state in the large and rambling house which Julia's parents once owned. Julia has come out of curiosity to see the house where she lived as a little girl, while Abner and Randolph have come as a matter of courtesy to pay their last respects to the deceased.

The three file past the body. Benton Wolf has put his brother in the coffin which he had kept for himself. Around the face of the dead man, as Abner observes, there is a ring of buckshot wounds which serve as a reminder in death of the manner in which Adam Wolf died. Julia is touched by the sight of gloves on the dead man's hands. "Look," she says to Abner. "They were full of holes, but his brother has knitted them up."

"Perhaps his brother's death will have softened Benton Wolf's heart," says Abner. "Let us ask him, Julia, if he is now prepared to return the estate to you." The three ascend the stairs to Benton Wolf's study. He greets them with surprise. A map of the estate, which hangs on the wall, indicates the man's love for the estate which he and his brother had obtained at Julia's expense. Abner asks Benton Wolf to deed over the land and house to Julia, but Benton Wolf vehemently and scornfully refuses. Ignoring this, Abner instructs Randolph to draw up a deed of transfer, and when this is done he places the document upon the desk before Benton Wolf and says, "If you refuse to sign, I will remove the gloves from your brother's hands."

Benton Wolf signs the document, though reluctantly, and the estate is returned to Julia. "But why did he sign?" Julia asks as she, Abner, and Randolph leave the house.

Your task is to answer Julia's question for her by forming a hypothesis which is relevant, adequate, simple, consistent with the known facts, and testable.

II. Identify these fallacies in the following passages: Accent, argument from force, ad hominem argument, argument to the people, argument from pity, argument from authority, complex question.

1. Just ask around. Everyone—I mean everyone—knows that higher education today just isn't what it ought to be.

2. Notice on a sack of popular snack food:

> This **NEW** 4.2-ounce package
> is a **LARGER SIZE**
> than the old 4-ounce package.

3. Attorney to Court: This tender youth, who is my client, was injured from flying glass when the window at Haggarty's Hardware was broken. His face and arms were cut, requiring over fifty stitches. Anyone who has had a single cut knows how painful they can be. My client has suffered horribly. He is not, I tell you, the individual who broke that glass.

*4. Statement by an elected representative: The attempt to tie the minimum wage to increases in the cost of living is very popular with the voters in my district. Therefore, it is sound economic policy.

5. Jim says to Joe, "Say, are you the only ugly member of your family?"

6. Cancer is caused by prolonged exposure to cold temperatures. I know this is true, because my uncle, who is a tour guide in Texas, swears it's true.

7. Either you agree that the earth is flat or I beat up your little sister.

8.

> **Erika:** The welfare system in the United States has created a class of individuals who expect the government to support them. I, for one, don't think that people should be given free handouts.
>
> **Robert:** I don't accept what you say. Look, you're wealthy and you'll never be on welfare. What's wrong with you is that you just don't want to help people.

*9. Your honor, my client is not guilty of the crime of which he is charged. I direct your attention to his condition. You see his pale demeanor. He is recovering from pneumonia. In addition, you'll notice the sadness of his eyes. His mother recently died.

10.

> **Jones:** Mr. Brady says that consumption of large amounts of alcohol over an extended period can be dangerous.
>
> **Smith:** Why would you want to listen to what Brady says? The old man's a hopeless alcoholic.

III. Identify these fallacies in the following passages: Accent, argument from force, ad hominem argument, argument to the people, argument from pity, argument from authority, complex question.

1.

> **Linda:** Nicole cheated on her exam in Astronomy.
>
> **Betsy:** How do you know?
>
> **Linda:** Susan told me.
>
> **Betsy:** Oh, then it's absolutely not true that Nicole cheated. You mustn't believe Susan. She hates Nicole. You've noticed that Nicole has been dating Bill. Well, Susan was dating him before the Homecoming Dance, but when Bill met Nicole at the dance he dropped Susan like a hot potato. Susan hasn't had a good thing to say about Nicole ever since.

2.

> **Linda:** Your speaking of that Homecoming Dance reminds me that I'm grounded for the rest of the month.
>
> **Betsy:** What on earth for?
>
> **Linda:** I got in from the dance about 1:30 in the morning and my father was furious.
>
> **Betsy:** Gosh. What did you do?
>
> **Linda:** Well, when Dad yelled at me I said, "Come on, Dad. Everyone stays out late for dances these days, so it's all right for me to do it, too."

3. A man walks onto a car lot and pauses by a car. A salesman approaches him and says, "Would you like for me to have the car undercoated or would you like to drive it home as it is?"

*4.

    Senator: Our president has developed a foreign policy notable only for its inconsistency.

    Citizen: So you say; but I haven't seen you doing anything in office which would strengthen our foreign policy.

5. Interrogating officer to person in custody: Unless you sign this statement stating that you stole the money from Ed's Fill 'er Up, the prosecutor will ask for the maximum penalty in court.

6. It was an election year in the United States. During the course of a particularly heated debate in the U.S. Senate, one senator accused another (who happened to be a candidate for President of the United States), of playing presidential politics. The senator who was a candidate subsequently gained the floor and said, in a voice heavy with sarcasm, "I have been accused of playing presidential politics in this debate, but I notice that they never play presidential politics over in the White House. No, over there, everything that's said is for the good of the nation and has nothing to do with winning elections."

7. This recording has sold over a million copies, so the music on it must be of a very high quality.

8. My brother says that I owe him fifty dollars and that as proof he is not going to allow me to borrow his car.

*9. Jane, a telephone volunteer at the drug rehabilitation center, in a conversation with a drug addict who is threatening to commit suicide: "Suicide is immoral. It must be so, since Mr. Dickerson, who is an experienced locksmith, says it is."

10. One student to another, "I am surprised that you want to study chemistry. Everyone knows that bio's the science to take. Just ask anyone in the dorm, and you'll find that out."

You may be interested to know that

there are further examples of informal fallacies in Appendix II.

(Notice the clever use of Accent.)

IV. The arguments in the following passages are not fallacious, although you might be tempted to identify some of them as examples of the kinds of fallacies examined in this chapter. Explain why the arguments cannot be classified as fallacious.

1. Retailer in telephone conversation with customer: I hold a signed contract indicating that you will pay me for the goods you purchased. I have sent you three bills for the goods and you have ignored them. Unless you pay me the money you owe me by the end of the week, I will take you to small claims court.

2. Label on a can of beer sold in the United States: Government warning: (1) According to the Surgeon General, women should not drink alcoholic beverages

during pregnancy because of the risk of birth defects. (2) Consumption of alcoholic beverages impairs your ability to drive a car or operate machinery, and may cause health problems.

3. Jane to Sally: I can't go with you to the movies tonight. My father refused to give me the money for a ticket.

*4. I think that it's possible (says William) for human beings to face death without fear. Eye witness accounts indicate that Seneca apparently did. It's said that he even aided his executioners in bringing about his own death.

5. Jerry was wrong in his belief that he could swim the English Channel. He drowned after swimming only a third of the way across.

Chapter 5

GROUNDS OF INFERENCE II
FACTS, GENERALIZATIONS, AND PRINCIPLES

As in Chapter 4, our theme in this chapter is fallacies and grounds of inference in practical everyday reasoning. We examine generalizations and principles, which are two of the five important grounds of inference identified in the introduction. By the end of the chapter, you should have a basic understanding of the functions of these grounds of inference and the errors which can occur in connection with their use.

GENERALIZATIONS

***Generalizations* tell us something about relations between facts, the way things behave, or their connections with certain other things.** Without generalizations we would not be able to pass beyond our present immediate experience with any degree of confidence. The following propositions are examples:

- Some snakes are poisonous.
- Some humans are not ambidextrous.
- All swans are white.

These generalizations are suggested by experiences with snakes and observations of humans and swans. Such generalizations can, of course, be either true or false. The first two propositions are true, but the last is false.

Let's look at *the connection between facts and generalizations* in order to better understand the origin and function of generalizations. It is our observation of facts or specific instances which leads us to make generalizations. This is true in the arts and sciences, as well as such trivial circumstances of everyday life as the one on page 67.

THE SMOKER

When I was a boy, one of my uncles was one of my heroes. I watched his every move, as youngsters do when they love and respect someone, and did my best to imitate him in my own way. *Nothing* my uncle did escaped my attention. (I wonder if he noticed!)

My uncle was a cigarette smoker. He rolled his own. After a meal, he'd pull out a pack of cigarette papers and a cloth pouch of tobacco. With the paper curled into a U, he'd sprinkle tobacco into the trough of the U and then seal the edges of the paper with moisture from his tongue. Afterward, he'd light the cigarette with a long wooden match and take a deep drag.

After observing my uncle for a long while, I began to notice that he lit a cigarette after meals and that he lit one cigarette not too long after he'd put out another. As my observations became more precise, I observed that he lit a fresh cigarette between twenty and thirty minutes after having put one out.

It seems strange to me that I made the observations I've just described, but I'll leave the analysis of my mental life for another occasion because I want you to notice what happened in the course of my observations of my uncle. At first in my observations, I saw isolated events—a cigarette smoked here, a cigarette smoked there, and nothing more. But at some point—I can't say when—I generalized from my observations. I said, "My uncle lights a fresh cigarette between twenty and thirty minutes after he's finished smoking another." That was my generalization, and when I made it, my isolated observations were no longer isolated. Instead, I saw a pattern of behavior in my uncle, and when I saw that pattern, my uncle's behavior became predictable to me. With regard to his smoking, I knew what to expect when we were eating, or riding in his truck, or walking together through the woods. Moreover, my generalization enabled me, if I'd ever wanted to, to estimate at any time of the day how many cigarettes my uncle had already smoked and how many he'd smoke before he went to bed that night. You see what generalizations enable us to do and why they're so very important: they enable us to pass beyond our immediate experience to draw connections between events and things. That's why we should make some effort to understand how we come to make and use generalizations and where we can go wrong in doing so. Let's look at generalization errors.

The errors we can make with generalizations fall into two categories. We can err either in forming or making generalizations or in applying them to particular cases. We begin by considering errors of the first sort.

ERRORS IN MAKING GENERALIZATIONS

In making generalizations we can err either by

- Drawing a conclusion from too few instances

or

- Selecting instances which have some characteristic which renders them unfit to ground the generalization

These errors arise in cases in which it cannot be assumed that the data gathered is like—or will indicate the same result as—further data which might be gathered. The first kind of error can be called *the error of insufficient sample*. It is easily illustrated. Suppose that an enormous opaque jar is set on a table before you and that you are told (correctly) that it is filled with black and white, and only black and white, marbles. You are asked to determine what percentage of the marbles are black and what percentage white. Your life has been dull and uninteresting until now and it occurs to you that this might be the turning point you've been waiting for, so you eagerly reach into the jar for a handful of marbles. You draw out ten, six of which are black. If from this handful alone you were to conclude that sixty percent of the marbles in the jar were black, your inference would be weak because it was based upon an examination of an insufficient number of marbles. For all you know, there were only six black marbles in the jar and you happened to capture them all in the single handful you drew from the jar. You will need to take further handfuls of marbles from the jar to increase your certainty that the marbles in your original handful are representative of the lot. Two handfuls of marbles with the same, or nearly the same, ratio of black to white would render your conclusion stronger, but your conclusion would be stronger still after three handfuls. The certainty that your conclusion is true increases with each successive handful (again assuming that the ratio of black to white marbles in later handfuls is the same, or nearly the same, as the ratio in the first).

The handfuls of marbles you took from the jar are referred to as **samples.** It is critical in inductive reasoning that we base our conclusions upon *fair samples*. One handful of marbles is not a fair sample since the marbles in the handful are too few in number, given the total number of marbles (remember that our jar is enormous). With each successive handful, our sample becomes more complete (more fair) and the inference we draw from our sample correspondingly more secure. **To say that a sample is fair is to say that it is *adequate* to ground the generalization.**

The samples on which we ground our generalization should be *relevant* as well as fair. The term most often used to indicate relevance in this connection is *representative*. A representative sample is one which is typical of the class being investigated.

DIANE'S PSYCHOLOGICAL PROFILE

Diane, who majored in philosophy in undergraduate school, enrolled in a master's program in psychology. In her first semester, she and several other master's degree psychology students volunteered to participate in a psychological profile study. When the tests were scored, the person in charge of the study called her in. "Your answers to the questions aren't like those of anyone else who took the test," he said. "I don't understand it."

"Neither do I," Diane replied. "I answered the questions honestly."

"Hm." The person in charge of the study tapped his fingers on his desk and gazed at the ceiling for some moments. At last, his eyes returned to Diane, and he said, "Did you major in Psych in undergraduate school?"

"No," Diane replied. "I majored in Philosophy."

"Oh, that explains it," said the person in charge of the study as he picked up Diane's test and tore it into shreds.

The implication of the person in charge of the study was that Diane's test was unrepresentative. As a Philosophy major in undergraduate school, her manner of thinking and her approach to problems were sufficiently unlike that of the other participants in the profile to justify throwing out her answers. Presumably, the other students in the profile study were Psychology majors in undergraduate school.

Although the person in charge of the study acted in full confidence that his conclusion was correct, it is not always possible to know whether available information provides a representative foundation for a generalization. After three dates with Joe, Carlotta might conclude that he is a pleasant and entertaining person to be around, but the pleasure she has in his company might have less to do with him than with the external circumstances of their dates. On one occasion she and Joe might have gone with another couple who, through their wit and charm, made the evening pleasant and memorable. On another occasion she and Joe might have seen a movie in which Carlotta's favorite actor played the leading role, while on still another occasion the couple might have dined at an elegant restaurant whose food, service, and atmosphere were sufficient to make her overlook certain irritating features of Joe's personality. Each of these dates, then, might have features which rendered them unsuitable as a foundation for a conclusion regarding the pleasure to be derived from Joe's company. If Joe is, in fact, not as pleasant and entertaining as Carlotta thinks he is after these dates, then Carlotta, in a common phrase, has not seen him in his true light.

The problem here is whether the data Carlotta has gathered is representative. In the case of the marbles, this problem doesn't arise. Since we are told at the outset that the jar is filled with nothing but black and white marbles, we know that each marble is representative, and consequently "fit to be counted." All we have to do is draw out several handfuls to ensure that we have a fair sample. In Carlotta's case, however, external circumstances could ensure indefinitely that she does not gather information which provides a reliable foundation for her conclusion about Joe.

Generalizations based upon insufficient samples or upon unrepresentative instances of a kind are fallacious. They are known as *hasty generalizations*.[1] Hasty generalizations are inductive fallacies since in induction the conclusion is rendered probable, not certain, by the premises. In the case of the marbles in the jar, as we saw, the probability that the conclusion that sixty percent of the marbles in the jar are black is true increases with each successive handful in which sixty percent of the marbles are black.[2] If it is possible for us to draw samples at random from the top, the middle, and the bottom of the jar, the likelihood that our samples are representative is increased. In Carlotta's case, matters are more difficult due to the complexity of the observations she must make.

---

[1] Another name for this fallacy is *converse accident*.

[2] The probability would also be increased by a draw in which the sample is 55 percent black followed by a draw in which the sample is 65 percent black.

College Professor: Commencements at this college are held on the lawn except in case of rain. If it rains, they're held in the gymnasium.

College Alumna: What do you mean? I've been to three commencements at this college and the skies were clear at each one. It never rains at college commencements.

In this example, the college alumna generalizes from her experience at three commencements. It is doubtful that the fact that the skies are clear on one arbitrarily chosen day of the year provides any basis for a generalization regarding the weather on the corresponding day of the next year. In this case, too, the number of years in which the skies have been clear on those arbitrarily chosen days is irrelevant. The instances chosen are unfit to ground a generalization.

A further example of the hasty generalization fallacy is as follows:

It has been proven that this consumer advocate was working for his own personal gain and not in the interest of consumers. From now on I will not trust any consumer advocate.

In this example, a generalization regarding the trustworthiness of consumer advocates has been made on the basis of one case. The conclusion has been drawn that no consumer advocate is trustworthy. The inference is fallacious because it is based upon an insufficient sample.

Even though hasty generalization is a fallacious argument, **it is necessary to distinguish between the grounding for a generalization and the truth of the generalization. A generalization can be true even though it is not well grounded.** A conclusion regarding the percentage of black marbles in the opaque jar which was based upon only one handful would not be well grounded, but it might nevertheless be true. The conclusion might be true, but given that it was not well grounded there would be little reason to believe that it was true. The probability that a conclusion based upon several representative samples is true is greater than the probability that a conclusion based upon only one sample is true. As the probability that a conclusion is true increases, one's justification for belief increases as well.

The fallacy of hasty generalization occurs in connection with an inference to a generalization. It is also possible for us to make mistakes in applying generalizations to particular cases. The fallacy that occurs when this is done is known as the *fallacy of accident.* An accident, or accidental feature or characteristic, is one that is irrelevant so far as the matter under consideration is concerned. That which is accidental is traditionally contrasted with that which is essential. Consider the following three paradigm examples of the fallacy of accident.

> Exercise is good for the heart. Therefore, cardiac patients should be made to jog in the halls of the hospital.[3]

In this example, the generalization is stated in the first proposition. The generalization holds for healthy individuals but is applied to a special case, that of cardiac patients. The care required for such individuals may include restrictions on physical activity, and a cardiac patient's condition might make jogging a life-threatening behavior.

> An inebriated alcoholic begs a bartender for one more drink, saying, "Come on, let me have a drink. One little drink won't hurt anyone."[4]

The generalization here is that one little drink won't hurt anyone. This generalization, like the generalization in the first example, is true. However, the generalization does not apply either to alcoholics, who cannot afford to drink at all, or to individuals who are already drunk. In the example, the individual is both inebriated and an alcoholic. These are the accidental circumstances that render the rule inapplicable.

BIGGER IS BETTER

When I was five I received five dimes for my birthday, a small fortune in 1947. Later that afternoon, I ran down the street to show a twelve-year-old friend my fortune. He said: "Bert, I feel terrible, I forgot that this is your birthday. Let me give you five nickels for those five dimes." What a grand deal! So I ran home to show my family that I had doubled my fortune and learned about the fallacy of accident: Bigger is not always better—a mistake that many communities and some universities have also made.[5]

[5] From Albert B. Randall, "The Ontological Significance of Laughter: A Phenomenological Exploration." Unpublished manuscript. Used by permission.

---

[3] I owe this example to Kenneth R. Merrill.

[4] Source unknown.

Bert, in this example, assumed that the generalization "Bigger is better" is always true and learned that in certain cases it is not. Nickels are larger than dimes, but they are worth less, not more, than dimes.

You probably have recognized that **the fallacy of hasty generalization is the opposite of the fallacy of accident. In accident, the generalization occurs in the premiss of the argument and is misapplied to a particular case.** The case has accidental characteristics that put it outside the scope of the generalization. **In hasty generalization, the generalization occurs as the conclusion,** or proposition derived from samples. As we have seen, **the samples used as the basis for the hasty generalization are either unfair or unrepresentative. If they are unrepresentative, they have accidental or irrelevant characteristics.**

PRINCIPLES AND RULES

We can learn something about our word **principle** by tracing it back to the Latin word *principium,* which means "beginning." Just as events in our lives have beginnings, arguments have premisses, many of which, as described by their content, are principles. Premisses so described are taken to be fundamental or foundational in some way or other. No wonder, then, that principles are sometimes referred to as *axioms* or *assumptions.* They are propositions whose truth is taken for granted in arguments.

Rule and *principle* are often used interchangeably, and in many cases there is no need to draw a distinction between these words. When a distinction is made, it indicates that one statement, which in the context is referred to as the *principle,* provides a ground or foundation for another, which in the context is called the *rule.*

Criteria and standards, which we examine in Chapter 8, can occupy the same logical position as rules or principles. They function as rules or principles when they guide us in making a judgment or when they serve to ground that judgment. They can, in other words, serve as our basic assumptions when we are thinking critically.

In general, rules and principles (and criteria and standards) become relevant or operative only when a certain situation emerges. Principles and rules would cease to have relevance if there were never any situations to which they could be applied. For example, the principles or rules

One good turn deserves another

and

One has a general obligation to relieve the suffering of others

would not be needed if no one ever did a good turn for anyone else and if no one ever suffered.

PROBLEM AREAS
OF PRINCIPLES

The analysis of principles leads us to consider these four problem areas:

- The principle utilized in the judgment may be relevant to the case considered, but defective.
- The principle may be true or unproblematic in itself but irrelevant or inappropriate to the case to which it is applied.
- More than one principle may be relevant to a particular case, but one may be of greater weight or overriding significance in the circumstances. We may err by giving undue weight to a principle.
- A case may incorrectly be seen as an exception to a principle or rule that is true or unproblematic in itself.

RELEVANT, BUT DEFECTIVE

Principles can be defective. This is the first problem area of principles. Some principles or rules that you might adopt work quite well as long as you do not announce to someone else that you have adopted them. One prime example is the rule "Make promises when you have no intention of keeping them." Only by keeping your adoption of this rule to yourself can you expect other individuals to trust you enough to enable you to act on it. Let us refer to rules of this sort as *self-defeating*.[6] **A self-defeating rule is one that works only when others do not know that you are acting on it.** Such rules have obvious limitations. In warfare it is important to keep one's plans a secret from the enemy, but in private life, rules that cannot be shared with others can create unnecessary divisions.

Other rules can be characterized as *self-frustrating* or *self-canceling*. **Self-frustrating or self-canceling rules can be followed only if they are not followed by all.** A trivial example is provided by the case of Joe, a smoker who, wishing to save himself some money, decides that he will no longer buy cigarettes but will only smoke those that he can get someone else to give him. Joe can act on his rule, and save himself some money in the process, but only if others do not adopt the same rule. If all other smokers were to follow his example, then no one would purchase cigarettes and in a short time there would be no one from whom Joe could secure a cigarette. If Joe's rule is to work, then other individuals must not be inclined to adopt it. The purpose for which the rule was designed is frustrated if everyone in the relevant class (the class of smokers) follows it.

---

[6] I owe this term, as well as the term *self-frustrating,* which I introduce in the next paragraph, to Kurt Baier. Baier argues that one condition of moral rules is that they must be taught to everyone. This condition enables him to identify self-defeating, self-frustrating, and morally impossible rules. See Kurt Baier, *The Moral Point of View: A Rational Basis of Ethics* (Ithaca: Cornell University Press, 1958), 195–200.

This example suggests that a rule of action ought to be one that everyone could follow in cases in which one is not interested in eliminating a particular practice. If one is interested in eliminating the practice of cigarette smoking, for example, then Joe's rule of action is a good one to follow. In that case, however, Joe needs to urge others to follow his example.

TRUE, BUT IRRELEVANT
OR INAPPROPRIATE

In some cases, **the principle itself is unproblematic but irrelevant or otherwise incorrectly applied. This is the second problem area of principles.** As an illustration of this problem area, consider the following case:

THE HISTORY PROFESSOR'S SALARY

A history professor at a small college resigned to take a position at another school. The dean of the college hired a man with comparable academic qualifications and experience to take the first man's place, but the newly hired professor was given a salary that was two thousand dollars higher than the history professor who was leaving would have been paid if he had stayed on at the school. This came to the notice of an interested third party who questioned the dean on the discrepancy in salary. The dean responded that the professor who was leaving was married but did not have children, while the man who had been hired to take his place was married with two children and consequently in need of more money.

The dean of the college had used the following principle: "Pay a person according to his needs." There is nothing wrong with this principle in itself and the dean no doubt felt himself quite benevolent in applying it. However, it is arguably the case that the dean made an error of judgment. He acted on a principle that simply was not relevant to the situation. Given current practice, colleges pay professors according to academic qualifications—which include degrees held, publications, and length of teaching experience—not family size. If professors were paid by the size of their families, a person with a master's degree, no teaching experience, and three children might be given a higher salary than a person with a Ph.D., ten years of teaching experience, and no children.

RELEVANT, BUT HOW WEIGHTY?

On some occasions, **more than one principle is relevant to a particular situation, and one is forced to weigh the relative importance of the principles. This is the**

third problem area of principles. Sometimes the choice between relevant principles is painful and controversial, as the following case illustrates.

LAST ON, FIRST OFF

For several years the city of Memphis, Tennessee, in an attempt to overcome past discrimination in hiring practices, actively recruited members of racial minority groups for service in its fire department. Quite a few blacks were hired as a result.

In May 1991, financial difficulties forced the city to lay off some of its firefighters. In accordance with its contract with the firefighters union, the city followed the last on, first off seniority rule according to which the last person hired is the first person to be laid off, the next to last person hired the next to be laid off, and so forth. As a result, many black firefighters were laid off.

The black firefighters sued, arguing that the affirmative action plan adopted by the city should have precedence over the seniority rule. Both a federal district court and a federal appeals court decided in their favor, but the U.S. Supreme Court overturned these decisions, ruling that seniority systems such as that followed by the city of Memphis fell under the protection of Title VII of the Civil Rights act of 1964 and could not be set aside for programs of affirmative action.

In this case, affirmative action principles that concern justice in hiring and firing practices had to be weighed against a seniority rule long followed in business. The decision was not an easy one, and not everyone was satisfied with the final Supreme Court ruling.

A LEGITIMATE EXCEPTION?

A fourth problem area of principles concerns exceptions to principles. We can err in a particular case by allowing an exception to a legitimate principle or rule. Authoritative bodies are often called on to make exceptions to rules, regulations, or requirements, but if a rule is just and duly constituted there should be a presumption against making an exception to it. It is not always easy for those in authority to distinguish legitimate exceptions and deserving cases from others, but in many cases the source of the error is favoritism due to special ties to one of the parties, a bias in favor of one party due to such considerations as religion, race or gender, or the exercise of power or influence by one party to the deliberations.

Individuals, like organizations, often make exceptions in favor of those they like or those who are like them, but individuals are often inclined to see themselves as special cases as well. People who steal, for example, want to be exempt from the principle "One should not steal" in order to act on the principle "Take what you want when you want it." However, they do not want others to be exempt from the no-stealing principle. In fact, they lock their doors when they leave home in order to encourage others to act on the no-stealing principle.

THE REQUIREMENTS
OF OBJECTIVITY

Our analysis in this section has not led us to a general theory as to what constitutes a well-grounded principle. Perhaps no general theory is possible at present and investigators will have to confine themselves to limited or regional statements designed to fit specific classes of principles. It is perhaps too much to expect of principles, and especially those of a practical sort, that they be not simply well grounded but absolutely certain. **Of principles designed to guide us in choices of alternative courses of action, it is our view that the requirements of objectivity are met when we determine what considerations there are that count against the principle and share them with other interested parties. It is also our view that a principle of action is worthy of adoption if the considerations counting against it are not overwhelming, which is to say that there are fewer objections to it than to some other principle that might be offered in its place.**

Summary

This chapter has examined these two grounds of inference in practical everyday reasoning: generalizations and principles. We have found that there is a close connection between facts and empirical generalizations. Facts provide the inspiration and basis for empirical generalizations, as well as the means by which we put them to the test. Just as the height of the tides varies with the position of the moon, so the trustworthiness of generalizations varies with the support provided them by facts. The connection is relatively simple, clear, and tight.

Generalizations originate in our observation of facts, but they enable us to pass beyond isolated facts to discern patterns of behavior in individuals and regularities in nature. Were it not for generalizations, much of our experience would be devoid of implications for the next moment. Generalizations, in short, assist us in grouping things together and making sense out of our world.

Two fallacies occur in connection with generalizations. The first is hasty generalization, which occurs either when a generalization is not grounded in a fair sample or when it is not grounded in a representative sample. The second is accident, which occurs when a generalization is applied to a situation or case that has special ("accidental") features that make the generalization irrelevant to it.

Principles enable us to make choices between alternative courses of action and to decide what is required of us in particular situations. While there is a close connection between facts and empirical generalizations, there is a close connection between particular kinds of situations or circumstances and principles. Situations in which we find ourselves call out principles for decision making, just as the cry of a baby calls its mother into action. We have examined four problem areas of principles. The first is principles themselves, which can be defective by being self-frustrating or self-canceling. The other three problem areas of principles are their irrelevance in particular situations, their relative weight when more than one is relevant in a particular situation, and special cases that seem to constitute exceptions to principles. These four problem areas remind us that while we cannot disprove principles by facts the way we can disprove false generalizations, we can make mistakes in the selection and application of principles to experience.

HELPFUL HINT

Hasty generalization fallacies are sometimes identified as accident fallacies, and vice versa. The following observations and suggestions help you distinguish these fallacies:

- Look for the conclusion of the argument. In the hasty generalization, the generalization is found in the conclusion. In the accident, the generalization is found in the premiss.
- The hasty generalization is an inductive fallacy. As such, it is subject to the two problems that faulty inductive arguments can have. First, the samples on which the generalization is based can be unrepresentative. (This is another form of the problem of relevance.) Second, the sample of evidence can be insufficient to ground the generalization. (This is another form of the problem of adequacy.) The term *hasty generalization* suggests that the problem of relevance was uppermost in the mind of the logician who coined the term.
- Accident, by contrast with hasty generalization, is a deductive fallacy. In accident, the chief problem is the inapplicability of the generalization to the case at hand. The fallacy consists in fastening on "accidental" or inessential features of the case to which the generalization is applied. The generalization is irrelevant to the essential features of the case.

A LOOK AHEAD

In Chapter 6, we examine the fourth ground of inference identified in the Introduction, which is analogies. In reasoning by analogy, we look for similarities and dissimilarities between things in order to move from familiar, safe ground to unfamiliar ground. Thus, when we observe that Gerald becomes angry when he is unable to balance his checkbook, we look for similar responses in other circumstances. Does he become angry when he dials a number repeatedly only to get a busy signal or when he discovers that the battery in his automobile is dead? If so, we are not surprised. Similarly, we reason by analogy when, in contemplating an investment, we infer that the performance of a company we have not examined will be like that of a company whose performance is known to us. For example, when we observe that the stock of a company in the paper industry is cyclical, and that the price of its shares rose over a five-year period before declining, we assume (perhaps incorrectly) that the stock of another company in the same industry will do the same. Analogical reasoning, like reasoning from generalizations, enables us to pass beyond our immediate experience, and for that reason it is extremely important.

Exercises

Answers to questions marked with an asterisk may be found in the back of the text.

I. Answer the following questions.

1. What are empirical generalizations?

2. What is the error of insufficient sample?

3. What is meant by saying that a sample is "unrepresentative"?

*4. Explain the difference between the claim that a generalization is true and the claim that it is well grounded.

5. What are two possible defects of principles or rules?

6. Can you provide an example from your own experience of a principle that was incorrectly applied?

7. Reread the case of "The History Professor's Salary." What principle should the dean have used in making his decision?

8. When are the requirements of objectivity met for principles that are designed to guide us in choices between alternative courses of action?

II. Identify any accident or hasty generalization fallacy in the following statements. Write "no fallacy" for any passage in which these fallacies do not occur.

1. I have my doubts as to the value of a college education. Abraham Lincoln didn't go to college, did he?

2. Communism has worked quite well in China.

3. You can judge a man by the company he keeps. Chief of police Harrison must be an unsavory character, for he is often seen in the company of criminals.

*4. John Stuart Mill defended liberty of thought and action and was concerned to eliminate what he called the "tyranny of the majority." I think that Thomas Jefferson would have approved of many of his views.

5. Sally says she did not enjoy the introductory course in physics and that if she had it to do over again she would not take the course. The conclusion I draw from this is that the course in physics is not universally popular.

6. Judge Timons has ruled against the defendant in the last twelve cases in which the defendant was a member of an ethnic minority. The defendant in this case is a member of an ethnic minority, so it is possible, and perhaps even likely, that Timons will rule against her.

7. Liberty of thought and action are cherished civil rights. I am justified, therefore, in interrupting Professor Peters's lecture on quantum mechanics to express my undying belief in God.

8. Eric plans to drive from New Orleans to Boston, but I have urged him to fly. Flying is in general a speedier mode of transportation than driving.

*9. The American passengers on the ship were rowdy and rude. All Americans, I suppose, are the same.

10. A person has a right to possess and use his own property, so you must return Johnnie's gun to her even though she plans to use it to shoot her man Frankie.

11. Our country is founded on the principle of free speech. Therefore, Rupert Kingsworthy should not have been punished for shouting "Fire!" in the crowded ballroom during the senior prom.

HELPFUL HINT

For further practice with accident and hasty generalization fallacies, try your hand at Parts II and III of the Chapter 7 exercises and the arguments in Appendix III. Some accident and hasty generalization fallacies are found in both places.

Chapter 6

GROUNDS OF INFERENCE III

ANALOGIES

As in the following case, in some inductive arguments the conclusion states a generalization from a sample of evidence.

DELORES GENERALIZES

When doing her weekly shopping for groceries, Delores bought a bag of cookies. At home, she opened the bag. The cookies at the top were covered with mold. "The cookies in this bag are all bad," she muttered to herself in disgust.

In this case, Delores does not examine every cookie, but draws a conclusion regarding every cookie in the bag from observation of the moldy cookies at the top. In a generalization from a sample of evidence, a conclusion about an entire class—in this case, the cookies in the bag—is based upon an examination of representative samples from the class—in this case, the cookies at the top. Delores's conclusion regarding the cookies in the bag was probably true, but nevertheless, there might have been a mold-free cookie somewhere in the bag.

Other inductive arguments are **analogical**—that is, they are grounded in a perception of a similarity or resemblance between two or more phenomena.

DELORES REASONS ANALOGICALLY

Delores, who was throwing a party, bought six bags of cookies. They were all the same brand and the same kind. At home, she opened one of them. The cookies at the top of the bag were covered with mold. "These cookies are bad," she said, "and I'll bet the cookies in every one of the other bags are bad as well."

In this case, Delores's inference is based upon the evident similarities between the bags of cookies. We are told that they were all of the same brand and type, but in addition, they might all have had the same expiration date stamped upon them. This would be another relevant similarity. In the previous example, Delores inferred that all of the cookies in the bag she opened were moldy. In this case, she infers that the cookies in the unopened bags are also moldy, and she does this because the other bags are similar in relevant ways to the one she opened. Her conclusion is probably true, but it is possible that the cookies in the other bags are mold-free. The bag she opened might be dissimilar to the others in an important way. For instance, it may not have been sealed properly, while the others were. In that case, mold might have formed in the bag she opened, but not in the others.

RELEVANCE

This simple example suggests that **in constructing and evaluating analogies, the considerations of paramount importance are the relevance and number of the observed similarities and dissimilarities.** In Chapter 2, *relevant evidence* is defined as "evidence which, if true, increases the likelihood that a proposition being defended is true." Irrelevant facts, of course, are those which neither increase nor decrease the likelihood that a proposition being defended is true. In connection with analogies, *relevant similarities* are those which increase the likelihood that the inference to a further similarity is correct, while *relevant dissimilarities* are those which decrease the likelihood that the inference is correct. *Irrelevant similarities and dissimilarities* are those which neither increase nor decrease the likelihood that the inference is correct.

Because irrelevant similarities and dissimilarities have no bearing upon the strength or weakness of the analogical inference, they should be disregarded. Suppose that we are comparing the quality of ride of one automobile with that of another. The fact that both automobiles are black has no bearing upon the inference. Neither would it make any difference if the automobiles were of different colors.

Although irrelevant similarities and dissimilarities should be disregarded, those which are relevant should be taken very seriously. Relevant similarities strengthen an inference, while relevant dissimilarities weaken it. To illustrate this point, let us consider the following list of facts regarding two individuals whom we will call "Terry" and "Tracey":

TERRY	TRACEY
1. Male	Male
2. Eighteen years of age	Eighteen years of age
3. Two years of high school Spanish	Two years of high school Spanish
4. Quarterback on high school team	First chair French horn, high school band
5. Graduate of Urban High School	Graduate of Urban High School
6. Top ten percent of graduating class	Top ten percent of graduating class
7. Score in ninetieth percentile, college placement exam in Spanish	Score on college placement exam in Spanish unknown

Terry and Tracey are similar in 1, 2, 3, 5, and 6, and dissimilar in 4. We do not know whether the two are similar with regard to 7. From these similarities and dissimilarities, *and these alone,* what can we infer regarding Tracey's performance on the college placement exam in Spanish? Can we infer that it is probable that his score is as good as Terry's? That it is likely? Possible? In order to come to a decision, we need to decide which similarities are relevant and which are irrelevant. We also need to decide whether the dissimilarity in 4 is relevant.

On reflection, it seems that the similarity in 1 is irrelevant and can be disregarded. Gender by itself has no particular bearing on the question asked. The dissimilarity in 4 also appears to be irrelevant, since there is no reason to think that Terry's experience as a football player, or Tracey's as a musician, contributed to their knowledge of Spanish.

The similarity in 3 is relevant, for it indicates the amount of experience the two have had in Spanish. The similarities in 6 and 5 are also relevant. Both students were near the top of their class in the same high school. This means that we do not have to consider whether their high schools or their courses in Spanish are of equal quality. The information given in 2 is relevant in that it enables us to infer that in all likelihood the two young men took the exam in the same year. This is important, since it means that we need not consider whether the exam taken by one was more difficult than that taken by the other. We can assume that in all likelihood the men took the same exam.

Given the facts available to us, and those alone, our analysis leads us to infer that it is likely, and even probable, that Tracey's score is as good as Terry's. However, we recognize that relevant dissimilarities unknown to us could reduce the likelihood that our inference is in fact correct. Suppose that, unknown to us, Spanish is spoken in Terry's home and that he learned Spanish as well as English as he was growing up, while only English is spoken in Tracey's home. In this case, Terry's knowledge of Spanish is surely much greater than that of Tracey, with the result that he can be expected to earn a higher score on the college placement exam in Spanish than Tracey.

KNOWN FACTS (AREN'T ALWAYS SUFFICIENT IN ANALOGICAL REASONING)

One Friday morning, the night watchman in Smith's Auto Parts is found bound and gagged. The alarm system has been expertly disconnected and the safe emptied of its contents. The safe is fullest on Thursday evenings and Fridays, since its contents are always taken to the bank at the close of business on Friday. These facts are consistent with the mode of operation of Spike Mallory, who has moved on from residential burglaries to burglaries in the automotive retail aftermarket. Faraday, who is at the scene with Inspector Marvel, says, "It must be Mallory, all right. This burglary is exactly like those he performed before we sent him to prison five years ago."

Marvel nods his head reflectively, and says, "Yes, the pattern is exact. You're right to see the similarities between the robberies. However, it's early days yet. We can't rule out the possibility that some one or more persons who are acquainted with Mallory's methods are imitating him."

"I hadn't thought of that," says Faraday. "And you think that the robberies might have been done by a gang?"

"It's possible," Marvel replies as he adjusts his hat. "It's possible."

ADEQUACY

Mention of the possibility of facts unknown to us prompts us to observe that **in constructing and evaluating analogies, the other important consideration in addition to relevance is the number of relevant similarities and dissimilarities.** We observed in Chapter 5 that we should avoid basing generalizations upon a small number of samples. Similarly, we should avoid inferences from one or a small number of resemblances between objects to some further resemblance. From the facts that Frank and Jesse are both from Oklahoma, eighteen years old, Baptists, love strawberries, and that Frank likes apple pie, it would be inept to infer that Jesse also likes apple pie. The inference would be inept because only one fact—their love of strawberries—is relevant to Frank and Jesse's shared tastes in food. The justification for the conclusion that Jesse, like Frank, likes apple pies would be much greater if it were also known that Frank and Jesse both like mince meat, rhubarb, cherry, and apricot pies.

In determining the number of relevant similarities, it is important not to count as separate those which are inseparably connected with one another. For example, the fact that two individuals have broken their legs and that each now walks with a limp should be taken together as one point of resemblance rather than separately as two. In general, the similarities and dissimilarities on which an inference is based should be independent of one another.

Summary

Analogies must be evaluated on a case-by-case basis, but **in general, any *analogy* is acceptable whose relevant similarities are greater in number than and/or more important than its relevant dissimilarities and whose similarities are sufficient in number to justify the strength of the conclusion drawn.** As is emphasized in Chapter 2, we should not claim more in a conclusion than is warranted by the premises.

GENERALIZATIONS AND ANALOGIES

The evaluation of analogical arguments is similar to the evaluation of generalizations, which are discussed in Chapter 5. Each must meet the conditions of relevance and adequacy. In making generalizations, we require that our samples be representative (relevant) and fair (adequate). Similarly, in analogical inferences we require that the similarities be such as to increase the likelihood that the inference is correct (relevant), and that the similarities be sufficient in number and importance, and greater in these respects than any relevant dissimilarities (adequate). The strength of the analogical inference is in proportion to the number and importance of relevant similarities in relation to relevant dissimilarities. As the number of such similarities increases in proportion to relevant dissimilarities, the inference becomes stronger.

A LOOK AHEAD

It is difficult to see how we could get along without an ability to reason analogically. When we lack experience in some area, we rely upon our ability to perceive similarities between the situation in which we find ourselves and previous situations in which we have made observations. Analogies are also sometimes the source of our thinking that two events or kinds of events are connected as cause and effect. This happens when we observe similarities between several occurrences of pairs of events in which one always follows the other. We examine causal reasoning in Chapter 7.

Exercises

Answers to questions marked with an asterisk may be found in the back of the text.

I. State the analogies in the following passages and critically evaluate them by reference to the relevance and number of similarities and dissimilarities.

1. Rick and Vick are cousins. Both are sixteen years old, play football and basketball on their high school teams, and are strong B students. Rick grew up on his parents' cattle ranch in Montana. Vick grew up in his parents' brownstone house in Brooklyn. Rick has a strong interest in cattle. Thus, Vick also has a strong interest in cattle.

2. Amanda and Zelda share a high-rise apartment in a large city. Each works as an accountant, though they are not employed by the same company. Amanda moved to the city from a small town, but Zelda grew up in the city. Each woman is in her late twenties. Amanda is five feet eight inches tall and weighs 148 pounds. Zelda is five feet four inches tall and weighs 120 pounds. As tenants in their apartment building, Amanda and Zelda have free access to athletic facilities, which include a heated swimming pool, sauna, and weight room. Amanda never uses these facilities and never exercises, but Zelda works out every other day. Zelda can bench-press 90 pounds with ten repetitions. We may conclude that Amanda could also bench-press 90 pounds with ten repetitions if she made the attempt.

*3.

Micki: Dear, have you ever had rhubarb pie?

Darrell: Yes, once.

Micki: Did you like it?

Darrell: I vowed to never have another piece of rhubarb pie as long as I lived.

Micki: You'd try a piece of my rhubarb pie if I made some, wouldn't you?

Darrell: Isn't that a little like asking a man who's broken his right leg if you'll allow him to break his left leg so he can find out if it hurts as much as the other break?

4.

Allen: Hon, that was a great dinner you fixed tonight. A gourmet's delight. The Harrisons enjoyed it, too. We should have them over more often, you know.

Betsy: I'm glad you enjoyed the dinner, dear, but now I could use some help cleaning up in the kitchen. It took me half the afternoon to make that dinner.

Allen: Oh, no you don't. You'll get no help from me.

Betsy: Why not?

Allen: Well, it's like this: When my uncle took me fishing as a boy we had a rule: If you catch it, you clean it. I had to clean all the fish I caught, and the same applies here. If you cooked the dinner, you have to clean up afterward.

Note: After this conversation there was a brief silence; then Allen heard the back door being opened and slammed shut and the car being started. There was a screech of tires as Betsy backed out of the driveway. This, and the dishes stacked in the kitchen sink, were testimony to her rejection of his argument.

5. "The planet Mars possesses an atmosphere, with clouds and mist closely resembling our own; it has seas distinguished from the land by a greenish colour, and polar regions covered with snow. The red colour of the planet seems to be due to the atmosphere, like the red colour of our sunrises and sunsets. So much is similar in the surface of Mars and the surface of the Earth that we readily argue there must be inhabitants there as here." (From W. S. Jevons, *Elementary Lessons in Logic: Deductive and Inductive*.)

6. Against Socrates' view that the soul survives the death of its body and is subsequently reborn in another body (the doctrine of reincarnation), Socrates' friend Cebes suggested that the soul might be likened to a cloak, which on the death of its owner is passed on to another person. The cloak thus survives the death of its owner but in the course of being handed on to other owners becomes worn and threadbare and is eventually discarded. Similarly, the soul might survive the death of this body but eventually wear out and fail to survive the death of a later body. On this analogy it appears that Socrates' view that the soul is immortal is untrue. (Plato, *Phaedo*)

7. A boy and his sister have been playing together. The boy becomes ill, and his mother learns from him that he has eaten some unripe fruit. Some time later, the boy's sister becomes ill. Her mother concludes that she has also eaten some of the unripe fruit. (Adapted from A. L. Jones, *Logic, Inductive and Deductive: An Introduction to Scientific Method*.)

*8. A conductor would never make his or her way through a symphony if he or she had to ask the members of the symphony whether they wanted to go on to the second or the third movement. Similarly, a political leader would never get anything done if he or she had to consult with the people. A political leader should forge ahead without regard to public opinion.

9. On becoming ruler of Syracuse, in Sicily, Hiero pledged to offer a golden crown to the gods, so a quantity of gold was weighed and a craftsman appointed to do the work. When the crown was delivered, Hiero had it weighed. When the weight of the crown was found to be the same as the gold which he had entrusted to the craftsman, Hiero was satisfied that he had not been cheated. Subsequently, however, someone suggested to Hiero that the craftsman might have mixed a little silver with the gold, thus producing a crown which was equal in weight to the original gold but not equal in value. This suggestion so disturbed him that Hiero called in Archimedes, the great scientist. "Find out whether silver has been mixed with gold in this crown," he ordered.

At first Archimedes did not know how to proceed. The presence of silver could not be detected through a visual inspection, since the crown was the color of gold, so other measures were required; but what could they be? According to ancient sources, Archimedes retired to his house to think, but no solution came to him until he lowered himself into his tub for a bath and observed the water rising on either side of him. Seeing the solution in this commonplace occurrence, he shouted "Eureka," which means "I have found it," and ran down the street dripping wet and—some say—naked.

Archimedes's insight was that some substances weigh more than others. The technical term for this is "specific gravity." Once he had this insight he was able to perform an experiment which answered Hiero's question. He took a jar and filled it to the brim with water. This jar was placed in a pan or another larger jar. A quantity of pure gold which was equal in weight to the crown was lowered into the jar of water, and the water which overflowed into the pan was collected and measured with care. The jar was then refilled and the process repeated with a quantity of pure silver equal in weight to the crown. The final stage of the experiment consisted in lowering the crown itself into the jar and measuring the overflow from it. The result was a conclusive answer to the question Hiero had ordered Archimedes to answer.

The specific gravity of gold is greater than that of silver. Therefore, a quantity of gold of a certain weight will be smaller than a quantity of silver of the same weight. Since it is smaller, it will displace less water than the corresponding quantity of silver. Archimedes demonstrated this when he placed first the gold then the silver in the jar and measured the results. When he lowered the crown into the jar, it caused more water to overflow the jar than the gold had done but less than the silver had done. Therefore, the crown was a mixture of gold and silver and Hiero had been cheated. The experiment added to Archimedes's fame and presumably sealed the fate of the craftsman as well.

10. Charles Albanese was convicted of murdering his father, his mother-in-law, and his mother-in-law's mother by arsenic poisoning. He was also convicted of the attempted murder of his brother. (Arsenic powder was found in his brother's cookie jar.) The prosecution presented evidence at Albanese's trial that he had wanted to gain control of the family's manufacturing business in order to support an extravagant lifestyle.

Throughout his trial, and later, Albanese maintained his innocence. With his execution scheduled for the morning of September 20, 1995, Albanese asked the Illinois Prisoner Review Board to clear his name or execute him. He said that he did not want his sentence changed from execution to natural life. In response to this request, Philip Prossnitz, a McHenry County, Illinois, prosecutor, stated that to protect the life of this convicted killer would be analogous to arguing that a cancer cell had a right to life. Albanese was executed early in the morning of September 20, 1995.

II. State the analogies in the following passages and critically evaluate them by reference to the relevance and number of similarities and dissimilarities.

1. My uncle doubled his money on a Canadian mining stock called Hard Rock Mining. Strike Three is a Canadian mining stock which is located in the same area as Hard Rock Mining. Perhaps I should invest some money in Strike Three Mining.

2.

    Micki: How's your leftover steak, dear?

    Darrell: Fine, just fine.

    Micki: Does it have more flavor now than it did the other night when we had it for the first time?

    Darrell: I can't tell that it does. Why?

    Micki: Well, when I marinate steak before I cook it, the herbs and spices I put in seem to soak into the steak so that the longer I let the steak marinate the more flavorful it is.

    Darrell: It's a good steak; that's all I can say. Pass the potatoes, will ya?

3. I blew my breath upon the window and moisture formed. I found moisture upon the grass outside my house this morning. It must have been caused by the wind blowing upon it.

*4. I was waiting for a cashier in a small drugstore to check the price on an item I wanted to buy. Business was slow, and the store was quiet, so I could hear an assistant manager discussing a problem with a new employee. "No, you don't understand," she said. "You are required to sign up for your coffee breaks. You can't take them whenever you want to. If every employee took a coffee break whenever he or she felt like it, there would eventually come a time when every employee was on a coffee break and no one was watching the store. We wouldn't have anyone to stock, or check, or do anything."

    This statement by the assistant manager reminded me of one of Thomas Aquinas's proofs for the existence of God. Aquinas observed that things in the universe came into existence at different times. At some previous time, then, there must have been nothing in the universe. However, there are things in the universe now, so at that former time there must have been some Being who brought things into existence. That Being, of course, is God.

5. As Micki and Darrell were eating brunch, the following exchange occurred.

    Darrell: That was quite an omelet, Micki. You're a great cook.

    Micki: Thanks, Hon. I love to cook, you know.

    Darrell: Yeah, I know. Say, these crumpets are excellent, too. There's nothing I like better than warm crumpets with butter, cream, and strawberry preserves.

    Micki: I like the crumpets, too, but I think I might try to make some of my own.

    Darrell: Why do that when you can buy crumpets like these at the store? It seems like a lot of trouble.

    Micki: Oh, I don't know. You like to play the guitar, don't you?

    Darrell: You know I do. What's your point?

    Micki: I might ask you why you go to the trouble of playing the guitar when there are so many good CDs of guitar music at the store.

    Darrell: Oh.

6.

    Teri: Mom, I'm so hot I don't know what to do.

    Teri's Mom: I'm sorry, Teri, but there's not much I can do about it. It often gets hot here in Texas in the summer.

Teri: By the way, Mom, you let Roxanna fly to Florida by herself to spend the weekend with one of her friends, so you ought to let me fly to California to spend the weekend with one of my friends. I'd be cool there.

Teri's Mom: Teri, your sister Roxanna is eighteen years old, but you're only five years old. I can't let you fly off by yourself.

Teri: Some day you'll regret this.

*7.   "I have avoided the inquiry into the Origin of the Moral Faculty . . . by the simple assumption (which seems to be made implicitly in all ethical reasoning) that there is something under any given circumstances which it is right or reasonable to do, and that this may be known. If it be admitted that we now have the faculty of knowing this, it appears to me that the investigation of the historical antecedents of this cognition, and of its relation to other elements of the mind, no more properly belong to Ethics than the corresponding questions as to the cognition of Space belong to Geometry." (From Henry Sidgwick, *The Methods of Ethics*.)

8.   Monsieur LaPointe speaks: Individuals in the gay and lesbian community argue that same-sex couples ought to receive the same treatment as married heterosexual couples. A gay person, for example, ought to be able to add his partner to his medical insurance plan. I agree. If individuals can will their money to institutions, such as colleges, and their pet dogs and cats, and if they can set up trusts for people to whom they bear no relation, then why can't a person add his lover to his medical policy?

9.   "Mark my words once for all, my dear friend, and be clever. Men are entirely self-centered, and incapable of looking at things objectively. If you had a dog and wanted to make him fond of you, and fancied that of your hundred rare and excellent characteristics the mongrel would be sure to perceive one, and that that would be sufficient to make him devoted to you body and soul—if, I say, you fancied that, you would be a fool. Pat him, give him something to eat; and for the rest, be what you please: he will not in the least care, but will be your faithful and devoted dog. Now, believe me, it is just the same with men—exactly the same." (From Arthur Schopenhauer, "On the Wisdom of Life: Aphorisms.")

10.   If you are given an A even though you failed the final exam, your grade point average is benefitted. If you are paid for a day's work even though you did nothing, your pocketbook is benefitted. Therefore, if you are allowed to practice surgery without having gone to medical school, your patients are benefitted.

11.   As Ted looks around his apartment he has these thoughts: "Hm. Look at these old records: Jefferson Airplane. David Bowie. Scuds Missel. I don't play these anymore, since I play CDs, so I'll toss them out. And these cracked and coffee-stained mugs in my kitchen cabinet. I don't use them anymore, so I'll get rid of them, too. Come to think of it, I'm never going to take another look at that stack of magazines in the corner cluttering up the room. Into the trash they go!"

Later, in his car, Ted reflects on his house cleaning as follows: "Boy, it feels good to be rid of all that useless stuff. From now on, my attitude is going to be this: 'If I don't use it, I'm going to lose it.' Down with clutter! Free me from the tyranny of things!"

As he utters these remarks, Ted looks at the center of his car's steering wheel and remembers that his car has an airbag. "No better time than now to act on my new principle," he says to himself. "I've had this car for two years and never used the air bag. I'm going to disconnect it right now!"

III. Supply counteranalogies for the following.

COUNTERANALOGIES

The technique known as *counteranalogy* consists in responding to analogies by providing alternate analogies which are as credible as the one proposed but which lead to a different conclusion. Here's an example:

Proposed Analogy: Marx argued that classes in society ought to be eliminated, but I disagree. Society is like an organism, and its classes are its parts. Just as an organism would be impaired if its means of locomotion or its means of thought and reflection were eliminated, so society would be impaired by the loss of its classes.

Counteranalogy: The relationship between the classes can be likened to that between a master and a slave, with the classless society being that society in which the slaves had been freed. Thus, society would be benefitted, rather than harmed, by its loss of classes.

---

1. I saw a man on television last night who was arrested for a brutal attack on a defenseless old woman. The man approaching me on the street just now is wearing the same type of clothes as the man who was arrested. He also combs his hair the same way. I'm afraid that I may be in danger.

2. Socrates argued that the citizens in a state occupied a position analogous to that of the father in the Greek family. The father nurtured the child, providing food, shelter, clothing, and other advantages; and when the father punished the child, the child would not consider that he or she had the right of retaliation even if he or she considered the punishment unjust. Similarly, the state provided protection from foreign invasion for its citizens, and the laws under which couples married and in accordance with which business and the affairs of state were conducted. The state had the right to require military service; and should the state charge a citizen with a crime and reach an incorrect verdict, the citizen had no right of retaliation and had to accept his or her punishment. This followed from the fact that the position of the citizen in relation to the state mirrored that of the child in relation to the father. (From Plato, *Crito*.)

3. There must be a moral faculty which enables us to know what is right and what is wrong. Unless we had eyes we would not be able to see physical objects, and unless we had a moral faculty we would not be able to tell right from wrong.

4. Sex offenders can change their behavior and be cured. Just as cigarette smokers can break the habit if they want to, so can sex offenders. Of course, it's helpful to the sex offender to have a strong support group during the cure process, but the most important factor is the offender's desire to change.

Chapter 7

GROUNDS OF INFERENCE IV
CAUSAL REASONING

In Chapter 4, we observe that facts are the ground for hypothetical reconstructions of events. We find in Chapter 5 that facts provide the ground for generalizations which in turn can be applied to particular cases. The facts we consider in Chapter 6 are observed similarities between objects which enable us to argue analogically to the existence of further similarities. Causal reasoning, which we consider in this chapter, is grounded in the factual observation that some pairs of events are constantly conjoined to one another. Causal reasoning can be viewed as a special form of analogical reasoning in that it assumes that what is true of one pair of constantly conjoined events is true of others which are similar to it in relevant respects. It is fitting, then, that we consider causal reasoning hard on the heels of our examination of analogical reasoning. In examining causal reasoning, we take up these topics:

- The distinction between necessary and sufficient conditions
- David Hume's rules for causes and effects
- The fallacy of false cause
- Two rules for identifying particular causes and effects

NECESSARY AND SUFFICIENT CONDITIONS

Some events seem to bear a special connection to one another. When I flip a switch upon entering my office, I expect the lights in the ceiling to go on, and when I drink a cold glass of tea on a hot summer day I anticipate that I will feel refreshed. Such commonplace expectations are an expression of our belief that events occur under certain conditions. I believe that the light in my office will come on only when I flip the switch, since there is but one switch, and that I will only seek out a glass of cold tea if I am hot or thirsty. **A *sufficient condition* for the occurrence of an event** like the light coming on in my office **is the *cause* of the event. The event itself is the effect, or necessary**

condition. Here is a proposition which will enable us to think through some of the uses of these terms:

If the scaffolding breaks, the painter will fall.

Propositions which have this form are referred to as "conditionals." The part following the word *if,* which is called the *antecedent,* indicates the sufficient condition, while the part following the comma, which is called the *consequent,* indicates the necessary condition. In this proposition it is claimed that the breaking of the scaffolding is a sufficient condition for the painter's falling and that if the scaffolding breaks the painter will necessarily fall. In a **conditional proposition,** the antecedent is always said to state a sufficient condition and the consequent a necessary condition.

The antecedent in the proposition above follows the word *if* and occurs in the first part of the proposition. Propositions with the same meaning may be written in a different order and with different words used to indicate the sufficient and necessary conditions. The following all have the same meaning as the proposition above.

The scaffolding breaks only if the painter falls.
The painter will fall if the scaffolding breaks.

***Only if* always indicates a necessary condition, while *if* always indicates a sufficient condition.** The previous two propositions can accordingly be rephrased and put into the same form as our example above.

We can extend our understanding of necessary and sufficient conditions by observing that the scaffolding's not breaking, but rather holding firm, is a necessary condition of the painter's not falling. It is a necessary condition, but not a sufficient condition, for the painter might fall even though the scaffolding held. He or she might faint, for example, or be blown off the scaffolding by a sudden gust of wind or slip on a banana peel thrown from an upper-story window by a malicious individual. When we express the idea that the scaffolding's not breaking is a necessary condition, we throw our original proposition into this form:

If the painter does not fall, the scaffolding does not break.

Notice that our proposition leaves a lot unsaid. When we think of the situation described, plenty of other conditions which are necessary to keep the painter from falling occur to us. Not only is it necessary that the scaffolding not break, it is necessary that the cable holding it to the building not fail. It is necessary as well that the painter not faint and not be blown off the scaffolding by a gust of wind or slip on a banana peel. Perhaps you can think of other necessary conditions as well. **When all necessary conditions have been met, that is equivalent to saying that the painter does not fall.** The necessity and sufficiency is not logical, but factual or *material,* which means that it must be discovered through observation. The language of cause and effect is commonly used when factual necessity and sufficiency is being considered.[1]

---

[1] In this chapter we tend to use *sufficient condition* interchangeably with *cause* and *necessary condition* with *effect,* but these respective pairs of terms are not synonyms. Sufficient condition and necessary condition are broader than the terms with which they are paired, since, for example, one can speak of logical sufficiency and necessity. No confusion should arise from our using the terms interchangeably in this chapter, since the focus of our discussion throughout will be on factual connections between events.

GRADUATION REQUIREMENTS

The language of necessary and sufficient conditions is applicable not only to events in the world but also to cases in which conditions are established by individuals or institutions. For example, one private undergraduate school sets these requirements for graduation:

- Satisfactory completion of 120 hours, including 30 hours in a major, specified general requirements, such as English, history, and mathematics, and miscellaneous electives
- Payment of applicable fees, including tuition, room, and board
- Completion of convocation or all school assembly requirements
- Attendance at commencement, unless excused

Each of these conditions, taken by itself, is necessary, but not sufficient, for graduation. On the assumption that the list of conditions is exhaustive, meeting each and every one of them is sufficient for graduation. The conditions are singly necessary but jointly sufficient.

HUME'S ANALYSIS OF CAUSE AND EFFECT

Since isolating causes and effects is an inescapable task of critical thinking, we examine four general rules which ably describe the relation. These rules, which should not be confused with the two rules for identifying causes and effects which we offer later, were first set forth by David Hume.[2]

HUME'S RULES FOR CAUSES AND EFFECTS

1. The cause and effect will be next to one another in space and time.
2. The cause will precede the effect.[3]
3. The cause and effect will be constantly conjoined with one another.
4. Like causes produce like effects.

---

[2] Hume set forth eight general rules for determining causes and effects. The first four, which are the ones we will discuss, are primary. The fifth and sixth serve to amplify the fourth, while the seventh and eighth bring out considerations which will occupy us in a later connection. For the most part, we have restated Hume's rules in our own words, but Hume's original formulations can be found in David Hume, *A Treatise of Human Nature,* Book I, Section XV.

[3] Occasionally, this Rule is amended to state that the cause will precede, or occur at the same time as, the effect.

FALSE CAUSE

The first of Hume's rules is sufficient to explain why we think there's no connection between my buttoning my overcoat and your pouring a cup of coffee. Few problems arise in connection with this rule, but the second rule can provide the occasion for faulty reasoning. **It is always the case that a cause precedes its effect, but it is an error to assume that one occurrence—call it "C"—is the cause of another occurrence—call it "E"—solely because C is temporally prior to E.** The following case illustrates why this should not be done.

THE CASE OF THE FARMER'S DOG

I once had a Brittany Spaniel. When one of my students showed me that she was losing hair around her nose, I took her to a veterinarian, who took a scraping from her nose and, by examining it under a microscope, determined that she had a demodex mite. This species of mite, which devours the dog's hair from inside its body, is passed from the mother to her pups and is not acquired in any other manner. The dog, in other words, cannot acquire the mite from anything in its environment.

After relating these facts, the veterinarian went on to say that a farmer had recently brought him a hunting dog which had lost hair over half its body. The farmer explained that he had placed fresh sand in the dog's pen in an effort to keep it warm during the winter, but shortly after had noticed that the dog was losing its hair. Concluding that the dog must be allergic to the sand, he had removed every grain of it from the cage. When the dog continued to lose its hair he consulted the veterinarian, who determined that the dog had the demodex mite and was near death. While dogs who are not treated for the demodex mite will eventually die, the case of the farmer's dog had a happy outcome; for after a period of intensive treatment the mite was destroyed and the dog went on to live a normal life.

"*Yee yee hee hee haw haw yip yip!*"

"*Yee yee hee hee haw haw yip yip!*"

False cause: "After this, therefore because of this."

The fallacy known as false cause occurs whenever some circumstance or cluster of conditions is mistakenly taken to be the cause of some other circumstance or cluster of conditions. In "The Case of the Farmer's Dog" a particular form of false cause fallacy known as **"post hoc ergo propter hoc"** is illustrated. The Latin phrase is translated as **"after this, therefore because of this,"** and the fallacy **consists in mistakenly assuming that one condition or cluster of conditions is the cause of another simply because it preceded the other.** While it is true that causes precede effects, it is not true that every event which precedes some other event is the cause of the later event. This observation is sufficient to show that some considerations other than those identified in Hume's first two rules are needed if we are to identify causes and effects with some accuracy.

THE CONSTANT UNION RULE

Hume stated that the most important of all the rules for identifying causes and effects is the third. **It is the constant union of cause and effect which chiefly marks the relation. No occurrence can truly be said to be the cause of another if the latter sometimes occurs when the former has not occurred.** There is only one light switch in my office. If the lights in my office were to come on occasionally when I had not flipped the switch, and when no one else had done so, I would be forced to conclude, contrary to my previous belief, that my flipping the switch was not the cause of the lights coming on.

Let us think of a string of lamps such as are used to decorate trees around Christmas time. These lamps may be wired in series—i.e., they may be connected to one another like a string of individuals who are holding hands. The bodies of the individuals are the lamps in this analogy and their arms and clasped hands are the wires which connect them. At either end of the string is an individual with one hand free. This part of the analogy corresponds to an electrical plug with two prongs. When the plug is inserted into an electrical outlet the lamps light up if these conditions are met:

C1. A sufficient supply of electricity is available at the electrical outlet.
C2. The wall socket is in good working order.
C3. The electrical plug is in good working order.
C4. There is a firm connection between the electrical plug and the electrical outlet.
C5. There is a firm connection between the electrical plug and the wires which run to the lamps.
C6. There are no breaks in any of the wires.
C7. Each wire is securely connected to each lamp socket.
C8. Each lamp socket is in good working order.
C9. Each lamp bulb is in good working order. (The filaments must not be burned through, for example.)
C10. Each lamp bulb is screwed securely into each lamp socket.

With these conditions before us, several observations can be made which enable us to underscore the significance of the requirement that there be a constant conjunction, or constant contact, between cause and effect. Discussion of the conditions also gives us more experience in handling the distinction between sufficient and necessary conditions.

1. Each of these 10 conditions is a necessary condition of the lighting of the lamps—i.e., every one of them must be met if the lamps are to light. If any one of them is not met, the lamps will not light.
2. No one of these conditions taken by itself is a sufficient condition of the lighting of the lamps. C10 might be met, for example, but unless C1 through C9 are met as well, the lamps will not light.
3. Taken all together, these ten conditions are both necessary and sufficient for the lighting of the lamps—i.e., when all these conditions are met, the lamps are lit; saying that all of these conditions have been met is equivalent to saying that the lamps are lit.

Points 1 and 3 can be expressed together by saying that the ten conditions are singly necessary and jointly sufficient to ensure that the lamps will light. *Singly* means "taken one by one."

There is more to be learned from our example about the distinction between sufficient and necessary conditions. Suppose the string of lamps is lit and we are enjoying the scene when suddenly the lamps go out. Our CD player, which is plugged into the same electrical outlet as our lamps, is still providing us with cool music, so we infer that C1 is a condition which is still being met. Next, we look at the wall plug, for our cat has been roaming restlessly about the room and might have knocked it out of the socket. The plug is still securely in the socket, so C4 is met. Which of the other conditions is not being met? We know that there must be at least one, and that there may be more than one, which is not being met, since we know that each one of the ten conditions is necessary for the lighting of the lamps.

We could check each condition in turn, but experience has shown us that the problem most likely lies with C9 or C10. We select a bulb near the plug for inspection and find that it is still screwed securely into its socket; but on taking it out of its socket for inspection we find that its filament is burned through. C9, then, is no longer being met. This knowledge enables us to state a fourth point, as follows:

4. A failure to meet a condition which is necessary but not sufficient for the lamps to light is sufficient by itself to ensure that the lamps do not light, but not necessary to ensure that this happens.

A failure to meet the condition is sufficient since the lamps do not light when the condition is not met, but the failure is not a necessary condition of the lamps not lighting since they might not light even though the condition is in fact met. If the condition is met but any one or more of the other conditions are not, the lamps will not light. For example, if C9 is met but one of the wires suddenly breaks, C6 is not met and the lamps go out.

We will not have learned everything which we might learn from our example until we set forth a fifth point; but to prepare ourselves for that point let us imagine once more that our lamps have just gone out. At this juncture, all we know is that one or more of the conditions necessary for the lighting of our lamps is not being met. We verify that C1 and C4 are still being met, just as before, but this time we discover that C9 and C10 are still being met as well. This interests us, so we work our way methodically through the other conditions until at last we come to C6. We are certain of our work to this point, so we conclude that there must be a break somewhere in the wire. If each and every one of the other conditions is being met and if we have succeeded in stating each condition necessary to the lighting of the lamps, then C6 must be the condition which is not being met. The fifth point is this:

5. A failure to meet any condition C1 through C10 taken at random is sufficient but not necessary to ensure that the lamps do not light, but when all other conditions but one have been excluded, the one remaining must be the one which is not being met.

Let us go back to our fourth point before going on to another matter. We said that a failure to meet a condition which was necessary for the lamps to light was sufficient to ensure that the lamps would not light but not necessary to ensure their not lighting, since a failure to meet some other condition might have the same effect. This failure to meet a condition necessary for the lamps lighting is a sufficient condition of the lamps not lighting. **Since an event like the lamps not lighting can have more than one sufficient condition, constant conjunction does not mean that the same sufficient condition will always be associated with an event. Constant conjunction does mean, however, that should a sufficient condition occur, a necessary condition, or effect, always follows.** In the case of our string of lights, as we have seen, there are ten conditions which would be sufficient to ensure that the lamps do not light. To say that there is a constant conjunction between a sufficient and a necessary condition in this case is to say that, when the lamps fail to light, the sufficient condition will be one or more of those ten and that there are no other conditions beyond those ten which can possibly be sufficient for the event's having occurred.

THE UNIFORMITY RULE

In our reasoning concerning matters of fact we take it for granted that the events which will follow the present situation or circumstance will be like those which have followed other similar circumstances. This is the essence of the fourth rule. We take the rule to be true because long experience has convinced us that nature acts in a uniform manner—i.e., that it has always acted in the manner in which we observe it to act at present and that it will continue to do so.[4] The assumption is crucial for reasoning concerning causes and effects.

IDENTIFYING CAUSES AND EFFECTS: TWO RULES

Having described the cause-effect relation with Hume's assistance, we can consider two rules for identifying particular causes and effects.[5]

RULES FOR IDENTIFYING PARTICULAR CAUSES AND EFFECTS

Rule 1: If you can eliminate or change a condition or circumstance without eliminating or changing the phenomenon in question, the two are not causally connected. Example: As you are driving down the road you hear a rattle in your car. Looking about, you discover a loose screw in the dashboard and tighten it up. Back on the road once more, you hear the rattle again. The loose screw and the rattle are not causally connected.

Rule 2: If a condition or circumstance cannot be eliminated or changed without eliminating or changing the phenomenon in question, the condition or circumstance is a cause or necessary condition of the phenomenon. Example: If a string of lights is unplugged from the wall, the lights go out. The source of power is a necessary condition of the lighting of the lights.

---

[4] The justification of our belief that nature is uniform is a matter of great philosophical interest, but our present purpose precludes our entering the discussion.

[5] All logicians who discuss these matters are indebted to John Stuart Mill. The two methods which are stated in this text are distillations of four methods for identifying causes and effects, which Mill described in admirable detail in his *System of Logic, Ratiocinative and Inductive: Being a Connected View of The Principles of Evidence and the Methods of Scientific Investigation* (New York: Harper & Brothers, Publishers, 1852), Chapter VIII.

Rule 2 can also be formulated in this way: If a phenomenon is eliminated or changed by eliminating or changing a condition or circumstance, the condition or circumstance is a cause or necessary condition of the phenomenon. Example: Your automobile engine is misfiring. In order to locate the problem, you disconnect the spark plug wires one by one. When you disconnect the wire to cylinder one, the engine runs even rougher than before, so you know that electricity is reaching the spark plug in that cylinder and that the plug is firing. Reconnecting the wire to cylinder one, you disconnect the wire to cylinder two and notice that the engine runs exactly as before. This suggests that the wire to cylinder two may be faulty, so you replace the wire. The engine runs smoothly again. A faulty wire to cylinder two was therefore the cause of the misfiring of your engine.

The word *change* is used in the statement of the two rules in order to indicate that the rules apply to quantitative or even qualitative modifications of phenomena as well as to their strict elimination. Observations of such modifications are common in our experience.

THE PASTA

Darrell: I want to say once more how good that rhubarb pie was that we had the other night.
Micki: Thank you, dear. How do you like the pasta we're having tonight?
Darrell: It's the best I've ever had.

Micki: Really?
Darrell: Really.
Micki: Even better than the last I made?
Darrell: Yes.
Micki: Why is that?
Darrell: I don't know. Perhaps your cooking skills are improving.
Micki: No, it's not that. I wonder what it could be.
Darrell: Did you use the same ingredients?
Micki: Yes, I. . . . No, that's not true. I used commercial tomato sauce this time rather than the sauce I canned myself. Say, I thought you liked my tomato sauce.
Darrell: I do, and this bread is good, too. By the way, did you hear about that wreck over on Main Street?

By Rule 2, if there is a change in a condition and a corresponding change in the phenomenon, that change is a cause of the phenomenon. The only change in Micki's recipe was the change in tomato sauce, so that change must be the cause of the change in the way her sauce tasted.

INTEREST RATES AND MARKET DECLINES

In periods of high interest rates in 1873, 1907, 1929, and 1974, the stock market declined. In 1979, however, interest rates rose but the market did not decline. Why was that the case? Market analyst Harold Finley observed that in the previous years the high interest rates were caused by supply and demand factors, but that in 1979 the interest rates had risen as a result of attempts by the Federal Reserve to prevent inflation. This difference accounted for the fact that the market had not declined in 1979. Since the increase in interest rates had a different cause than in the previous years, the failure of the market to decline on this occasion as a result of high interest rates was understandable.[6] By Rule 1, if a condition changes without there being a corresponding change in the phenomenon in question, there is no causal connection between the two. Finley's analysis suggests that the relevant point was not the change in interest rates itself but the factor which caused that change. When the interest rates rose not as a result of supply and demand, but as the result of another factor, the market was not affected. It is not always easy in analyzing a case to determine which facts are relevant.

Summary

- In conditional propositions, the antecedent states the sufficient condition and the consequent states the necessary condition. *If* indicates a sufficient condition, *only if* a necessary condition.
- Causes are sufficient conditions. Effects are necessary conditions.
- According to Hume's rules for causes and effects, causes and effects are next to one another in space and time, causes precede effects, there is a constant conjunction between causes and effects, and like causes produce like effects. The constant union of causes and effects is the most important of the four rules.

---

[6] See Harold Finley, "These High Interest Rates Are Different," *Chicago Tribune,* September 27, 1979, section 6, 12.

- In the fallacy of false cause, one event is mistakenly identified as the cause of another. In a special case of false cause, one event is mistakenly identified as the cause of another simply because it precedes the other. This is known as post hoc ergo propter hoc.
- Causes and effects can be identified by means of these two rules: (1) If a condition can be eliminated or changed without eliminating or changing the phenomenon, the condition and the phenomenon are not causally connected. (2) If a condition cannot be eliminated or changed without eliminating or changing the phenomenon, it is a cause or necessary condition of the phenomenon.

A HELPFUL HINT AND A LOOK AHEAD

Conditional propositions, which are described in this chapter, assume great importance in Chapter 13. Don't forget the meaning of *antecedent* and *consequent* or the important distinction between *if* and *only if*.

In the next chapter, we examine criteria, or aids in making judgments. There are many sorts of criteria, but for an immediate example of one common kind, suppose that you are presented with two rooms in a house and asked to state which is the larger. If the rooms differ greatly in size, you can identify the larger room by a simple visual inspection. However, if the rooms are very nearly the same size, you may not be able to tell which is larger in this way. You may need to obtain a tape measure and measure each room. The measurement provided by the tape is your criterion for stating which is the larger room.

Exercises

Answers to questions marked with an asterisk may be found in the back of the text.

I. Identify the necessary and sufficient conditions in the following statements.

1. If today is a holiday, the mail will not be delivered.
2. The lamp will not light if the switch is defective.
3. You will not make it home by 9 o'clock unless you start immediately.
*4. If it fails to rain, the crop will be lost.
5. I can purchase aspirin only if the store is open.
6. Only if you send him the money can he buy a bus ticket home.
7. If you've had a raise, then you've been on the job at least six months.
8. Rock-a-bye baby, in the tree top. When the wind blows, the cradle will rock.

*9.

> **Darrell:** I'm sick and tired of doing all the work around this house.
>
> **Micki:** You said that yesterday, and the day before that, and the day before that. It's just not true that you do all the work, and if you say that one more time, I'm going to scream.

10. The VCR should switch on at 8:00 P.M. if I have the timer set correctly.

II. Except for 12, identify the fallacies of false cause, accident, and hasty generalization which occur in the following. (The fallacies of accident and hasty generalization are explained in Chapter 5. You may need to review those sections before completing this exercise.) If a false cause fallacy is of the post hoc ergo propter hoc variety, indicate that. If a passage contains no fallacy, indicate that. Number 12 contains a fallacy familiar to you from Chapter 4.

1. I regret that the surgeon general's report on AIDS was published. You'll notice that the number of reported cases of AIDS has increased annually since it came out.

2. More tequila is produced in Mexico than in any other country. The value of the peso is currently at an all-time low. Let us preserve the strength of our own economy by not producing tequila in our country.

3. Jim's running shoes are a lot newer than mine and he can run a lot faster than I can. I want to run as fast as he can. Why can't I have new running shoes?

*4. Medical students are allowed to repeat courses in medical school if they fail, so surgeons, who were once medical students, should be allowed to repeat operations if they botch them up.

5. On December 5 one year, the city manager in a southern city asked residents to restrict the use of water sprinklers. He hoped thereby to avoid a water shortage. On December 6 the city had the first rain it had had in more than a month. On December 20 the city manager again asked residents to conserve water, and again it rained the next day. In early January the city manager repeated his request for a third time. Once more, it rained the next day. When interviewed by the local newspaper, the city manager stated that he hadn't been surprised by the rain.

6. In 1873, 1907, 1929, and 1974 when interest rates went up, the stock market went down. Interest rates are up now, so the market is going to go down.

7. Everyone has a right to make his or her views known; that's basic freedom of expression. Therefore, professors at State University are justified in devoting several classes each semester to the exposition and defense of their religious beliefs.

8. Recent studies have shown that students who drop out of college without completing their degrees chew nearly three times as much gum as those who go on to graduate. It seems clear that chewing gum makes it difficult for individuals to do college-level work.

*9. Professor Cohen requires two texts in her philosophy of law class. I'll bet she requires at least two texts in all the courses she teaches.

10. We've counted all but three of the one hundred and fifty ballots in this election, and all but six of them are for the reelection of Mayor Weakley. There's a strong probability that the last three will be for Mayor Weakley.

11. Scene I

Darrell: Hey, Hon, aren't you going to eat your dinner?

Micki: No; not now, at least. I don't feel well. It's this cold and this hacking cough, I guess.

Darrell: You have been coughing a lot. Here, let me clear the dinner dishes, and you lie down.

Micki: Thanks, I think I will. It's 7 o'clock. Do you want to watch that program? [Coughs]

Darrell: The one about the history of cheese? No, I'm not in the mood.

Scene II

Micki: Wow, it's 10 o'clock, and I've been lying here on the couch since dinner with this hacking cough!

Darrell: Yeah, and you haven't even slept.

Micki: I know. I think I'll take a pill to help me sleep. I have to get some rest.

Scene III

Micki: [Shaking Darrell] Come on, come on; it's time for you to get up.

Darrell: What time is it?

Micki: It's 6 A.M.

Darrell: Oh, no! I have to go to work, and I've hardly slept at all. You coughed all night long.

Micki: Yeah, I know. It must have been that sleeping pill I took.

Darrell: Yeah, I guess so. Don't take one tonight, and maybe you won't cough so much.

Micki: All right.

12. Scene IV [It is 6 P.M., the same day. Darrell is returning home from work.]

Micki: Oh, Hon, you look so tired! It's because I kept you awake last night, isn't it?

Darrell: Yes, but you mustn't blame yourself. It's not your fault that you had that hacking cough. Just don't take one of those pills tonight.

Micki: I don't think it was the pill which made me cough. I talked to the man who repairs the plumbing in the apartment building, and he said those pills won't make you cough.

Darrell: Well, maybe, but it seems to me that plumbers are always a little too willing to pipe up.

Micki: Please, you'll make me start coughing again.

Darrell: I won't say another word.

III. Identify the fallacies of false cause, accident, and hasty generalization which occur in the following. If a false cause fallacy is of the post hoc ergo propter hoc variety, indicate that. If a passage contains no fallacy, indicate that.

1. People everywhere have a right to listen to whatever music they please. Therefore, B. J. has the right to play his boom box at peak volume at 2 A.M. in the hospital corridor.

2. Abe typed his term paper on a personal computer, but the hard drive failed and he had to type it all over again. That wouldn't have happened with a typewriter. Computers are much less efficient than typewriters.

3. My dog, who is suffering from worms, hasn't eaten any of her dog food. It seems obvious that she doesn't like this brand of dog food.

*4. Whoever exceeds the speed limit should be punished by law. Officer Singh exceeded the speed limit in pursuit of that hit-and-run driver. Therefore, he should be punished by law.

5. Last semester, Sakurai smoked two packs of cigarettes per day, but this semester he's cut back to a half a pack a day. Sakurai's grade point average last semester was A. This semester his average is C. If Sakurai knows what's good for him, he'll smoke more cigarettes next semester!

6. Twenty-five students are taking the course in Shakespeare. Dolores is one of them. By the way, she made an A on the last exam, as did Jacques and Madeline. I think every student in the class made an A.

7. When Lakshmi's father died, she wept for several hours. She must be a sad and melancholy sort of person. That's a shame, since there's so much in this life to be happy about.

8. Each student is responsible for obtaining a copy of the text for the course. Therefore, Jack, who threw Patricia's text into the river, should not be forced to buy her a new copy of the text. Patricia should buy the text herself.

*9. When Beth visited the city, she repeatedly kicked the man on the street who attempted to snatch her purse. Therefore, Beth is dangerous in that she is prone to violence, and I don't want my children to hang out with such a person.

10.

Victoria: Thanks for inviting me over for afternoon tea.

Rebecca: I'm glad you could make it. How do you like my new tea cozy?

Victoria: It's beautiful. I wish I had one.

Rebecca: Perhaps Shaun will get you one for your birthday.

Victoria: And perhaps cows can fly.

Rebecca: [After a slight pause] I love tea, but I think I'm allergic to it.

Victoria: Why so?

Rebecca: I performed an experiment. For two weeks last month I drank two cups of tea each day at four. Afterward, I experienced a swelling sensation in my throat.

Victoria: What kind of swelling sensation?

Rebecca: The sort you have before you get a sore throat.

Victoria: Hm.

Rebecca: And that's not all. For one week after that, I drank water at four P.M., and no tea at all.

Victoria: Not any at any time of the day?

Rebecca: No. None.

Victoria: What was the result?

Rebecca: No swelling.

Victoria: That's interesting. Are you experiencing swelling today, after all the tea you've drunk?

Rebecca: Yes.

Victoria: Then I guess you are allergic to tea. Say, if you were to tell Shaun that I desperately wanted one of those tea cozies, maybe he would get me one. Will you do it?

Rebecca: Sure.

IV. Answer the following questions.

1. Early one morning, Paul struggles out of bed and stumbles to the lavatory to wash his face. He turns on the hot water faucet, but the water which comes out is cold. He holds his hand under the water. Gradually, the water becomes warm, then hot. What cause-effect relation is evident here—i.e., what conditions brought about the change in the temperature of the water?

2. Early in 1970, Dr. Oscar Auerbach, pathologist at New York Medical College, reported on the results of autopsies performed on 971 men who had died at the Veterans Administration Hospital in East Orange, New Jersey, from causes other than larynx cancer. The results were as follows:

   a. 519 of the men had smoked at least one pack of cigarettes a day. Autopsies revealed that every one of them had cell damage in his larynx.

   b. Of the 519 men, 85 percent had smoked two or more packs of cigarettes a day. These men had more advanced cell damage. Also, 4 of the 519 had cancer which had not been detected at the time of death.

   c. The 452 remaining men were nonsmokers. Of those who had never smoked, only 4 percent had any cell damage at all.

   d. Of the 452 remaining nonsmokers, those who had quit smoking for at least five years before their death had fewer cell changes than those who smoked up until the time of their death. It was discovered that new living cells were gradually replacing dead ones in these cases.[7]

   Describe these research results using the language of cause and effect—i.e. identify the cause-effect relations indicated in the study. What general conclusions might you draw from the study?

3. According to William P. Castelli, M.D., the director of the Framingham Heart Study, Seventh Day Adventists—whose religion requires them to be vegetarians, to exercise regularly, and not to use alcohol, caffeine, or tobacco products—live longer than other U.S. citizens. The men live on average seven years longer, and the women five years longer. The heart attack rate of Seventh Day Adventists is only 15 percent of the population at large and the cancer rate only 40 percent.[8] What conclusions regarding causes and effects do you draw from Castelli's statement?

*4. A series of murders have been committed on Montmartre Boulevard. Inspector Marvel is called to investigate. Several of the individuals who live in the area report having seen a tall man dressed in black on the street. In each case, the

---

[7] "New Cigarette Danger Found," *The Sunday Oklahoman*, January 11, 1970, section A, 1–2.

[8] Ilene Springer, "Castelli Speaks from the Heart," *AARP Bulletin* 33, no. 5 (May 1992), 16.

man was seen shortly before a murder was committed. No other elements common to the murders emerge in Marvel's investigation. Was the tall man dressed in black the murderer?

5. On occasions k, l, m, n, and o, Martha threw a party for her friends. Along with Gary, who was her date, these couples attended: Peter and Peggy, Ralph and Carlotta, Billy Bob and Wanda, Lance and Iris, Pietro and Phyllis, and Carlos and Linda. At each of these parties everyone had a good time. On occasion p Martha threw another party. She invited the persons listed above, but in addition invited Mike and Donna. No one had a good time, and most of the couples went home early. What do you conclude? On which of the two rules for determining causes and effects are you relying?

6. On occasions q, r, s, t, and u, Martha threw a party for her friends. Along with George, who was her date, these couples attended: Peter and Peggy, Ralph and Carlotta, Billy Bob and Wanda, Lance and Iris, Pietro and Phyllis, and Carlos and Linda. At each of these parties everyone had a good time and stayed until all hours. On occasion v Martha threw another party. She invited the persons listed above, but this time Carlos and Linda were unable to attend. Everyone had a good time and stayed until all hours. What do you conclude? On which of the two rules for determining causes and effects are you relying?

7. What cause-effect relation is described in the following passage? Briefly restate the argument presented and classify it as "very weak," "weak," "strong," or "very strong." Explain why you place the argument in the category you choose.

I think that when people know they run a risk of losing money in an investment they exercise more caution than otherwise. For example, I wouldn't give much thought to the purchase of a bond from the government because I'd be confident that I'd get my money back with interest. On the other hand, if I were thinking of buying a stock whose price fluctuated within a wide range, I'd proceed with caution since I'd realize that I might lose money on my investment.

Something similar holds in other areas as well. Back when I was in college, one of my professors told the class that any student who wished to could retake one exam, excluding the final exam. He said that the grade on the retake would replace the grade on the original exam in every case. This meant that a student had a chance to improve his or her grade but that he or she also risked lowering it. The professor said that the first time he offered retakes he told his students he'd count the higher of the two exam grades. Under that arrangement, no student raised his or her grade, so he introduced the risk factor the following year. In that year, six students who took retakes raised their final grade by one letter, so he concluded that the system worked. The professor's experience is evidence for my thesis that if you know you have something to lose you'll work a little harder than otherwise.

8. What cause-effect relation is described in the following passage? Briefly restate the argument(s) presented and evaluate it (them) by applying one or the other of the rules for identifying causes and effects. Classify the argument(s) as "very weak," "weak," "strong," or "very strong." Explain why you place the argument(s) in the category you choose.

It is sometimes argued that capital punishment will deter crime. A very rich person will not be deterred from parking in a no parking zone, for the fine attached to the offense in that case is minimal. However, any individual will be deterred from killing another person if that individual knows that he or she will be put to death for the act. That's the argument, at least; but I don't think that capital punishment has that effect. Albert Camus cites a writer named Koestler who said that at the public execution of a pickpocket in England there were pickpockets in the crowd of spectators around the scaffold who were hard at work picking pockets. The threat of capital punishment didn't have a deterrent effect on those individuals. Camus also observes that 170 of 250 persons who were hanged early in the twentieth century in England had attended one or more executions. The threat of capital punishment didn't deter them, either.

There are still other considerations offered by Camus which are relevant. He cites the report of the English Select Committee of 1930 to show that where capital punishment was abolished there was no significant increase in crime and that where capital punishment was reinstated there was no significant decrease in crime. Some violent crimes, moreover, are acts of passion. If a man catches his wife in the arms of another man, he might fall into a rage and kill that man. Capital punishment won't deter crimes like these, because the person doesn't know beforehand that he's going to commit the crime. I rest my case; capital punishment doesn't deter crime.[9]

9. What cause-effect relation is described in the following passage? Briefly restate the argument presented and classify it as "very weak," "weak," "strong," or "very strong." Explain why you place the argument in the category you choose.

I notice that there are quite a few more murders in Los Angeles and Chicago than there are in the little town where I live. This convinces me that the murder rate increases with increases in population density. What I mean is this: when you increase the number of people who live in close proximity to one another, the number of murders per capita increases proportionally.

10. What cause-effect relation is described in the following passage? Briefly restate the argument(s) presented and evaluate it (them) by applying one or the other of the rules for identifying causes and effects. Classify the argument(s) as "very weak," "weak," "strong," or "very strong." Explain why you place the argument(s) in the category you choose.

Our mental capacities, including our ability to reason, remember, and control our emotional behavior, are determined by our bodies, and in particular by our brains. There's no getting around the fact that our intelligence is determined by our genetic inheritance. Not only that; look at the effect of Alzheimer's disease on a person's memory, and look at the way syphilis reduces a person's ability to make decisions and assume responsibility for actions performed. If memory and those other abilities weren't determined by the brain, those diseases wouldn't have any effect on them.

11. What are the necessary and sufficient conditions for (a) the operation of a household flashlight and (b) a cherry pie?

---

[9] For Camus' arguments see Albert Camus, "Reflections on the Guillotine," in *Resistance, Rebellion, and Death*, Justin O'Brien, Trans. (New York: The Modern Library, 1960), 142–46.

Chapter 8

GROUNDS OF INFERENCE V

CRITERIA AND STANDARDS

The last of the five grounds of inference listed in the Introduction is criteria and standards. That ground is the subject of this chapter. We cover these topics:

- Criteria in judgments
- Criteria and standards in comparisons and rankings
- Errors in rankings (two rules for ranking scales are provided)
- The process of forming a judgment utilizing criteria and standards
- Background conditions (the assumptions we make in any particular situation regarding the conduct to be expected from others)
- The evaluation of criteria and rules (four guidelines are presented)

JUDGMENTS AND CRITERIA

THE CASE OF PAT BLOOD

Pat Blood, who ran an employment agency, was interviewing a young woman who had previously held several jobs as a waitress and who had been released from each of them after only three or four days of work. Pat, who rarely misjudged the individuals he interviewed, was puzzled by this. The woman before him in his estimate would make a model employee. Under further persistent questioning by him, the woman confessed that she was pregnant and had been fainting on the job. Her work required her to be on her feet most of the time, but that made her dizzy. It also emerged that the woman's husband had left her and that she was attempting to make ends meet by working in spite of her condition. This confirmed Pat's judgment that she was a steady and dependable person. He found her a job which did not require her to stand.

Every day we make a wide variety of **judgments.** As Pat Blood did, we judge the character of other people. We also render judgments on the appropriateness of actions, and judge distances, speeds, and the value of objects. But how do we make these judgments? When we are not able to say, we chalk our judgments up to experience or say that we make them "by feel." Nevertheless, even in these judgments with anonymous foundations it is likely that we rely upon at least one criterion. **"A *criterion*, strictly speaking, is an aid by means of which a correct judgment is reached. . . ."**[1]

There are many kinds and uses of criteria. **Generalizations, principles, and rules** such as those we examine in Chapter 5 **function as criteria when they aid us in making judgments. Other criteria are properties whose presence indicates or implies the presence of some other property or properties.** For example:

- The position of the fluid in a thermometer is a criterion for stating whether someone has a fever.
- The oil (or lack of it) on the dipstick of an automobile engine is a criterion for the amount of oil in the crankcase of the engine.
- The listing of a book in the card catalog or database of a library is a criterion indicating that the book is held by the library.
- Outside the setting of a hospital or clinic, we can determine whether an unresponsive person is breathing by holding a small mirror to his or her mouth and nose. If the person is breathing, his or her breath fogs the mirror. The fog on the mirror is our criterion for judging that the person is breathing.

SIGNS AND SYMPTOMS

In medicine, a distinction is drawn between a sign and a symptom. A sign is an indication of a disease or other condition which can be observed by a physician or other knowledgeable person, while a symptom is a sensation or other evidence of a mental or physical condition or disease which is perceived by the patient. In "Chinese restaurant syndrome" (CRS), which results from eating too much salt, one may experience a pounding in one's head, tautness in one's neck and shoulders, and a backache. These are symptoms. In CRS one's arteries are dilated. This condition would not be observed by the average patient, but only by a physician and would thus be said to be a sign of the syndrome. Signs and symptoms are criteria.

---

1 *Webster's Dictionary of Synonyms,* 1st ed. (Springfield, MA: G. & C. Merriam Co., 1951), 781.

The following case suggests one invaluable function of criteria.

THE CASE OF O. B. BRADFORD

O. B. Bradford was performing the four thousand mile checkup on my Volkswagen. I told him that the engine had begun using a lot of oil. With the car raised on a lift and the engine idling, he placed his hands close to the pencil-tip mufflers, felt the beat of the exhaust against his palms, and listened for a moment to the swishing, hissing, and clicking of the engine. He then turned to me and said, "Number three piston is scalded."

O. B. took the engine out of the car and an apprentice mechanic disassembled it. "Yep, that piston's scalded," the apprentice said as he held out the offending part for my inspection.

"What piston is that?" I asked.

"Number three," he answered. I looked at O. B. and saw that he was grinning.

O. B. Bradford's skill at diagnosing the trouble with an automobile engine was so great as to approach the intuitive. Another individual would need to disassemble the engine to locate the difficulty by a visual inspection, but O. B. was able to pinpoint the difficulty without doing that. The engine sounds and the rhythmic exhaust puffs were the means by which he inferred that the piston was scalded. They were the criteria he used in his diagnosis. O. B's. diagnosis illustrates that **criteria enable us to come to a judgment when we are unable to do so by means of a direct inspection of the object we are examining.** Further illustrations of this are found in the examples listed above and marked by bullets. We use thermometers, for instance, because we are not able to tell by direct hands-on inspection whether a person has a fever or how high the fever is.

We use criteria not only when diagnosing conditions like scalded pistons and fevers, but **also in coming to judgments about events which take place over time.** For example, pedometers enable us to know approximately how far we've walked, and stopwatches enable us to determine how fast we've run. The readings on pedometers and stopwatches are criteria.

In some cases, **criteria come into play when considerations of prudence, precision, or procedure require that we base our judgment upon a foundation open to the inspection of all concerned.** In a deliberative assembly, for example, the chair allows the members to vote by voice, by show of hands, or by written or electronic ballot upon measures introduced. The oral expression of approval or disapproval, the show of hands, and so forth, are criteria for determining whether a majority of the voting members favor a motion. When it is impossible in a voice vote to tell by listening whether the affirmative votes are more numerous than the negative, a show of hands might be requested by the chair or by some member of the assembly. The show of hands is a more precise criterion than the voice vote.

We should note that **some properties are not infallible criteria for the presence of other properties.** A dipstick as in the example given above is practically infallible, but the card catalog or database of a library is not. Bertrand Russell (from whom we have taken this illustration) reminds us that a book might be held by a library but not be entered in its card catalog (perhaps because it is a recent acquisition), or that it might be entered in its card catalog but lost. Still, the criterion, though fallible, can be useful.

> Speaking abstractly, we may say that a property A is a *criterion* of a property B when the same objects possess both; and A is a *useful* criterion of B if it is easier to discover whether an object possesses the property A than whether it possesses the property B. Thus being mentioned in the catalogue is a *useful* criterion of being in the library, because it is easier to consult the catalogue than to hunt through the shelves.[2]

Before passing to our consideration of comparisons and rankings, which gives us an opportunity to discuss criteria in more detail and to distinguish them from standards, let us observe that **the criteria we use in making decisions do not become the focus of our attention until we experience some difficulty in reaching a decision.**

---

[2] Bertrand Russell, "Transatlantic 'Truth,'" in *The Albany Review* II, no. 10 (1908), 401. This article has been reprinted under the title "William James's Conception of Truth," in *Philosophical Essays* by Bertrand Russell (New York: Simon and Schuster, 1968).

In these cases we either apply our criteria with self-conscious attention to detail, subject our criteria to critical analysis, or cast about for a criterion which will enable us to make our decision. In disputes of a criteriological sort, which we examine in Chapter 9, the disputants differ as to the criteria they use in making their judgments.

COMPARISONS AND RANKINGS

WILT CHAMBERLAIN VERSUS MICHAEL JORDAN: HOW DO THEY COMPARE?

In his career, Michael Jordan scored over 50 points in a game in 34 games. Wilt Chamberlain scored over 50 points in a game in 47 games in one season. Does this mean that Chamberlain was a better player than Jordan?

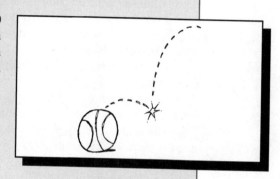

Comparisons take this form: This is _____ than that. *Than* is a sure indicator of a comparison. The blank may be filled in with such words as *smaller, taller, better,* and *more expensive.* **A comparison always involves two things or classes of things. A ranking involves one thing or class of things. In ranking, something is given a place on a scale.** After a brief description of such scales, we will examine comparisons and rankings in more detail.

Some scales utilized in rankings admit of degrees. Some words which indicate places on a scale admitting degrees are these:

- Tall, medium, short
- Good, indifferent, bad

The extremes of such scales appear as opposites to one another. Good and bad and tall and short are opposites in this way, but such **opposites at the ends of scales with degrees are unlike other opposites which admit of no degree.** *Alive* and *dead* and *officer* and *nonofficer* are examples of such opposites. One may be near death, of course, but there are no degrees of death. One is either dead or alive, but not both. Similarly, one can be an officer or a nonofficer in an organization, but not both.

Three or more degrees or positions can typically be distinguished in ranking scales which admit of degrees. The place-indicating words highlighted by the bullets above are illustrative. **However, no more than two positions are necessary for a ranking.** The 1936 Chevrolet automobile, for example, had only two models, the Standard and the Deluxe.

Some scales indicate ranges of a certain kind, while others indicate arbitrarily assigned characteristics. Cold, medium, and hot as applied to the temperatures of objects indicate ranges, as do small, medium, and large. A cold drink might be said to be between approximately thirty-three and forty-seven degrees and a medium-sized male Collie dog one which weighed between sixty-five and sixty-nine pounds. Standard and Deluxe as applied to 1936 Chevrolets, by contrast, do not indicate a range but fixed characteristics which have been determined by the manufacturer. These characteristics, as our selection of an antique automobile is intended to underscore, cannot be determined without observing the models or uncovering a reliable source of information on them. There is another difference between the two kinds of rankings. If I know that a cold drink is one in the range of temperatures indicated above, I can estimate the range of temperatures for medium and hot drinks. With a description of only one model of the 1936 Chevrolet, however, I have no basis for deducing the features of the other. Suppose I have a description of the Standard. Can I then say that the Deluxe is larger than the Standard? That it has a more powerful engine? A transmission with one more gear than the Standard? An extra tail light sportily positioned in the rear window? These questions are unanswerable with nothing more to go on than a description of the Standard.

The scales discussed in the last paragraph can be expanded as needed with further degrees or positions indicated by such words as *cool* or *tepid* or *Super Deluxe*. You'll observe that these scale words and those already mentioned indicate positions or mark out places within the scale. (Some scales utilizing words which do not indicate positions are mentioned farther on in our discussion.) However, the words used in the scale for the models of Chevrolets indicate value as well as position. *Cool* implies nothing about a drink until we know what kind of drink is under consideration. Soft drinks are ordinarily served chilled in the United States and coffee is served hot (though there are exceptions). If we are talking about soft drinks, then *cold* implies a higher value or more desirable drink; but if we are talking about coffee, the order of value of the scale is reversed. Standard and Deluxe indicate an order of value, however, even before we learn that they are model names for 1936 Chevrolets. We know immediately that the Deluxe ranks higher than the Standard whatever we happen to be talking about. Given this order of value we are also certain that the lowest point on the scale is indicated by Standard. The case of Chevrolets illustrates this. We can be certain that *Substandard* was never considered as a possible model name for a Chevrolet.

CRITERIA IN COMPARISONS

The preceding remarks on scales prepare us to consider comparisons and rankings in more detail. Let us begin with comparisons. When you are comparing two things you can often make your comparison simply by using one or more of your senses. For example, you may simply see that one man is taller than another or feel that one drink is colder than another. On some occasions, however, you cannot make a comparison directly by means of your unaided senses. For example, you may not be able to tell whether one drink is colder than another. I grant that when drinks are that close in temperature one usually does not care which is the colder, but if you needed to know for some reason, you could go to the extreme of placing a thermometer in each glass. In that way you would determine whether one drink is colder than another or whether they are equally cold. To introduce a thermometer is to introduce a criterion for determining the coldness of the drinks. The criterion for the coldness of the drinks is the expansion of mercury in a glass tube. The coldness of the drinks is correlated with the extent of the expansion of the mercury.

It is important to notice the use of criteria in making comparisons. **Criteria enable you to make comparisons indirectly by correlating what you would like to know, but cannot know directly, with what you can know.** Suppose you are interested in whether one house is larger than another. Some comparisons like this are unproblematic. I can easily see that my house is smaller than Monticello. Sometimes, however, houses are close enough in size that we can be deceived as to which is the larger. In those cases we have to resort to criteria in order to make the desired comparison. Our criteria of bigger can be longer, wider, or higher, or they can be more rooms or larger rooms, or the volume of the house, which is the product of its length, width, and height. If I were to use the first of these criteria and you the second, we might disagree as to which house is the larger, and I might be right on my criterion and you right on yours. There is little room for disagreement about the volume of the house if we have measured correctly. However, knowing the volume of the house might not be as useful as knowing how much usable space the house has, and in that case we may be driven back to the criterion of the number of rooms and their sizes.

Houses are visual and tactile objects, but not all the objects we compare are phenomena of that sort. Some are abstract entities. It is readily seen, for example, that in comparing the size of two corporations the data on which we rely is numerical. The sales of the corporations, as expressed in thousands or millions of dollars, is one criterion for determining the relative sizes of corporations. For such entities, our knowledge of size is always indirect and thus dependent upon a criterion.

STANDARDS IN RANKINGS

Criteria can be used in rankings as well as comparisons, but they need not be. Just as you can compare some things directly, so you can rank some things directly. Seeing the Sears Tower in Chicago you can without hesitation say that it is a tall building. However, **while you may be able to get along without criteria in rankings, you can never get along without standards.**[3] How standards differ from criteria becomes apparent

[3] In distinguishing *criterion* and *standard* I am following the lead of Kurt Baier, whose influence is evident in this chapter. See Kurt Baier, *The Moral Point of View* (Ithaca, NY: Cornell University Press, 1958), Chapters 2 and 3. Cited hereafter as Baier.

Not every use of criterion and standard is considered in this chapter. In discussing the classification of disputes in Chapter 9, we turn to a further consideration of the meanings of these terms.

when it is recalled that **ranking terms are relative. The meaning of ranking adjectives varies with the objects to which they refer.** A large dog is not a large elephant, an expensive guitar is not an expensive pipe organ, and so forth. Our standard for the use of *large* varies from dogs to elephants and our standard for the use of expensive varies from guitars to pipe organs.

THE MANY MEANINGS OF STANDARD

Criterion and *standard* are synonyms in some uses, but we distinguish the two in order to clarify rank orderings. We find that standards are essential in fixing the meanings of relative terms. However, the word *standard* is sometimes used in the place of *requirement.* A job applicant who does not satisfy all the requirements for a position may be said not to meet the standards set by the employer. Again, it is occasionally claimed that a product has been manufactured in accordance with exacting standards. Products which do not meet those standards do not, as is sometimes said, "measure up." The phrase in quotes is revealing. A standard is a measure.

Our standard for the use of *relative terms* can also vary within a single class of things. Within the class of dogs our standard for the use of *large* varies from breed to breed. A short German shepherd is one which falls below the average for German shepherds, but a short German shepherd is a tall dachshund. **For some members of a class,** however, **there are no specific standards to which we can appeal.** Since their ancestry is random and indiscriminate, there are no standards for mongrels within the class of dogs. We would consequently never say, "That's a large dog for a mongrel." Such a statement would betray a lack of understanding on our part. We might, however, say "That mongrel is a large dog." This statement makes good sense, for in this case there is a standard for the use of large. That standard is derived from the class of dogs without specific reference to any particular breed.

The case of dogs prompts us to observe in passing that **standards emerge under conditions of need or desire.** Mongrel is not a classification for which it would be useful or fruitful to state standards. However, mongrels or mixed breeds can evolve into breeds in their own right. The black and tan coonhound, which is noted for its speed, stamina, keen sense of smell, and ability to withstand extremes of temperature, was a mongrel which the American Kennel Club recognized as a breed in 1945. Standards, then, can be developed for specific purposes. We have occasion to observe at a later point that standards can also evolve over time.

STANDARDS IN COMPARISONS ACCORDING TO RANK ORDERINGS

Standards **play a role in some comparisons, but their role differs from that played by criteria.** Let us suppose that we are presented with two German shepherds who are so close in height that we cannot tell which is the taller without measuring. Through the use of a measuring device we can determine which animal, if either, is the taller. The measuring device provides our criterion in this case. Without a standard for the height of German shepherds, however, we would be unable to say which of the two dogs we had measured most nearly approximated the average for the breed. Would it be the taller of the two dogs or would it be the shorter? We would have no way of knowing. **Standards, we see, are irrelevant to comparisons in size, but indispensable to comparisons according to a rank ordering.**

This holds for abstract entities as well as those we can observe through our senses. If we were contemplating the purchase of common stock in a corporation, we might be interested in determining the price-earnings ratio of the stock. The *P/E ratio,* as it is called for short, is determined by dividing the price per share of the stock by the earnings per share of the corporation. Let us suppose that the stock of a corporation is selling for forty dollars per share and that the earnings per share of the corporation are two dollars. The P/E ratio of the stock is then forty divided by two, or twenty. Is this a good P/E ratio? Is it high? Is it low? We cannot answer these questions unless we have a standard. We can compare the P/E ratio of this corporation with that of another corporation, but we cannot know whether the P/E ratio of either is high or low without a standard. The P/E ratio is useless information until we have a standard by which to evaluate it.

How is that standard determined? We can take the average of the P/E ratios of the companies in a particular industry or that of the chief competitors within an industry. For some comparisons we utilize a weighted mean rather than an arithmetical mean, but that is determined by other considerations into which we do not enter here.

CHANGES IN STANDARDS

P/E ratios provide us with an example of one way in which **a standard can change.** As P/E ratios vary with investor interest in a corporation and with the earnings of the corporation, so the average of P/E ratios in a class can change and with them the standards we use in evaluating companies.

For another example of the way in which standards change, let us cast a backward glance to 1976. In that year *Newsweek* magazine ran an article in which incomes in the United States were placed on a descriptive scale that had been developed by urban sociologist Richard Coleman. Here is that scale, along with the incomes corresponding to it:

- The Success Elite—$50,000 minimum.
- People Who Are Doing Very Well—$30,000 minimum.
- The Middle-American Dream—$19,000 minimum.
- The Average-Man Comfortable Existence. $15,000 minimum.
- The World of Just Getting Along—$9,500 minimum.
- Having a Real Hard Time—$5,750 minimum.
- The Poor—$4,500 maximum.[4]

Suppose that *Newsweek* were to run another article utilizing this scale the week that you are reading this.[5] What do you think would be the range of salaries corresponding to the positions in the scale?

We should also observe that **the scale in the article exhibits an order or progression as well as an order of value.** The higher the income, the better the existence of the individual and the higher the social status.

Some relative terms are position-indicating. With them no standard is needed to know that objects are being located on a scale. When someone tells you that Martin guitars are expensive, you understand what that individual is saying—that is, you know that the individual is ranking Martin guitars at or near the upper limit on the scale of price. However, unless you know the standard for ranking guitars as expensive or inexpensive, you do not know how much the Martins cost. Is $150 expensive for guitars? $1,000? $5,000? (For your pocketbook, guitars at any of these prices may be expensive; but your pocketbook is another standard.)

Here is another example of the role of standards in fixing the meaning of relative terms: If someone tells you that Norton is a poorly paid pilot for a commercial airline, you know what that person means—that is, you know that your confidant is placing Norton at or near the bottom of the scale. However, unless you know what such pilots make, you have no idea of Norton's income. You lack the key to the scale of ranking for the income of airline pilots—i.e., you do not know the current standards for the salaries of such pilots. Notice that your ignorance of the standards for the salaries of airline pilots would also have been evident to you if you had been told not that Norton was poorly paid but simply that he earned $40,000 a year. In that case you would not have known whether you would have looked uninformed if you had said, "Hey, that's pretty good for an airline pilot."

CRITERIA IN RANKINGS

In all of the examples of rankings we have examined until now, the name of the rank has indicated its position on the scale. The words *large, expensive,* and *highly paid* indi-

---

[4] Kenneth L. Woodward and Mary Lord, "Making It in America," *Newsweek,* January 5, 1976, 67.

[5] If the scale were to be used again, the name of the fourth category from the top would probably be changed to "The Average-Person Comfortable Existence" to bring it into line with current usage.

cate a ranking near the top of a scale, while *small, inexpensive,* and *poorly paid* indicate a ranking near the bottom. However, **the words used in rankings do not always indicate their place in the scale.** Prime examples of this are the model names manufacturers give their products; for manufacturers want to rank their products without saying that any one of them is better or worse than any other. In England two ranking names for apples are super grade and extra fancy.[6] Which would you suppose is the higher of the two ranks? One company has two models of staple guns. Which do you suppose ranks the highest, the high compression or the heavy duty?

When non-place-indicating ranking labels **such as these are used, criteria are generally involved in fixing the ranks.** (In some such rankings the lower in rank on one set of criteria can be higher on another. For example, a less expensive guitar can have a better tone quality than a more expensive one.) The difference between the top of the line and the bottom of the line of a product is not always obvious when non-place-indicating ranking labels are used, but this is sometimes the case even when the ranking names do indicate an order. For example, Kohno guitars have been classified as the Model 15, the Model 20, the Model 30, and the Model 50. The model names indicate an order of some sort, but if you placed guitars from each of the ranks side by side the average person would not be able to tell one from another. What are the criteria for distinguishing the models?

There are criteria for distinguishing the models of Kohno guitars; they concern the materials used in the guitars and certain niceties of design. It is worth noting, however, that when models are not ranked according to their function (as the models of Kohno guitars are not), it is not always clear what criteria are genuine or relevant. Those who are unacquainted with Kohno guitars might not know, as we do, that the various models are ranked by the quality and kind of materials used and by their design.

The particular interests or purposes of individuals often provide simple and direct clues to the criteria which are relevant for ranking purposes. In this connection let us continue to think of guitars. For a practicing guitarist, the quality of the sound of the instruments and the ease with which they can be played are the prime considerations or criteria in ranking them, but a collector of guitars who is not interested in playing them might rank them by age, maker, condition, or the fame of their previous owners. One guitar played by Eddie Lang, a jazz guitarist from the 1920s, is reportedly kept in a bank vault in California. The value of this instrument is determined by the prestige of its owner. The value or rank order of other guitars is determined by a combination of the previously mentioned criteria.

RANKING ERRORS

It is possible to make mistakes in ranking things. Mixing or confusing one ranking scale with another is one common mistake. Another consists in omitting

---

[6] I owe this example to J. O. Urmson. See his "On Grading," in *Logic and Language* (First and Second Series), ed. Antony Flew (Garden City, NY: Doubleday, 1965), 389.

relevant places in the ranking scale. Here are two questions from a course evaluation form which was used for many years at a small college:

A. Organization of Course

    a. Excellent

    b. Good

    c. Adequate

    d. Confusing

B. Instructor's Attitude Toward Student

    a. Usually considerate

    b. Sometimes inconsiderate

    c. Usually inconsiderate

In A there is a shift from one ranking scale to another. "Adequate" and "Confusing" are not parts of the same scale as "Excellent" and "Good." A student might find that the organization of a course is poor, but nevertheless not be confused by it, while either a good or fair organization might be adequate. The choices in A ought to be these, if we adopt a scale with "Excellent" at the top:

    a. Excellent

    b. Good

    c. Fair

    d. Poor

    e. Very poor

In B, on the instructor's attitude toward students, there is no shift from one scale to another, but the scale is incomplete. Isn't it possible that some professors are always considerate and that some are always inconsiderate? With these two additions, the scale in B would be expanded to five positions.

    With the errors just illustrated in mind, let us state the following rules.

RULES FOR RANKING SCALES

- There should be one scale per ranking. Do not mix or confuse ranking scales.
- The ranking scale should be sufficiently complete for the purpose at hand. Do not omit relevant places in the ranking scale.

RANKINGS AND RANKS

Rankings indicate positions on a scale, while ranks in organizations indicate positions within a hierarchy, which is a type of scale. The meaning of ranking terms is determined by standards. The responsibilities and privileges of an office in an organization, as well as the qualifications one must meet in order to be eligible for that office, are determined by the constitution or bylaws of the organization. Some rankings admit of degrees, which imply a range, but ranks in organizations do not. A lieutenant colonel is simply one rank above a major and one rank below a colonel.

FORMING A JUDGMENT UTILIZING CRITERIA AND STANDARDS

Having clarified comparisons and rankings, we can consider a case in which a judgment is being formed. Let us make our case a simple one (for there is perhaps less to be learned at this point from a complex example than from a simple one) in which something is being evaluated. Let us ask ourselves what would be involved in evaluating a compact disc, or "CD," player for our sound system.

How do you evaluate CD players? First, you take their specifications into account. You want to know their frequency response, their wow and flutter characteristics, their signal-to-noise ratio, and their power output. Of course, there are other relevant specifications, and we will come to some of them, but two comments are in order with the mention of these. The first is that in order to know the meaning of the specifications you must know how the manufacturer arrived at its figures. For example, did the manufacturer use NAB standard equalization or some other? This is to say that in order to get anything of value out of the specifications you have to have the ranking standard. The second comment, which is closely related to the first, is that you cannot make a legitimate comparison of the specifications of two CD players unless you know that the specifications of each were determined by the same standards of testing. This is another illustration of the importance of standards in ranking.

A sufficient number of specifications have been mentioned to illustrate how you might go about comparing one CD player with another. Assuming the same standards were used in arriving at the specifications, the specifications are legitimate criteria for determining which of two CD players is the better. However, the specifications mentioned so far are not the only criteria for evaluating CD players. This becomes immediately apparent if you imagine yourself shopping for a CD player. In that case, in addition to the specifications already mentioned you will want to know what kind of speakers (if any) the CD player will drive and what sort of microphones (if any) it will take. The size and weight of the CD player may also be a consideration, as may be its general appearance. In addition, you will want to know what kind of warranty the CD player has and whether the store from which you can buy it is in a position to honor the warranty. You will want information concerning the performance record of the CD player. Does it require frequent servicing or does it give many years of service without needing major repairs? Last, but probably not least, you will want to know how much the CD player costs.

Notice the sequence of reasoning. First, when you were simply comparing the electrical specifications of CD players, and those were your only criteria, any CD player in the world would have been fair game for your comparison. However, once you decided to buy a CD player you limited your class of comparisons to CD players you could afford, CD players for which service was available, and so forth. This is an important point: **every comparison is limited to a class.** The best CD player in the world may not be the best CD player for you.

Second, when buying a CD player **some of the relevant criteria are more important than others and you have to weigh the relative importance of each against the other.** For example, you will have to balance the specifications against the price and your expectation of dependable service. If you know that a dealer stands behind his product, you may buy it even if its specifications are not quite as good as those of a product sold by another dealer; or if you have a choice of two dealers, and neither has a service department but you decide to buy anyway, you will choose the product with the best combination of specifications and price.

Notice that the considerations operative in your decision apply to any case in which an individual is considering the purchase of a CD player. Anyone about to purchase a CD player should consider the electrical specifications, availability of service, and price of the CD players he or she considers. However, the weight of these considerations in any particular case will vary. Suppose that you have narrowed your choice of CD players to CD player A and CD player B and that the specifications of A are better than those of B. In that fact you have a reason for buying A and a reason against buying B. If A and B are comparable in price and if service is available on each of them, you will surely buy A. If you can only get service for B in your area, then in that fact you have a reason for buying B and a reason against buying A. Moreover, if the specifications of A are not much better than those of B, the fact that you can get service on B but not on A will probably be of sufficient weight to make you buy B. When you can only get service for B and when the prices of the CD players are comparable, the service consideration outweighs the electrical specifications, but when the prices are comparable and you can get service on both machines, the electrical specifications are the deciding factor. This shows that **the relevant considerations, or facts to be weighed, apply to any purchase situation, but their weight or importance varies from situation to situation.**

We have now taken an important step in understanding the process of making practical judgments; for in considering which CD player to buy we have outlined the process we go through any time we consider alternative courses of action. That process consists of two stages, which are

- The surveying of the relevant facts
- The weighing of the considerations (reasons) for or against the course of action.[7]

---

[7] Baier, 93, f.

In surveying the facts about CD players we examine the electrical specifications, the availability of service, the price, and so forth. In these facts we have reasons for or against buying CD player A or B. In the second stage of deliberation we weigh these facts. In other practical judgments we go through the same stages, though of course the relevant facts are different. Suppose, for example, that we are not deciding which CD player to buy, but whether to buy a CD player. In the first case our goal, which is buying the CD player, was set, but in this case we are choosing our goal, and the facts relevant here are facts about ourselves. If we enjoy listening to music, we might like to have a CD player. However, we should weigh our interest in having one against other of our interests in order to determine whether we ought to buy one.

In some cases, the task of weighing relevant considerations is not easy. An employer, for example, is interested in having employees who are skilled, knowledgeable, dependable, and able to get along with others. Each of these considerations is important, but suppose that of two employees under consideration for a promotion one is very skilled and knowledgeable but undependable, while the other is very dependable but relatively unskilled and prone to error. The employer has a choice between one employee who works well when he is on the job but often misses work and another who never misses work but whose work leaves something to be desired. The choice between these employees can be very difficult because it is difficult to determine whether it is best to have an employee who is always there but who does mediocre work or one who does excellent work but is often absent.

WEIGHING COSTS AND BENEFITS

The task of weighing relevant considerations in choosing between alternative courses is sometimes difficult. In business, the costs of a proposed course of action are weighed against the benefits to be derived from it, but some costs and benefits are not easily measurable or compared with other costs and benefits. Suppose that engineers employed by an automobile manufacturer design a brake system which is superior to the brake system currently in use but that this system would be much more expensive to produce than the current one. Use of the new system would undoubtedly save lives since it enables automobiles to stop in a shorter time from any speed, but how can the value of those lives be calculated? If the new system would ensure increased sales, and if this were the only consideration which needed to be weighed in the balance, the decision as to whether to produce the new brake system or retain the old one would be simple, since the added cost of the new system could be weighed against the number of additional cars which would be sold. When the value to be weighed against the cost of the new system is human lives, however, how is the calculation to be made?

BACKGROUND CONDITIONS

We rarely act or make decisions in a vacuum. If we reflect upon the circumstances in which we find ourselves, we discover that we have already made several assumptions regarding conduct which is appropriate. If we are studying in a library, we assume that it is not appropriate to place a boom box on the table and turn it to full volume. If we are in business, we assume that others will act in their own best interest or (in an extension of this egoistic position) in the interests of their company. These assumptions provide the background conditions under which we act and make our decisions.

***Background conditions* are the assumptions which can be made in any particular situation regarding the conduct to be expected from ourselves and others.** The assumptions made in warfare, politics, or business differ from those made between friends and family members. At an auction, for instance, it is assumed that individuals understand that they have an opportunity to inspect the items which will be offered for sale prior to the time at which the bidding begins. If one individual perceives that an item is defective and another person does not, he or she is under no obligation to tell that person about the defect, since he or she may be bidding against the individual when the sale begins. At auctions it is understood that one person is pitted against another in the bidding process and that the purpose of each is to secure the items each wants at the lowest possible price. Between family members or friends, the background conditions are different. If a mother shopping for groceries with her daughter places a leaking carton of milk in her shopping basket without noticing the defect, it is assumed that the daughter will point out the defect to her mother if she notices it herself. This understanding differs in marked ways from the understanding which people have at auctions.

Our understanding of background conditions in decision-making situations can be compared to our understanding of the way characters ought to act in stories. Years ago I recall seeing an article on science fiction in which the writer reviewed rules for the behavior of robots in science fiction plots. I have been unable to find that article, but "The Three Laws of Robotics" in Isaac Asimov's *I, Robot* conveys the idea. The first law states that robots are never to bring harm to humans and that they are to protect them from harm.[8] Willard Huntington Wright, in a similar vein, suggests some rules for the detective novel. These concern permissible clues, the number of detectives in the story, and so forth.[9] Of course a writer cannot lay down rules such as these for other writers, but if he or she is respected in a particular genre, the rules may come to be accepted.

Readers of stories and novels and viewers of plays and films come very quickly to understand and accept the rules of operation of characters. Characters, after all, behave in characteristic ways. In addition, readers and viewers understand that particular actions are not possible in plots. In a story set in the 1850s, a person in danger cannot telephone

---

[8] See Isaac Asimov, *I, Robot* (Garden City, NY: Doubleday, 1950), 11.

[9] S. S. Van Dine (Willard Huntington Wright), "Twenty Rules for Writing Detective Stories," in *Philo Vance Murder Cases* (New York: Charles Scribner's Sons, 1936), 74–77.

for help or fly a plane from one place to another. These limitations follow from the period in which the story is set. Stories, then, provide us with (1) characters who operate according to certain rules and (2) settings which limit the scope of possible actions. These rules and limitations are background conditions for stories. Analogous background conditions operate in decision-making situations in which criteria and rules are applied.

In most cases, the understanding of these **background conditions is not explicitly spelled out, but tacitly understood. They are taken for granted.** Michael Polanyi speaks of a "structure of tacit knowing" in perception.[10] A man riding a bicycle, for instance, may be talking to a friend riding along beside him without being aware that he is moving the handle bars of the bicycle back and forth all the while. Similarly, an individual's understanding of a situation can be informed, or molded, by background conditions even though he or she is not explicitly aware of them. These background conditions are, we might say, a "structure of tacit understanding."

Background conditions can also be compared to light, which enables us to see and goes largely unnoticed so long as it is adequate, but becomes the focus of our attention when suddenly extinguished. Light, like the motion of the handle bars of the bicycle, is something of which we are aware, but not directly. Background conditions, like these phenomena, are perceived but not noticed.

When something goes wrong, or questions are raised about a particular decision, background conditions come to the focus of attention. An individual appeals to them when he or she wants to argue that certain criteria or rules ought not to be applied. The mother in the grocery store might argue, for example, that her negligent daughter should have pointed out the leaky milk carton to her. "After all, I'm your mother," she might say. "You're supposed to help me out."

EVALUATING CRITERIA
AND RULES

When selecting the criteria or rules which are applicable to a situation, we are guided by background conditions—i.e., we are guided by our tacit understanding of the situation. It is equally important to observe that without some situation or other which calls them out, criteria and rules lack point and purpose. An examination of this point enables us to understand how criteria and rules come to be called into question and evaluated.

Criteria and rules have meaning in and through the situations to which they are applied. In this respect, they are similar to solitary statements like this: "I think I ought to go to town today." What can be said regarding the truth or falsehood of this statement, taken by itself? Nothing whatsoever. We do not know who has made the statement, and because we do not know that, we do not know what reasons the individual might have

---

[10] Michael Polanyi, *The Tacit Dimension* (Garden City, NY: Doubleday, 1967), 9.

for making it. When the individual says "ought," is the individual referring to some moral obligation which he or she has or perceives himself to have? Does the person need to pick up supplies for a home repair project or perhaps buy a loaf of bread? We do not know, and are prevented by our lack of knowledge from entertaining some judgment regarding the truth or falsehood of the statement.

In the analogy I'm constructing, the criterion or rule occupies the logical position of the single statement. It comes to seem relevant and appropriate when some situation to which it can be applied is supplied. Without that situation, the criterion or rule can be understood (just as the single statement in the last paragraph is understood even though we have no idea of the situation or circumstance in which it is purportedly uttered), but no determination can be made as to its truth value. **Criteria and rules, and the situations to which they are applied, are cosuggestive—that is, criteria and rules suggest situations to which they can be applied, while situations suggest criteria and rules which seem relevant to them.** Criteria and rules without situations are like empty forms awaiting contents, while actual situations without criteria and rules are like paintings in a gallery awaiting a visitor to observe them in one way or another to give them a meaning.

One purpose of these remarks is to take us beyond the view that it is possible to intuit the acceptability of criteria or rules taken by themselves without reference to some circumstance or state of affairs. Like the premises of inductive arguments which can suggest more than one conclusion, criteria and rules can suggest several possible applications. However, they cannot be evaluated apart from their actual or envisioned application to some situation in which they are supposed to provide a response to a problem. They are rather like chairs which must be placed in a room for evaluation. "Is the color right?" a wife asks her husband as they shop for a chair; "and is it the proper size for the living room?" "I don't know," replies her husband. "I'd have to see it in the room to be sure." There is even something curious about the notion of a criterion or rule which bears no relation to some case. **A criterion or rule can no more be evaluated apart from some case (application), real or imagined, than a patch of color can be imagined which has no shape whatsoever.** Let us look further at the matter of calling criteria into question.

It is helpful to think of the process of questioning a criterion as analogous to that in which an individual is called to account for his or her actions. When an individual has been charged with following a rule or discharging a duty, that individual is called to account when the rule is broken or the duty not discharged. Another individual who has not been charged with following the rule or discharging the duty is not called to account when the rule is broken or the duty not discharged. For example, a stock person in a grocery store is called to account when the shelves have not been stocked, but a checker in the store is not, since it is not the checker's duty to stock the shelves. Similarly, a criterion or rule comes to be questioned when a problem persists which it is designed to solve.

A criterion or rule is evaluated, in the nature of things, from the perspective of a problem. Just as a cleaning agent is put to the test by applying it to a stain on a dress, so a criterion or rule is put to the test by applying it to a particular problem. **If the problem is adequately solved by application of the criterion or rule,**

the criterion or rule thereby passes the only sort of test to which it can be put. In principle, any criterion or rule is subject to critical evaluation through application to problem situations. The desire for criteria and rules which cannot be called into question is one which is not likely to be satisfied. **In the ideal case, the criterion or rule which is applied is not one which is beyond all possible question but simply the one which, in the circumstances, has the most to recommend it.**

Our purpose has been to outline the process by which criteria and rules come to be evaluated. Criteria and rules cannot be evaluated in advance of their anticipated or actual application. However, in a particular case in which you are evaluating criteria and rules, you may find that one or more of the following guidelines are relevant and worthy of being followed:

GUIDELINES FOR EVALUATING CRITERIA AND RULES

Evaluation of criteria and rules should be based upon

- A knowledge of the situation which is as complete as possible
- An acquaintance with, and evaluation of, criteria and rules applied in similar situations
- A judgment as to whether application of the criteria will solve the entire problem or only a part of it
- A judgment as to whether the criteria will solve the problem but create other problems
- An estimate of the possibility of actually applying the criteria in the situation

---

Summary

- Criteria are aids to making judgments. For example, in comparing the relative size of two objects we can resort to a measuring stick when we cannot tell by visual inspection which is the larger.
- Standards give meaning to ranking terms, such as small, medium, and large. For example, the average size of adult elephants provides a standard for determining whether a particular elephant is large for its class.
- Some ranking scales indicate ranges. Others indicate arbitrarily assigned characteristics.
- Some relative terms indicate orders of value.
- The two stages of deliberation are the surveying of the relevant facts and the weighing of the considerations for or against the course of action.

- Two common errors in ranking scales are (1) mixing or confusing one ranking scale with another and (2) omitting relevant places in the scale. There should be one scale per ranking and the scale should be complete enough for the purpose at hand.
- Background conditions are the assumptions which can be made in any particular situation regarding conduct to be expected from ourselves and others.
- Criteria and rules are evaluated when the problem they're designed to solve continues.
- In evaluating criteria and rules, we should ask whether (1) we know as much as we can about the situation, (2) we know how criteria and rules are applied in similar situations, (3) the criteria will solve the whole problem, (4) application of the criteria will create other problems, and (5) the criteria can actually be applied.

A LOOK AHEAD

Our examination of criteria and standards prepares the way for our examination of disputes in Chapter 9. Some of the most interesting and important disputes requiring critical thought are those in which criteria and standards are not fixed or generally agreed upon. Such issues as whether a fetus is a person, a particular motion picture is a work of art, an executive is overpaid, or one president is greater than another are quite common, but cannot be settled without the introduction of some criterion or criteria or some standard or standards. Several cases in which criteria are at issue are introduced in exercises in order to underscore this logical point and provide practice in resolving disputes.

Exercises

Answers to questions marked with an asterisk may be found in the back of the text.

I. Provide answers to the following.
   1. How do comparisons differ from rankings?
   2. How do standards differ from criteria?
   3. Explain the role of standards in comparisons according to rank orderings.
   4. Explain the steps of deliberation, either using the example of buying a CD player or one of your own.
   5. Explain what is meant by a *background condition*.
   6. Outline the process by which criteria and rules come to be evaluated.

7. What guidelines might be followed in evaluating criteria and rules?

8. You are employed with a steady income and some investments in stocks and bonds, but virtually nothing in savings due to a recent purchase of a new car. In filling out your income tax forms you discover that your tax bill is $4,000. It is April 1, and your federal and state tax returns are due on April 15. You will have to borrow money or sell some of your stocks and bonds in order to pay your taxes, since the bulk of your salary this month will be used to pay for current living expenses and homeowners insurance.

   a. What criteria will you use in deciding whether to borrow money or sell some of your holdings?

   b. Assuming that you decide to sell some of your holdings, what criteria will you use in deciding which holdings to sell? Will some of these criteria be of greater weight than others?

9. You are planning to purchase new carpet for your house. What criteria will you use to determine the quality of the carpets you examine for possible purchase?

10. Two hundred and fifty jobs are ranked in *The Jobs Rated Almanac*.[11] Actuary is ranked first, economist fiftieth, flight attendant one hundredth, surveyor one hundred and fiftieth, plasterer two hundredth, and migrant worker two hundred and fiftieth. What criteria do you suppose were utilized in deriving these rankings?

II. Classify the following as comparisons or rankings. For each ranking statement it will be possible to specify a scale or ranking order.

   1. Al plays golf, but he is a novice.
   2. Although Al is a novice at golf, his swing is better than Jerry's.
   3. Elephants are heavy animals.
   *4. Stephanie is a third-rate student.
   5. Stephanie is a better student than Foster.
   6. Alaska is larger than Texas.
   7. These are Grade A large eggs.

III. For many years the students at a private college were asked to complete the following course evaluation form in each of their courses at the end of each semester. The form is reprinted here without revision. (a) Indicate which, if any, of the rules for ranking scales are broken in Questions 1 through 13. (b) Where a rule is broken, state a revised scale which would eliminate the defect.

   There are two questions which you might ask yourself as you examine the evaluation form. These questions do not concern the ranking scales used in the form, but they are relevant to determining the adequacy of the form as an instrument of evaluation. The questions are these: (1) Are any of the questions or required responses redundant? (2) Is each question relevant to every college or university course you can think of, or are some questions relevant to some courses but not others?

---

[11] Les Krantz, ed., *The Jobs Rated Almanac* (New York: World Almanac, 1988).

STUDENT EVALUATION OF COURSE

COURSE _____

PROFESSOR _____

This evaluation should be based upon your perception of this particular instructor in this particular course. Consider carefully before making your evaluations. Circle the most appropriate response to each item. Feel free to comment on the reverse side.

1. ORGANIZATION OF COURSE:
   a. Excellent
   b. Good
   c. Adequate
   d. Confusing

2. ASSIGNMENTS:
   a. Reasonable
   b. Of a "busy work" variety
   c. Too hard
   d. Too easy

3. TEXTBOOKS:
   a. Essential
   b. Helpful as supplement to lectures
   c. Somewhat useful
   d. Worthless

4. INSTRUCTOR'S ABILITY TO COMMUNICATE KNOWLEDGE:
   a. Stimulating
   b. Satisfactory
   c. Poor

5. INSTRUCTOR'S PRESENTATION OF SUBJECT MATTER:
   a. Clear
   b. Satisfactory
   c. Obscure

6. INSTRUCTOR'S MANNER OF ANSWERING CLASS QUESTIONS:
   a. Full and direct
   b. Adequate
   c. Unsatisfactory
   d. Scornful

7. INSTRUCTOR'S ATTITUDE TOWARD STUDENTS:

   a. Usually considerate
   b. Sometimes inconsiderate
   c. Usually inconsiderate

8. YOUR OWN KNOWLEDGE OF THIS SUBJECT—gained from this course:

   a. A great deal
   b. A fair amount
   c. Very little

9. GRADING: The number of items (exams, papers, etc.) used to determine grade was

   a. Sufficient
   b. Larger number than necessary
   c. Too few

10. GRADING ON INDIVIDUAL TESTS AND PAPERS: The professor was

    a. Too generous
    b. Fair and reasonable
    c. Severe
    d. Unreasonably severe

11. RETURNING ASSIGNED MATERIAL: The instructor returned tests and papers

    a. Promptly
    b. Within a reasonable time
    c. After unreasonable delay

12. THIS COURSE, COMPARED WITH OTHER COURSES AT THIS LEVEL, WAS:

    a. Very difficult
    b. Difficult
    c. Average
    d. Easy
    e. Very easy

13. MY OVERALL RATING OF THIS PROFESSOR:

    a. Excellent
    b. Good
    c. Average
    d. Poor
    e. Unacceptable

14. Please WRITE COMMENTS ON STRENGTHS AND WEAKNESSES OF THIS COURSE, AND MAKE SUGGESTIONS AS TO HOW THE COURSE MIGHT BE IMPROVED:

Chapter 9

THE SUBJECTS AND KINDS OF DISPUTES

Socrates: And what sort of difference creates enmity and anger? Suppose for example that you and I . . . differ about a number; do differences of this sort make us enemies and set us at variance with one another? Do we not go at once to calculation and end them by a sum?

Euthyphro: True.

Socrates: Or suppose that we differ about magnitudes, do we not quickly put an end to that difference by measuring?

Euthyphro: That is true.

Socrates: And we end a controversy about heavy and light by resorting to a weighing-machine?

Euthyphro: To be sure.

Socrates: But what differences are those which, because they can not be thus decided, make us angry and set us at enmity with one another? . . . I will suggest that this happens when the matters of difference are the just and the unjust, good and evil, honorable and dishonorable. Are not these the points about which, when differing, and unable satisfactorily to decide our differences, we quarrel, when we do quarrel?[1]

Disputes are familiar to us all, and to take an interest in them is a sure means of entering into the life of the nation or the world. Within our own country we dispute the morality of some social practices, the legitimacy of governmental funding of services and projects, and the responsibility of government and business as citizens and consumers. We also dispute or are witnesses to disputes between nations. Some of those disputes are:

- Should a woman be allowed to have an abortion on demand?
- Should immigration laws establish strict limits to the number of individuals allowed to become citizens of our country?
- Should tariffs on the goods exported to other nations be reduced?
- Should aid and comfort be given to one side or the other in clashes between other nations?

---

[1] Plato, *Euthyphro*, Trans. by B. Jowett.

Disputes such as these are driven by a wide variety of considerations. The participants or disputants in some may be motivated by principle or by a desire that the truth be recognized. This may be the spirit in which a scientist opposes a hypothesis set forth by a colleague or an attorney defends a client. In others, the disputants may be concerned for social justice, as in the controversy regarding slavery in the United States in the nineteenth century and the Civil Rights movement in this century. The chief motive of some may be the well-being of other individuals. This is undoubtedly the case with many of those who are concerned about environmental pollution, endangered species of animal life, and global warming. Still others who find themselves embroiled in a dispute are moved by the consideration that they personally have something to lose or gain in the matter at issue. The interest or advantage perceived to be at stake may be as calculable as a salary or an inheritance or as incalculable as the respect and admiration of others.

These motives can be at work in the quiet of an apartment or a scientific laboratory, in a board room or a court room, on the streets of our cities, or on the world stage; for all of us, no matter how humble our station or heavy our responsibility, are drawn at some time or other into a dispute. None of our lives are completely untouched by controversy. Neither our governments nor our churches and synagogues nor our schools, families, or friendships are safe havens from questions and misunderstandings which may lead to conflict and dispute. It is for this reason that we all have something to gain from a better understanding of the nature of disputes and from considered and systematic practice in resolving them.

There are signs, moreover, that a study of disputes is not only useful, but one to which many men and women can be drawn. In spite of wars, and in spite of all the violence we see in our society and in others, the desire of persons to avoid the exercise of physical force, which signals the failure of other methods to resolve differences, is profound and widespread. We see this in our country in the willingness to work for change through the political process and in the use of the courts as a means of settling disputes. If disenchantment with the political process or with our legal system is widespread and thoroughgoing we might expect either to fall into neglect through disuse. However, no major election in our country lacks enthusiastic candidates, and our courts are crowded with individuals who had rather settle their disagreements peacefully than through a bloody feud.

Two warnings, however, are in order. The first is that no painless shortcuts or simple recipes for understanding and resolving disputes are to be found in the pages that follow. It is unlikely that there are any. Disputes can be quite complex and difficult. On occasion disputants who come to understand each other are able to resolve their differences, but understanding sometimes exposes differences more fundamental than any which the disputants had anticipated. At the other extreme, a resolution to one dispute may simply be the basis for another.

The second warning is that **the present approach to disputes makes no assumptions regarding the rationality of individuals who enter into disputes.** It is certainly not expected that everyone who becomes a party to a dispute is able to identify the kind of dispute in which he or she is participating by means of the classification of disputes to be presented in this section. Neither is it thought that the inability of some individuals to use the classification is an objection to it. Some individuals are not able to distinguish plants or animals in accordance with the classifications utilized by biologists, but that does not mean that those classifications are useless. They are, on the contrary, very useful to those who are able to appreciate them. With these caveats in mind, let us seek the conditions for the existence of a dispute.

THE CONDITIONS FOR THE EXISTENCE OF DISPUTES

The parties in a dispute differ from one another in some manner. However, **differences, or perceived differences, are a necessary but not a sufficient condition for a dispute.** This observation is captured in a distinction preserved by the phrases *differ from* and *differ with*. **In a dispute, individuals who (think they) *differ from* one another *differ with* one another. In other words, they set themselves in opposition to one another.** Persons may differ from one another in a variety of ways, but until one takes a stand against another and the other responds, those differences are merely descriptive. One individual, for example, may believe that automobiles made in one country are better than those made in another while another individual believes the opposite, but those opinions are not made a matter of dispute until one takes it upon himself to demonstrate the truth of his or her belief and the falsehood of the other and until there is some response to this attempted demonstration. In short, for a dispute to exist there must be these three factors:

- A difference of opinion
- An argument by one party to the effect that its opinion is true and the opinion of another party false[2]
- A response by the other party, or by someone interested in the issue, to this argument

This account makes the actions of individuals in opposing one another the fundamental dispute-producing condition. Of course, an individual can carry on an inner dialogue with himself or herself which conforms to the pattern of a dispute in which two or more individuals have set themselves in opposition to one another. In this case, the solitary individual can be undecided as to the truth of some matter or as to the best course of action in some circumstances and can alternately be drawn to one position or another in the course of an inner struggle to make up his or her mind. There is no reason why this process cannot be called an *inner dispute* or *inner debate,* for the individual in such a case is aware of a difference between two possible opinions and of the tension of opposition between them. Nevertheless, the process of disputing can best be observed in cases in which two or more individuals are seen to express differing opinions and to set themselves against one another, and so our illustrations of disputes

---

[2] This condition is sufficient to distinguish the disputes which are our concern from altercations, squabbles, spats, or tiffs.

in this text typically involve two or more persons. **Let us call the act of individuals in opposing the opinion of others the *existential condition* for the dispute in order to underscore the point that it is this act which brings the dispute into existence.**

WHAT CAN BE DISPUTED?

Notice that no suggestion has been made as to the possible subjects of disputes. On the contrary, it is assumed that any matter of perceived importance to individuals which inspires them to search for reasons why another should agree with them can become a subject of dispute. This may seem a small enough point, but the view is widespread that some matters fall outside the range of possible dispute. A prime instance of this is found in the claim "tastes cannot be disputed" (*de gustibus non est disputandum*). This thesis is passed from one generation to another as if it is an incontrovertible axiom even though it is easily shown by the most trivial examples that tastes no less than other matters can be subjects of dispute.

Since the sort of taste which supposedly cannot be disputed is not specified, let us assume that the claim might be directed either to tastes of a gustatory sort or to tastes in the arts. It is clearly the case that two individuals can choose different desserts at dinner or have different tastes in music and think nothing of it, but those individuals can and might, on an evening when the conversation is slow, debate the merits of their choices and tastes. The individual who chooses rhubarb pie can argue that his dessert is better because it has fewer calories than the sour cream raisin pie ordered by his dining partner, while his dining partner in turn can argue that hers is better because it is fresher than the rhubarb and because it enhances the flavor of the coffee she has chosen much more than the rhubarb would have done. Similarly, one individual might argue that the music he enjoys is superior because its rhythms are intricate while another of a differing opinion might argue that the music she enjoys is superior because its melodies and harmonies, which incidentally are not obscured by intricate rhythms, are rich. This suggests that tastes can be disputed. Some further consideration of the matter might even yield the conclusion that the disputes which tastes might occasion can be many and varied.

It might be objected, however, that the argument of the last paragraph misses the point. A critic could suggest that the claim that tastes cannot be disputed is not that individuals cannot argue about tastes but that individuals do not change their tastes no matter how much they might happen to be debated. This is an *empirical claim,* or in other words a claim which is open to proof or refutation with evidence gained from experience and observation. A response to it might be that tastes do change. Individuals who enjoy some forms of popular music in their teens and twenties sometimes find as they enter early middle age that they have developed a taste for music of a less recent vintage and that the music they previously enjoyed now seems trivial to them. Many individuals, moreover, frankly assume that their tastes can be improved, as evidenced by their enrollment in courses in art appreciation or workshops in wine tasting.

Hearing these considerations, however, our critic might observe that the claim that tastes cannot be disputed is not so much that individuals do not change their tastes as it is that those tastes are not changed by argument. After all, what argument can alter the taste buds of the diner who ordered sour cream raisin pie? To this there are two replies. The first is that while the taste buds of the diner are not changed, the dispute might nevertheless draw the attention of one party or another to considerations which eventually lead to a change in taste. Tastes, as we know, are developed over time. The second reply is that the subject of the dispute in the illustration was the superiority of the dessert chosen in the circumstances and that in this matter possible reasons favoring one choice over the other can be found. The person who chose sour cream raisin pie might be led to regret her choice and even agree with her dining partner that his choice was superior by the consideration that it had fewer calories than the pie she chose, while her dining partner who chose rhubarb might come to regret his choice by being reminded that sour cream raisin pie and coffee are a delightful combination. Reasons related to choices involving tastes, then, can be given; but where reasons can be given, error is possible, so we find that in tastes, as in other areas of our experience, it is possible to find that one has erred.

This conclusion might prompt our critic to say that even if it is possible to change tastes through argument, to do so would be coercive. As a matter of etiquette, if not of morality, people ought to be left alone in their tastes. Openness to the tastes of others is something which as a matter of courtesy we owe them. What are we to make of this claim? Let us respond to it with a suggestion of our own, which is that you and I (and everyone else) ought to be left free to form our own tastes so long as those tastes do not lead us into actions which bring harm to other individuals. The problem of the harmful effects of tastes should be handled in the same way as any other harmful effects are handled.

The preceding discussion indicates that tastes can be discussed. There is more to the discussion of tastes, after all, than the attempt to bring someone around to our own view. The truth is that by discussing food and clothes and works of art we enlarge our own understanding. While some of our tastes are unimportant in themselves the question of taste itself ought not to be dismissed lightly. Our tastes, it can be argued, are an expression of our judgment. Just as we can be a poor or a fine judge of distances or of character, so we can be a poor or fine judge of art or music. Vaclav Havel, the former president of Czechoslovakia, argued "that good taste is a visible manifestation of human sensibility toward the world, environment, people."[3] It might also be argued that our taste is a measure of our capacity for appreciating and enjoying the world, ourselves, and others.[4] Of course, **the present logical analysis leaves the determination of the importance of matters disputed to those who enter into a dispute.** Logicians as well as nonlogicians are well advised not to attempt to dictate beforehand what issues individuals might judge worthy of dispute.

---

[3] Lance Morrow, "I Cherish a Certain Hope," *Time,* August 3, 1992, p. 48.

[4] Another (pragmatic) answer to the claim that tastes are unimportant is provided by aesthetician Monroe C. Beardsley, who notes that the prevailing level of taste in a society has much to do with determining what works will be produced and available for viewing, listening, or reading and that consequently we all have a stake in the tastes of others. See "Can We Dispute About Tastes?" in *Introductory Readings in Philosophy.* Marcus G. Singer and Robert R. Ammerman, Editors. New York: Charles Scribner's Sons, 1962, 326.

KINDS OF DISPUTES

In asking whether tastes can be disputed we inadvertently introduced the three logical dimensions of disputes, which are these:

- The participants or disputants: The individuals or groups who differ with one another
- The subject: That about which the disputants differ
- The ground: The basis of the differing judgments made by the parties to a dispute

In the heat of debate or even in the cool of analysis these logical features can be difficult to separate, but the difficulty can be overcome with sufficient reflection.

The possible grounds of disputes is the basis of the classification of disputes we offer. Grounds, which can be facts, principles, criteria, standards, or linguistic ambiguities, are of fundamental significance. We classify disputes in accordance with their possible grounds as factual, criteriological, verbal, or mixed.

FACTUAL DISPUTES

A factual dispute is a dispute over some fact. **A *fact* can be described as a state of affairs or an existing condition which is not in doubt, or which has been verified in some way.** These propositions state facts:

- Babe Ruth died in 1948.
- George Washington was the first President of the United States.
- Seven plus five equals twelve.
- For every action there is an equal and opposite reaction.
- Cigarette smoking can cause cancer.

Not all facts, as these examples suggest, are of the same order. However, there is little controversy as to how the truth of the claims made in these propositions might be established. In every case the criteria and attendant evidence are well fixed and unproblematic, with the result that any dispute which might arise over their truth can be resolved by established means.

CRITERIOLOGICAL DISPUTES

Criteriological disputes are those which arise over the appropriateness of a criterion or standard, generalization, principle, or rule. Standards, as explained in Chapter 8, are determinations as to the meaning of relative terms used in ranking scales. Criteria can be properties which point to or imply other properties, but generalizations, principles, or rules function like criteria in that they provide the foundation for judgments and the basis for logical divisions and classifications. When disputants differ with one another over the appropriate criterion, standard, generalization, principle, or rule, the dispute is criteriological. The dispute which might arise over the following claim would almost certainly be criteriological:

- Executives who receive salaries of over $200,000 a year are overpaid.

What criteria should be used to determine whether executives in this salary range are overpaid?

Possible criteria are:

- The amount of the salary as compared with that of other executives within the same country.
- The amount of the salary as compared with that of other executives in companies of approximately the same size.
- The amount of the salary as compared with that of other executives in companies within the same industry.
- The amount of the salary as compared with the salaries of the lowest paid employees within the same company, the salary of the highest paid executive not to exceed that of the lowest paid employee by some determined percentage.

You can probably think of other possible criteria in addition to these. In deciding the question, a combination of criteria, rather than only one, might well be used.

The following claims might also give rise to criteriological disputes:

- A fetus is a person.
- Rap music is a high art form.

One possible source of criteriological disputes is the principles in logical divisions. Logical division (as opposed to the mathematical operation of division) is the process of separating or dividing classes into subclasses. The foundation for a division is a principle known as the *fundamentum divisionis,* or principle of division. Disputes which arise over the principle of division of a class are criteriological, since in such cases it is the principle of division which is at issue.

Another source of criteriological disputes is classifications, which are based upon some differentiating characteristic of a collection of objects. Books, for example, can be classified according to their size or age. Living species are classified by a combination of their numbers and rate of decline in numbers as endangered, threatened, or extinct. In this text, disputes are classified according to their ground. The purpose you have in mind determines the principle of classification which you use.

Criteriological disputes over principles of classification arise because some phenomena are difficult to classify according to a single principle. (When more than one principle is used in a classification, the result is a *cross classification.*) In biology, for example, should groups be classified according to characteristic traits such as the length of their legs or the color of their skin (a *phenetic* hierarchy) or by evolutionary descent (a *phylogenetic* hierarchy)?[5] Disputes over classifications also arise because value considera-

---

[5] On this issue see Mark Ridley, *Evolution and Classification: The Reformation of Cladism* (London: Longman, 1986), 3–5.

tions are an inherent part of the classification process. For example, should the sickle cell trait be classified as a disease? Consider this observation by Geoge J. Agich:

> The *sickle cell trait* (a condition, usually asymptomatic, caused by heterozygosity for hemoglobin S) may be advantageous (that is, promote survival) in an environment where malaria is endemic and antimalarial drugs are unavailable since it confers a resistance to malaria; the same trait, however, would be a disabling and perhaps life-threatening condition in high mountain villages since the sickling of red blood cells and attendant vascular difficulties occur when the cells are deprived of oxygen. Here, *adaptation* is the key to explaining why the sickle cell trait might be regarded as a disease in one instance and a constitutent [*sic*] of health in another.[6]

FACTUAL OR CRITERIOLOGICAL?

In some cases it is difficult to decide whether a dispute is factual or criteriological. One reason for this is that the difference between a fact and its criterion is often blurred. It is typically the case that the more a phenomenon is accepted as a fact, the less we think about the criterion which establishes it as such. Thus, when a workman measures a house for carpet it doesn't occur to anyone to question his use of a tape measure. We accept this as a criterion for length. Of course, we can question the workman's *application* of the criterion. If his or her measurement seems odd, we might say, "Are you sure about that measurement? Did you read the tape correctly?" But we won't question the criterion itself. It is usually when we are uncertain about what might count as a relevant fact that we begin to think of criteria. The following interchange helps in explaining this point.

AMALGAMATED INDUSTRIES: ASSET OR LIABILITY?

Aaron: Amalgamated Industries certainly is an asset to our community, isn't it?

Amy: An asset? You must be joking! Amalgamated's smokestacks have filled the air of our city with pollutants.

Aaron: Yes, but think of the jobs Amalgamated has created.

Amy: Amalgamated has created jobs, all right. We've had to expand our police force to patrol the streets where Amalgamated workers live, and our drug rehabilitation center is now overcrowded. Some asset!

---

[6] George J. Agich, "Disease and Value: A Rejection of the Value-Neutrality Thesis," *Theoretical Medicine,* IV (1983), 31.

Both individuals in this conversation know what it means to say that Amalgamated Industries is an asset: if it is an asset, it is valuable to the community. However, Aaron and Amy disagree as to whether it is an asset. What criterion enables them to decide? Neither Aaron nor Amy would disagree for long about how much space was occupied by the Amalgamated Industries plant or about how many persons were employed at the plant, since the criteria for getting an answer to those questions are agreed upon and secure. Neither do Aaron and Amy disagree about whether Amalgamated's smokestacks pollute the air or whether Amalgamated created jobs in the community, whether those jobs were in the factory itself or on the police force or in the drug rehabilitation center. Again, all those matters are matters of fact. The point of disagreement between Aaron and Amy is this: Do those facts count for or against the proposition that Amalgamated Industries is an asset to the community? The dispute is about criteria, not facts—i.e., it is a dispute as to which of these considerations should be the criterion for determining whether Amalgamated is an asset to the community. Is it Amalgamated's effect on the quality of the air in the community, or is it its effect on the expansion of the local economy or the safety of the streets? Or is it some combination of these possible criteria?

Reflection on this example provides an opportunity to examine a hitherto unobserved relation between criteria and facts in disputes, which is that **criteria determine which facts are relevant in a particular case.** As already observed, none of the facts about Amalgamated were in doubt. What was in doubt was whether those facts counted for or against the thesis that the company was an asset to the community. When a criterion is selected, certain facts immediately become relevant. If it is decided that air quality is a relevant consideration in determining whether the company is an asset to the community, then data as to the effect on air quality of the company's smokestacks immediately becomes relevant. If it is decided that the creation of jobs is the relevant criterion, then the number of jobs created becomes the relevant fact and air quality becomes irrelevant.

WHICH CRITERION WOULD YOU CHOOSE?

If Amalgamated Industries were located in your community, perhaps you know where you would stand on the issue of whether it is an asset. It is not difficult, however, to envision disagreement on the issue. If you were an employee of the company you would be inclined to emphasize the fact that it created jobs—your job, in fact!—in deciding whether it is an asset. On the other hand, if you were an elderly person with asthma you might choose the criterion of air quality.

Let us consider another criteriological dispute. In this one, principles function as criteria.

THE DISCRIMINATORY RESTAURANT

A man and a woman were planning on going out to dinner together. The woman objected to a restaurant suggested by the man. When the man asked for the woman's reasons for objecting, she replied that at one time the restaurant had refused to serve women. "That was a long time ago," the man observed in response. "Women are served there now. Besides, the food at the restaurant is very good." These considerations did not overcome the woman's objection to the restaurant, so the man suggested another restaurant in the area.

The man and the woman in this case agreed that women should not be excluded from public restaurants, but it was the man's view that the injustice had been corrected years before and that the mistakes of the past should be forgotten. The woman's view, by contrast, was that the restaurant should be boycotted for all time. It made no difference to her that no one associated with the restaurant at present had been associated with it during the period in which it had not served women. The rule on which the man's decision seems to have been based was "Let bygones be bygones," while the woman's decision seems to have followed from some rule like this: "Once wrong, always wrong." On the rule followed by the man, the fact that the restaurant no longer refused to serve women was relevant, but on the woman's rule it was not. This illustrates once more that criteria function to determine which facts are relevant.

It is generally the case that **when facts are established, criteria are unproblematic, and when criteria are problematic or unsettled, it is not clear what counts as a relevant fact.** When a disputed claim encourages a search for more data, the dispute is generally factual, since factual evidence should settle the issue. On the other hand, when a disputed claim results in asking what *kind* of evidence might count for or against it, the dispute is generally criteriological, since there is uncertainty about the sort of data which is relevant. You often question the relevance of data even as you gather it, but if you apply the distinction you observe that in some cases there is more concern with determining what counts as evidence than with gathering evidence, and in that case the problem is generally criteriological.

VERBAL DISPUTES

Now consider disputes of the *verbal* sort. The description which follows differs in some respects from the one traditionally given by logicians. Traditionally, logicians treated disputes in connection with an analysis of the nature of definition. It was typically pointed out in logic texts until recently that some disputes are verbal while others are real. The former were considered to be disputes of a lesser order than the latter in that they could be resolved by clarifying the way in which some key term was being used by one or another of the disputants. When that was done, the disputants would cease talking at cross purposes and harmony (at least in the textbook examples) would be restored. Real disputes, which could not be resolved by defining a key term, were sometimes said to be those which involved a question of fact, but beyond that not much more was said by way of analysis.

In the classification of disputes presented here, the traditional prejudice against verbal disputes is not retained. Such disputes are considered to be genuine even though some disappear when the language used by the disputants is clarified. This is because the existential condition of disputes is the active opposition of one individual or group to another and not the presence or absence of linguistic ambiguity.

THE FAR SIDE   By GARY LARSON

"Well, of COURSE I did it in cold blood, you idiot!...I'm a reptile!"

A verbal misunderstanding, not a verbal dispute.

Misunderstandings such as those produced by linguistic ambiguities should not be conflated with disputes. Such misunderstandings can lead to disputes, but they need not do so. When an individual takes a word or phrase to have a meaning other than the one it was intended by its user to have, communication breaks down. **A breakdown in communication**, however, **is not a dispute.** Individuals can fail to understand each other but not enter into a dispute. This is easily illustrated. Walter Stace, in explaining verbal disputes, asks us to imagine that some individual believes that the correct definition of *man* is "five-legged animal." (It is unlikely, of course, that any person would entertain this definition of man, but that is nothing against Stace's illustration.) The man surveys the world, finds no five-legged animals in it, and concludes that there are no men. The person's misunderstanding will be cleared up, Stace correctly says, when someone supplies the person with the correct definition of man.[7] The illustration enables us to observe the difference between a verbal misunderstanding and a verbal dispute. Stace takes himself to be illustrating a verbal dispute, but based on the distinctions made in this text, he has given us a verbal misunderstanding, not a dispute. Disputes arise when the existential condition is satisfied, which is to say when individuals set themselves in opposition to one another.

Not only are verbal misunderstandings not verbal disputes, it can even be the case that disputes are avoided because individuals, having misunderstood one another, think that they are in agreement when they are not. Misunderstandings can be a necessary condition for some (verbal) disputes, but they are not sufficient conditions for disputes.[8]

The traditional characterization of verbal disputes is not rejected entirely in our analysis. We reject the distinction between verbal and real disputes, but retain "verbal" as a category of disputes. Individuals can misunderstand one another due to a linguistic ambiguity of some sort, but verbal disputes arise when and only when individuals set themselves in opposition to one another as a result of that ambiguity. This way of describing verbal disputes clarifies the role of linguistic ambiguities in disputes while making it clear that disputes arise only when the existential condition is satisfied.

"Most of the disputes in the world arise from words."
WILLIAM MURRAY, FIRST EARL OF MANSFIELD AND CHIEF JUSTICE IN *MORGAN V. JONES* (1773)[9]

---

[7] W. T. Stace, *Religion and the Modern Mind* (Philadelphia: J. B. Lippincott Company, 1952), 249.

[8] If traditional logicians are thinking of verbal misunderstandings when they speak of verbal disputes, it is understandable that they do not classify them as real. The mistake, if there is one, consists in confusing a misunderstanding with a dispute.

[9] This quotation is taken from the front cover of the *CBA Record* for September, 1994. William Murray's insight is profound.

In the following analysis, we distinguish these two kinds of verbal dispute:

- The disputants use a term with different meanings without realizing that they are doing so and thus talk past one another. In this case there is a two-party equivocation on the term.
- The disputants cannot agree upon one of two or more recognizable meanings of a term.

TWO-PARTY EQUIVOCATIONS

In distinguishing verbal disputes from other sorts of disputes, close attention must be paid to the way in which words enter into disputes; for most disputes involve words in one way or another. We have seen that when individuals set themselves in opposition to one another they may use words with different meanings, thus thinking they are in disagreement with one another when they are not. They may also use the same word but with different meanings, thus coming to think that they are in agreement with one another when they are not. The last of these points is illustrated by the following case.

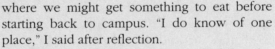

THE GRODY RESTAURANT

I once took a group of students to hear a lecture by an eminent philosopher. The lecture was given at a school a hundred miles away from the college where I was teaching, so I drove one car filled with students while a philosophy major drove a second car which was also filled with students.

After the lecture, which ran late into the night, the students and I were rather tired and restless. The philosophy major asked me whether I knew of a restaurant where we might get something to eat before starting back to campus. "I do know of one place," I said after reflection.

"Is it a good place to eat?" asked the philosophy major.

"I'd say it was pretty grody," I replied.

At this, the philosophy major's face lit up and he said, "All right; we'll go there." This response surprised me, since in high school my friends and I had used the word *grody* to indicate that something was very bad, but I obediently led the way to the restaurant.

The restaurant that hot spring evening was grody without doubt, and the philosophy major shot me inquisitive glances as we ate our rather unappetizing snacks. In the parking lot afterward he touched my arm and said, "I thought you said that restaurant was grody."

"I did," I replied, "and it was. The food was terrible, my silverware was dirty, the cushion in my booth had a tear in it, and the service was slow."

"Oh," said the philosophy major, "when you said the restaurant was grody I thought you meant it was a good place to go—a fun place, with good food."

"Not at all," I said.

"Next time I'd better check on the meaning of your words," said the philosophy major. He walked away, shaking his head in wonder.

The incident in the box illustrates a verbal misunderstanding, not a verbal dispute, but the sort of misunderstanding which occurred might just as easily have occurred in a dispute. In such cases there is **a two-party equivocation upon a term, with one party using a term with one meaning, the other with another. In such cases, the disputants talk past one another. This is one form of verbal dispute.**

LACK OF AGREEMENT REGARDING RECOGNIZABLE MEANINGS

In a second form of verbal dispute, the disputants are unable to agree on one of two or more recognizable meanings of a term. William James recounts one such dispute.[10] He was with a camping party somewhere in the mountains (probably the Adirondacks). Upon his return from a solitary walk he found several of the other campers engaged in a heated discussion. They were imagining that a squirrel clung to a tree opposite a man. As the man moved around the tree the squirrel shifted its position so that it remained out of the man's sight. The campers, who were evidently weary and bored, had begun disputing whether the man went round the squirrel as he walked round the tree. When James appeared they appealed to him to settle their dispute.

The dispute could be resolved, James suggested, through a decision as to what the campers meant by "going round." Did going round mean that the man stood first on the north then successively on the east, south, and west sides of the squirrel or did it mean that the man faced the belly of the squirrel then, in sequence, its right, back, and left sides? The answer to the question, and the consequent resolution of the dispute, depended upon the adoption of one or the other meanings of the term. Notice that these meanings were clearly distinct and that all the campers had to do was select one or the other of them.

---

[10] William James, *Pragmatism* (New York: Longmans, Green, and Co., 1907), 43–45.

IF A TREE FALLS IN THE FOREST . . .

A dispute which hinges upon a decision between more than one recognized meaning of a term is implicit in the question "If a tree falls in the forest with no one around does it make a sound?" The answer to the question, and the consequent resolution of the dispute, can be found by asking what one means by *sound*. If by sound one means vibrations in the air, or sound waves, the answer is yes. If, on the other hand, one means such vibrations actually perceived by the auditory sense of some living being, the answer is no.

One day on entering a classroom for a lecture, I found two students engaged in a heated dispute as to whether President of the United States Richard M. Nixon had been impeached. Each student was frustrated with the other and thought that the other was unaware of certain historical facts. It emerged that by *impeach* one student meant "attacks upon an individual with the intent to discredit the individual" while the other meant "formal charges of misconduct or wrongdoing before a court of justice." When these differing meanings were discovered, it became possible to end the dispute.

In disputes like these, nothing much seems to hinge upon the adoption of one meaning of a term rather than another. It is sufficient that the disputants clarify their disagreement. In other disputes, however, a determination of the meaning of the term might have implications for further decisions of a theoretical or practical nature. In the dispute last mentioned, a decision to use *impeach* in the sense of to bring charges of wrongdoing before a court brought in its train the factual question of whether such charges were lodged against Richard M. Nixon.

SOME DISPUTES INVOLVING WORDS ARE NOT VERBAL DISPUTES

In addition to the disputes just identified there are others which have words as their focus but which are nevertheless not verbal disputes. Of these, some are factual while others are criteriological. We examine cases of each.

Factual Disputes Involving Words

In factual disputes involving words, the words have an established meaning or usage. These disputes can be resolved when the meaning of the words in question is determined to the satisfaction of those concerned. In Stace's example, the understanding of the word *man* is clearly wrong given established usage. The dispute between my students as to whether Richard M. Nixon was impeached would have developed into a factual dispute if one student had denied, for example, that *impeach* can simply mean "to attack or discredit." In that case, in order to resolve the dispute it would have been necessary to consult a dictionary. Disputes over the meaning of words which have established uses are factual.

Criteriological Disputes Involving Words

Other disputes focusing on words are criteriological. The issue once again is the correct usage of the word, but in these disputes the meaning of the words is not established, at least to the satisfaction of all concerned. The interest in some of these disputes is primarily theoretical, as when philosophers dispute the definition of *knowledge, justice,* or *beauty.* In other cases the interest is primarily practical in that the goal of the disputants is the application of the term to some case. It is illuminating, for example, to devise criteria for the use of the word *obscene* in order to determine whether a book or motion picture can appropriately be placed in that category.

This illustration recalls the distinction between vagueness and ambiguity which we made in Chapter 3. If we do not know how to use a word, or are not able to apply it under certain circumstances, and that not simply because we have never encountered it or gone to the trouble to learn its meaning, it may be vague. Some examples of words which are vague in some uses are *tall, living, obscene, absolute,* and *beard.* On one level, obviously, we know the meaning of these words and can apply them without difficulty. There are borderline cases, however, in which it is not clear whether the word is correctly used. *Beard* provides the classic example of this. At one extreme it is obvious that a bewhiskered individual has a beard, and at another that an individual is clean shaven. In the middle, however, there are individuals who cannot be classified with certainty. The reason for this is that it is impossible, without being arbitrary about the matter, to specify how many hairs it takes to make a beard.

The vagueness of some words can be eliminated by establishing a standard. *Tall* is a ranking word whose vagueness can be so eliminated. However, a vague word can lead to a dispute of another sort. If two individuals cannot agree as to the standard which ought to be used to determine whether an individual is tall, then the dispute is criteriological. Disputes, such as the one mentioned earlier, over the standards to be applied in determining whether a work is obscene are notorious in the law and provide an excellent example of a dispute involving words which we would classify as criteriological. Other relevant examples in the law are cases in which it is necessary to establish criteria for "fair division of property" or "fair determination of child support."

While a vague word, as we have seen, is one which we don't know how to apply in certain circumstances, a word (or a statement) is ambiguous when (1) it has more than one meaning and (2) it is impossible to determine from the use of the word which meaning is intended. Words which have only one meaning must surely be outnumbered by those which have several, so the second condition is critical.

As indicated in Chapter 3, words which have more than one meaning can be used in an equivocal manner. *Pen,* for example, can mean a writing instrument or an enclosure for pigs, while *bar* can mean a rod of some kind, a place to get a drink, or a legal body. When an individual deliberately or unconsciously shifts from one meaning of a word to another, that individual is said to *equivocate.*

Equivocations are possible (though not common) on the word "is" in propositions. *Is* can be used in the sense of predication, as in "Mark Twain is an author," or in the sense of identity, as in "Mark Twain is Samuel Clemens." Equivocations are also possible (and more common) on relative terms such as *small* and *heavy.* There are few individuals who would be so inept as to argue that a small elephant is a small animal since all elephants are animals, but the illustration shows how an equivocation on a relative term might be made. Ambiguities of this sort can be eliminated by establishing a standard. Disputes involving relative terms are classified as criteriological.

This discussion reveals three sorts of dispute which involve words but which would not be classified as verbal.

- One party uses a term with an established meaning while the other does not. In this case, the dispute might develop as a factual dispute, with one party introducing evidence that he or she is using the term in a recognized sense.
- The parties are concerned with the criteria which are relevant to the application of a term in a particular context. Disputes in the law as to "obscene" or "fair division of property" are examples.

■ The parties are employing relative terms, such as *large* or *excessive,* which, in the absence of standards, are ambiguous.

MIXED DISPUTES

The last type of dispute in our classification is the mixed. **Mixed disputes are those in which two or more of the kinds of difficulties which define the other classes of disputes are encountered. A mixed dispute,** in other words, **contains subdisputes of a verbal, factual, or criteriological nature.** Many, if not most, disputes are mixed. They should be handled in piecemeal fashion. Separate the linguistic from the factual or criteriological difficulties and address each in turn.

Mixed disputes sometimes proceed through moments or periods which are identifiable by the kinds of consideration which happen to be the focus of attention. A dispute, for example, can be verbal in its inception but then come to center on some question of fact or some criteriological consideration when the verbal ambiguity has been eliminated. In these cases, elimination of the verbal ambiguity serves the function of exposing a point of disagreement which then becomes the subject of a dispute. In other cases, a dispute of a criteriological sort leads to a verbal dispute. When agreements on principles or criteria are not possible, nations are sometimes able to bring their active opposition to one another to an end through shifts in the language of the treaties or pacts on which they are working. This is one reason why so much in negotiations can hinge on a single word.

Summary

■ Individuals can differ *from* one another in some way, but not differ *with* one another. When individuals differ with one another, they set themselves in opposition to one another.
■ The *existential condition* of disputes is the act of individuals in opposing the opinions of others.
■ The three logical dimensions of disputes are the subject, the ground, and the participants or disputants.
■ Disputes are classified by their possible grounds as factual, criteriological, verbal, or mixed.
■ There are two kinds of verbal disputes, which are those in which the disputants use a term with different meanings without realizing that they are doing so and those in which the disputants cannot agree upon one of two or more recognizable meanings of a term.
■ Mixed disputes are those which contain subdisputes of two or more of the other kinds of disputes.

A LOOK AHEAD

Having stated the logical dimensions of disputes and classified them by their grounds, we are prepared to analyze disputes in more detail. We consider negotiations and resolutions in Chapter 10 and tactical maneuvers in Chapter 11.

Exercises

Answers to questions marked with an asterisk may be found in the back of the text.

I. Provide answers to the following.

1. Explain the distinction between *differing from* and *differing with*.
2. What is the *existential condition* for disputes?
3. What conditions must be met for a dispute to exist?
4. The claim that tastes cannot be disputed is not entirely unambiguous. What are some of the possible meanings of that claim?
5. Give a specific example of a dispute over a matter of taste, and identify the ambiguities in the claims made in the dispute.
6. What are the logical dimensions of disputes?
7. Two kinds of verbal disputes are distinguished in this chapter. What are they?
8. Three kinds of disputes which involve words but which are not verbal are distinguished in this chapter. What are they?

HELPFUL HINT

You probably won't have much difficulty in Exercises II and III below, but if you do have difficulty, it will probably be with classifying disputes as verbal. It would be a good idea to restudy the part on verbal disputes before doing the exercises.

II. Classify the following disputes as verbal, factual, or criteriological. ("Mixed" is not suggested as an option here, since the disputes are relatively simple.)

1.

Joyce: My uncle Charles was a highly educated man. He taught himself plane geometry and was an expert on Roman history.

James: I happen to know that your uncle didn't even have a high school diploma. I don't call that highly educated!

2.

> **James:** I don't think that human beings are determined. I agree with William James, who argues for free choice.
>
> **Joyce:** Of course human beings are determined! Haven't you noticed the legions of young executives who struggle to rise to the top of their companies?

3.

> **Joyce:** I've heard that the American Civil Liberties Union claims that the use of the death penalty in a state can actually increase the homicide rate in that state.
>
> **James:** That's bizarre. The death penalty will limit the homicide rate by serving as a deterrent. If you know you might fry for your crime you'll think twice. It stands to reason.

*4.

> **Joyce:** I think it's a crime the way Jim treats Sue. They've only been married a couple of months, but he often comes home late at night with no explanation.
>
> **James:** Show me the statute which says it's a crime for a man to come home late at night and I'll agree with you.

5.

> **James:** I just saw *Blazing Hockey Puck* at the Uptown Cinema. It's a great movie.
>
> **Joyce:** I wouldn't call any movie great that relied upon gratuitous sex and violence and glorified drug use by athletes.
>
> **James:** Of course it's a great movie. You don't have to take my word for it. *Blazing Hockey Puck* has grossed more than any other sports-centered film in the last decade.

6.

> **Kay:** Slavery as an economic system is immoral since it is demeaning to the individuals who are held as slaves.
>
> **Mark:** Capitalism is also an immoral economic system since it makes slaves—wage slaves—of the workers.
>
> **Kay:** Nonsense. The workers in a capitalist economy are not wage slaves; they're free to quit one job and take another any time they want to.

7.

> **Joyce:** I'm impressed by the decisiveness of World War I. When you examine the battles in that war you discover vast changes in combat techniques. For instance, the Allies developed a unified supply system for arms and materiels.
>
> **James:** I agree that there were great advances in combat technique in World War I. However, I don't think that the war can properly be said to have been decisive. Were any historical trends reversed? Were the nations of the world set on a new course? I think not. In fact, the indecisiveness of the war is shown by the fact that the nations of the world found it necessary to fight another world war twenty years later.

8.

> **James:**   Israel, as indicated by recent statements out of Washington, has supplied arms to China.
>
> **Joyce:**   Israel hasn't supplied arms to China, for that would constitute a violation of its arms purchase agreements with the United States.

*9.

> **Joyce:**   That was a great performance of Rakhmaninov's *Rhapsody on a Theme of Paganini,* wasn't it?
>
> **James:**   Are you kidding? The performance was totally lacking in spontaneity.
>
> **Joyce:**   It was a technically perfect performance, with not one note missed. I say it was great.

10.

> **Joyce:**   I see you're refinishing your uncle's antique chair. You should use an 800-grit sandpaper on the last coat of varnish for a really smooth finish.
>
> **James**   800-grit sandpaper?
>
> **Joyce:**   Yes.
>
> **James:**   I don't think there is an 800-grit sandpaper.
>
> **Joyce:**   You won't find it in all the stores, but it's made.
>
> **James:**   No, it's not. I'm sure that 400 is the finest grit sandpaper that's made.

III.   Classify the following disputes as verbal, factual, or criteriological. ("Mixed" is not suggested as an option here, since the disputes are relatively simple.)

1.

> **Joyce:**   The health care available in the United States is second to none. We are able to perform organ transplant surgeries and other difficult procedures which can't be done in other nations.
>
> **James:**   The health care available in the United States is hardly as good as you seem to think. In many countries every citizen is guaranteed access to basic medical services, but many individuals in the United States don't get basic health care because they can't pay for it.

2.

> **James:**   Under capitalism the rich get rich and the poor get poorer. More and more wealth becomes concentrated in the hands of fewer and fewer persons.
>
> **Joyce:**   Nonsense. Under capitalism everyone benefits. Both the rich and the poor increase their wealth.

3.

> **Joyce:**   Japan has fewer tariffs on manufactured goods than does the United States.
>
> **James:**   Nonsense. Japan has imposed more tariffs on manufactured goods than any other country in the world.

*4.

> **James:**   Japan is more open to foreign business competition than is the United States.

Joyce: How you can say that is beyond me. Japan has erected many more barriers to foreign trade than has the United States.

5.

Joyce: Les is a racist. He is suspicious of all individuals who are not black.

James: Yes, Les is a racist. He is interested in improving the material and social circumstances of blacks.

6.

James: Dogs are more intelligent than cats. A dog will come to you when you call it, but a cat is too stupid to do even that.

Joyce: You're wrong. Cats are more intelligent than dogs. You mistake the independence of cats for lack of intelligence. Cats don't come when they're called because they refuse to be dominated by humans.

7.

Joyce: The *Gazette* is biased in favor of the Republican party. Stories about Republican candidates for political office are always accompanied by a picture of the candidate. Photos of Democratic party candidates are never run.

James: That may be because Democratic party candidates don't submit photos to the paper.

Joyce: Oh, come now.

James: I'm serious. Anyway, I disagree with you. If you look at the amount of space the paper gives to Democratic candidates you'll find that it's about the same as that given to Republican candidates.

8.

James: My car gets good gas mileage. I drove it around for a week without filling up the tank.

Joyce: Are you kidding? I checked the car the last time we took a trip, and it only got nine miles to the gallon.

*9.

Joyce: The federal deficit is a disgrace. So long as our country runs a deficit, long-term interest rates are going to rise.

James: Quite the opposite of what you say is true. In most cases, long-term interest rates decrease with increases in the deficit.

10.

James: The best way to get good gas mileage with your car is to hold it to a steady speed on the highway.

Joyce: What do you do when you're going up steep hills?

James: You hold your car to a steady speed.

Joyce: I don't think so; you'd burn a lot of gas going up hills if you did that.

James: Oh, yeah? Well, what do you recommend?

Joyce: Instead of keeping a steady speed you hold the accelerator pedal to one position. That way, you don't give the car any more gas going up hills than you do going down, so the mileage is better.

James: The mileage isn't better. With your method, you'd slow down to a near crawl on some hills. To get good gas mileage you have to go somewhere, not simply creep along.

11.

Jesus: "Truly, truly, I say to you, unless one is born anew, he cannot see the kingdom of God."

Nicodemus: "How can a man be born when he is old? Can he enter a second time into his mother's womb and be born?" (John 3:3–4.)

Chapter 10

NEGOTIATIONS AND RESOLUTIONS

Chapter 9 distinguishes the various kinds of disputes. In this chapter, we examine negotiations and resolutions, whose importance becomes clear after we reflect on cases like the following:

- Suppose that a group of butterflies was killed off from eating genetically engineered corn. This would raise the question of whether the corn would be harmful to humans. Proponents of the genetically engineered corn would probably argue that the danger to humans was unknown, so humans might as well eat it. Moreover, they would argue, genetically engineered corn helps small farmers by producing a higher crop yield. Without competitive yields, such farmers might go out of business. Opponents would argue that since the dangers to humans were unknown, the corn shouldn't be sold and humans shouldn't eat it.

- It is common practice for colleges and universities to offer scholarships to promising high school athletes, but suppose that leagues were formed that would pay students to participate in college athletics. On this system, which would undoubtedly have to be underwritten by corporations, students would sign contracts specifying that they would play on the team and only go to school part time. For years, educators have disagreed as to whether college athletics takes students away from their studies and causes some athletes to perform poorly in the classroom when they could otherwise do well. Some would undoubtedly argue that under the new league system the students' classroom work would undoubtedly suffer, while others would defend the system by observing that it would allow students to attend college who otherwise could not afford it.

- Suppose a sports figure punches his coach in the face, but is not suspended because he is a top player. Should he have been suspended? Some will say yes, arguing that employment as a professional athlete is no different from other kinds of employment in which common courtesy and respect between employer and employee are required. Others will argue that the relationship between coaches and their players is different from ordinary employment relations. Passions run high in athletics, and it is to be understood that conduct that would seem violent in the staid halls of an insurance company is not out of the ordinary on the field of play. This being the case, the decision not to suspend the athlete is appropriate.

Can disputes like these be resolved? Are the issues in them subject to negotiation? Our purpose in this chapter is to offer some help in distinguishing negotiable from non-negotiable issues and to shed some light on what constitutes a resolution to a dispute. In some of the exercises at the end of the chapter, you will be given an opportunity to devise some dispute resolutions of your own.

DISTINGUISHING NEGOTIABLE FROM NONNEGOTIABLE ISSUES

A NEGOTIATION?

In the summer of 1999, government authorities raided a student hostel at the University of Tehran, leaving one person dead and twenty injured. In response, thousands of outraged students poured into the street to protest against the hard-line clergymen who largely controlled the government in the Islamic Republic of Iran. Many waved photographs of moderate President Khatami to show support for his reform policies. The protests, which began on July 7 and lasted for six days, were thought to be the largest in Iran since those that preceded the overthrow of the Shah of Iran in 1979. Did these protests constitute a negotiation?

In discussions of cases like the three mentioned, it is important not to ignore the significance of public discussions in fashioning public opinion. "Unless we make ourselves hermits, we shall necessarily influence each other's opinions" wrote the American philosopher C. S. Peirce in 1877.[1] The observation remains true, but in the second half of the nineteenth century the chief influences on U.S. citizens were books, newspapers, and conversations with friends and acquaintances in church or synagogue or at the corner grocery store. Today the conversational circle has been so expanded by radio and television that the potential for our opinions to be molded by individuals with whom we will never have living contact is greater than at any moment in human history. Moreover, it is possible that we are more conscious of or concerned with the opinions of others than any generation before us. The public fascination with surveys, polls, and market analyses would probably be a source of wonder to human beings from an earlier age.

Public discussions and exchanges of opinion of the sort to which these remarks draw attention should be distinguished from negotiations. Opinions can be changed through ne-

---

[1] Charles Sanders Peirce, "The Fixation of Belief," in *Philosophical Writings of Peirce,* ed. by Justus Buchler (New York: Dover Publications, Inc., 1955), 13.

gotiations, but they need not be. Negotiations often have nothing to do with an individual's opinions, as in the case of a member of Congress who allows a provision he or she detests to be tacked onto a bill in order to secure its passage. Public discussions, moreover, lack one of two elements that must be present for there to be a negotiation.

- A negotiation requires at least two parties.
- The parties must have the authority to accept or reject proposals or propositions.

It is the second element that public discussions lack. Discussions between individuals on a street corner or on a talk show, or statements by public figures, are profoundly important parts of the process by which public opinion is formed, but they are not negotiations for this reason. Individuals who are disputing a matter can speak for themselves or through a representative such as an attorney. Groups speak through professional associations such as a union. In the absence of individuals or bodies empowered to act on behalf of parties like these, however, negotiation is an impossibility. This consideration of negotiation in relation to the process by which opinions are formed paves the way for consideration of the kinds of issues that can be resolved through negotiation.

BRINGING PRESSURE TO BEAR

Groups speak through organizations like the American Medical Association or even through trusted charismatic leaders. The spokespersons for such groups attempt to influence public opinion, lobby for causes, and in general exert pressure on (for example) politicians and governmental agencies. It should be noted, however, that such efforts are not negotiations in the strict sense of the term since the spokespersons in question lack the authority to reject decisions by the individuals or agencies to whom they are making their wishes known. Automobile manufacturers, for instance, lack the authority to reject emission standards for automobile engine exhaust systems that have been set by the Environmental Protection Agency. Bringing pressure to bear is, then, not equivalent to negotiation (though in some cases it might be every bit as effective). Attempts by negotiators to put pressure on the other party to the negotiation are accompanying circumstances of negotiations, but they are not defining characteristics of them.

The first observation is that some kinds of issues cannot be resolved through negotiation. Some issues, of course, cannot be settled through negotiation because one or the other of the parties to the discussion refuses to allow them to be considered. An individual who has offered a used car for sale may tell a prospective buyer that the price is "firm." That means that he or she is not willing to barter. *Nonnegotiability by decisional fiat,* as this can be called, is not the sort of nonnegotiability meant in saying that some kinds of issues cannot be settled through negotiation. **The sort of nonnegotiability meant concerns** matters that cannot be settled through negotiation *due to their nature.* There are two such matters:

- Factual issues
- The meanings of words set by the collective action of persons who use the language

Factual issues provide the most uncomplicated examples of matters that cannot be settled through negotiation. Suppose that you and a companion are passing an old church on an afternoon walk and you comment that the steeple of the church is at least 210 feet high. Your companion demurs, saying that it cannot be over 180 feet high. The difference of opinion between you concerns a matter of fact. The steeple is as high as it is no matter what either of you thinks, so negotiation is simply out of place. You might change your companion's mind through special pleading, but his or her agreement with you would not ensure that your belief was correct.

Some disputes arise over the meanings of words. These disputes are either factual or criteriological. Negotiation does not have a role in disputes of the former sort, but it can have a role in the latter (as is explained below). A brief examination of the ways in which words gain their meanings enables us to distinguish factual from criteriological disputes over the meanings of words.

The first point to be noted is that the meanings of words are fixed and changed in the course of being used by individuals in their interactions with one another. Given these interactions the meanings of words are, by and large, not a function of the whim of a single individual or even of a group of individuals, but rather a function of the collective action of those who speak the language. In English, *bachelor* indicates an unmarried male. A single individual can arbitrarily use the term with some other meaning, but he or she does so at the cost of being misunderstood by individuals who know English. Friends can use the word with some other meaning among themselves if they choose, but that does not change the meaning which that word has outside their circle. Even if they use *bachelor* with a special meaning with one another, they are forced to use it in the sense of unmarried male in speaking with strangers since communication requires shared meanings.

This suggests that, **by and large, the meanings of words cannot be determined through negotiation. The authority for the meanings of words is collective and resides in the group that uses the language.** It is for this reason that the meanings of words are reported, but not stipulated, in dictionaries.

This is not to deny that the meanings of some words are assigned to them by individuals or groups. Occasionally, individuals coin a new word or find reason for expanding the usage of an old one. The test of a coinage or an expansion, however, is acceptance by those who use the language. Once a coinage becomes accepted, even the person who originally coined it cannot change its meaning since it has become a part of the common understanding of those who use the language.

Some words are singled out by individuals or groups for special functions. Researchers in a specialized area as well as parties to a discussion or dispute sometimes stipulate that a word or phrase has a special meaning in their communications. Cases like these are of special interest, for they are instances in which the meanings of words depend on decisions made by individuals under conditions in which negotiation might be a possibility. Whether the individuals concerned actually do engage in negotiation depends upon whether negotiation is a means of making decisions which those individuals have recognized.

Are criteria or standards subject to negotiation? The answer to this question must be affirmative, since some disputes over the meanings of words are criteriological, and since negotiation can, given the decision-making procedures accepted in the group in which the dispute has arisen, be considered an appropriate procedure.

Negotiations often occur in connection with balloting. When the members of a group have advance notice that a measure will be introduced in a meeting, negotiations regarding it often take place before the meeting is called to order. In addition, balloting (and other methods such as the drawing of straws) can be an effective means of bringing disputes to an end when the parties concerned are unable to reach a consensus based on the clarification of language, available empirical evidence, or modifications of their conflicting demands.

According to the previously stated classification, **disputes are verbal, factual, criteriological, or mixed. What role does negotiation have in each of these kinds of disputes?**

- Verbal disputes are not resolved by negotiation but by making linguistic usages plain. This does not contradict the earlier observation that the meanings of technical terms can be negotiated. Disputes over the meanings of such terms are criteriological.
- Factual disputes are not resolved by negotiation but by the verification or falsification of the claims made by the disputants. (This is not to say that the resolution of factual disputes is always a simple matter. The evidence which would resolve the dispute can be difficult or impossible to obtain, or the evidence might be available but one party be too stubborn to acknowledge it).
- Criteriological disputes, by contrast with the first two kinds of disputes, are resolved through negotiation or through a combination of verification of fact and negotiation.
- Negotiation can contribute to the resolution of mixed disputes which contain one or more criteriological subdisputes.

Before leaving this topic it is helpful to consider a criteriological dispute in which negotiation is appropriate and inescapable but in which considerations of fact are relevant. It is not difficult to imagine such a dispute. For example, a spokesperson for a labor union argues that a fair contract with a particular company for the union's members should include increases in salary and in health and retirement benefits as well as a guarantee of sick leave. In response, a spokesperson for the company argues that the salaries of the employees are already well above the industry average and that the company will not consider an increase in salary without corresponding decreases in health and retirement benefits. The issues in this dispute, as in others like it, may change as its participants present further arguments, but considering the dispute at this stage of its development it seems clear that its central issue is the criteria by which the fairness and acceptability of the contract will be measured. It also seems clear that resolution of the dispute does not depend upon the verification or falsification of the factual claim made by the company spokesperson even though that claim, either by being sustained by the company or refuted by the union, may have the effect of strengthening the position of one side or the other and thus influencing the outcome of the dispute. Here, then, is a criteriological dispute in which both negotiation and the verification or falsification of factual claims are all appropriate.

The example shows that facts can be relevant in disputes regarding criteria, but it is equally worth remembering that criteria can determine which facts are relevant. If a high school diploma is a requirement for a job, then the educational status of applicants is made relevant by that requirement. The relation between facts and criteria, however, is complex. In other cases, as observed in Chapter 9, it is impossible without criteria to determine what constitutes a fact.

IN SEARCH OF RESOLUTIONS

In the beginning stage of a dispute, one or more individuals express their view that something is true or false or right or wrong, or that something ought to be encouraged or discouraged or mandated or prohibited. At first, these statements are often nothing more than an expression of the individuals' feeling that something is true or that some events or practices are not in their interest or that something ought to be done about something. If no one takes them seriously or if the individuals lack some recognized medium such as a court to make others listen to them, nothing is done and no dispute emerges; for a dispute is at the minimum a two-party relation. However, if the individuals are taken seriously a dispute emerges. The dispute is marked by debate in which each side presents evidence for its position. The most intractable disputes are usually the criteriological, in which individuals differ on the criteria which are used to determine whose claims ought to be recognized as justified. Disputes can go on for years without resolution. In some cases, however, ways of resolving the dispute are finally found and the dispute brought to an end.

In the remainder of this chapter we consider dispute resolutions. We begin by distinguishing between resolutions in principle and resolutions in practice. This leads us to examine the concept of a resolution.

POSSIBLE RESOLUTIONS

A possible resolution of a dispute is a resolution in principle. A resolution of that sort requires knowing what would be required to end the dispute. A resolution in practice occurs when the requirement or requirements for a resolution have

been met. Some disputes can be resolved both in principle and in practice, while others can be resolved in principle but not in practice. Still others can be resolved neither in principle nor in practice. Some, however, can be resolved in practice though not in principle if the disputants' agreement to end their dispute without settling the matter between them is considered a resolution.

REQUIREMENTS FOR RESOLUTIONS

The requirements for the resolution of a dispute are determined by the kind of dispute. In criteriological disputes, facts can be irrelevant to the resolution because the determination of a criterion or criteria is necessary in order to determine what constitutes a fact. Note, for example, that an object is as long as it is no matter the system used to measure it, but until the concept of a foot is introduced and a standard set for the foot, it cannot be a fact that the object is a foot long. It is a measure of success in establishing criteria and standards in some areas that they are taken for granted as uncontroversial facts.

Of course, **facts are relevant to the resolution of a factual dispute, but the facts which are materially necessary or sufficient to resolve the dispute are a function of the connection between the claims made by the disputants. For some disputes,** for example, **a demonstration that the claim of one or the other of the disputants is false is not sufficient to settle the matter and end the dispute.** If I claimed that an individual known to both of us has been married five times and you claim that she has only been married four times, a demonstration that your claim is false would not be a demonstration that mine was true, and we might pursue the matter until we had determined how many times the person had been married. On the other hand, if I were to claim that all of the chief executive officers of the Fortune 500 companies are over the age of fifty-five and you were to claim that not all of them are over that age, finding one who was fifty-five or younger would be sufficient to end the dispute in your favor.

Factual disputes are often easy to resolve since the criteria or standards to be applied in determining the truth or falsehood of factual claims are relatively unproblematic. That is the case in the example of the height of the church steeple. However, **some factual disputes are irresolvable in that the claims in question cannot be verified or falsified in practice.** It is possible in principle to settle the truth value of the possible claim that the average weight of the members of the United States Congress is 170 pounds, but unless every member of the U.S. Congress agrees to be weighed—an unlikely possibility—one can neither verify nor falsify the claim in practice. Similarly, in a factual dispute one may not be able to get the data needed to bring the dispute to an end. A consideration of this sort will affect one's estimate of the likelihood that a dispute of this sort will be resolved; but this requires looking further at the concept of a resolution.

THE CONCEPT OF A RESOLUTION

To this point *the concept of a resolution* has been left unanalyzed. It is not, however, completely unambiguous. Some of its ambiguity can be eliminated and the way cleared for a consideration of the exercises at the end of the chapter by considering it from the standpoint of each of the three logical dimensions of disputes outlined in Chapter 9.

Those dimensions are the subject, the ground and the participants or disputants. We begin with resolutions from the standpoint of the disputants.

As observed in Chapter 9, individuals often differ *from* one another without differing *with* one another. A difference between two or more parties is a necessary but not a sufficient condition for a dispute. **A dispute arises only when individuals set themselves against one another on some matter. This setting against or active opposition of individuals to one another is the existential condition for a dispute. Disputes are resolved in one sense of *resolution* by eliminating this condition.** For example, an atheist and a theist who have been disputing the matter of God's existence with one another can simply agree to let the matter drop. As is sometimes said, the disputants "agree to differ."

Notice that it is not the cessation of the discussion in this case which marks an end to the dispute, but the decision of each side to drop its opposition to the other. The atheist and the theist continue to hold their respective beliefs and thus continue to disagree with one another, but they do not stand to one another as disputants. This reminds us that there is a distinction between a disagreement and a dispute. Disputes are disagreements, but not all disagreements are disputes.

In relations between warring countries, a cease-fire or period in which the countries agree not to do battle with one another is sometimes obtained. This is not a condition like that between the atheist and the theist of our example, for the warring countries still satisfy the existential condition for a dispute by standing in opposition to one another. It is true that the atheist and the theist still differ from one another on the question of God's existence, but this difference is no longer a point of contention between them and neither is straining to convince the other that he or she is correct and that the other's view is false. This shows that **a resolution to a dispute is possible even when it is not possible to secure agreement on the matter on which the disputants disagree.**

Such resolutions are, in fact, more common than one might expect. There are many familiar cases in the law in which charges are brought against an individual and then dropped for lack of evidence. The bringing of charges satisfies the existential condition for a dispute, but when the charges are dropped for lack of evidence the dispute is ended without determining whether the charges are true. No one interested in negotiation should forget that some disputes can be ended without determining whether one or either of the parties to the dispute is correct in its claims.

This discussion anticipates in a helpful way a consideration of the sense of resolution which emerges when disputes are considered from the standpoint of their subject. Imagine once again that an atheist and a theist have each determined to convince the other that his or her position is true and that the position of the other is false. This time, however, the result is different. Each presents the reasons for his or her position and in the end one becomes convinced that the other's position is correct and his or hers incorrect. That individual changes his position accordingly and the dispute is resolved. In this case the issue is settled for the disputants by their coming to hold the same opinion on the matter being discussed. The issue between them is settled by their agreement. This sense of resolution is often captured in the phrase "the matter is settled." (It cannot be said that the matter is settled for those who agree to differ.)

It is important to note that individuals can share a belief but not hold their shared belief for the same reasons. This circumstance leads to considering the resolution of disputes from the standpoint of the grounds of disputes. For an example, think this time not of an atheist and a theist but of two theists. One believes in God on the authority of the religious body in which he or she was raised while the other, who belongs to no religious body, has been convinced by a personal experience that God exists.[2] The belief is the same, but the reasons for the belief are not.

On occasion, individuals who share a belief but do not share the same reasons or grounds for that belief find that their sphere of agreement is small. This is often the case in politics when, for instance, two individuals vote for the same candidate for widely differing reasons. If one individual picks the candidate because she is a woman and the other because she has had experience in holding other offices, and if these are the overriding criteria of each voter, then in a subsequent election in which there is a female candidate with no previous experience the voters may be led to different choices.

A resolution to a dispute, then, **might consist in a joint agreement by the disputants to end the exchange with no agreement on the matter on which they differ or it might consist in an agreement on the matter under dispute with or without agreement on the grounds which led to that agreement. Agreement on the matter under dispute but without agreement on the grounds which led to it is better in most practical matters than no agreement at all, but if individuals can also agree on grounds, then agreement in principle is achieved, and with that, a cessation of the opposition of one party to the other.**

Summary

- Negotiations require at least two parties, and someone with each party must have the authority to accept or reject proposals.
- Some issues are nonnegotiable because one or all of the parties involved refuse to negotiate. This is *nonnegotiability by decisional fiat.*
- Factual issues cannot be settled through negotiation.
- For the most part, the meanings of words cannot be determined through negotiation.
- Criteria and standards are subject to negotiation.
- Disputes pass through stages. In the first stage, individuals express their dissatisfaction about something. In the second stage, someone responds to these expressions of dissatisfaction. In the third stage, the dispute is either resolved or forgotten.
- A resolution in principle is a possible resolution. A resolution in practice occurs when the resolution has been implemented.

---

[2] I have been told of a nonbeliever who became a believer when the cancer which he was diagnosed to have went into remission. This instance fills our need for a believer whose belief is not grounded in the teaching of a religious body.

- Disputes can be resolved in practice though not in principle by disputants simply giving up their opposition to one another.
- Verbal disputes can be resolved through an analysis of language.
- Factual disputes can be resolved through verification or falsification of claims.
- Criteriological disputes can be resolved through negotiation.

A LOOK AHEAD

Since important issues are often at stake in disputes, since disputes can last a long time, and since human beings can be impatient, competitive, and unscrupulous, it is understandable that some disputants seek means for securing an advantage over their opposite numbers. In the next chapter, we survey the tactics or tricks which disputants use to get the better of the other side.

Exercises

Answers to questions marked with an asterisk may be found in the back of the text.

I. Answer the following questions.

1. What are two necessary elements of negotiations?
2. What is meant by *nonnegotiability by decisional fiat?*
3. Are there any kinds of issues which by their nature cannot be settled by negotiation? If so, what are they?
4. What is a *resolution in principle* of a dispute?
5. In what ways can disputes be resolved?
6. Read dispute 5 in Exercise III below. Taking the arguments presented there, and adding more of your own as seems appropriate, write a brief essay in which you defend either the thesis that overpopulation is a problem or that it is not. Your assignment is to build as strong a case for your thesis as you can.

II. For the purpose of this exercise, let us stipulate that an issue is negotiable if it can be settled or decided by the mutual agreement of two parties, and that the parties in question in the exercise are individuals rather than organizations or institutions. Some issues will be negotiable in principle though not in practice. These issues, we may say, are nonnegotiable by decisional fiat. A general contractor who offers an estimate on remodeling a kitchen might be willing to change the estimate in negotiation or might decide to not discuss a change in the estimate. This is an example of a matter which is negotiable in principle though perhaps not in practice. On the other hand, the height of a church steeple is fixed. Its height is unaffected by the opinions of individuals as to its height. Consequently, when two individuals differ as to the height of the steeple their disagreement cannot be settled by negotiation.

In this exercise, indicate by "NN" which matters are nonnegotiable (i.e., negotiable neither in principle nor in practice). Indicate by "N" those matters which are negotiable in principle though perhaps not in practice.

1. Sign in a medical doctor's office: Payment must be made at the time of consultation.
2. When two gametes unite a zygote is formed.
3. When a human ovum is fertilized a person comes into existence.
*4. Eric will drive you to Boston in his car, but you must buy the gasoline for the trip.
5. Persons whose cholesterol rating is 150 are generally not subject to heart attacks.
6. Obscene films are those which contain scenes of nude human bodies.
7. Attorney to state's attorney: My client will plead guilty to the misdemeanor if you will drop the felony charges against him.
8. A student must complete 120 hours of course work in order to be awarded a bachelor's degree.
*9. Those whose blood line indicates that they are one quarter American Indian may receive benefits provided by the Department of the Interior.
10. John is more handsome than Jack.
11. Christmas occurs on December 25 each year.

WHAT CONSTITUTES A SOLUTION TO THE EXERCISES IN PART III?

The chief value of the exercises in Part III is the practice they provide in enabling you to state the issues in disputes, appreciate the interests of each party to the dispute, and think of possible resolutions. The classification of disputes provided in Chapter 9 should be useful as a guide to determining the type of dispute, but in working through the exercises, rely upon your own ability to read and understand an argument in finding the issues which emerge.

You're asked to present a possible resolution of the disputes. This is a sufficient ground for ending the dispute or one or more considerations which could possibly take the dispute a step closer to resolution. For factual disputes it may be possible to supply a resolution of the former sort, but for criteriological disputes no more than a resolution of the latter sort is expected. Remember that the resolution of many disputes which you will encounter will depend not upon the discovery of an unquestionable truth or a flawless procedure but only a claim or a procedure which is sufficient to enable the disputants to put the matter behind them.

III. Classify the two-party disputes in the following narratives as verbal, factual, criterio-logical, or mixed and complete the narratives with clarifications, facts, or criteria which provide a sufficient ground for resolving the disputes or which would carry them to a new level. The latter is accomplished with the introduction of a consideration which did not occur to either of the disputants. This consideration might be a clarification of a word, a fresh fact, or a criterion, but in any case your task in writing a resolution is to have the parties work out, or begin to work out, the differences between them.

1.

Phil: I've been reading about the case of Jerry Smith, the man who murdered and dismembered fifteen men.

Sophia: I remember that case. Smith's murders were discovered when a visitor to his house discovered a head in the refrigerator, weren't they?

Phil: Yes. It was a fortunate discovery for him, for I suspect that otherwise he would have been Smith's next victim!

Sophia: The whole affair makes me feel a little queasy.

Phil: Understandably. Murders as gruesome as those committed by Smith should be punished by execution, don't you think?

Sophia: I don't know. Didn't Smith plead insanity at his trial? I'm inclined to think that if someone is insane and thereby unable to control his actions he should receive treatment for his disability rather than death.

Phil: That's very noble of you, I'm sure.

Sophia: Don't be sarcastic. I'm serious in this. It's well recognized both in our morality and in the law that an individual is not responsible for actions over which he has no control. Suppose that when I'm driving down a residential street well within the speed limit a child chasing a ball runs in front of my car and I hit him because I am unable to stop in time. Even if the child dies I won't be held responsible because it was physically impossible for me to stop. Similarly, if individuals are unable through some mental defect to refrain from certain forms of conduct they're not held morally or legally responsible for that conduct.

Phil: Maybe not, but isn't it a little difficult in cases like Smith's to establish lack of control? In your case you didn't plan to hit the child; on the contrary, you were taken by surprise when the child ran out in front of you. Smith, by contrast, had to lure those men to his residence. That took forethought. Smith, in fact, had an established plan of action for gratifying his perverse desires and he carried it out over a period of weeks and months. I say that actions which exhibit such purposefulness imply a great deal of control.

Sophia: I'm willing to admit that in a particular case it may be difficult to establish that an individual lacked the requisite control, but I still think I have a point. If an individual was unable to control his actions I don't think he should be punished for them. On the contrary, he should be given some help.

Phil: You raise an interesting point. Let's suppose that someone like Smith is unable to help himself and that he acts under a compulsion so powerful that he cannot but persist in killing others. You would say, I suppose, that such an individual ought to be treated in an institution rather than put to death?

Sophia: Yes, I would. Wouldn't you be of the same opinion?

Phil: That depends. Are we to say that someone like Smith can be cured of his illness?

Sophia: I'm not sure that a cure is possible in cases like his.

Phil: Neither am I. For the sake of our discussion, however, let's suppose it to be an established scientific fact that someone like Smith cannot be cured. In that case I'd say he should be put to death.

Sophia: I'm of the opinion that you're altogether too willing to snuff out human life.

Phil: I assure you that the thought of putting someone to death doesn't appeal to me. It simply seems to me to be the best course in the circumstances.

Sophia: I don't see how.

Phil: Well, look at it this way: Why should you give someone free room and board for the rest of his life as the price for keeping him from killing someone else? We put mad dogs to death after they've given someone rabies because they're a danger and because there's no value in keeping them in a cage for the rest of their lives.

Sophia: But a human being is not a dog!

Phil: No, obviously, but the damage a human being like Smith can do greatly exceeds the damage the dog could do. We should tell him that we're very sorry but that he's unfit for society and an expense we can ill afford and then put him to death.

Sophia: I don't know. I just don't know. If someone can feel remorse for his crimes, as Smith apparently did, he has some human feelings, and I can't help but think that if we put people like him to death we might eventually go after other members of society who pose an inconvenience to us.

2. Carlotta and Peutrell are going out for a drive. Peutrell does not put on his seat belt before starting his engine and pulling away from the curb. Carlotta is reluctant to say anything, but thinks the matter important and tells Peutrell that he ought to put on his seat belt. Peutrell puts on his seat belt but responds to Carlotta's suggestion with some feeling. This is the conversation that follows:

Peutrell: I remember when driving was a simple matter. No seat belts, no airbags, no buzzers or bells when you opened the door, and, in short, no governmental interference in your private life.

Carlotta: You may not like to wear your seat belt, but seat belts do save lives and frankly I think it's irrational not to use them when the technology's available.

Peutrell: Not only is the technology available, it's stuffed down your throat. I don't think society has any business telling me I have to wear a seat belt. In the vast majority of cases anyway seat belts are not needed. If I drive two blocks to the Gas 'n' Go to buy a six pack I have to put on a seat belt, and I barely make thirty miles an hour the whole trip. That's really life threatening, isn't it? Who do you think is benefitting the most from all of this? It's not me and it's not you. It's the seat belt manufacturing industry. We have people out on the streets in our country with no place to sleep but the gutter, and we're spending our energies on cutesy ads to get people to buckle up. It's makes me sick.

Carlotta: Interestingly enough, we might not be wearing seat belts today but for the power of the automobile industry. I understand the technology for airbags was available even before seat belts were mandated by the government but were not made mandatory due to the opposition of the automobile industry, which argued that airbags would drive up the cost of cars.

Peutrell: I don't want anyone mandating anything for me.

Carlotta: It is a beautiful day for a drive, isn't it?

Peutrell: If you say so.

Carlotta: Look. Like I'm sorry I mentioned the seat belt. I happen to agree with you that in perhaps the vast majority of cases one doesn't need to wear one, but there are times—such as when you're on the highway in heavy traffic—that you're at great risk and need one. It would be great if we could depend upon people to put on their seat belts in such circumstances, but we can't. People are forgetful, so we have to have laws to force them to form the habit of putting on their seat belts. You might put on your seat belt for the rest of your life without being in an accident, and you could say that that was a nuisance and an intrusion, but if you had just one accident and your life were saved by your seat belt you'd sure as heck be glad you'd bothered to put it on.

Peutrell: Yeah, I guess you're right on that, but I hate having the government telling us what to do in so many areas of our lives. Every time you make a law like the seat belt laws you take away a decision that people ought to be able to make for themselves. Let's suppose I don't put on my seat belt when I'm on the highway in heavy traffic. That's my problem, or it should be. We ought to be left to make our own decisions and live with the consequences. Children grow to adults by learning to make decisions, but not by having others make decisions for them.

Carlotta: It's interesting that you mention children. I think the strongest possible case can be made for requiring parents to strap their infants into safety seats. Infants don't have the maturity to make such decisions for themselves, and lacking such maturity there's no reason they should be made to suffer for the consequences of an accident. Even if you're right that adults shouldn't be required by law to buckle up, I still think the laws in place to protect infants are a good idea.

Peutrell: I'm inclined to agree with you on that point. Say, that looks like an accident ahead, doesn't it? That black sedan must have been passing on a hill.

Carlotta: There's maturity of judgment for you. To think that you might meet some nut like that on the road.

Peutrell: Yeah.

3. Jim and Sue have been married for two months. They are having their first argument. Sue is the first to speak:

"Do you realize that you expect me to fix six vegetables for every dinner? Every night I'm standing over that four-burner stove fixing black-eyed peas, cabbage, carrots, corn, green beans, and squash."

Jim is mildly surprised, for Sue has listed the vegetables in alphabetical order. He makes a note to compliment her on that later; but now they are in the midst of an argument, and so he says, "I also like okra."

"Oh!" Sue's eyes flash in anger. "Most of the time you only eat one of the vegetables. I've never seen you eat more than two!"

"That's true," Jim agrees amiably, "but you can't expect me to know which vegetable I'll want before dinner. When could I make up my mind? Certainly not after breakfast. One cannot think of vegetables on top of cereal and toast. After that I'm off to the brokerage house, and when Mr. So-and-so calls wanting to know whether he should buy into Pepp Boys Auto or IBM, I can't very well be caught thinking of vegetables, now can I? No, the only time to think of vegetables is at dinner."

Sue's hand is tightly gripped around a spatula and her knuckles have turned white, but she manages to speak in an even tone. "There's something else that bothers me. Before we got married you said you believed in regular church attendance, but we haven't been to church since our wedding. In fact, you don't even get up most Sunday mornings after watching videos and drinking beer until all hours of the night on Saturday."

"But I do believe in regular church attendance," Jim says with exaggerated dignity. "Why, every Easter Sunday you'll find me in church, regular as clockwork."

Sue now grasps the other end of the spatula, bends it into the shape of a horseshoe, and walks out the back door. As quiet settles over the kitchen Jim chooses the corn, takes a bite, and reflects that it tastes like canned corn rather than fresh. He decides not to mention it to Sue until she has calmed down.

*4. The scene is a cafeteria at a major institution of higher education. Sam and Teri are seated at a table together as other students wander by with trays piled high with food. There is a long silence which is finally broken by Teri.

Teri: You look awful. You look as if you haven't slept in days.

Sam: No, it's not that. Last night I went down to O'Houligan's with Jack. It was a mistake, for Jack was determined to drink the night away. I hung around hoping to find a ride back to campus, but I didn't see anyone I knew except Doris and Carlotta.

Teri: Surely Doris would have driven you back.

Sam: Yeah, I thought so, too, but Jack queered that by buying a pitcher for the entire table.

Teri: I'm surprised Carlotta was there.

Sam: So was I. It was a weird scene.

Teri: Weird because you'd never seen her drink?

Sam: No, it wasn't that so much as it was her line of conversation. She was talking about her great grandfather who lived back during the Great Depression. It seems he had a small dairy and delivered milk to regular customers. Times were hard and he was having trouble making ends meet, so he began watering the milk.

Teri: Wouldn't his customers notice that?

Sam: I guess he added just a little water at first, and gradually increased the amount over time. Anyway, Jack was feeling his drink a little and told Carlotta in a loud voice that her great grandfather was a crook and Carlotta got very upset. She emphasized that times were tough during the Great Depression and that if her great grandfather's dairy had gone under he'd not have been able to support his family. Jack, who didn't care one way or the other, baited her on. He said that of course her great grandfather would want to support his family, but he was misrepresenting his product and that was the same as lying. He was a lying thief in Jack's estimate.

Teri: What did Carlotta say?

Sam: Well, she surprised me. You know how quiet she is. Well, she slammed her mug down on the table and asked Jack if he'd please let her finish. Jack said "Sure," stretching it out in an exaggerated way, and leaned back in his chair with a pasty smile. Then Carlotta said that as soon as he was back on his feet her great grandfather went to each customer, explained what he'd been doing, and promised it wouldn't happen again. That proved that he was basically an honest man, she said. Jack wouldn't let it go. He said that this confirmed his worst suspicions about Carlotta's great grandfather. It showed not only that he was a cheat but that he used the truth when it was convenient to him.

Teri: I imagine Carlotta could have replied to that by saying that her great grandfather felt a great deal of guilt for watering the milk and that that showed how important it was for him to be honest.

Sam: That's basically what she did say. Also, she said that her great grandfather was able to point out that his milk was still better than the milk sold in stores, since his customers continued to buy it.

Teri: That's a good point. I imagine it took a lot of courage for her great grandfather to go around to his customers in that way. How did his customers respond?

Sam: Carlotta said that most of them quit.

Teri: So honesty's not the best policy?

Sam: I guess that depends on when you're honest. If he'd told his customers up front that he was going to offer a lower grade of milk at a reduced price and watered that milk, he probably could have priced the product to make money and avoided all the guilt and loss of customers down the line.

Teri: Sounds good to me; but when did you get back from O'Houligan's?

Sam: I don't know. Very late. After the conversation about her grandfather Carlotta wasn't about to hang around, so I walked her back to campus.

Teri: Jack was pretty abrasive, huh?

Sam: Yeah, you could say that.

Teri: Sometimes I wonder about him.

Sam: How do you mean?

Teri: I think he might be an alcoholic.

Sam: He's only about twenty-two.

Teri: You can be an alcoholic at that age. It all depends on how long you've been drinking and how much you've drunk.

Sam: I thought alcoholism was inherited.

Teri: Like blue eyes? That's ridiculous.

Sam: No, of course not like blue eyes. I mean that you can inherit a tendency to become an alcoholic. It's a matter of your body's being able to digest the alcohol. Something about enzymes.

Teri: Well, I know someone who has a lactose intolerance. That means he can't digest milk, but he's not a "milkic," or whatever you'd call someone who couldn't stop drinking the stuff.

Sam: People don't develop a craving for milk. Isn't your comparison between milk and alcohol a little ridiculous?

Teri: Probably. But still I do get tired of hearing how alcoholism is inherited. I heard of a doctor—a doctor, mind you—who said of an alcoholic I happen to know that he was an alcoholic from the moment he took his first drink. As if after having one drink the man who became an alcoholic even had a desire to take another. No, if you become an alcoholic it's because you drink and drink and drink.

Sam: Well, if that's true—and of course I've never seen an individual become an alcoholic without drinking—what makes the individual who takes the first drink take another?

Teri: There's the social factor. People drink because they're put in situations where other people are drinking.

Sam: You mean that if you fall in with fast companions you'll go downhill to ruin.

Teri: Well, that could happen, but I wasn't thinking just of that. Alcohol is very respectable. You see it everywhere. There's a whole ethos. In business you drink to close a deal and you go to one cocktail party after another.

Sam: I never had that problem as a sack boy at IGA.

Teri: You know what I mean. I'm thinking of salespeople and business executives. Moreover, you have to recognize the influence of advertising. There are all those beer ads directed at young men between the ages of eighteen and twenty-three that picture drinking as a very masculine thing to do.

Sam: Oh, look. There's Jack now.

Teri: Wow. Like I see what you mean. He looks like he was hit by a truck!

5.

Sophia: Have you heard the news? This morning Alice gave birth to a baby girl!

Phil: Didn't she already have five children?

Sophia: As a matter of fact this is her seventh baby. Why do you ask?

Phil: It seems to me that Alice isn't doing much to help us with our problem of overpopulation.

Sophia: You're disgusting. Having a baby is one of the most wonderful and important events in a woman's life.

Phil: I don't deny that, but I do deny that it's an event a woman has to experience seven times.

Sophia: Well, if you're such an expert, how many times should she experience it?

Phil: I'd think that once would be enough.

Sophia: You're presumptuous in addition to being disgusting. Who do you think you are, deciding how many children women should have?

Phil: I admit that I sounded presumptuous, but I am worried about the overpopulation of the planet and think that it has reached such serious proportions that we must take steps to limit the reproduction of the species. That, in turn, means reducing the size of families.

Sophia: Alice had every right to have every baby she did.

Phil: No doubt, but not every right which one has is one which ought to be exercised. Suppose I own an empty house. I have a right to keep it empty, but if there are people who need housing it may not be right of me not to rent it.

Sophia: I thought we were talking about overpopulation. What's this about renting houses?

Phil: I'm talking about the exercise of rights. Look around the world and you'll see poverty, malnutrition, and starvation on a large scale. And why? Overpopulation. My point is that even if Alice and every other woman does have a right to have babies that doesn't mean she, or they, should have babies.

Sophia: Don't you think the solution to those problems you mention is our caring for other people and sending them the food and supplies they need?

Phil: No doubt we should do what we can to help others, but that will only take us so far. The sad fact is that if we help those poor starving people to survive they'll simply have more children and make our overpopulation problem worse than it already is.

Sophia: You're overly pessimistic. With the technology we're developing in this country we'll be able to grow more and more food on less and less land, and that will take care of the problem of starvation as well as free up more land for people to live on.

Phil: I hope that I'm less pessimistic than you are optimistic. I think you're living in a dream world. However, even if you're right that we'll develop that technology, don't you think we should take steps to limit population growth in the meantime? People are dying right now.

Sophia: I understand that people are dying, and I'm sorry about that, but I stand by my previous solution. I think that when people see the problem, as those people in those other countries surely must by now, they'll take steps to solve the problem. I mean if we really had that problem of overpopulation over here, Alice would see that and not have children.

6. In the state of Illoway a power company by law cannot cut off the power of a customer who has not paid his or her bill if the temperature is below thirty degrees Fahrenheit. The law ensures that poor people who cannot pay their power bills do not freeze to death.

Each year Illoway Power Company loses approximately $100,000 in revenues due to this law, but Red Microwatt, a rising young executive in the company, has come up with a plan to reduce these losses. He suggests that Illoway Power form the "Energy Assurance Foundation" in order to raise money through donations to pay the power bills of needy people who cannot pay their own. In ads promoting the work of the foundation there will be no mention of the law prohibiting power cutoffs for nonpayment of bills, but the ads will mention that some people do not have money enough to pay their bills and that Illoway Power will match every dollar contributed to the foundation.

Microwatt's superiors in the company think that his plan is brilliant. The money contributed to the Energy Assurance Foundation will go directly to Illoway Power and will reduce its outstanding revenues. Moreover, by matching those contributions Illoway will secure a tax write-off for charitable contributions, which will reduce its losses still further. "We've found a way to get the general public to reduce our losses for us," smiled one Illoway executive.

Red's wife Sally, however, was not pleased to learn of the plan. At dinner the evening of Red's meeting with the top brass of Illoway Power the following conversation ensued.

Sally: On your plan John Q. Public shells out money which is supposed to be paid by Illoway Power. I love you, but this is deceitful in the extreme. How many people would contribute money to the foundation if they knew who it was really helping?

Red: Wow, I don't believe this! This is the coup of my career. I'm undoubtedly going to get a big promotion out of this and you're worried about whether the public is going to be deceived?

Sally: I'm just as worried about you. Does rising in the company mean so much to you that you'd sell your soul for a public relations gimmick? Someone's going to put two and two together, you know, and when that happens the chances are good that you'll be hung out to dry.

Red: I don't think so. Anyway, my action helps everyone.

Sally: I can see how it helps the company.

Red: It also helps the general public. Illoway Power has to show a profit to its shareholders. If it reduces its losses, that increases its profits.

Sally: I don't call the shareholders the general public.

Red: No, of course not, but I wasn't finished. Don't you see that if Illoway Power doesn't reduce its losses the company will have to go to the state and ask for an increase in the rates it can charge? My plan should help it reduce its losses. Anyway, if it works the company can put off a request for a rate increase for quite some time. So it helps everyone—the company, the shareholders, the general public.

Sally: Well, I do admit you're ingenious. However, I'm still uneasy about this.

7.

Shopkeeper: May I help you?

Jane: Yes, I think so. My aunt from out of state sent me this Bobbie Brooks blouse, but it's too small for me, you see, so I'm hoping to exchange it for another just like it but in a larger size.

Shopkeeper: Did your aunt buy the blouse at one of our other stores?

Jane: I don't know.

Shopkeeper: Perhaps we could get the name of the store from your receipt.

Jane: I don't have a receipt. Auntie wouldn't send one because she wouldn't want me to know how much she paid for the blouse. However, the blouse is still in its original package, as you can see, and I've found another here in the same color but in my size. We could simply trade.

Shopkeeper: But you don't have a receipt and the blouse wasn't purchased at this store, so a trade in merchandise would be highly unusual.

Jane: Yes, but the blouse I have hasn't even been taken out of its wrapper, and the blouses are identical except for their size.

Shopkeeper: I can't see that it would be in our interest to make a trade.

Jane: I notice the blouses are the same price no matter what their size.

Shopkeeper: I'm sorry, but I simply can't help you.

8.

Sophia: While shopping in Clancy's Department Store yesterday I saw a woman nabbed for shoplifting. She put on a belt in the dressing room and attempted to wear it out the door. Such a small item.

Phil: I wonder if she'll go to jail.

Sophia: I don't know, but perhaps she won't if she's a first-time offender.

Phil: Even first-time offenders can go to jail in some cities, but I read somewhere about one city which set up classes for shoplifters.

Sophia: Classes! You mean like a school for shoplifters?

Phil: Yeah. As I recall, if you were a first-time offender you'd have a choice of going to jail and paying a fine or paying a fee to attend a class on how to quit shoplifting. If you chose the class you could avoid a conviction record.

Sophia: That's the most ridiculous thing I ever heard of. I can see taking classes on scuba diving or playing the piano because those are skills that require instruction and practice, but what sort of skill is—for lack of a better term—"not shoplifting"? I can see it all now. We used to say, "She's getting pretty good on the piano. I heard her play 'The Blue Danube,' and that's a tough tune." Now we'll say "She's getting pretty good at not shoplifting. I saw her go through Clancy's without stealing a thing, and that's a hard store to not shoplift in."

Phil: I think you're getting carried away. Are you short on sleep or something?

Sophia: Maybe, but don't you think the whole idea is stupid?

Phil: Not necessarily. People go to classes to learn how to quit smoking or lose weight, don't they? Those are classes on how to change your behavior. The classes on shoplifting could be a lot like them.

Sophia: Well, I say the best thing to do with shoplifters is put them away. That'll teach them. Besides, it won't work.

Phil: You mean the classes won't work?

Sophia: That's right.

Phil: Well, the more I think about it the more I think they will.

Sophia: What will you believe next?

*9. Peutrell has just overhauled the accelerating pump system in his carburetor. He replaces the carburetor on the intake manifold, bolts it down, and attaches the fuel line. All this time he is feeling quite pleased with himself; for he has done the whole job without referring once to the sheet of instructions which came with his accelerator pump rebuilding kit. "This ol' boy knows his carburetors," he tells himself. Meanwhile, Carlotta, an interested onlooker, picks up the discarded carton of the accelerator pump rebuilding kit. A tiny silver ball, looking like a ball bearing from a tiny antique roller skate, rolls out of the carton and bounces across the driveway. This conversation follows:

Carlotta: What was that?

Peutrell: Don't worry about it. We'll be rolling in five minutes.

Carlotta: I don't think so. I don't think your carburetor is going to work.

Peutrell: You've never overhauled a carburetor. You've never even changed a tire.

Carlotta: That's true, but I still say your carburetor isn't going to work.

10.

Lacey: I've heard that 52 percent of the people in the United States are females.

James: That may not be the exact percent, but I have heard that there are more females than males.

Lacey: I think that that percentage, whatever it is, should be reflected in our institutions of higher learning.

James: In what way?

Lacey: Let's say that 52 percent is correct. In that case 52 percent of the professors in colleges and universities should be females. Don't you agree?

James: No, I don't agree. You might as well say that because, oh, 48 percent of the people in the country are under the age of 21 that 48 percent of the professors should be under that age.

Lacey: I expected that from you because you're not very sympathetic to women.

James: It's not that; it's just that I'm not convinced that we should worry about what percentage of professors are male or female.

Lacey: That's easy enough for you to say, but if you look at the history of education in America you'll find that it's dominated by men and that as a result women's' issues have been neglected.

James: How is it dominated by men? I didn't have a male teacher until I was in the ninth grade. If anything, the educational system is dominated by females.

Lacey: It's dominated by males because males are the ones who do the hiring.

Chapter 11

TACTICAL MANEUVERS

If everyone who is likely to engage you in a dispute knew how to think and was a disinterested seeker after the truth, disputes would be much more pleasant affairs than they usually are. However, many of the disputants you encounter are unscrupulous. In this chapter, accordingly, it is important to examine some of the tactics or tricks which such disputants might use to secure an unfair advantage. An awareness of the tactics is very important; truth and right can be distorted by the use of these tactics and made by your opponent to appear to be otherwise. Observers of the dispute can be led by the tactics to conclude that the other disputant has gotten the better when that is not in fact the case. Even you might be thrown off by the tactics and unable in the moment to think of an appropriate response. The cross section of tactics which follows should help in confronting the unscrupulous disputant.

Tactics **is the method or technique for securing a goal.** Of course the goal an individual attempts to achieve can be a worthy one, and the tactics used quite unexceptionable. In this chapter, however, we examine less respectable uses of tactics. Therefore, put from your mind the painstaking processes of gathering evidence and constructing arguments in an honest attempt to discover the truth, and think instead of strategies for winning battles and coming out on top regardless of truth and right. The purpose is to discover the means by which individuals can be led to assent to propositions without regard to their truth or falsehood or take actions without regard to considerations which ought to count for or against them.

TACTICS

The tactics which an individual might use to secure an unfair advantage in a dispute can be divided into these four broad groups:

- Tactics by which a disputant attempts to divert someone from the issue of the dispute to a side issue. These are diversionary tactics.
- Tactics designed to make one assume that the other disputant has the advantage of authority or evidence on his or her side. These can be called tactics of presumption or assumption.

- Tactics of control, by which the other disputant attempts to manipulate or coerce in some way.
- Modeling tactics, in which the disputant attempts to secure an advantage through an imaginative or fanciful construction either of the issue under dispute or of the course its discussion is taking.

Success in defending oneself against these tactics depends upon the ability to recognize them in use and respond to them in an appropriate manner. This may not be as easy as one might think, for these reasons:

- Textbook examples are able to isolate tactics for consideration, but in disputes these tactics might be obscured by a forest of distracting details.
- One can reexamine the textbook examples as often as desired, but in the course of an actual dispute there may be little time for reflection and response. Tactics can be simple to identify but difficult to counter.
- Disputes are not static affairs, but exchanges in process in which meanings and understandings can shift and change with startling rapidity. A response which is relevant at one point in a dispute may not be relevant later. Examination of the following tactics should be accompanied by an attempt to observe instances of their use in disputes which you witness or participate in.

ISSUE-RELATED DIVERSIONARY TACTICS

There are several tactics by which another disputant can seek to divert one from the issue of the dispute. **First, the disputant can distort one's position or misrepresent what has been said.** This can be accomplished by generalizing a position in ways never intended. Suppose one were to claim that individuals should be allowed to purchase sexually explicit literature or videos. An opponent might respond by saying that this would contribute to the corruption of minors and hence must not be allowed. To this one would have to reply that one was speaking of persons of legal age and never intended to suggest that children should be allowed to purchase such materials. The defense to a generalization of a position beyond what is intended is a careful restatement of the position with proper qualifications. A careful statement of a position with proper qualifications is no sure defense against an attempt to generalize it. Even if one had said at the outset that adults should be allowed to purchase sexually explicit materials, one's opponent might nevertheless have responded that such a suggestion would contribute to the corruption of minors. Unless one is persistent in restating one's position, it is liable to be forgotten by those who are observing the dispute.

The disputant can distort or misrepresent one's position by emphasizing certain parts of the statement at the expense of others or by quoting one's remarks out of their original context. This is the technique of *accent,* which we discussed in Chapter 4.

A second tactic for diverting attention from the issue in the dispute consists in switching to an issue closely related to, or closely associated in the popular mind with, the issue under discussion. This is the tactic of *shifting the issue.* In a discussion of the problem of overpopulation, a disputant who wanted to eliminate the problem recommended that individuals use birth control techniques, including sterilization. A disputant on the opposite side immediately stated that she was against genocide and was shocked that the other disputant approved of techniques whose use was advocated by individuals who wished to wipe out certain ethnic minorities. Here there was an attempt to draw attention away from what individuals on their own might decide to do to what an unprincipled and tyrannical group of individuals might attempt to do to others.

Some years ago, a reporter asked a candidate for president of the United States whether the people of a particular country were oppressed. The candidate replied that the people of that country did not think of themselves as being oppressed and that they had often expressed their love of freedom. Of course, oppressed people can express a love of freedom, and people can be oppressed in fact when they do not think they are, so the politician did not answer the question. However, the reporter did not press the candidate on these points, so the candidate's attempt to shift the issue was successful.

Just as it is possible to miss the point of a statement or action, so it is possible to draw the wrong conclusion to an argument. This error is known as the *irrelevant conclusion.*[1] In other fallacies described in Chapter 4, the premises do not prove that the conclusion is true because they are logically irrelevant to it. That is the case with the irrelevant conclusion as well, but there the similarity ends. In other fallacies, the disputant has the conclusion to be defended firmly in mind but selects premises which do not provide evidence for its truth. In the irrelevant conclusion, the disputant presents an argument which may in fact be quite good, but draws the wrong conclusion from it. The disputant, from either ignorance or design, misreads the argument.

I first became aware of this fallacy—though without knowing the technical name for it—when I was in elementary school. One of the local business clubs sponsored a contest at my school for Best All Around Girl in the Sixth Grade Class and Best All Around Boy in the Sixth Grade Class. Two boys and two girls were selected as finalists in the contest. I do not remember the names of the girls, but Bill Brown and I were the boy finalists. It was very exciting, since Bill was my best friend.

The members of the business club asked the girls, and Bill and me, to join them at their luncheon meeting on the Thursday before the Monday on which the winners were to be announced at a schoolwide assembly. I remember that all of us dressed up, since the luncheon was a special occasion. Bill and I wore suits and ties, and the girls wore dresses with lace. I also remember that each of us was asked to say a few words about ourselves after the luncheon plates had been cleared away. All of us received polite applause from the business club members.

On the day of the assembly, the entire school filled the large auditorium, while the school principal, the president of the business club, the two girls, Bill, and I occupied

---

[1] The Latin name for this fallacy is *ignoratio elenchi*. This term literally means "ignorance of the conclusion."

the large elevated stage at the front. We seemed to be far removed from the laughter, conversation, and shuffling of feet of the students and teachers in front of us. Finally, the principal strode to the large wooden speaker's stand at the center of the stage, tapped the microphone to make certain it was on, and asked for silence. The noise of conversation subsided and the room gradually fell silent. The principal welcomed the students to the assembly and reminded them of what was to take place. He then introduced the president of the business club, who announced the winners of the contest.

I cannot tell you who was chosen Best All Around Girl in the Sixth Grade Class, since I cannot remember the names of the two finalists, but I can recount the speech in which the business club president announced the Best All Around Boy in the Sixth Grade Class. It went something like this:

> All of you know Gerald Brown. Gerald is a pillar of the First Baptist Church and a member of our city council. He owns and operates Brown's Grocery down on Main Street, and of course any one who has shopped there knows that he sells the freshest meat and produce in town and that his prices on canned goods are as low as can be found in the entire county. Yes, this community is much the richer for the presence of Gerald Brown. Accordingly, Bill [here the president of the business club turned to Bill, who sat beside me], it should come as no surprise to you to learn that you're the Best All Around Boy in the Sixth Grade Class.

As Bill walked to the platform to receive the award I clapped and cheered with everyone else, but inwardly I was in shock. I kept thinking to myself that Bill was being given the award, but that Gerald Brown, his father, had won it. The speech had been about the father, not the son. The logical conclusion to the speech was that Gerald Brown was a respected member of the community, but the conclusion drawn was that Bill, his son, was the Best All Around Boy in the Sixth Grade Class.

"Senator Vest's Tribute to a Dog" provides another example of an irrelevant conclusion.

SENATOR VEST'S TRIBUTE TO A DOG[2]

Senator Vest, of Missouri, was urged by the attorneys in a dog case to help them. Voluminous evidence was introduced to show that the defendant had shot the dog in malice, while the evidence from the other side went to show that the dog had attacked the defendant. Urged to speak, Vest arose, scanned the face of each juryman for a moment, and said:

Gentlemen of the jury: The best friend a man has in the world may turn against him and become his enemy. His son or daughter that he has reared with loving care may prove ungrateful. Those who are nearest and dearest to us, those

---

[2] Source unknown.

whom we trust with our happiness and our good name, may become traitors to their faith. The money that a man has he may lose. It flies away from him, perhaps, when he needs it most. A man's reputation may be sacrificed in a moment of ill-considered action. The people who are prone to fall on their knees to do us honor when success is with us may be the first to throw the stone of malice when failure settles its clouds upon our heads.

The one absolutely unselfish friend that man can have in this selfish world, the one that never deserts him, the one that never proves ungrateful or treacherous, is his dog. A man's dog stands by him in prosperity and poverty, in health and sickness. He will sleep on the cold ground, when the wintry winds blow and the snow drives fiercely, if only he may be near his master's side. He will kiss the hand that has no food to offer; he will lick the wounds and sores that come in encounter with the roughness of the world. He guards the sleep of his pauper master, as if he were a prince. When all other friends desert, he remains. When riches take wings and reputation falls to pieces, he is as constant in his love as the sun in its journey through the heavens.

If fortune drives the master forth an outcast in the world, friendless and homeless, the faithful dog asks no higher privilege than that of accompanying him, to guard against danger, to fight his enemies; and when the last scene of all comes, and death takes the master in its embrace, and his body is laid away in the cold ground, no matter if all other friends pursue their way, there by the graveside will the noble dog be found, his head between his paws, his eyes sad, but open in watchfulness, faithful and true even in death.

Senator Vest sat down. He had spoken in a low voice, without any gesture. When he finished, judge and jury were wiping their eyes. The jury returned a verdict in favor of the plaintiff for $500. He had sued for $200.

The conclusion to "Senator Vest's Tribute to a Dog" is this: "The one absolutely unselfish friend that man can have in this selfish world, the one that never deserts him, the one that never proves ungrateful or treacherous, is his dog." The conclusion which the judge and jury drew from the speech, however, was that the defendant had shot the dog in malice and that the plaintiff deserved damages. The irrelevant conclusion was drawn by them, rather than Senator Vest, for in his speech Senator Vest never referred to the case at hand.[3]

Along with accent, shifting the issue, and irrelevant conclusion, the **straw man** can be classified as an issue-related diversionary tactic. This consists in someone stating another disputant's position in a form which is easily refutable. Any of the previous tactics can be considered to be straw man tactics and are described as such when cast in a form for which a ready-made refutation is available. If a position can easily be refuted when generalized in unintended ways, then it becomes a straw man which can easily be knocked down. If mention of one problem causes some individuals to think of another, then a refutation of a weak position regarding that other problem might be taken as a refutation of a position regarding the first. The stand against genocide as a response to the problem of overpopulation, which is mentioned above, is an example.

It should not be thought that the straw man tactic relates only to particular arguments. In political campaigns an attempt may be made by one side to define the position of the other in the media. Just as an advertiser attempts to create an impression of a product in the public mind, so political campaigners can attempt to create an unfavorable image of the opposition candidate, or attribute views to the candidate which the candidate may not hold. If the candidate does not respond to clarify his or her position, the public may come to believe that he or she in fact holds the position imputed to him or her by the opposition. This particular application of the straw man technique is sometimes referred to as *defining the other side.*

A further issue-related diversionary tactic consists in directing attention from the issue of the dispute to the disputant on the other side. This tactic is the resort of individuals who are unable or unwilling to consider issues or who realize that the disputant on the other side is getting the better of them. This approach is discussed in Chapter 4 in connection with the **ad hominem argument** and thus needs no further amplification here.

TACTICS OF PRESUMPTION OR ASSUMPTION

A second group of tactics used in disputes is tactics of presumption or assumption. **These are designed to encourage the belief that a disputant has knowledge or authority or that certain tasks or responsibilities are to be borne by one disputant rather than another.**

---

[3] We should, however, not forget the context in which the speech was made. If Senator Vest was called to speak by the plaintiff, judge and jury may very well have assumed that he was taking it for granted that the plaintiff's case had already been established. Farther on in this chapter we discuss tactics of presumption and assumption.

SUBSTANTIVE TACTICS TO CREATE
AN IMPRESSION OF KNOWLEDGE
OR AUTHORITY

The importance of selecting a proper authority in those cases in which we lack the knowledge or experience necessary for making an informed decision on our own is underscored in Chapter 4. The argument from authority, for example, consists in mistakenly identifying an individual or source as an authority, while the argument to the people consists in appealing to popular opinion, which shifts like the wind, as a ground for believing one thing rather than another. In this connection, it is important to examine some of the ways in which disputants attempt to get other disputants to come to think that they have knowledge or authority. Such knowledge helps avoid being fooled by them.

An analogy indicates the importance of this discussion. In the Trick of the Chinese Rings, which C. S. Peirce described in the nineteenth century, a magician shows two metal rings to the audience, announcing as he does so that he will link them together. He then moves his hands swiftly in an elaborate manner and afterward holds the rings above his head to show that they have in fact been joined like two links in a chain. The

magician then immediately hands the rings to a member of the audience, who verifies that there are no breaks or gaps in either ring by which they can have been joined. While it is tempting to ask how the rings were joined, we should rather ask what the trick consists in, for it consists not in joining the rings but in leading the audience to believe that they were not connected to begin with. As a matter of fact, the rings were linked all along, but the magician spoke of them as if they were not. He led his audience to assume that they were unconnected. It is because the members of the audience made this assumption that they were led to the conclusion that the magician had put the rings together. The techniques we now describe are designed to cause one to view the other disputant in particular ways; they are designed to make one perceive another as having knowledge or authority. The point is very significant; for just as the magician's audience was inclined to believe that the rings had been joined once they had been brought to think that they were separate to begin with, so one is inclined to believe that what another says is true, or to yield to his or her decision on some point, when one perceives the other as being knowledgeable or having authority.

There are an indefinite number of ways in which individuals attempt to encourage others to believe that they know something or have authority in some matter, but all of them share this in common: they are attempts to create an appearance of one sort or another. Appearances inevitably influence the formation of judgments, but it is notoriously the case that appearances can deceive; that is why attention must be given to them.

Individuals attempt to create an impression of knowledge or authority in and through their surroundings. An employee of some rank in a company will, for example, have a larger desk or a finer computer than someone of lower rank. Possessions, too, are used to create impressions of knowledge or authority. For many individuals, the most important possession in this regard is an automobile. In the United States, many individuals of modest means whose housing is none too elegant nevertheless purchase a very fine vehicle. In some cases, one factor in this choice is the desire of the individual that others think that he or she is wealthy. Others are supposed to believe that since it takes a lot of money to buy a fine automobile, the individual who drives one must have a lot of money. The desire to appear to have a lot of money is in turn driven by the observation that wealthy individuals typically command the attention if not the respect of others.

Perhaps more than in any other way, **individuals attempt to create the appearance of knowledge or authority by modifying their personal appearance.** By the way in which they wear their hair, and through their clothes and jewelry, individuals attempt to determine the way in which others perceive them. In "Davis's Wingtips" we imagine a world in which clothes, more than any other consideration, are the driving force in judgments.

DAVIS'S WINGTIPS

Scene: The fifty-fourth floor of the Metropolitan Building; office of the president of F-X Corporation.

Characters: William Dirkson, president of F-X Corporation; Paul Franks, executive vice president of F-X Corporation.

Dirkson: Since Smith has resigned, we'll need someone to take over the aerospace account. What do you think of Hawthorne?
Franks: She could handle the account, but my choice would be Davis.
Dirkson: Davis! You surprise me. I thought I saw him wearing wingtips the other day.
Franks: That's Davis's sense of humor. If you'd seen his hosiery you'd have appreciated the powerful bridge between shoes and pants which they effected. Moreover, he'd chosen a Half Windsor for the knot of his tie.

Dirkson: A Half Windsor?

Franks: That's right. Given the current width of ties, it was an interesting choice, and one which altered the design of the tie in a manner which suggested the single-mindedness which, in my estimate, the aerospace account requires.

Dirkson: Hm. That's very impressive. Anything else?

Franks: Only the silver of his cufflinks, which served to emphasize the appearance of maturity conveyed by the streaks of silver hair at his temples.

Dirkson: All right, that's enough for me. Give Davis the aerospace account.

Franks: Done.

If this dialogue seems ludicrous, that is because the characters assume that clothes are the sole measure of a person. On the other hand, it would not be correct to assume that humans do not take clothes into account in evaluating others. People do think that the way in which individuals dress provides clues to their values and perceptions. If nothing else, clothes provide an indication of an individual's ability to present himself or herself in a manner which others consider appropriate.

But clothes can enable an individual to do more than that. By setting a certain standard in dress, an individual may be able to lead others to think that they are subject to his or her judgment or that he or she controls the conditions of interaction and the rules of decision making in the situation. The reasoning process involved is somewhat as follows: The one who sets the standard in clothes—referred to as the "smart dresser"—says, "I know how to dress, so I know how to handle this matter. You obviously don't know how to dress, so you don't know how to handle the matter." The not-so-smart dresser, who picks up the clues from the smart dresser, thinks to himself or herself, "I'm inappropriately dressed, so I obviously don't have as firm a grasp of the situation as that person does. I would rather not do things the way that person says we're going to do them, but I look so shabby by comparison with that person that I don't think that anyone would listen to me." The reasoning of the not-so-smart dresser may not be good, but the psychological effect which the smart dresser has had is powerful and effective.

One defense against an attempt to gain control of a situation by dressing in a particular manner is the reflection that it is usually easier to appear to have knowledge and authority by dressing in a particular manner than it is to actually be knowledgeable or have authority. While appearances can deceive, a sure test of an individual's knowledge and authority is what he or she in fact says and does over a period of time.

This may seem a simple enough point, but even here there is the danger of being drawn to doubt the hard evidence of another disputant's words and deeds, especially when there is long-term contact with the other disputant. On countless occasions, individuals have been gullible enough to allow others to explain away even the most callous

THE FAR SIDE By GARY LARSON

"Well, we're lost. I knew from the start that it was just
plain idiotic to choose a leader based simply on the size
of his or her respective pith helmet. Sorry, Cromwell."

Appearances Can Deceive

negligence, betrayal, and error of judgment. In "You Were Always on My Mind,"[4] a song
which was popular some years ago, the singer tells his lover that even though he has
slighted her and neglected her it is, nevertheless, the case that she was always on his
mind. The singer wants his lover to believe that he loves her even though the love
which he says is always present in his own mind has rarely or never been translated into
specific words and deeds of the sort which would indicate his love. "Appearances to the
contrary," he says in effect, "I love you." The song is a very good song of its kind, but its
appeal, though attractively presented, is specious. If a man loves a woman, then over
time he will express that love in words and deeds whose meaning is inescapable. Simi-

---

[4] See Willie Nelson, "Always on My Mind" (New York: Columbia Records, 1982).
     The manufacturer's number for this record is AL37951. According to the credits on the record itself,
"Always on My Mind" was written by J. Christopher, W. Thompson, and M. James. The song's publisher is not
given either on the record or on its cover.

larly, if an individual acts over time in a neglectful and faithless manner, then that individual is a neglectful and faithless person, and that is all there is to it. Occasionally, even the best of persons errs in his or her conduct with another, but over time a pattern of behavior is established, which is as certain a test as is available of a person's character. While appearances can deceive, then, a person can be known by specific actions over time. In a dispute with another, you should never be distracted by appearances.

SUBSTANTIVE TACTICS TO UNDERCUT KNOWLEDGE OR AUTHORITY

The tactics just discussed are designed to create an impression of knowledge and authority; but there are also tactics which are designed to create the impression that an individual lacks knowledge and authority or cannot be trusted. There is, for example, the tactic known as **poisoning the well.** No one who knows that the water in a well is poisoned will drink it unless forced to. Similarly, if an individual's credentials or reputation have been undercut, no one is inclined to listen to the individual. The most common ways to undercut the authority of an individual are these:

- Demonstrate that the individual has a questionable past.
- Demonstrate that the individual has special interests or that it would be to his or her advantage if what he or she says is true (or false) is actually true (or false). This suggests that the individual has an ulterior motive for saying what he or she says.
- Demonstrate that the individual has erred in other judgments. Set forth as many errors as possible.

In court proceedings, the credibility of witnesses can be of critical importance. Just how critical is illustrated in the trial of Augusto Falcon and Salvador Magluta on charges "of smuggling 75 tons of cocaine into the U.S. and amassing a fortune of $2.1 billion."[5] The prosecution presented "evidence that included detailed drug ledgers," but the defense team attacked "the credibility of accomplice witnesses, most of whom were promised reduced sentences," and secured a federal jury verdict of not guilty on February 16, 1996.[6]

Given that the outcome of cases can hang on the credibility of witnesses, the cross-examination of witnesses to determine their credibility is an important task of attorneys. However, is it fair to lay a person's entire past before the court in sordid detail or to suggest by innuendo or through a bullying attack upon the witness that he or she is guilty of the grossest immorality? Some attorneys have taken the position that their obligation to their client justifies any attack upon the witness which can serve to destroy his or her credibility. Francis L. Wellman, however, observes that the witness has no opportunity to defend himself or herself from the witness box and that a vicious cross-examination to suggest that the witness ought not to be believed can unnecessarily damage the

---

[5] See "Big Defense Team Wins Big," in *The National Law Journal* (March 4, 1996), 8.

[6] *Ibid.*

reputation of a witness. He sets forth some guidelines taken from Sir James Stephens's Evidence Act for determining which questions are fair and which not.[7] These guidelines are of some interest in disputes outside the courtroom as well as within, as the following discussion indicates.

A question is generally taken to be fair if what it implies would, if true, affect the credibility of the witness in the matter on which he or she is giving testimony. The truth of the imputation in the question and its relevance to the matter at hand are, in other words, essential criteria of fairness. Suppose a man is called to testify for the defense in a case in which a corporation executive is charged with insider trading. The charge is that the corporation executive bought securities on the basis of market moving information which was not available to the general public and which she had only as a result of her special position within the corporation. Suppose further that the man who is brought to testify for the defense is guilty of adultery, though not with the corporation executive who is charged with insider trading. Would the attorney for the prosecution be justified in asking questions of the witness which would suggest that he was an adulterer? The man is an adulterer, so the questions meet the criterion of truth. However, it is not clear that the man's adultery is relevant to the case of insider trading, so the second criterion is not met.

Consider a modified version of the example in the last paragraph. The witness for the defense has been having an affair with the corporation executive who is charged with insider trading. He and she have been seeing each other behind the backs of their spouses for years, and the attorney for the prosecution has evidence of that. In this case, is the man's adultery relevant? If the special relationship of the witness to the defendant is such that he is likely to want to give false testimony in an attempt to aid her defense, then the answer is yes.

Three criteria are suggested for determining whether questions regarding the credibility of a witness are unfair:

- Did the incident or circumstance referred to occur so long ago that it is not likely to have an effect upon the opinion of the court? Some incidents which attract a great deal of attention at the time of their occurrence come to seem insignificant with the passage of time. Moreover, individuals who make mistakes at one point in their lives often earn the forgiveness of their fellows over time. Reminding the court of errors which have been forgiven has little effect.
- Is the incident of a nature or character which is not likely to have an effect? If the incident is one which would embarrass the witness but not one which would cause the jury to doubt the truth of his or her statement, the mention of it is gratuitous if not unfair.
- Is the gravity or importance of the incident or circumstance outweighed by that of the evidence to be given? If the incident seems insignificant or trivial by comparison with the evidence to be given, the question should not be asked. If the witness has relevant evidence that the defendant is guilty of treason to his country, questions regarding the times he has written checks with insufficient funds to cover them probably does not carry much weight.

---

[7] Francis L. Wellman, *The Art of Cross-Examination,* 4th ed. (New York: Collier Books, 1962), 202.

This is not to say that it is always possible to predict what seems significant in court. Some years ago, a man from Massachusetts was arrested for drunken driving in Dallas, Texas. Out of fear that he would lose his driver's license, he consulted an attorney who subsequently examined the report of the arresting officer. This report included the time the ticket was given and the time the report was filed. However, it was evident to the attorney that the report was not entirely accurate, since the distance between the point of arrest and the station where the report was filed was so great as to preclude the possibility that the officer could have reached the station and filed the report at the stated time. When the case was heard, the attorney put the officer on the stand and emphasized not only the great distance but also the speed limits on the roads which would be taken and the level of traffic on those roads at the indicated time. The defendant, who in fact had been drunk, was found not guilty on the ground that it was intolerable for a police officer to falsify a report.

PROCEDURAL TACTICS TO UNDERCUT AUTHORITY

The tactics for undercutting authority or discrediting testimony which we have mentioned thus far are substantive—that is, they concern specific kinds of responses which might be made to another disputant. Other tactics for undercutting authority are procedural rather than substantive. The first of these is the tactic of *refusing to recognize* the *authority* of the other disputant. This can be done by refusing to speak to the other disputant. In negotiating with a body of individuals or an institution one can refuse to speak to a particular representative and demand to speak to a person of higher rank.[8]

In addition to attempts to create the presumption, or make others assume, that a disputant has, or lacks, knowledge or authority, there are other tactics of presumption or assumption which concern the *allocation of* certain *tasks or responsibilities* to one disputant rather than another. One important responsibility in a dispute is the demonstration that one side or the other is correct. If Disputant 1 can cause Disputant 2 to think that the responsibility for proving that Disputant 2's position is correct lies with Disputant 2, while Disputant 1 has no responsibility for proving that Disputant 1's position is correct, then Disputant 1 has achieved a great strategic victory; for his or her position will then be presumed to be correct until proven otherwise. In courts of law, one party or the other is presumed to have the burden of proof. In disputes which are pursued outside the courtroom, however, there are often no clear understandings as to who has the burden of proof, with the result that one disputant may lead the other to think that he or she has the burden of proof when in fact there is nothing in the nature of the dispute or the circumstances surrounding it to indicate that this is so.

---

[8] For understandable reasons, it is considered poor form for an attorney to speak to an opposing attorney's client.

Our current topic is tactics for undercutting the authority of disputants, but it can be observed that in negotiations one should always determine whether the individual with whom one is speaking is in a position to make the desired decision. If the person cannot make the decision, then speak to a person who can.

According to the *argument from ignorance,* a claim is false since it hasn't been proven true, or true since it hasn't been proven false. A disputant can choose one or the other of these versions of the argument depending upon his or her interests at the moment. The argument is fallacious in either version, since an unproven thesis can nevertheless be true and a thesis can be false even though it has not been shown to be so. As a tactic in a dispute, however, the argument from ignorance can be very effective. For example, the inability to offer a relevant proof can be construed as a justification for continuing to hold to a position. Nevertheless, the argument from ignorance can be countered with the observation that the inability to demonstrate that a position is false (or true) does not by itself constitute a proof that the position is true (or false). A lack of a refutation is not itself a proof, and a lack of a proof is not itself a refutation. The argument can also be countered with the observation that the sort of argument or evidence needed to make a case may be forthcoming shortly.

TACTICS OF CONTROL

A third group of tactics encountered in disputes are called "tactics of control." These are used when a disputant wishes to take charge of the course of the dispute in particular ways. Tactics of timing are included in this category.

TACTICS OF TIMING

Stalling is one tactic of timing. **It consists in the attempt to forestall the adoption of a proposal in the hope either that others who presently support it lose their enthusiasm for it or that others can be brought to the view that it lacks merit.** During the discussion of a proposed resolution of a dispute an individual can say something like this: "This proposal has obvious merit, but is this the time to implement it?" In some cases it can be difficult to determine the intentions of the individual who makes this statement. Does the person approve of the proposal but think that it would be better to adopt it at another time, or does the person want to prevent the proposal from being adopted no matter its merit? Is the person interested in doing what is best for all concerned, or does he or she want to further his or her own narrow interests? It is not always possible to know, but it is possible to evaluate the reasons an individual gives for delaying an action. If the reasons are not good ones, the proposal should be adopted without delay. There is no practical distinction between a proposal which is delayed and one which is denied.

What are good reasons for delaying the adoption of a proposal? There may be insufficient information available to determine whether the proposal is a good one. It may be necessary to gather more information. Those considering the proposal may not have had an opportunity to consider the information which is available. Other anticipated or hoped-for proposals or actions by individuals might render it unnecessary to act on the proposal. If the proposal is not adopted immediately but publicized for some time before being approved, it might be better understood and more easily accepted by those who are affected by it. Any one of these might be a good reason in some situation for delaying the adoption of a proposal. However, if there is no good reason for delay, action on the proposal should occur.

In order to delay the adoption of a particular resolution, an individual can introduce consideration after consideration in an effort to wear down its proponents. He or she can also suggest that a committee be formed to consider the feasibility of the resolution. This is a particularly effective move if the considerations previously mentioned seem to be relevant. In proposing the committee, the individual interested in delaying the adoption of the resolution should not suggest a time for the committee to report, for without a deadline it is possible that the committee will extend its work for an indefinite period.

During a negotiation between two disputants, the disputant who wishes to prolong the process refuses to reply to proposals by the other side unless forced to, or replies only after a delay and with further demands.

An individual who favors a proposed resolution to a dispute wishes to thwart attempts to delay action on the proposal. The tactics he or she uses might be called *tactics for rushing to judgment*. If the other side in a deliberative assembly succeeds in securing approval of a committee to study the resolution, the individual who favors the resolution proposes a deadline for the committee's report.

Other tactics for rushing to judgment are illustrated in the practice of attorneys. Suppose that the attorney on one side is prepared to go to court, but that the attorney on the other side is unprepared. In this case, the attorney who is prepared will push for an early court date in order to give the other attorney little time to prepare his or her case.

Attorneys sometimes combine stalling tactics with tactics of rushing to judgment. In the beginning stages of negotiation, for example, an attorney can be noncommittal as to what he or she is going to offer the other side by way of a settlement, then at a later stage make a surprise offer on the eve of trial. This is called an *offer on the courthouse steps*. Attorneys who use this tactic choose a time which is convenient for themselves but not convenient for the other side. It is recognized that some offers which seem good on first inspection may not seem so after reflection. This tactic, like others in which an attorney attempts to force the other side to a quick decision, is designed to eliminate the opportunity for reflection so far as possible.

TACTICS OF PSYCHOLOGY

The tactics of timing discussed above are designed either to delay or to hasten a resolution of a dispute. Now consider other tactics of control which we call *tactics of psychology*. All the tactics discussed have psychological effects, but those which we classify in this way are intended specifically to create anxiety or despair in the other disputant.

When a disputant knows the disputant on the other side particularly well, it is often possible for him or her to play upon the disputant's ignorance or insecurity. *Psychological tactics ad personam*—or, in other words, psychological tactics directed to the person—can be very effective if the disputant on which they are used is known to have a particular dislike, fear, or aversion. But even in the absence of a specific knowledge of another disputant's particular fears and aversions, it is possible to appeal to certain motives for action which are widely known to inspire action and influence behavior.

Perhaps the most important of these motives for action is social approval. All humans to some extent, and most to a great extent, seek the approval of fellow human beings. Even in cases in which the approval of others is not a good reason for doing something, it is human to take courses of action which are calculated to win the approval of others or at least avoid expressions of disapproval from others.

Few persons think that they lack independence, and most can point to actions which they have taken even though knowing that they would be met by others with disapproval. In order to appreciate the force of social approval in influencing actions, however, contemplate the prospect of wearing clothes which are quite different from those worn by friends. While braving the disapproval of some persons all of the time and of others some of the time, few can brave the disapproval of those in their inner circle except in exceptional circumstances. Social approval, then, is a powerful motivator, and the disputant who can bring it to bear upon his or her adversary wields a powerful weapon.[9] Other motives for action are adventure, security, and ownership. In considering one's personal desires and those of others, further motives for action undoubtedly come to mind.

MANIPULATION

The tactics of timing and the psychological tactics previously discussed are widely used tactics of control. A further tactic of control consists in the attempt to manipulate the other party by intentionally misrepresenting relevant facts. This can be done simply by **withholding relevant information.** *Relevant* here means information which can reasonably be expected to have an effect on a decision.

The practice of withholding relevant information has the same effect in everyday life as it does in disputes. College and university students often sell their textbooks to fellow students at the end of a semester. One semester before final exams I announced to the students in one of my classes that I would be using another text in the course the following semester. One of the students in the class then sold his text to a student who had signed up for the class the next semester. When this student subsequently learned that I had told the previous class I would no longer be using the text, she was not pleased. Referring to the student who had sold her the old text, she asked, "Why didn't he tell me?" Of course the answer to her question was painfully obvious; the student knew that she would not buy the text if he supplied her with that information. Since the information would have influenced her decision, it was relevant.

Persons who withhold relevant parts of the truth are said to be lacking in candor. These persons do not specifically utter an untruth, but their intention is to deceive others. Liars also intend to deceive others, but they do so by intentionally making statements which they believe to be untrue. It would be difficult to estimate the measure of control which one disputant can exercise over another by the simple device of *telling a lie.*

---

[9] While clothes can be used to create a presumption of knowledge or authority, the present discussion suggests that in general clothes can be used to create ad hoc the presumption that those who do not dress in a particular manner fail for that reason to measure up—i. e., that they are not quite acceptable in the circumstances.

Regarding the use of lies in disputes, there are two schools of thought. According to the first, one should tell "big lies," which consist in bold and sweeping statements. These statements are believed, it is argued, because people think it unlikely that anyone would have the nerve to make them if they were not true. According to the second school of thought, one should mix small but significant lies with statements which are true. It is argued that by associating the lies with so many true statements, a presumption can be created that the lies are true. This approach can be combined with the technique of making a statement one day which is retracted the next, as in the case of a seller of kitchen cabinets who told a customer that there would be no extra charge if she chose to have her cabinets made of hickory. When the customer phoned the salesperson a week later to place her order, the seller told her that there was an extra charge for hickory and denied having said otherwise. Every other statement the salesperson had previously made remained the same.

Both schools of thought agree that the best lie is the one whose falsehood cannot be determined. "Tell the lie which cannot be shown to be a lie" is the rule which these liars follow. In the last example, the customer had not had the seller put his original statement in writing, so she had no proof that her memory was correct.

It is not always easy to tell when someone is lying. Some believe that a sure indicator that a person is lying is his or her inability to look them in the eye, but liars are as aware of this common belief as others, and many of them develop the habit of looking others directly in the eye when they are lying to them.

These are all tactics by which one party to a dispute might manipulate another. In the perfect manipulation, the individual being manipulated is moved like a puppet by invisible strings and does not realize that he or she is being manipulated. If the individual becomes aware of the manipulation, the manipulator may continue to have an influence over him or her, but that influence is not, strictly speaking, manipulation.[10] In manipulation there is a lack of recognition on the part of the person being manipulated.

COERCION

Coercion, by contrast with manipulation, consists in the use of force, or the threat of the use of force, to influence the behavior of another. In manipulation, the influence of another is undetected, while in coercion the influence (the appeal to force) must be detected to be effective. The force can be either psychological or physical. *Psychological* is used here in a broad sense to include any use of pressure short of actual physical contact, but there are borderline cases in which it may not be clear whether the force exerted is psychological or physical. If a large man backs a small woman into a corner and threatens to beat her up if she does not sign a contract, is that form of coercion psychological but not physical? Would the man have to make physical contact with the woman for his act to be classified as physical?

---

[10] In some cases, an individual in an ongoing relationship comes to a dawning realization that the other party to the relationship is a manipulator who has repeatedly influenced his or her behavior. Does this realization bring with it an end to the other party's ability to influence the individual's behavior? Not always. Whether from force of habit, or a desire to avoid conflict, or weakness of will, some individuals continue to allow the other party to determine their behavior.

Cases of psychological coercion are not difficult to imagine. Consider the following: There is an opening for the position of public defender in a small judicial district, and two attorneys apply for the position. One attorney has two years of experience and is not highly respected in the legal community, while the other has been in practice for five years and has earned the respect of other attorneys in the community. The attorney with two years experience is related to an influential businessman in the community who lets it be known that he wants his relative to have the position. The law firm which handles legal matters for the businessman then throws its support behind the attorney with two years of experience, with the result that he is hired for the position. A case like this is clearly a case of psychological coercion.

The previous examples concern the use of force to gain the upper hand without regard to truth and falsehood or right and wrong. The **argument from force,** which is examined in Chapter 4, can be viewed as a particular form of coercion. This sort of argument is fallacious by virtue of the fact that the premiss, in which there is an appeal to force, is irrelevant to the truth of the conclusion. If the law firm employed by the businessman in the last example had argued that the attorney with two years of experience deserved the position because the firm would lose the businessman's account if the relative were not hired, the argument would have been an argument from force. However, the question of whether the attorney deserved the position did not come up in the example. Instead, force was used by the individuals simply to get their own way.

MODELING TACTICS

A fourth group of tactics for securing an advantage in disputes is **modeling tactics. These consist in imaginative constructions of the situation, circumstance, or state of affairs which is the focus of the dispute.** Modeling tactics bring the power of images and myths to bear upon the dispute.

THE SLIPPERY SLOPE

One oft-used model in disputes is known as the **slippery slope.** According to this model, a particular resolution or demand may appear to be innocent or unproblematic in itself, but nevertheless if adopted or granted leads to further resolutions or demands which are less innocent or unproblematic but which have to be adopted or granted since the original resolution or demand was adopted or granted. Adoption of the original resolution is like taking a first step on a slippery slope. When that step is taken, one's foot slips, and since it does, another step becomes necessary. With that step, one's foot slips again, necessitating still another step. Eventually, since each successive step requires another, one ends up at the bottom of the summit from which one began. According to the slippery slope argument, once the first step is taken, it is inevitable that one will slip to the bottom of the summit.

Slippery slope, or simply slippery soap?

The claim made by the slippery slope is sometimes expressed with different images. There is, for example, the image of "The Camel in the Tent." The faculty of a small college were considering a proposal to admit student members to a committee of the faculty. Several faculty members spoke in favor of the proposal, but one who was opposed secured the floor and told his colleagues that if they let the camel get its nose in the tent it wouldn't be long before it was the tent's sole inhabitant. The image was arresting. One could imagine the tent's original inhabitants fleeing its shelter as the camel worked its way inside.

An image similar to that of the camel in the tent is evoked by the phrase "If you let him get his foot in the door, then . . ." Still another phrase used to express the same idea as the slippery slope is *the thin end of the wedge*. Obviously, if one allows the thin end of the wedge to be inserted it is possible to drive the wedge all the way in. This general idea is sometimes expressed as the *wedge principle*.

A historically important argument which expresses the slippery slope idea is called the *domino effect*. Imagine a long line of domino tiles standing on edge in a close line. If the first tile in the line is tipped over, it will hit the second, which in turn will fall, hitting the third tile and knocking it against the fourth, and so on until the last domino in the line has been struck and felled by the preceding domino. The fall of the last domino is as inevitable as the descent of an individual to the bottom of the slippery slope. In the 1960s in the United States it was argued that if South Vietnam fell to the Chinese communists then one nation after another would fall until all of Southeast Asia would fall. In the 1980s when the United States sent advisors to El Salvador, it was observed in *The New Yorker* magazine that the same argument was revived to justify that action. Here is the relevant editorial in which this view is expressed:

Ever since the United States first sent advisers to El Salvador, people have been debating whether or not El Salvador is "another Vietnam." If one looks at the two countries themselves, few similarities emerge. Whereas Vietnam was largely Buddhist, El Salvador is largely Catholic; whereas Vietnam had a population of about eighteen million, El Salvador has a population of only about four million; whereas Vietnam was a divided country, El Salvador is not; whereas Vietnam was in Asia, twelve thousand miles away from the United States, El Salvador is nearby, in what we are pleased to call our "back yard;" and so on. However, if one looks not at the two countries but, rather, at American policies toward them, similarities of all kinds suddenly emerge. The Administration in power in Washington has applied the domino theory to El Salvador, as it did to Vietnam. According to that theory, the fall of South Vietnam was supposed to be the first step in a takeover of Southeast Asia by the Communist Chinese—a step to be followed, perhaps, by a whole string of losses, leading up to a moment when (it was said at the time) "we would have to fight them at the Golden Gate Bridge." Now Jeane Kirkpatrick, the American Ambassador to the United Nations and a leading spokesman on our Latin-American policy, has stated that there is in existence "a plan to create a Communist Central America." And Assistant Secretary of State Thomas Enders has stated, even more grandiosely, that "the battle for the Western Hemisphere is now under way in El Salvador." (Apparently, the Eastern Hemisphere will remain unaffected.) Ambassador Kirkpatrick has even resurrected the "psychological" variant of the domino theory which was characteristic of the justifications for Vietnam. According to this line of thinking, the fall of a country not only puts pressure on its geographic neighbors but also destroys confidence in the United States among the leaders of countries all over the world. Thus, in phrases that hark back to Richard Nixon's expression of fear that the United States would become a "pitiful, helpless giant," she has described the Central American crisis as one of "ultimate importance," for "if we can't use American power in this case, which is so clear-cut, there is going to be a general assumption in the world that the United States can't use power anyplace." As in Vietnam, therefore, the credibility of American power in its entirety is seen by her to be at stake. As in Vietnam, the local, political aspects of the struggle, which appear to be the most important ones, are interpreted solely in terms of global, military significance. Finally, as in Vietnam, there is a large disparity between the immense, "ultimate" catastrophe supposedly to be avoided and the modest means that at any given moment are requested to do the job—a disparity that invites the suspicion that when, as seems likely, these means prove inadequate, larger and larger sacrifices will be asked for, as happened in Vietnam. For instance, Ambassador Kirkpatrick, while speaking of "ultimate" stakes, tells us that mere "money" is going to be "the key" to our success, and so urges Congress to pass legislation giving increased financial aid to El Salvador.

It appears that these striking doctrinal similarities—similarities in which the striking differences between the countries in question appear to be overlooked—are being mirrored in the details of our actions on the ground in El Salvador. In a recent issue of the *Village Voice*, the writer Marc Cooper describes what has happened to the city of Berlin, in the Salvadoran countryside. In late January, the guerrillas took the town over. Two days later, government forces took it back, in the process flattening large parts of it with artillery and air strikes. Since then, in an effort to ingratiate the government of El Salvador with the people of Berlin, the United States Agency for International Development has arrived with a million dollars or so in hand and has proposed to build up the center of the city again. In this way, the United States hopes to win the hearts and minds of the people of El Salvador, and so win the battle of the Western Hemisphere. Meanwhile, in the capital, San Salvador, an American public affairs officer told Mr. Cooper, "We want to encourage political and economic reforms. And we want to build the democratic center." Whatever El Salvador may be, this strange mixture of indiscriminate firepower, philanthropy, and sheer political fantasizing is pure Vietnam. Standing cities, especially ones in different hemispheres of the earth, tend to look different. Flattened ones all look the same. El Salvador is not another Vietnam, but with a little more effort along the lines of our present policy we may make it one before long.[11]

---

[11] "The Talk of the Town," in *The New Yorker,* May 2, 1983, 29.

There are two stages in the response to slippery slope arguments. The first is to determine if the inevitable progression to disaster which is envisioned in the argument is a real possibility. In some cases it may be a real possibility, but in a great many cases it is not.[12] Once satisfied that there is no such danger, proceed to the second stage by observing that the disastrous consequences envisioned are not an inevitable consequence of the resolution at hand, and that the resolution should be considered on its own merits and not on the merits, or lack thereof, of other resolutions which might someday be introduced. In this stage, a proper response is, "Let us consider the resolution before us and no other." It is also helpful to point out to others that should a proposal be introduced in the future which would have disastrous consequences, the assembly can, and should, vote it down.

PERCEPTION DETERMINING DESCRIPTIONS

In considering modeling tactics it is important not to omit perception determining descriptions of individuals and classes of individuals. Some of the most important of these suggest power relations. The disputant who can successfully describe the disputant on the other side as an oppressor and himself or herself as one who is oppressed or who can describe the other as one of the advantaged and himself or herself as a disadvantaged person secures thereby a tactical advantage over the other disputant.

Sociologists have long observed the power of labels in determining how individuals and groups are perceived and how they behave. Perhaps the best response to an ill-suited description is a lively and easily remembered alternative description of the individual or group.

MODAL CONSTRUCTIONS

Modal constructions are important modeling devices. There are three modes, which are necessity, possibility, and impossibility. To say that an action is necessary is to say that it must be done, while to say that it is possible is to say that it can be done. To say that an action is impossible is to say that it cannot be done. **In disputes, as elsewhere, actions which are quite possible are often described as impossible.** A sign on a wall in a business, for example, reads, "We are sorry that we are unable to cash checks." Of course the business can cash checks! The truth of the matter is that the management has decided not to. A spokesperson for one side in a dispute says, "My hands are tied. The people I represent cannot agree to your proposal." Cannot? Perhaps the hands of the spokesperson are tied, but those of the individuals he or she represents are not; it is simply the case that they choose not to accept the proposal. **The power of the modal construction lies in its assumption of a condition or state of affairs which does not exist but which forces the individual to make the statement in question.** Management could simply say, "We won't cash your check," but it is more effective to suggest

---

[12] It is appropriate to mention here that the proposal to admit student members to the faculty committee, which was mentioned above, never led to the disaster envisioned by the professor who spoke against it. Two student members to the committee were approved by the faculty; and fifteen years later the number of student members remained the same and no student member had expressed an interest in removing faculty members from the committee.

that the matter is beyond the control of management. If reality is such that management cannot cash checks, then management is surely not to blame for not doing so.

Images of motion and rest are a ready source of tactical models in disputes, as well as in public campaigns of persuasion. In presidential politics in the United States, for example, observers often speak of a candidate's "momentum." A candidate who is gaining momentum is one who is rising in the public opinion polls. Similarly, an administration or an officer can "move forward" with a program. These are images of motion, but images of rest are sometimes used. It is said sometimes that an individual stands by tradition, or holds fast to proven principles. How a particular situation is described depends on the position one occupies. Person 1, who is resisting change, says, "I am standing firm against disruptive influences." Person 2, who is seeking change, says, "In my attempts to effect change, I have been blocked by Person 1, who is blind to the need for fresh ideas and alternative courses of action."

One interesting modal trick consists in characterizing a single event as a trend. One event does not make a trend, but one event is all that is needed for a disputant to begin to speak of a trend.

THE TREND

There was once a country in which the ruler was elected by popular ballot. The term of office was four years, and no ruler was allowed to serve more than two terms in succession. For decades, the rulers of the little country were elected without exception to two terms in succession, and then Euphorius was elected to serve for a term and was defeated in a bid for reelection to a second term. Immediately, one of Euphorius's supporters announced that there was a trend to single-term rulerships.

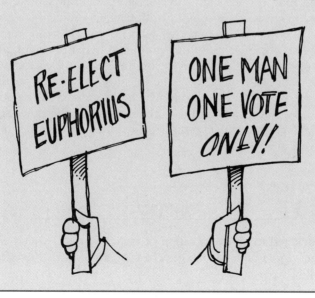

Euphorius's supporter was attempting to make the simple defeat of Euphorius seem as if it were part of a recognizable historical pattern. A proper response to the announcement would be the observation that *three or four* single-term rulerships which occurred in succession would be evidence of a trend, but not one by itself.

WINNING SOCIAL AND POLITICAL DISPUTES

In this text it is emphasized that disputes—at least the more intractable ones—are not static momentary events but processes over time. It is also emphasized that the ideal resolution is the one in which the disputants overcome their differences and find a basis for agreement. **In social and political disputes,** however, **it is often the case that one side or the other is not willing to change its position for any reason. In those cases, the apparent winner—often after a considerable period—is simply the disputant who had the persistence to keep the dispute alive by replying to the statements made by the opposing side.**

Social and political disputes are generally won by changing the perceptions of individuals rather than by supplying new facts. In these disputes there are generally two classes of participants, which are the active spokespersons and the observers. The tendency of many observers is to incline to one side and then the other as one side or the other appears to be getting the upper hand in the dispute. In the end the side which prevails is the one which is able to secure, for a time at least, the support of the majority of the observers. This being the case, the active spokespersons must use every means at their disposal to rally the observers to their side if they are to win the dispute. If one is an active spokesperson in such a dispute, then one must be prepared to reiterate his or her position again and again. Never rely upon the good sense of the observers to perceive who is right. Instead, reply to statements which seem to be so obviously false that no one in his or her right mind could possibly believe them to be true. Constantly be on the lookout for fresh ways to make the desired meaning plain. This must be done because social and political disputes are won or lost on the basis of perceptions which are created in the course of the dispute. If one chooses not to respond to a claim made by the other side, it must only be because it is in fact not being taken seriously by anyone who is in a position to affect the outcome of the dispute.

Summary

This chapter is devoted to an examination of tactics or tricks which unscrupulous disputants use to secure an unfair advantage. The tactics are divided into four classes, as indicated in the following table.

TABLE OF TACTICS

I. Issue-related diversionary tactics
   A. Accent
   B. Shifting the issue
   C. Irrelevant conclusion
   D. Straw man
   E. Defining the other side
   F. Ad hominem argument
II. Tactics of presumption or assumption
   A. Personal appearance
   B. Poisoning the well
   C. Refusing to recognize authority
   D. Allocation of tasks or responsibilities
   E. Argument from ignorance
III. Tactics of control
   A. Stalling
   B. Rushing to judgment
   C. Psychological tactics ad personam
   D. Withholding relevant information
   E. The big lie
   F. The little lie
   G. Argument from force
IV. Modeling tactics
   A. Slippery slope
   B. Perception determining description
   C. Modal constructions

This table reveals that the tactical use of some informal fallacies examined in Chapter 4 is considered in this chapter. These fallacies are accent and the argument to the person. Poisoning the well is also considered. In addition, some informal fallacies not previously considered in the text are introduced in this chapter. These are the irrelevant conclusion, the straw man, the argument from ignorance, and the slippery slope.

A LOOK AHEAD

Logic is commonly divided into two great branches, which are the informal and the formal. Propositions and arguments are examined in both branches, but there the similarity ends. Informal logic treats the content, or matter, of propositions and arguments, and, to the extent necessary to understand them, the context in which they are presented. Formal logic, by contrast, treats their structure, or form. The form of a proposition or argument is that part of it which remains unchanged while its content, or matter, is varied. Just as coins of different metals can be shaped by the same die, so arguments on different subjects can nevertheless have the same form.

All of the preceding chapters emphasize the importance of understanding the content of arguments as well as the context in which they are presented. In the next three chapters—for the rest of the text—we enter into the formal branch of logic and ignore the content and context of arguments so far as is practicable. This enables us to determine the validity of several kinds of arguments. Validity? It's easy to forget what that consists in, so let's remind ourselves. As we stated in the section headed "Deductive Arguments" in Chapter 2, valid arguments are those whose conclusions cannot be false when their premisses are true. In invalid arguments, by contrast, the truth of the premisses does not ensure the truth of the conclusion.

Exercises

I. Answer the following questions.

1. What are some perceptions determining power descriptions?
2. What are modal constructions?
3. What are the chief tactics of timing?
4. What are three guidelines for determining which questions are fair and which are not in examining the credibility of witnesses?
5. What are three common methods of undercutting the authority or credibility of a witness?

II. Follow the instructions in each of the following.

1. Provide an example from your own experience of a use of one of the tactics in each of the four categories of tactics discussed in this chapter. See the "Table of Tactics" in the chapter summary for a list of all the tactics.
2. Each of the following is a dispute of long duration:

   - Ulster versus the IRA
   - Israel versus Palestine
   - Serbia versus Bosnia

   Select one of these disputes for critical analysis. Describe the origins and causes of the dispute, the chief impediments to its resolution, and the tactical maneuvers by which each side attempts to secure an advantage over the other.

   To get started on your research, see the relevant volume of Andrew C. Kimmens, ed., *The Reference Shelf* (New York: The H. W. Wilson Co., 1989). *The*

Reference Shelf volumes are anthologies of articles, with each volume devoted to a single topic. Also, see the Subject Index on *Facts on File World News CD-ROM* (1997). This research tool has many hyperlinks. Both of these sources should be available in your library.

3. Identify any occurrences of the fallacies of irrelevant conclusion, argument from ignorance, and slippery slope in Appendix III: Informal Fallacies and Tactical Maneuvers: Fifty Arguments for Analysis and Discussion.

Chapter 12

CATEGORICAL LOGIC

This chapter is devoted to categorical logic, which is sometimes referred to as *traditional logic* because it assumed its present mature form long before truth functional logic—the subject of Chapters 13 and 14—came of age. The father of traditional logic is the Greek philosopher Aristotle.

Categorical logic is so called because it examines arguments whose premisses and conclusions assert things "categorically," or without qualification. A **categorical proposition** says, for example,

Socrates is brave.

rather than

Socrates is *either* brave *or* not brave.

or

Socrates is brave, *if* reports of his conduct in battle are true.

There's no *either-or,* or *if, and,* or *but* with categorical propositions.

We identify four forms of categorical propositions and explain how to determine the validity of arguments called *syllogisms.* When you've completed this chapter, you'll be acquainted in an introductory way with the bare essentials of what until relatively recently was considered the chief jewel in the crown of formal logic. You'll also see Arthur and his friends in action in a tense drama.

CATEGORICAL PROPOSITIONS: FORMS, DIAGRAMS, AND TRANSLATIONS

DR. WINSLOW'S ERROR: EPISODE I

On the day of its first meeting, Arthur was one of the first to arrive for his logic class. He chose a desk on the inner aisle and toward the rear of the room. There were about fifty desks in the room. Twenty minutes after Arthur's arrival, nearly every one of them was filled.

The professor in Arthur's class was in her early to mid-thirties. At the stroke of the hour, she strode into class, her arms laden with papers and books. After placing these on her desk, she surveyed the class and smiled. Arthur noticed that her eyes crinkled nicely when she smiled, and liked her instantly.

"I'm Dr. Winslow," said Arthur's professor. "We will concentrate on formal logic this term. Because I'm interested in the roots of logic, and think that it has some practical applications, we will begin by examining categorical logic."

Dr. Winslow turned to the chalkboard behind her and scooped a piece of chalk from the tray. Her head darted back and forth between the board and the class, and she didn't pause in her remarks as she scrawled the following in large white letters on the board:

THE FORMS OF CATEGORICAL PROPOSITIONS

AFFIRMO	NEGO
A: All S are P.	**E: No S are P.**
Examples: All chocolates are delicacies.	No beggars are wealthy persons.
I: Some S are P.	**O: Some S are not P.**
Examples: Some merchants are poets.	Some operas are not comedies.

"These four propositional forms are easy to remember if you think of the two Latin words." Here, Dr. Winslow pointed to *affirmo* and *nego* on the board, and Arthur copied the words into his notebook. He thought he'd better, since they were Latin. "*Affirmo* has the letters *a* and *i* in it," Dr. Winslow went on. "That's the source of the names of the A and I propositions. *Nego* has an *e* and an *o* in it. That's where the names of the E and the O come from.

"These words help you remember something else, too," Dr. Winslow went on. *Affirmo* means 'to affirm,' and **the A and I propositions are classified as *affirmative.*** The A affirms that all of class S, whatever it is, is included in class P, and the I affirms that a part of S is included in P. *Nego* means 'to deny,' and **the E and O are classified as *negative.*** The E denies than any S is included in P, and the O claims that some S is not included in P."

"Can I ask a question?" asked a coed several rows to Arthur's left. By leaning forward in his seat, Arthur could see that she wore thick-lens glasses and had close-cropped hair.

"Of course you can," said Dr. Winslow with a laugh. "I've been rushing along because I'm double-parked behind Perkins Hall and afraid I'll be towed. Ever since the administration turned the staff parking lot into tennis courts, I've had a tough time finding a place to park. But don't worry about that. Tell me your name, and ask your question."

"All right. My name is Maggie Bristow, and I want to know what 'S' and 'P' in those diagrams stand for."

"Good question," responded Dr. Winslow. "S stands for 'subject term,' and P for 'predicate term.' To derive a proposition, simply replace S and P with terms. But 'What are *terms?*' you're going to ask. **Terms are nouns or noun phrases which denote classes of things.** Check out the first example above. *Chocolate* is the subject term, and *delicacies* is the predicate term. The second example has *wealthy persons,* which is a noun phrase, as its predicate term, so you see that terms can be more than one word."

"Thank you," said Maggie. "That makes good sense, but now I have another question: What are we going to do with these propositions?"

"We're going to put them into **arguments with two premises,** which **are called syllogisms,** but first we need to examine them in more detail." Saying this, Dr. Winslow turned to the board, scooped an eraser from the tray, and wiped out her previous writing in a wild and undisciplined manner. Then, a piece of chalk appeared between her fingers like a card slipped from the sleeve of a card shark, and she drew the following diagrams with broad and sweeping strokes:

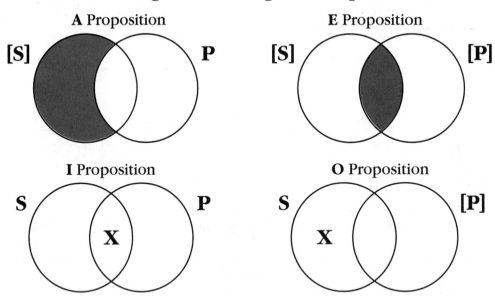

Venn Diagrams for Categorical Propositions

A Proposition [S] P

E Proposition [S] [P]

I Proposition S X P

O Proposition S X [P]

Brackets enclosing "S" and "P" indicate that the term is distributed.

Dr. Winslow dropped the chalk in the tray and wiped the dust from her hands by clapping them together in an up and down motion. "There," she said with satisfaction. "Follow those charts to diagram categorical propositions and also to understand what the propositions enable us to assert. **The subject term of each proposition is represented by the circle on the left and the predicate term by the circle on the right. Shading indicates empty areas.** Like pastures with no cows, **empty areas are areas which contain no individuals.** Thus, in the diagram for the A, the shaded area indicates that there are no individuals in class S who fall outside class P. In other words, all members of class S are members of class P. In the diagram for the E, the shaded area indicates that no individuals in class S are individuals in class P. There is no overlap between the two classes S and P in E propositions.

"For our purposes, *some* means *at least one.* **The x in the diagrams for I and O propositions tracks the one or more individuals being referred to.** In the diagram for the I, the x in the overlapping part of the two circles indicates that at least one member of the subject class is a member of the predicate class. In the diagram for the O, the x outside the circle for the predicate class indicates that at least one individual in the subject class is not a member of the predicate class.

"The diagrams also show us the distribution of terms. **If a term is *distributed,* the proposition refers to the entire class denoted by the term. If a term is *undistributed,* the proposition refers to only a part of the class. In the diagrams, any term whose circle has an x in any part of it is undistributed, and any circle with shading in any part of it, or with neither an x nor shading, is distributed."**

Dr. Winslow paused, picked up a stack of papers from her desk, and surveyed the class. "That's enough for now. We need to discuss course requirements. This syllabus which I'm passing out indicates the dates of your exams and the exact topics which will be covered on them."

Immediately after copying down the Latin words, Arthur had been distracted from Dr. Winslow's remarks; for a striking young woman with long black hair which fell over her shoulders and trailed down her back had entered the room and taken the desk to his immediate left. Arthur, whose spontaneous friendliness was evident to all who knew him, had smiled in her direction, but to all outward appearances, the young woman was unaware of his presence.

Following her introduction to the course, and her distribution of the syllabus, Dr. Winslow called the class roll. The young woman answered to the name "Maria Ramirez." After class, Arthur turned to her and said, "It looks as if this is going to be an interesting class, doesn't it?"

"Perhaps," said Maria, walking quickly away.

In the next class meeting, and the one after that, Arthur looked for Maria, but she didn't attend. When two weeks had passed, and she still hadn't come to class, Arthur decided that she must have dropped the course.

On the day of the first exam, however, Maria was in her desk when Arthur arrived. Arthur was greatly surprised and a little concerned. He wondered whether Maria could pass the exam without having come to class. Taking his seat beside her, he said, "I'm afraid that I'll forget the distribution of terms. Are you?"

"No," said Maria.

"I'm also afraid that I won't be able to translate the propositions into standard form. However, I made this chart to spell out how you do it." Arthur held out his notebook to

Maria and pointed helpfully to the chart below. "I made up these rules myself," he said with some pride."

TRANSLATING CATEGORICAL PROPOSITIONS INTO STANDARD FORM

- Make certain that the proposition begins with *All, No,* or *Some* and that it uses nothing but nouns and noun phrases.
- Decide whether the proposition is affirmative (A or I) or negative (E or O).
- Use *is not* or *are not* with O propositions and *is* or *are* with all others.
- Translate "Not all S are P" forms as "Some S are not P."
- Replace *Only* and *None but* at the beginning of propositions with *All,* and reverse the subject and predicate terms.

"It's the last of these rules that I always forget," said Arthur with enthusiasm. "See, you have to translate 'Only employees are allowed in the warehouse' as 'All persons allowed in the warehouse are employees.'"

But Maria wasn't listening. "I'm sure you'll do just fine," she said. Arthur saw her eyes dart briefly in his direction, then return quickly to the chalkboard. He also noticed that her hair glistened in the light from the windows.

Moments later, Dr. Winslow arrived, carrying a stack of examination papers. She divided the exams and handed several to the first person in each row. When Arthur received his, he found that the first question, as he had feared, concerned the distribution of terms. The instructions read, "Translate the following propositions into standard form, and draw a circle around each distributed term." The following propositions looked complicated to Arthur, but he began to work his way methodically through them.

Glancing to his left, Arthur saw that Maria was working her way through the exam with no apparent difficulty. She was writing almost as quickly as she would have been if she had been writing a letter. Exactly twenty-three minutes after the examination had begun, she handed in her paper. Arthur was just beginning the third of five sections of the exam. "Either she did extremely well," he thought to himself, "or she wrote down whatever came to her mind."

One week later, Dr. Winslow returned the exams. Once again, Maria was in her seat. She took her paper with a smile, and laid it on her desk in plain view. Arthur read "98 out of a possible 100" at the top of her exam. When he received his paper, Arthur found that he had made 90. "Hm," he said to himself. "I made an A, but I had to work a lot longer for mine than Maria did for hers."

CATEGORICAL SYLLOGISMS: TRANSLATING INTO STANDARD FORM AND TESTING BY VENN DIAGRAMS

DR. WINSLOW'S ERROR: EPISODE II

Maria Ramirez, the student who sat to Arthur's left in logic class, did not attend class from the day the first exams were returned until the day of the second exam. On that day, however, she was once again in her desk when Arthur arrived. When he received his copy of the exam, Arthur turned it face down and wrote out some memory aids. Maria, by contrast, began writing almost immediately. She handed in her exam at twenty-five minutes after the hour, and when the exams were returned the next week, her score was 98. Arthur, by contrast, made 84. "Hm," he said to himself. "I wonder how she does it."

One evening nearly a month later, Arthur and Papita Bodogovich, a student he'd met in English composition class, met at the school cafeteria for dinner. Like lost sailors searching the distant horizon for land, they stood with food trays in hand looking left and right for vacant seats when they heard a nearby voice shouting over the din of music and conversation saying, "Come sit with me." It was Maggie Bristow.

Arthur and Papita eagerly accepted Maggie's invitation. "Thanks," said Papita.

"Don't mention it," said Maggie. She smiled at Papita, then turned to Arthur with a look of concern. "Say, where have you been all week?"

"My grandfather died, and I went to his funeral."

"I wish I could have gone," said Papita, "but it was so far away."

"I'm sorry," said Maggie.

"Thanks. Say, did I miss anything this week?" Arthur evidently wanted to change the subject.

"In logic? I'll say! You missed a huge amount of material, but don't worry. I can help you. I have it all right here." Maggie tapped her cranium and winked as she spoke.

"Well, I'm sure you do have it all in your head," said Arthur in friendly exasperation, "but what good does your famous photographic memory do me?"

"Relax," said Maggie. "I have it all written down." She dipped into her shoulder bag, which rested beside her chair, and pulled out several sheets. "Here it is—the categorical syllogism in a nutshell."

"Great," said Arthur, "but can you take me through it? Our third exam is upon us."

"Sure," said Maggie, sliding her low-riding glasses up the bridge of her nose with a practiced index finger. "How about now?"

"Go ahead," said Papita. "I have to study French anyway." At this, Arthur nodded and slid his chair around to Maggie's side of the table.

HISTORY'S MOST FAMOUS SYLLOGISM

All humans are mortal beings.
Socrates is human.
Therefore, Socrates is a mortal being.
Minor term: Socrates. Major term: mortal beings. Middle term: human.

"Where did you leave off?" Maggie asked. "Do you know the names for the terms in the syllogism?"

"Oh, let's see," said Arthur. "I haven't been thinking about this."

"Right. Then let me tell you, just to save time. **There are three terms in the syllogism. The *minor term* is the subject term of the conclusion, the *major term* is the predicate term of the conclusion . . .**"

"**And the *middle term* is the one term which the two premises share in common,**" Arthur contributed.

"Right you are. Keep those terms in mind. They'll help you put the syllogism into standard form, and Dr. Winslow says you have to know the term names to test the validity of syllogisms by the rules technique."

"Okay, I'll remember them," said Arthur. "What's next?"

"This," said Maggie, tapping the following chart with her forefinger. "Even the most recalcitrant syllogisms fall into line when you follow this guide."

STEPS IN PLACING CATEGORICAL SYLLOGISMS IN STANDARD FORM

1. Translate each proposition into standard form as necessary.
2. Identify the conclusion.
3. Write the premiss with the major term first and the premiss with the minor term second.

   Example: Some horse lovers are jockeys, and only individuals under six feet in height are jockeys, so some horse lovers are under six feet in height.

becomes

   All jockeys are persons under six feet in height.
   Some horse lovers are jockeys.
   Therefore, some horse lovers are persons under six feet in height.

"Hm," said Arthur. "This is pretty good, but how did you identify the conclusion?"

"See that word *so*?" Maggie asked.

"Oh, that's right," Arthur responded. "We studied indicator words for premisses and conclusions back in Chapter 1."

"Yes," said Maggie. "Any further questions?"

"Why did you add *persons* in the first premiss and conclusion?"

"Just read the propositions without it," said Maggie a little impatiently— *under six feet in height* isn't a class term. You have to add something like *persons* to make it one."

"Gotcha," said Arthur. "Well, that just about wraps it up, I guess."

He stretched elaborately and reached for his food tray, but Maggie said, "Are you kidding? I haven't shown you how to test for validity yet."

Arthur, who was tired, looked across the table to Papita for some means of escape, but Papita was happily engrossed in French verbs. "All right," Arthur said gamely. "If you're willing to help me some more, I'm willing to learn."

"That's the spirit," said the indefatigable Maggie. "Dr. Winslow says that we have all sorts of arguments thrown at us, and many of them with a great deal of fuss and to-do, but that if they're **categorical arguments** they **can all be tested by the *Venn diagram* technique. With this technique, we take two overlapping circles, just as we did when we diagramed categorical propositions, and then add a third one,** like this:

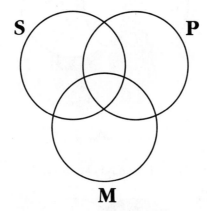

S, P, and M indicate the minor, major, and middle terms, in that order."

"These three circles remind me of the circles on beer coasters," Arthur observed irreverently.

"Yeah, me too," said Maggie. "It makes you think that John Venn, the British logician who thought up the technique, must have been sitting in a pub having a pint of bitters when he got the idea. But never mind that: the technique is simple and effective. It works as follows. **Once you've put a syllogism into standard form, you diagram the premisses using the x's and the shading for categorical propositions. You don't diagram the conclusion. If the syllogism is valid, the conclusion is automatically diagramed in diagraming the premisses, and if it's invalid, it isn't diagramed."**

"So for valid syllogisms," Arthur observed, "diagraming the premisses is like scraping away the black stuff from contest tickets to reveal the winning prize."

"And for invalid syllogisms," Maggie continued, "diagraming the premisses is like scraping away the black stuff to reveal that you ain't got nothing."

"Well," said Arthur, who was forgetting his fatigue, "give me some examples."

"Right you are," said Maggie, reaching into her bag for a pen. "We'll start with this syllogism." Maggie's hand flew across the page as she scribbled the following:

All marigolds are prize winners.
All flowers behind the patio are marigolds.
Therefore, all flowers behind the patio are prize winners.

"To test this syllogism, we draw and label a circle for each term and then diagram the premisses. **If one of the premisses is either an A or an E and the other is either an I or an O, we diagram the A or the E first.** For this syllogism, it doesn't matter which premiss we diagram first, so we start at the top. 'All marigolds are prize winners' is diagramed like this:

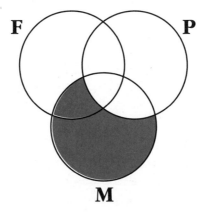

'All flowers are marigolds' is diagramed like this:

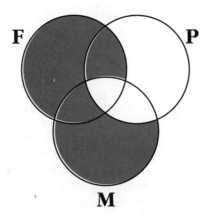

"This completes the work of diagraming. Next, we read the diagram to determine whether the syllogism is valid. In this case, the conclusion is diagramed, so the argument is valid. "All flowers behind the patio are prize winners" is diagramed like this:

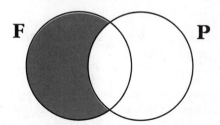

If you mentally lay this diagram on top of the three circle diagram above, you see that all the necessary parts are shaded."

"I can see that," said Arthur, "but there's even more shading than is necessary to diagram the conclusion."

"Don't worry about that," said Maggie, digging into a piece of cake with a bent fork. Like a little extra icing on a cake, that's unnecessary but quite all right. **It's too little shading, not too much, that dooms a syllogism to invalidity.** Let me show you. The diagram for

All hamsters are pets.
All dogs are pets.
Therefore, all dogs are hamsters.

looks like this:

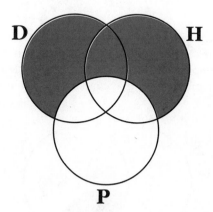

"Is this syllogism valid? No, for the conclusion is not diagramed. All of the D circle which falls outside the H circle must be shaded, but one part of that area—the part D shares with P—is unshaded."

"You're a good teacher, Maggie. I'm amazed at how well you know this material."

"In other words, you're ready to be done, huh?"

"No, not really. I'm getting into it now. Besides, you haven't shown me how to do diagrams with I or O propositions."

"Right," said Maggie. "I almost forgot those. I'll have to give you two examples of those in order to show both valid and invalid syllogisms and to explain how to avoid problems in placing the X. Here's my first example:

> No episodes of *Northern Exposure* are feature presentations.
> Some reruns are feature presentations.
> Therefore, some reruns are not episodes of *Northern Exposure.*

"In cases where one premiss is an I or an O proposition, it makes a difference which premiss is diagramed first. In this argument, the second premiss is an I. If we diagram it first, we run into trouble. To show why, I'm going to label the diagram for the argument and number the spaces within the circles.

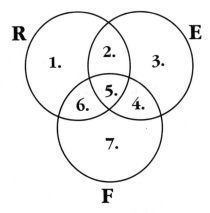

In order to diagram the I proposition, we must place an X in the overlapping parts of the R and F circles. This area includes spaces 5 and 6. Which do we choose? Our choice makes a difference, since space 5 overlaps with the E circle, while space 6 does not. Fortunately, we solve our problem in this case by diagraming the E proposition first, like this:

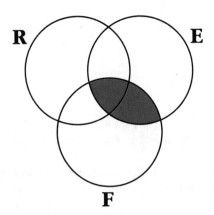

With the E proposition diagramed, it is evident that the X for the I proposition must go in space 6, for that's the only space left where it can go. In general, **when one premiss of a categorical syllogism is either an I or an O proposition, diagram it last.** Here's our completed diagram:

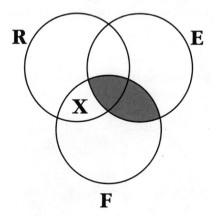

The argument is valid, for the X in space 6 diagrams the conclusion.

"In this example, we found out where to put the X by diagraming the A proposition first. However, **diagraming the A or the E proposition first in cases in which one premiss is an I or an O won't always tell us where to put the X.** In class, Dr. Winslow used this example:

All dentists are highly skilled technicians.
Some highly skilled technicians are sports heroes.
Therefore, some sports heroes are dentists.

We label the circles of our diagram, and diagram the A proposition as follows:

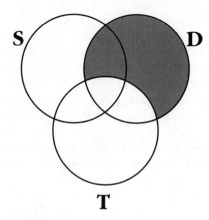

This leaves us wondering where to put the X for the second premiss."

"Yeah," said Arthur. **"In cases like this, the X has to go in the overlapping portion of the S and the T circles, but that's divided into two spaces.** Space 6 is in the area between the S circle and the T circle, and space 5 is in the overlapping area of all three circles. **So what do we do?"**

"You see the problem exactly," said Maggie approvingly. "With no more information than is given in the premises of our argument, we can't decide between the two spaces."

"We're like refugees on the boundary between three countries who don't know which way to run," said Arthur.

"So **we play it safe by placing our X upon the line between spaces 5 and 6,"** said Maggie. As she spoke, Maggie completed the diagram:

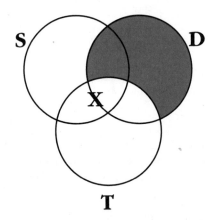

"Well, Arthur, is the argument valid?"

"I don't know."

"I'll tell you, then. It's not valid. For the conclusion to be diagramed, there must be an X in the empty space between S and D, but our X is on the line."

"I think I'm going to enjoy Venn diagrams," said Arthur.

"I love them," said Maggie. "Dr. Winslow says that **the Venn Diagram technique works for all syllogisms which contain three terms used with the same meaning in each of their occurrences.** Apart from determining whether that's the case, the technique allows you to test the validity of syllogisms without reference to their content. **The rules technique,** which I'll show you next, also **requires you to check for three terms,** but it frees you from the need to draw little circles on the palm of your hand or an available napkin when you're thinking under pressure. The only downside of **the rules technique** is that it **requires you to distinguish between affirmative and negative propositions and to know the distribution of terms within propositions.** You remember distribution, don't you Arthur?"

Maggie's voice trailed off, for she saw that Arthur was distracted by a couple walking by. "What is it?" asked Papita, who also noticed Arthur's distraction.

"Do you know that couple?" Arthur asked, nodding toward the table across the aisle.

"I don't know the guy," said Papita, "but the young woman is Maria Ramirez. She's in my French class."

"It's interesting," said Arthur. "The guy's name is Mike. He was my first roommate in the dorm, but we didn't get along, and I managed to get myself moved to another room. Maria is in the logic class with Maggie and me. She never shows up except for exams and when the professor returns exams. Counting the first class, she's only been to five classes all semester. It's amazing. It only took her twenty to thirty minutes to complete each of the first two exams, and she made a high A on each one. It took me the whole class period to finish the exams, and I had to struggle to get some of the answers. I don't know how she does it."

"Neither do I," said Papita. "She attends every class in French, but she's not doing very well."

"Some people do better in some subjects than others," Maggie observed.

"I suppose," Papita replied thoughtfully, "but in her case I wonder."

"Well, we'd better be going," said Arthur.

"Wait," said Maggie, who could sense that the lesson was over. "Take this sheet of rules for testing syllogisms. You may need them."

"Thanks." Arthur absent-mindedly stuffed the sheet of rules into his pocket. Had he known that his future as a student would hang on his knowledge of those rules, he would have been more grateful to get them.

CATEGORICAL SYLLOGISMS: TESTING BY RULES

DR. WINSLOW'S ERROR: EPISODE III

On the night before his third exam in logic, Arthur and Papita walked by Humanities Hall hand in hand. Nodding toward the building, Papita said, "Are you ready for your exam?"

"I think so. I've been studying. This exam covers the categorical syllogism. I hope Dr. Winslow doesn't have us test syllogisms by the rules technique. I sometimes forget the names of the fallacies."

"I'm afraid I can't help you there," said Papita, squeezing Arthur's hand.

"Never mind," said Arthur. "Let's walk under the trees."

"Are your eyes blinded by the porch lights of Humanities Hall?"

"Yes," Arthur said with a smile. "It's the long hours of study."

Arthur guided Papita into the shadows under one of the trees which lined the walkway leading up to Humanities Hall. He slipped his arms around her waist and leaned toward her, as if to give her a kiss, then straightened suddenly and stared in the direction of Humanities Hall.

"What is it?" asked Papita, who saw the sudden change in his demeanor.

"Look," said Arthur, pointing with one hand and guiding Papita to the far side of the tree with the other. "The bottom window on the right."

Papita's eyes followed the line indicated by Arthur's outstretched hand, and saw a shadow in the window. "Someone's climbing out," she said. "But that building's locked for the night."

"Right you are," said Arthur.

Papita and Arthur stood motionless under the tree. After several minutes, the figure who had climbed out of the window strode from the bushes into the light of the porch. "That's Mike!" whispered Arthur.

"And that explains a lot," Papita whispered in return.

"What do you mean?"

"Don't you get it? How do you think Maria Ramirez does so well on her exams? She has help."

"You mean that Mike . . . "

"That's exactly what I mean. Isn't Dr. Winslow's office in Humanities Hall? And isn't it likely that she makes up her exams the day before she gives them and stores them in her office overnight?"

"Yes, but how would Mike . . . ?"

"I don't know."

"Come on, Papita. We have work to do."

"What work?"

"We're going to check out Dr. Winslow's office."

"Are you crazy? What if you're caught?"

"You'll be there to defend me. Come on."

"I don't like this," Papita said; but she followed Arthur down the walk and into the shadows of the window from which Mike had emerged.

Under the window, Arthur found two cement building blocks, which made it relatively easy for him to reach the window ledge and pull himself inside the building. Once inside, he reached out his hand to Papita and helped her in.

It was nearly midnight by this time, and Arthur had the disquieting feeling that he would not be rested for his exam the next morning—assuming he wasn't caught and charged with breaking into Humanities Hall. He took Papita's hand, and they climbed the stairs to the second floor, their way lit by red exit signs. Once on the second floor, they walked to the end of the hall.

"That's Dr. Winslow's office on the left," Arthur whispered. "If you're right, Mike must have gotten in there; but how?" Arthur tried the door, touching it gingerly with a handkerchief-covered hand. It was locked.

Papita turned toward the window at the end of the hallway and said, "Look." She pointed upward. Following her hand, Arthur saw a false ceiling, made up of squares of light material resting in square frames. One square was slightly askew.

"You're a genius, Papita. Mike climbed onto the window ledge and pulled himself through the false ceiling." Arthur bent over the window ledge and in the dim light saw black marks, which could have been made by rubber-soled shoes. "There's one way to find out," he said.

"Don't do it," said Papita. "We have enough to go on. Let's call Dr. Winslow." But it was too late. Arthur was already pulling himself through the false ceiling.

Positioning himself on the steel frames of the false ceiling, Arthur crawled to Dr. Winslow's office, pulled back an insulated square, and peered into the room below. He was directly over Dr. Winslow's desk. "Mike could have dropped down on the desk, found the exam, and let himself out through the door, leaving it locked behind him," Arthur reasoned. Then he lowered himself onto Dr. Winslow's desk and slipped to the floor.

At that moment, Arthur heard footsteps outside the door and someone speaking to Papita. She answered, but he couldn't make out her words. Arthur's heart caught in his throat. "Oh, no," he muttered to himself. A key turned in the door, a hand switched on the office lights, and there before Arthur stood Dr. Winslow. She wasn't smiling. "Arthur, I don't remember our having an appointment this evening," said Dr. Winslow laconically.

"I'm afraid we didn't," Arthur said weakly.

"Then what are you doing in my office?"

"I know this looks bad, but I can explain."

"What you say had better be good. Otherwise, we'll have to have a word with the campus police."

Arthur blinked and glanced at Papita, who was wringing her hands. In the next few minutes, with her assistance, he outlined the course of events which had led to his climbing into Dr. Winslow's office.

"What you say is very interesting," said Dr. Winslow when the two had finished. "But why should I believe you?"

"Well, how do you explain the fact that Maria never comes to class except for exams, but always makes an A?"

"That's easy. She studies on her own."

"Yes, I thought so, too, at first."

"But then I told him," said Papita, "that she wasn't doing well in our French class. That doesn't prove anything by itself, but I'll bet that if you checked with her other professors you'd find that she was struggling along."

"All right, that's something I can check," said Dr. Winslow, "but why shouldn't I conclude from your presence here, Arthur, that *you* wanted a copy of tomorrow's exam?"

"Because I don't need it," Arthur said bravely.

"Don't need it?"

"No. I've studied."

"But I don't know that."

"Then ask me some questions," said Arthur in a sudden inspiration.

Dr. Winslow's eyes narrowed thoughtfully, and she took down a book. "All right," she said. "Sit down, the both of you. I'll do just that." Arthur and Papita obediently sat in chairs opposite Dr. Winslow's desk, but Dr. Winslow remained standing by the door, her face grave.

After some moments, she spoke. "Tell me whether this argument is valid: 'A crime is punishable by law. The way Jim treats Jane is a crime. Therefore, the way Jim treats Jane is punishable by law.'"

Arthur swallowed hard on hearing this argument. Suddenly, his throat was dry. "It's not in standard form," he stammered.

"That's right," said Dr. Winslow. "You'll have to put it in standard form."

"Oh," said Arthur. "In that case, could I have some paper to write out the argument and draw Venn diagrams?"

"You won't need paper," Dr. Winslow said coldly. "You'll do it in your head and use the rules technique."

Again Arthur swallowed, and his mind raced to the crumpled sheet of paper which Maggie had given him in the cafeteria. He did his best to visualize it, but to no avail. If he could have visualized it, he would have seen the rules and fallacies in the box below.

RULES AND FALLACIES OF THE CATEGORICAL SYLLOGISM

- Each term of the syllogism must occur twice and only twice, and be used with the same meaning in each occurrence. If there is a shift in meaning in the use of a term, the **fallacy** is **Four Terms.**
- The middle term must be distributed at least once. If it isn't, the **fallacy** is **Undistributed Middle.**
- Unless a term is distributed in a premiss, it may not be distributed in the conclusion. If a term is distributed in the conclusion, but not in the premiss, the **fallacy** is **Illicit Distribution.**
- At least one of the premisses must be affirmative. If neither premiss is affirmative, the **fallacy** is **Exclusive Premisses.**
- If one premiss of a categorical syllogism is negative, the conclusion must be negative. If the conclusion of an argument with one negative premiss is affirmative, the **fallacy** is **Negative Fallacy.**
- No syllogism can have an I or an O proposition for a conclusion unless it has an I or an O proposition for a premiss. If the conclusion is an I or an O proposition, but neither premiss is an I or O, the **fallacy** is **Existential Fallacy.**

"Do you just want to know whether the syllogism's valid?" asked Arthur.

"Yes, and if it's invalid, I want to know what fallacy it commits."

"Could you repeat the argument?" Arthur was stalling for time, but Dr. Winslow complied, saying,

"A crime is punishable by law.
The way Jim treats Sue is a crime.
Therefore, the way Jim treats Sue is punishable by law."

Arthur closed his eyes in thought. He could feel a tautness in his neck. Finally, he said, "It's a *Fallacy of Four Terms.* There's an equivocation on *crime.*"

Arthur's answer was correct, but Dr. Winslow didn't tell him so. Instead, she nodded inscrutably and said, "For your next argument, I'll give you the premisses and ask you to supply the conclusion. Understood?"

"Understood," said Arthur.

"Very well," said Dr. Winslow. "Here are the premisses:

'Only students who break into their professors' offices are expelled.
Arthur broke into his professor's office.'

What conclusion follows from these premisses?"

"The conclusion is painfully clear to me," said Arthur, his face indicating more clearly than words that he was resigned to the worst. "It's 'Arthur is expelled.'"

"Yes, that's the conclusion, all right. Is the argument valid?"

"Yes, it is."

"Are you certain?"

"Yes."

"That being the case," prompted Dr. Winslow, "translate this proposition into standard form for me: "Only men are husbands.""

"Oh," said Arthur, his eyes suddenly shining. "I see what you're getting at. I forgot to reverse the subject and predicate terms in 'Only students who break into their professors' offices are expelled.' The correct translation is 'All students who are expelled are students who break into their professors' offices.'"

"Does your new translation affect the validity of the argument?" asked Dr. Winslow.

"Yes," Arthur responded quickly. "The argument is invalid. It's an example of the **fallacy of Undistributed Middle.** Still, there's something about the argument I don't understand." Arthur made this last statement with some hesitancy and with a slight tremor in his voice. Papita wondered why Arthur didn't stop speaking when he'd named the fallacy and let well enough alone, but she said nothing.

"What is it you don't understand?" asked Dr. Winslow, her countenance softening somewhat.

"Well, if you translate the first premiss correctly, as 'All students who are expelled are students who break into their professors' offices,' then it's false. I mean, not all students who are expelled are students who break into their professors' offices. There are other reasons besides that for expulsion."

"That's true," Dr. Winslow replied, "but the point of translating propositions into standard form is not to make them true, but to express what they actually say."

"Oh, of course that's right," said Arthur, shaking his head.

"But since you raise the question of truth," Dr. Winslow went on, "I want to ask you this: Is it possible for a valid syllogism to have one or more false premisses?"

"Oh, that's easy," Arthur responded. "The answer is yes."

"Why?" asked Dr. Winslow. "If valid arguments can have false premisses, what's the point in having valid arguments?"

"**Validity is a matter of form.**" Arthur was slightly more relaxed now than he had been. "**Valid forms ensure** one thing and one thing only."

"What's that?"

VALID ARGUMENTS

Valid arguments can have false premisses with either true or false conclusions, and they can have true premisses with true conclusions, but they cannot have true premisses and false conclusions.

PREMISSES	CONCLUSION
True	True
True	False (Impossible)
False	True
False	False

"That the conclusion cannot be false when the premisses are true."

"Good man," said Dr. Winslow. "You're doing well, but I have other questions for you. Is this syllogism valid:

'All voters are concerned citizens.
No members of the Midnight Raiders are voters.
Therefore, no members of the Midnight Raiders are concerned citizens.'"

"That's invalid—the fallacy of **Illicit Distribution.**"

"That's right," said Dr. Winslow. "For your next problem, I'm going to give you the premisses of an invalid argument, but not the conclusion. The premisses by themselves are sufficient to indicate the invalidity of this argument. I want you to name the fallacy. Are you ready?"

"Yes, I'm ready."

"Here are the premisses:

'No areas of Circle A are areas of Circle B.
No areas of Circle B are areas of Circle C.'"

"That's easy," said Arthur confidently. "It's **Exclusive Premisses.**"

At this, Dr. Winslow smiled, and laid down her book. "I have only one more syllogism for you, Arthur. First, **suppose that a syllogism's premisses are A and E propositions and that its conclusion is an A.** Do you have enough information to decide on the validity of the argument?"

Arthur paused in thought, and silence filled the room. Papita, whose spirits had improved with each of Arthur's correct answers, became concerned. Finally, Arthur said yes and when Dr. Winslow shook her head affirmatively, Papita sighed with relief.

"What's the fallacy?"

"The **Negative Fallacy,**" said Arthur.

Dr. Winslow smiled broadly and shook Arthur's hand. "Well, Arthur, you know the material for the exam. I never doubted that you did, but I couldn't take that for granted in the circumstances."

"I understand."

"Now," said Dr. Winslow, looking back and forth between Arthur and Papita, "you must not say a word to anyone about anything you have seen tonight or anything we have discussed. Is that understood?"

Papita and Arthur nodded their heads in understanding, then Arthur asked, "What do you intend to do?"

"Since you're students, my telling you what I'm going to do might put you in a difficult position. But I can tell you this much: tomorrow I intend to catch a cheat or two. Now let me see you out of the building. I have work to do."

"Did you suspect anything before now?" asked Papita as the three walked down the stairs.

"I don't make a practice of coming to my office at midnight, if that tells you anything," Dr. Winslow replied. "Oh, by the way, Arthur; one more thing: tomorrow I want you to take your exam as usual, but don't do anything which you wouldn't ordinarily do. It's very important that you act in a normal manner. All right?"

"You bet," said Arthur.

Papita took Arthur's hand as they walked down the front steps of the Humanities Building. "Whew," she said. "We were really lucky, weren't we?"

"You don't know how lucky," said Arthur in reply. "I was on shaky ground with that last question. I kept wanting to say that it was the **Existential Fallacy,** but now I remember that **you have that fallacy only when the conclusion is an I or an O proposition and the premises are both A's or E's or some combination of the two.**"

"I've had enough of fallacies for one night!" said Papita. "We'd better get some sleep."

"Right," said Arthur.

DR. WINSLOW'S ERROR:
EPISODE IV (CONCLUSION)

When Arthur showed up for his third logic exam, Maria Ramirez was already in her seat. Arthur nodded at her but did nothing more. Dr. Winslow's instructions, given the night before, were not easily forgotten. Neither was Dr. Winslow's test of Arthur's knowledge of logic easily forgotten.

Precisely at the appointed time for class to begin, Dr. Winslow entered the room and distributed the exams. When Arthur received his, he wasted no time in reading the instructions. The first section dealt with Venn diagrams, while the other dealt with the rules technique. Arthur began with the Venn diagrams. The first syllogism had to be translated into standard form, but Arthur managed to do that and test its validity without undue difficulty. Maria, however, had not even written her name on her paper by the time Arthur had completed the problem. He noticed, in glancing her way, that her jaw was set, and that she sat motionless, her pencil clasped tightly in both hands. At the end of the period, she handed in her paper without having written a word. "Hm," Arthur muttered to himself.

"Could you follow me to my office?" Dr. Winslow asked when Arthur turned in his paper. "I have something to tell you."

"Sure," said Arthur.

When Arthur reached the top of the stairs with Dr. Winslow, he saw Papita standing at the end of the hall. "I've asked Papita to join us," Dr. Winslow explained.

Arthur and Papita followed Dr. Winslow into her office and took the chairs they'd occupied the night before. This time, however, Dr. Winslow sat behind her desk and leaned toward them with a smile. "I can fill you in on what's been happening, but you must maintain complete confidence if I do. Is that understood?"

"Yes," Arthur and Papita said in unison.

"Good. I noticed early on that Maria did well on her exams but was rarely in class. Good students can pass my exams without coming to class, but they generally don't do as well as she did, so I was surprised by her performance. After the second exam, however, I knew the young lady was cheating."

"Pardon me, but how did you know?" asked Papita.

Dr. Winslow smiled. "It was an error I made which showed me she was cheating."

"What was that?"

"After I write an exam, I take it myself, as if I were a student. Generally, if I can't complete the exam myself in twenty minutes, I know it's too long for my students, who, after all, can't be expected to know the material as well as I. My copy of the exam becomes the key which I use to grade the exams. Well, the second exam wasn't too long, but I made a mistake in the answer to the last question, which I didn't catch at the time I made out the key. I only caught the error when I graded the exams. And you know what? Alone of all the students, Maria made the same error in exactly the same words as I did. For me, that was strong circumstantial evidence that she'd obtained a copy of the key."

"That was strong evidence, but there was another problem," Arthur interposed.

"Yes," Papita broke in. "Once she had the key, how could she use it? Commit it to memory?"

"Not likely," said Dr. Winslow. "I don't make up the exams until the afternoon before I give them, which wouldn't have given her much time. Moreover, students who cheat generally don't want to do the work which memorization requires."

"But how, then?" asked Arthur. "I sat beside her in each exam, and think that I would have noticed it if she'd had notes, or answers written on the cuffs of her blouse, or something like that."

"Precisely," Dr. Winslow agreed. "I watch my classes on every exam I give, and I didn't notice suspicious behavior on the part of any student on either of the two logic exams. Still, she got the answers; and halfway through the second exam I knew how."

"How?" Arthur and Papita asked in unison.

"By means of a two-way radio."

"What?"

"Yes. She wore a hearing aid in her left ear which was attached to a radio receiver hidden somewhere on her body. I'd guess she had it strapped to the inner side of one of her thighs, since it wouldn't show in that position."

"But who read her the answers?" asked Arthur.

"Oh, come on," said Papita, tapping Arthur lightly on the shoulder. "Isn't that obvious."

"Oh, yeah. It is."

Dr. Winslow smiled. This morning, the dean of students and Brandon Sweeney, who is Mike's dorm counselor, waited outside Mike's room in the dorm. At precisely five after the hour, they knocked and Mike said, 'Come in.' How careless and overconfident can you get? The dean and Sweeney strode into the room and saw Mike with a transmitter in hand and a copy of my exam key on his bed before him. When confronted in that way, he confessed to everything."

"Wow," said Papita. "What will happen to them?"

"I'm sure they'll be expelled."

"Serves them right, I'd say," said Papita, shaking her head. "But I have one more question. Mike obviously didn't take your copy of your key, or you'd have known that it had been stolen. How did he make a copy?"

"He simply took pen in hand and copied the answers onto a sheet of paper. The answers to the problems aren't long; it's deciding what to write which takes most of your time on a logic exam."

"That's why Maria always finished her exams so quickly, while it took me the entire period to finish my exam. She didn't have to think, but I did."

"Precisely," agreed Dr. Winslow.

"Could I ask another question?" This came from Papita.

"Certainly."

"Where did you keep your exams?"

"In the filing cabinet behind me. The lock doesn't work, unfortunately, but after this I think the dean will make certain that it's repaired. Well, that's it, I guess." Saying this, Dr. Winslow rose from her chair.

Arthur and Papita mirrored her action, but Arthur paused before walking to the door. "I also have another question," he stated.

"What is it?"

"What was your clue? I mean, what made you think that Maria was receiving a radio transmission? Her long hair completely covers her ears, so you surely didn't *see* anything."

"That's right, but I did see her put her hand to her left ear on several occasions. That reminded me of one of my uncles who wears a hearing aid. The motion was exactly the same, so then I knew."

"That raises another question," said Papita. "Why didn't you confront her after the exam, if you were certain?"

"I needed proof. Moreover, I didn't know whether she was acting alone. For all I knew at that point, she might have been using a battery-driven cassette player instead of a radio device. If she was using a cassette player, she might have been acting alone, but if she was using a radio device, she had an accomplice. I wanted to find out which it was. Also, I didn't think I had the authority to make her uncover her ear in class. I could have asked her, I suppose, but she could simply have said no."

"That makes sense to me," said Papita. "Come on, Arthur. Let's get some lunch."

"Sounds good to me. Would you like to join us, Dr. Winslow?"

"I'd love to, but I'm late for a meeting with the dean. I have to provide evidence, you see. But thanks for the invitation. And thanks for your help."

"Some help," said Arthur as he and Papita walked away. "We could have mucked everything up."

"But we didn't, old boy; we didn't," said Papita.

"'Old boy?'"

"Yeah; didn't you notice how slow you were in crawling through that false ceiling last night?"

"Well, maybe. But I aced my logic exam this morning."

"It's not everyone who has a private review session with the professor," Papita observed.

"I guess not," said Arthur, "but I don't want another one like that one."

"I don't blame you, kiddo. Why don't we celebrate by driving downtown for lunch?"

"You're on."

Summary

In looking back over the material in this chapter, we find that the chief topics are categorical propositions and arguments. We have identified four standard forms of categorical propositions and explained how to translate sentences in ordinary language into one or the other of these four forms. We have also examined categorical syllogisms. Of particular interest is our description of the Venn diagram and rules techniques for distinguishing valid from invalid categorical syllogisms. In the following remarks, we recall the chief theoretical points in the chapter, trusting that the exercises which follow will help you put this theory into practice. We begin with categorical propositions, continue with syllogisms, and conclude with the techniques for determining validity.

In considering categorical propositions, the first point to remember is that their subject and predicate terms, which are nouns or noun phrases, denote classes of things. The second point to remember is that they either affirm or deny that all or a part of one class is included in another. A propositions affirm that the entire subject is included in the predicate class and E propositions deny that any member of the subject class is also a member of the predicate class. I propositions affirm that at least one member of the subject class is a member of the predicate class, and O propositions state that at least one member of the subject class is not a member of the predicate class. A and I propositions are affirmative. E and O propositions are negative.

Arguments with two premises are syllogisms. Those whose premises and conclusions are categorical propositions are categorical syllogisms. Each categorical syllogism contains three terms. The middle term occurs in each of the premises, but not the conclusion. Each of the other two occurs in both a premise and the conclusion. The minor term is the subject term of the conclusion, and the major term is the conclusion's predicate term. In placing a syllogism in standard form, make certain that each proposition is in standard form, find the conclusion, and make the proposition with the major term the first premise, and the proposition with the minor term the second premise in the syllogism.

Distributed terms refer to the entire class denoted by the term, and undistributed terms refer to only a part of the class. Venn diagrams for the four categorical propositions indicate that the subject terms of A and E propositions are distributed, as are the predicate terms of E and O propositions. All other terms are undistributed.

To determine the validity of a syllogism with the Venn diagram technique, draw three overlapping circles with two side by side on top and one somewhat underneath the other two. The top circles, from left to right, are for the minor and major terms, respectively, and the bottom circle is for the middle term. Diagram the premisses by shading or entering X's, then determine whether the conclusion has been diagramed in the process. If it has, the argument is valid. If not, the argument is invalid.

In diagraming the premisses, start with the A or E if the other one of the two premisses is an I or and O proposition. In diagraming I and O propositions, place the X upon the line when you don't have enough information to decide between the spaces on either side. Also, for syllogisms whose conclusions are A or E propositions, remember that the entire areas necessary to diagram the conclusion must be shaded for the syllogism to be valid, and that it's fine if more than that area is shaded.

Of the six rules for determining validity, one concerns the number of terms in the syllogism, and shifts in their meaning. When this rule is broken, the Fallacy of Four Terms occurs. Two rules relate to the distribution of terms. If the middle term isn't distributed at least once, the result is Undistributed Middle, and if a term is distributed in the conclusion but not in the premiss in which it also occurs, the result is Illicit Distribution. Two rules specify the possible arrangements of affirmative and negative propositions in valid categorical syllogisms. If neither premiss is affirmative, the fallacy is Exclusive Premisses. If a syllogism with a negative premiss has an affirmative conclusion, the Negative Fallacy occurs. The sixth rule states that a syllogism can have an I or O proposition for a conclusion only if it has an I or O proposition for a premiss. Syllogisms which break this rule commit the Existential Fallacy.

A LOOK AHEAD

Standard form categorical syllogisms are nice enough arguments—they use only four forms of propositions and have only two premisses—but when we listen to the way we argue, we find that we use a lot of propositions which aren't categorical propositions by any stretch of the imagination. Notice how these propositions differ in form from A, E, I, and O propositions:

The lights are out in Brooklyn and it is snowing in Philadelphia.
Either she calls to apologize or she can find someone else to throw her shower.
If you take off ten percent and throw in the twelve-inch speakers, then it's a
    deal.
Not replying to my request is equivalent to saying no.

In categorical propositions, we link subject and predicate terms, but in propositions like these, we string together complete units of thought by means of words like *if, then, either, or, and,* and *is equivalent to.* In Chapter 13, we examine propositions which use such words. Our two purposes are to set forth the conditions under which they are true and false and to learn how to symbolize them.

Exercises

Answers to questions marked with an asterisk may be found in the back of the text.

1. Identify the form (A, E, I, O) of each of the following propositions. State whether the proposition is affirmative or negative, identify its subject and predicate terms, and draw a circle around each distributed term.

   1. No motherly kisses are coquettish contacts.
   2. All terrorists are enemies of society.
   3. Some autobiographies are creative fictions.
  *4. Some press releases are not trustworthy documents.
   5. Some musicians are not performing artists.
   6. No accrued dividends are earnings which have been paid.
   7. Some paupers are victims of a cruel fate.
   8. All viaducts are bridges.
  *9. No moot questions are questions which require an answer.
  10. All subject terms of A propositions are distributed terms.

II. (a) Translate the following as A, E, I, or O propositions. Choose the translation which best retains the meaning of the original sentence. (b) Identify the distributed terms within the propositions.

   1. Penguins are not four-legged animals.
   2. John Q. Public is not wealthy.
   3. Not every cat is wild.
  *4. Only graduate students can receive advanced degrees.
   5. Birds fly.
   6. Cats are feline animals.
   7. This board is green.
   8. Philosophers are reflective persons.
  *9. They jest at scars who never felt a wound.
  10. Not all apples are ripe.

III. The following syllogisms are in standard form. Test the validity of each by means of a Venn diagram. Write "Valid" by the diagram for each valid syllogism. State the fallacy committed by any invalid syllogism. Label the circles of your Venn diagrams with the words in **bold.**

1. All ballet dancers are graceful persons.
   All basketball players are **graceful persons.**
   Therefore, some basketball **players** are ballet **dancers.**
2. Some market analysts are not technicians.
   Some **technicians** are investors who ignore the P/E ratio of stocks.
   Therefore, some **investors** who ignore the P/E ratio of stocks are not market **analysts.**
3. No saints are scoundrels.
   Some **scoundrels** are athletes.
   Therefore, some **athletes** are not **saints.**
*4. All restaurants are establishments subject to inspection by the Department of Health.
   All establishments which cannot ignore the threat of roaches are establishments subject to **inspection** by the Department of Health.
   Therefore, some establishments which cannot ignore the threat of **roaches** are **restaurants.**
5. No programs of historical importance are programs filled with idle **gossip.**
   Some programs filled with idle gossip are not newscasts.
   It follows that some **newscasts** are programs of historical **importance.**
6. No psychiatrists are neurotic persons.
   Some **psychiatrists** are eccentric persons.
   Therefore, some **eccentric** persons are not **neurotic** persons.
7. Some ambidextrous individuals are not switch hitters.
   All **switch hitters** are baseball players.
   Therefore, some baseball **players** are ambidextrous **individuals.**
8. No members of Quantrel's Raiders are autograph seekers.
   All **autograph seekers** are hero worshipers.
   Thus, no hero **worshipers** are **members** of Quantrel's Raiders.
*9. Some art forms are not things popular with the masses.
   Some felicitous combinations of sights and sounds are **art forms.**
   Accordingly, some felicitous **combinations** of sights and sounds are not **things popular** with the masses.
10. All strategists who tend to dispense with craft and guile are strategists who demand concessions from the opposition.
   All strategists who negotiate from positions of strength are strategists who tend to **dispense** with craft and guile.
   Therefore, some strategists who **negotiate** from positions of strength are strategists who **demand** concessions from the opposition.

IV. Test the validity of each of the following by means of a Venn diagram. Write "Valid" by the diagram for each valid syllogism. State the fallacy committed by any invalid syllogism. Translate into standard form as necessary. Label the circles of your Venn diagrams with the words in **bold.**

1. Some decisions hastily made are decisions regretted. All decisions which are John's decision to gamble are decisions **regretted.** Therefore, all decisions which are **John's decision** to gamble are decisions **hastily made.**

2. No one who saw Carlotta that night is one who will ever forget her. No John is one who will ever **forget** her. So, all **John** is one who saw **Carlotta** that night.

3. All those who die young are good people. No members of the Order of the Onion are those who **die young.** It follows that no **members** of the Order of the Onion are **good people.**

*4. All those who are interested in the gas mileage of their cars are poor persons. All **poor persons** are those who spend beyond their limit. Therefore, all those who **spend** beyond their limit are those who are interested in the **gas mileage** of their cars.

5. All birds in the spring are birds who have nest eggs. Some robins are not birds who have **nest eggs.** Therefore, some **robins** are **birds** in the spring.

6. Since **virtuous** actions should be practiced and **temperate** actions are virtuous, they should be **practiced.**

7. Vegetables should be stored in cool places, so **trees,** which are **vegetables,** should be stored in **cool places.**

8. No **languages** are **perfect** because they're inventions of humans and no **human** inventions are perfect.

*9. **Sacrificers** of honor are to be **pitied,** for the sacrifice of honor is inconsistent with happiness and those who are **unhappy** are to be pitied.

10. Those who ignore human rights are to be detested, but only **tyrants** are persons who **ignore** human rights, so some persons to be **detested** are tyrants.

V. Test the validity of each of the following by means of a Venn diagram. Write "Valid" by the diagram for each valid syllogism. State the fallacy committed by any invalid syllogism. Translate into standard form as necessary. Label the circles of your Venn diagrams with the words in **bold.**

1. Some Rotarians are devout persons and some Catholics are **devout persons,** so some **Catholics** must be **Rotarians.**

2. All dogs are mammals, since carnivores are **mammals** and **dogs** are **carnivores.**

3. All rottweilers are dangerous, so since children shouldn't be allowed to have **dangerous things,** no **children** should be allowed to have **rottweilers.**

*4. No hobos are persons with elaborate plans, but some **hobos** know how to spin elaborate yarns. Some persons who can spin elaborate **yarns,** then, are not persons with elaborate **plans.**

5. All inventors are dreamers and some **dreamers** use **power tools.** It may thus be concluded that some **inventors** use power tools.

6. Some gangs practice the techniques of terrorism; but since **gangs** are a city phenomenon, the **groups** which practice the techniques of terrorism are **city phenomena.**

7. Some individuals who marry for money are not **interested** in the person they marry, and not all individuals who marry for love also marry for **money,** so some individuals who marry for **love** are not interested in the person they marry.

8. Religious individuals are not superstitious because it is obvious that while no **religious** individuals are **blasphemous,** all blasphemous individuals are **superstitious.**

*9. Some **retired sailors** are superstitious, for they believe that it is **bad luck** to have a woman on board ship and everyone who believes that is **superstitious.**

10. All who follow laws are solid citizens. **Nature** follows **laws,** so things which are nature are **solid citizens.**

VI. Test the validity of each of the following by means of a Venn diagram. Write "Valid" by the diagram for each valid syllogism. State the fallacy committed by any invalid syllogism. Translate into standard form as necessary. Label the circles of your Venn diagrams with the words in **bold.**

1. Only those who have fallen on hard times are people who have been forced to declare bankruptcy. Everyone who has been forced to declare **bankruptcy** sings the praises of thrift. I conclude from this that everyone who sings the praises of **thrift** has fallen on **hard times.**

2. Inasmuch as only **industrious people** get ahead in life, all **lawyers** are people who **get ahead** in life—assuming, of course, that they're industrious.

3. No news is good **news,** but since **terrorist threats** are no news, they're **good news.**

*4. Only harmful stimulants should be **avoided,** but all **coffees** are harmful **stimulants,** so it stands to reason that we should avoid coffee.

5. All **foreign ambassadors** make **mistakes,** but some of them are not insensitive persons, so some people who make mistakes are not **insensitive** persons.

6. Social problems are complex phenomena, but it could hardly be denied that many **complex problems** can be **understood.** For example, molecules are complex, and today we know a great deal about them. Thus, **social problems,** like molecules and other complex phenomena, can be understood.

7. Americans believe in equality, but this means that some **Ku Klux Klan** members believe in **equality,** since they're **Americans.**

8. All friends in good times are fair-weather friends. Some friends in **good times** are friends who don't know you when you're down and out. Therefore, some friends who don't know you when you're **down** and out are **fair-weather** friends.

*9. All rapists are inhuman. Those who pollute the environment are **rapists.** Therefore, those who **pollute** the environment are **inhuman.**

10. Not all fleet of foot are runners, but only **runners** are allowed on the cinder track. Accordingly, some persons allowed on the **cinder track** are **fleet** of foot.

Chapter 13

PROPOSITIONAL LOGIC I
TRUTH FUNCTIONAL PROPOSITIONS

The purpose of this chapter and the next is to introduce a branch of formal logic which has undergone considerable development in the past one hundred and fifty years. This branch is alternately referred to as *sentential logic, propositional logic,* and *truth functional logic*. It examines arguments in which simple propositions are combined with one another by means of **operators,** or **truth functional connectives,** to form compound propositions. In this chapter, we define these connectives by means of truth tables, introduce symbols for them, and show how they and selected letters from the alphabet are used to capture the truth functional meaning of propositions expressed in ordinary language. The connectives are defined in the story entitled "Blue," and the material in boxes illustrates the process of symbolization.

DEFINING THE TRUTH FUNCTIONAL CONNECTIVES

It was a Saturday evening. I boarded the plane in Cincinnati a little after 8:30. My seat was next to the aisle. In the seat by the window sat a thin young woman whose dark black hair lightly brushed her shoulders. As I sat down next to her, she smiled my way and smoothed out her dress, which fell nearly to her ankles and bore a pattern of golden brown leaves. The dress reminded me of autumn.

I'd been attending an academic meeting in Cincinnati, and was eager to get back to my work on this text, so I pulled a pen and a clean white sheet of paper from my black zipper satchel, slid the satchel under the seat in front of me, and wrote out the forms of truth functional propositions. My purpose was to define each of the connectives for each proposition by means of a truth table. I began with this one:

Truth Table for Conjunction

P	Q	P • Q
T	T	T
T	F	F
F	T	F
F	F	F

In categorical propositions, subject and predicate *terms* are joined together by *is* or *is not*. In truth functional logic, complete units of thought, represented by capital letters, are strung together, like pearls on a necklace, by truth functional connectives.

When I'd gotten this far, the young woman startled me by saying, "What are you doing? What's this?" She put her finger on the truth table as she spoke.

"I'm writing a chapter on propositional logic for a text in critical thinking. Ordinarily, I don't write on planes, but I have a contract deadline to meet."

"What's 'propositional logic'?" she wanted to know.

"It's a part of logic developed by the Stoics, and . . . "

"The who?" she asked, breaking in.

"No, not the Who," I replied, thinking she was referring to the old rock group. "The Stoics; but never mind. The idea is that **we combine simple propositions with one another in various ways to make compound propositions.** Right now I'm writing a section in the text which explains the possible combinations of truth values for such propositions."

"Can you give me an example?"

SYMBOLIZING CONJUNCTIONS

- Victor swims and Victor works out with weights.   S • W
- Ruth is an athlete and a musician.   R • M
- Fran and George are the valedictorians of their classes.   F • G

In addition to *and,* these words indicate conjunctions: *but, besides, as well as, although.*

And indicates a relation rather than a conjunction in "Matthew and Francis are adversaries." Symbolize as "A" (for "adversaries").

Some conjunctions contain negations.

- Although John is ambidextrous, he is not a great drummer.   A • ~D

"Sure," I replied. "What's your name?"

"Let's say my name is 'Blue.'"

"All right," I said. "Let's say my name is 'Red.'"

"Is your name really Red? You don't have red hair."

"My name is Red just as surely as your name is Blue," I said with a broad smile.

"All right, fair enough," Blue replied. "Just give me the example."

"The truth table you've put your finger on," I said cooperatively, "is for the conjunction. **Conjunctions are 'both-and' propositions. For example, 'Blue sits next to the window, and Red sits next to the aisle' is a conjunction.**"

"Well?"

"Well, the point for propositional logic is that **such propositions are true if and only if both of the simple propositions, which are called 'conjuncts,' are true.** The proposition as I stated it is true, but if I were not sitting next to the aisle it would be false." To demonstrate, I got out of my seat, stood in the aisle, and leaned on the back of the seat in front of mine, smiling with professorial self-satisfaction. "See what I mean?" I went on. "'Blue sits next to the window' is still true, but 'Red sits next to the aisle' is false, since I'm standing up. That makes the entire conjunction false."

"I'm sorry, sir, but you'll have to sit down and fasten your seat belt," said a stern voice behind me. "We're about to take off." It was a flight attendant, calling me into line.

As I sat down again, Blue asked, "Are you always like this on planes?"

"Always," I said. "Now where was I? Oh, yeah. Just **look at the truth table. If you substitute 'Blue sits next to the window' for p and 'Red sits next to the aisle' for q,** you see what I'm talking about. **'Blue sits next to the window and Red sits next to the aisle' is true only when both of the propositions** we've **joined by *and* are true.**"

"Why should I believe that?" Blue asked.

I looked at Blue for a moment, wondering whether she was serious. She seemed to be, so I said, "You should believe it because we use *both* and *and* to assert that the two propositions we join by these words are true. We don't mean that one of them is true, or that the other is true, but that . . . " Here my voice trailed off, because I realized that I was about to use the word *both* again, which wouldn't be very helpful. Then I had an inspiration, and said, "It's like those vending machines which require you to put in two coins. If you put in one coin, the machine won't give you the newspaper or the soft drink. It only gives you the newspaper or soft drink when you put in two coins."

"Most of the machines I've seen take four or five coins," Blue observed.

"Yes, but the principle's the same. Each and every one of the conjuncts must be true for the conjunction to be true, just as the required number of coins must be inserted for the product to be delivered."

"All right, I see what you mean, but what's the story with the, uh, truth table? Why do you need that?"

"First, the truth table provides a way of defining the truth functional connectives. Second, it provides a way of determining the validity of arguments."

"Do you mean that you can determine the validity of arguments with just that little truth table there?"

"Well, no. The truth table must be constructed to suit the purpose."

"So not all truth tables are like that one?"

"No, some are simpler than this one, and some are more elaborate."

"Well, show me."

"Really? You want to sit here on the plane and do truth tables?"

"It can't be worse than reading the airline magazine," said Blue.

"Or playing tic-tac-toe," I said. "All right, you're on. First, I'll show you **the simplest truth table of all.**" My hand flew across the page, with this result:

Truth Table for the Curl

P	~P
T	F
F	T

"You see that little symbol before the p?" I asked. "It's called **the 'curl,' or the 'tilde.'**"

"Yeah, I've seen that on computer keyboards," said Blue with interest. "What does it mean?"

"It means *not*. It's the symbol for negation. The truth table shows that whenever p is true, not p is false, and whenever p is false, not p is true."

"I can see that," said Blue, "but I'm wondering why you only have two rows of Ts and Fs in this truth table. You have four in the truth table for the conjunction."

"Say, how did you know those **Ts and Fs arranged from left to right are called 'rows'?**" I asked suspiciously. "Do you already know about truth tables? Are you putting me on?"

"No, honestly," said Blue, her eyelids fluttering and her head shaking as she spoke. "It was just a lucky use of words, I guess."

"Hm," I said, still a little suspiciously. "Let's try your luck again. What would you call **the lines as they run from top to bottom?**"

"I don't know."

"Take a stab at it."

"Ok, let's see. Oh, I know; I'd call them 'pillars.'"

"That's very good," I said. **"Logicians call them 'columns,'** but the idea's the same."

"You still haven't answered my question," said Blue.

"What was it?"

"Why do you have two rows in the truth table for the curl and four in the truth table for the conjunction?"

"Propositional logic is a logic of truth values," I replied, **"and there are only two of those."**

"True and false?" asked Blue.

"That's right," I said. "Say, are you absolutely sure you don't already know about truth tables?"

"No, honest," she said. "I just couldn't think of anything else that T and F might stand for."

"All right," I said, "let me answer your question. **The truth table is supposed to show all possible combinations of truth values. One proposition is either true or false, so there are only two rows for the p in the truth table for the curl. For two propositions, however, there are four possible combinations of truth values.** Here, I can illustrate with some coins."

I pulled down the tray table from the back of the seat in front of me and laid down eight quarters, in this pattern:

H	H
H	T
T	H
T	T

"Say, look at those quarters," said Blue. "You musta been buying soft drinks from the same machines I have."

"Yeah," I said. "Think T for the heads and F for the tails and you'll see the pattern. This gets all the possible combinations of truth values for two propositions."

"What if you have three propositions instead of two?" asked Blue.

"I don't have enough quarters for that!"

"You don't need them. I think I can see the pattern. **For one proposition you need two rows, and for two propositions you need four.** That means that **for three propositions you need eight rows of T's and F's.**"

"Yes," I said, "but how would you lay them out?"

"Just the way you did with the quarters," said Blue, pointing to my quarters as she spoke. **"You start with the right column and alternate heads and tails, or rather T's and F's. Then you move to the left and double up.** You have two T's and two F's, then two more T's and F's. And **then you move to the third column and double up again.** You have four T's and then four F's."

Truth Table Showing Three Columns with Ts and Fs

P	Q	R
T	T	T
T	T	F
T	F	T
T	F	F
F	T	T
F	T	F
F	F	T
F	F	F

"You're very good at this," I said. "Say, I . . . " Suddenly I became aware of movement to my side. Blue looked up, and I followed her gaze to the aisle.

"Pardon me, sir," said the flight attendant in a weary voice. "We're preparing for takeoff, and I've been asking that tray tables be stored upright behind the seat backs." She began to turn away, then cast a look at the quarters and said, "By the way, sir, you're not gambling on the plane, are you? I'm not sure that Ohio regulations allow that, though I could check if you'd like."

"No, don't bother," I said. "We're just doing truth tables."

"All right, but wait for the Fasten Seat Belt sign to go off before doing any more, OK?"

"Ok," I said.

Blue and I sat back in our seats and prepared for takeoff. I looked over at her and saw that she was staring straight ahead. "I've flown a hundred times," I thought, "and not spoken three words to the person beside me, and now . . . " Then Blue looked my way and caught me staring at her.

SYMBOLIZING DISJUNCTIONS

- Either Joshua is promoted, or Danielle is given a raise.   J ∨ D
- Tickets for the season and/or individual performances are available.   S ∨ P
- I don't go to the ball unless my fairy godmother swings into action.   B ∨ G
- My carriage turns into a pumpkin unless I get home before midnight.   C ∨ H

"You can tell me some more without the quarters," she said.

"All right, I will," I said. "In addition to conjunctions, there are **disjunctions. Those are either-or statements like 'Either the airline serves dinner on this flight or it serves snacks.'"**

"Or," Blue broke in, "like 'Either Red stays in his seat or the flight attendant gets rough.'"

"That's right," I laughed. "The truth table for the disjunction looks a lot like the one for the conjunction. Here, let me show you." I put the paper on the armrest next to Blue and drew this:

Truth Table for Disjunction

P	Q	P ∨ Q
T	T	T
T	F	T
F	T	T
F	F	F

"That symbol between the p and the q," I said, **"is called the *vee* or the *wedge*. The symbols are read simply as 'Either p or q.'"**

"Hm," said Blue, pulling the sheet into her lap. **"The disjunction is false only when both the p and the q are false."**

"Yes, and **in propositions like these, the p and the q are called *disjuncts*."**

"All right, that makes sense, except that I thought that when you said 'either p or q' you meant that only one or the other was true. Like us getting either dinner or a snack, but not both."

"That's called the 'exclusive' disjunction," I said. **"The wedge is the symbol for the 'inclusive' disjunction, which means 'either p or q or both.'"**

"Could you give me an example?"

"Sure. If we were on an international flight, we might get both a dinner and a snack, so in that case the *or* in 'Either the airline serves dinner on this flight, or it serves snacks' would clearly be inclusive."

Blue nodded her head, then pointed ahead. "The Fasten Seat Belt sign is off. We'll find out about the dinner before long."

"Right." I was so wrapped up in my little lecture that I hardly heard what Blue said. "The next kind of statement," I went on, "is the conditional. Here, hand me the paper." Blue obliged, and I drew this truth table upon it:

Truth Table for the Conditional

P	Q	P ⊃ Q
T	T	T
T	F	F
F	T	T
F	F	T

SYMBOLIZING CONDITIONALS I

If you've already studied Chapter 7, you know that in conditional propositions we assert that the truth of the antecedent is a *sufficient condition* for the truth of the consequent, and that the truth of the consequent is a *necessary condition* for the truth of the antecedent. The antecedents of conditional propositions always express sufficient conditions, and the consequents always express necessary conditions.

Necessary condition indicators: *only if, unless,* implies, then* (The simple propositions following these words are always placed to the right of the horseshoe.)

Sufficient condition indicators: *if, since, provided that, in case, assuming* (The material following these words is always placed to the left of the horseshoe.)

SYMBOLIZING CONDITIONALS II

In the following examples, the letters in bold indicate the capital letters used in the translations. Notice how the correct order of the conditional propositions is determined by the necessary and sufficient condition indicators.

If the water **f**reezes, the pipe **b**ursts.   F ⊃ B

The **c**ar careens out of control if the **d**river falls asleep.   D ⊃ C

Only if the password is not **a**ccepted is her access to the mainframe **d**enied.
   D ⊃ ~A

Mark travels by **p**lane only if he has the **m**oney.   P ⊃ M

Yolanda buys a **c**ar in the event that she receives the **r**aise.   R ⊃ C

Provided that **M**ark speaks the truth, the **s**ecretary distributes the Minutes.
   M ⊃ S

If Molly **a**nswers the phone, then Jerry **l**oses his courage and **h**angs up.
   A ⊃ (L • H)

If Brad's **g**rade slips from B to C, then either Erin does not share her **n**otes
   or Brad skips the **r**eview session.   G ⊃ (~N ∨ R)

---

*Don't forget that it's usually easier to symbolize propositions with *unless* as disjunctions. See the discussion of disjunctions above.

"In this case," I said, **"the symbol between the p and the q is called the 'horse-shoe,' and the statement is read 'if p then q.'"**

"I have my own example for that one," said Blue, catching my eye.

"What is it?" I asked.

"'If John acts like a louse, then Blue leaves Cincinnati,'" said Blue.

"Oh," I said, not knowing quite how to respond. "That's a good one, all right."

"Yeah, and the first row shows it's true, which it is. I can also understand why the second row shows it's false. If John acts like a louse but Blue doesn't leave Cincinnati, then it has to be false. The fourth row makes sense, too, where it's false that John acts like a louse and that Blue leaves Cincinnati. She wouldn't have any reason to, if he didn't act like a louse. But I don't get the third row. If it's false that John acts like a louse, then why does Blue leave Cincinnati? Why doesn't she stay?"

"I don't know," I said. "Maybe she goes shopping in Chicago. No, seriously, the thing to think about is the meaning of the conditional."

"I thought that's what I was doing," said Blue.

"Well, you were, but hear me out. **The conditional does just one thing: It rejects the possibility that the p statement, or 'antecedent,' is true when the q statement, or 'consequent,' is false. It allows all other possibilities, but rules that one out."**

Blue sat in silence for a moment, then nodded her head. "So **just so long as the consequent isn't false while the antecedent is true, the conditional is true?"**

"That's it. Remember the disjunction? It did something similar. It ruled out the possibility that both disjuncts could be false and the disjunction nevertheless be true."

"Watch out," said Blue. "Here comes the flight attendant."

Blue and I pulled down our tray tables and waited for the flight attendant to come to our row. "We're only getting snacks," I observed.

"And I'm hungry," Blue said. "I haven't had anything since morning."

"You can have my peanuts," I said magnanimously.

"What a guy," said Blue.

The flight attendant offered coffee, tea, and a variety of soft drinks, but Blue and I both chose orange juice. I passed my peanuts to Blue, and she didn't refuse them. "Are you getting off in Chicago?" I asked.

SYMBOLIZING BICONDITIONALS

In biconditionals, each statement on either side of the three-bar line expresses both a sufficient and a necessary condition of the other. This explains why "if and only if" indicates a biconditional.

- Passing the **e**xamination is equivalent to passing the **c**ourse. $E \equiv C$
- Sarah **w**ins the lottery if and only if her number is **d**rawn. $W \equiv D$

"No, I'm going on to Oklahoma. I have a sister in Oklahoma City. I'll stay with her and her husband for awhile."

"And what then? I know it's none of my business."

"I don't know. I suppose I'll get a job or something. That's what one does, isn't it?"

"Yes," I said. "That's what one does."

For a few minutes, Blue and I sat in silence, then she said, "What about you? Are you getting off in Chicago?"

"Yes, that's the end of the journey for me."

"Then you'd better get busy, hadn't you?" Blue's tone of voice made her question a statement.

"Whatever do you mean?" I asked in surprise.

"I mean you'd better finish telling me about propositional logic," she said. "You don't have much time."

"No, I guess I don't," I laughed. "Tell you what: I'll tell you about biconditionals, or equivalences."

"All right."

"We need another truth table." I turned over the sheet and drew this:

Truth Table for Material Equivalence

P	Q	P ≡ Q
T	T	T
T	F	F
F	T	F
F	F	T

"This is the truth table **for material equivalence. The symbol between the p and q is called the 'three-bar line.' Statements like this are read 'p is equivalent to q.'** What do you notice about the truth table?"

Blue stared at the truth table for a moment, then said, "Well, in the last column the statement is true even though both p and q are false. That's strange."

"Not 'even though,'" I prompted. "Think about it some more. Something else is going on."

Blue knitted her brows, then her face lit up. "Oh, I see," she exclaimed. **The statement is true whenever p and q have the same truth value."**

"Exactly," I said. *"**Equivalent** statements are ones which have the same truth value."*

"But you said this is material equivalence," said Blue. "What does that mean?"

"We could also use the term 'factual,'" I said. "The point is that **the propositions are materially equivalent when they just happen to have the same truth value.** Look at your cup of orange juice, for example. You've drunk half of it. By contrast, I haven't touched mine. In this analogy, our cups of orange juice aren't equivalent. Get it?"

"Of course," said Blue impatiently.

"All right, now watch." I picked up my cup and drank it half down. "Now our cups are equivalent, right?"

"Right. As a matter of fact, they're equivalent, but they don't have to be. I could drink the rest of my juice, or you could drink the rest of yours, and then they wouldn't be equivalent anymore."

"Exactly. But **there's another type of equivalence in which two propositions always have the same truth value no matter what.**"

"How could that be?"

"It could be, and is, because the equivalence is a matter of the form of the propositions, and not their content, or 'material' part."

"All right, show me."

"This time we'll construct a truth table with more columns than we've used before, and we'll use the curl, too."

"It's about time," said Blue.

With Blue watching, I drew out the following truth table. I'm numbering the columns in the order in which I filled them out, so you can see exactly how I did it. I filled out the "~p" by reference to the "p" and the "~q" by reference to the "q."

Truth Table for (p ⊃ q) ≡ (~q ⊃ ~p)

2	1	3	4	5	6	7
p	q	~p	~q	p ⊃ q	~q ⊃ ~p	(p ⊃ q) ≡ (~q ⊃ ~p)
T	T	F	F	T	T	T
T	F	F	T	F	F	T
F	T	T	F	T	T	T
F	F	T	T	T	T	T

When I was finished, I passed the sheet to Blue, and she stared at it for awhile. "Hm," was all she said. That was sufficient encouragement for me to offer some explanation.

"You see," I said, **"there's never any case in which p ⊃ q and ~q ⊃ ~p differ in truth value, so there's a solid row of Ts under (p ⊃ q) ≡ (~q ⊃ ~p). That's a logical equivalence."**

"That's actually very interesting," said Blue, her eyes bright. "Are there any more of these logical equivalencies?"

"Yes, there are quite a few of them. They're very useful forms. **Since they always have the same truth value, you can replace the form on one side of the three-bar line with the one on the other.**"

At this point, Blue and I heard a bell above us, and noticed that the Fasten Seat Belt sign had come on again. In a matter of seconds, the flight attendant collected our cups, and the captain announced that we were preparing to land in Chicago. We didn't say anything else until we felt the wheels of the plane hit the runway.

"A good landing," I said, but Blue simply nodded.

We taxied to a halt by the terminal, and passengers stood up to collect their bags from the overhead racks. Blue looked out the window. Soon, I pulled my satchel from under the seat in front of me, and said, "I wish you luck in Oklahoma City."

Blue looked my way and held up the sheet of truth tables. "May I have this?" she asked.

"Of course," I said, and started down the aisle. Toward the front of the plane, I glanced back, but Blue was staring out the window again, her chin resting on her left palm. Then someone behind me poked me in the back to get me moving again, and I left the plane. In the terminal, I headed left in search of the baggage area, where I found that my suitcase had gone on to Oklahoma City.

Summary

In this chapter we have considered the truth table definitions of the connectives for conjunctions, disjunctions, conditionals, and material equivalencies. (You should memorize these truth table definitions.) We have also considered the distinction between material and logical equivalencies. Material, or factual, equivalencies are a function of the truth value of component propositions, whereas logical equivalencies are a function of the form of the component propositions. The rules of replacement, which we examine in Chapter 14, are logical equivalencies.

A LOOK AHEAD

In Chapter 14, we discover that the truth functional compound propositions which we have examined in this chapter are the bricks out of which many arguments are constructed. As we learn to distinguish those which are valid from those which are not, we find that the truth tables examined in this chapter provide the groundwork for techniques for demonstrating both validity and invalidity. We also show how to construct demonstrations of validity known as *formal proofs*.

Background Information for the Exercises

When the truth value of one or more component propositions is known, it is possible to determine the truth value of some compound propositions by relying on the truth table definitions of the connectives. Practice in doing this is useful in remembering the truth table definitions. In addition, the ability to determine truth values in accordance with the definitions of the connectives is essential to the technique of demonstrating the invalidity of arguments by assigning truth values. This becomes evident in the next chapter.

Some of the propositions in the exercises below are punctuated with brackets as well as parentheses. We use brackets when we need punctuation to surround a part of a proposition in which simple propositions are already grouped together by parentheses. This proposition illustrates the need for brackets in addition to parentheses:

$$(A \equiv B) \lor X \supset Y$$

Without brackets, it is impossible to know whether the proposition is a disjunction or a conditional. When brackets are added, however, the answer becomes plain, as you can see from this:

$$[(A \equiv B) \lor X] \supset Y$$

The proposition is clearly a conditional.

In general, brackets are easy to use. The chief point is to make certain that they always surround parentheses, like this:

$$[(\;)]$$

You want to avoid punctuation like this:

$$[(]$$

With this punctuation, you can't tell what's enclosing what.

A technique known as *looping* can be helpful in determining the truth value of relatively complex propositions. To illustrate the technique, we assume that in this proposition A and B are true and X and Y are false: $[\sim(\sim A \bullet B) \bullet A] \lor X$.

To determine the truth value of a proposition, work from the inside out. In our example, begin with $\sim A \bullet B$, then proceed to $\sim(\sim A \bullet B)$, then $\sim(\sim A \bullet B) \bullet A$, and then to the statement as a whole. A and B are given as true, so $\sim A$ is false. Utilizing loops, we derive the following:

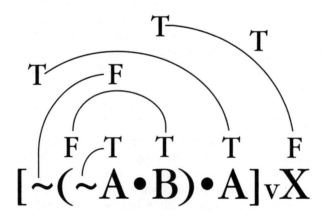

Now you're ready to do the exercises which follow.

Exercises

Answers to questions marked with an asterisk may be found in the back of the text.

I. Assuming that A and B are true and X and Y are false, which of the following are true?

  1. A • X

  2. A • (B ∨ Y)

  3. A ∨ ~Y

  *4. B ∨ Y

  5. ~B ∨ Y

  6. ~(B ∨ Y)

  7. A ≡ X

  8. A ≡ (B ∨ Y)

  *9. A ⊃ ~Y

  10. B ⊃ Y

  11. ~B ⊃ Y

  12. ~(B ⊃ Y)

  13. (A ∨ B) • X

  *14. (A ∨ B) • (~X • Y)

  15. (~A ∨ ~B) • (~X ∨ ~Y)

  16. (A • ~B) • (X • ~Y)

  17. ~(A • ~B) ∨ ~(~X • Y)

  18. (~A • ~B) ∨ (X ∨ Y)

  *19. [(A • B) ∨ X] ∨ Y

  20. (A ⊃ B) ≡ (~X • Y)

  21. (~A ∨ ~B) ≡ (~X ⊃ ~Y)

  22. (A ≡ ~B) ≡ (X ≡ ~Y)

  23. ~(A ≡ ~B) ⊃ ~(~X ≡ Y)

  *24. (~A ≡ ~B) ∨ (X ⊃ Y)

  25. [(A ≡ B) ∨ X] ⊃ Y

II. Assuming that A and B are true and X and Y are false, which of the following are true?

   1. ~X • ~Y

   2. (A • X) ∨ (A • Y)

   3. (A • ~X) • (A • Y)

  *4. A • (~X • Y)

   5. (A • B) • (X • Y)

   6. (A ∨ B) • (X ∨ Y)

   7. (A ∨ B) • (X • Y)

   8. ~X ⊃ ~Y

  *9. (A ⊃ X) ≡ (A ⊃ Y)

  10. (A ⊃ ~X) ⊃ (A ⊃ Y)

  11. A ⊃ (~X ⊃ Y)

  12. (A • B) ⊃ (X • Y)

  13. (A ≡ B) ⊃ (X ≡ Y)

 *14. (A ≡ B) ⊃ (X • Y)

  15. [(~A • ~B) ∨ ~X] ∨ ~Y

  16. (A ∨ ~A) • (~B • ~X)

  17. ~[A • (B ∨ X)] ∨ (A • B)

  18. ~(~X • Y)

 *19. X • [(A • B) ∨ (X • Y)]

  20. X ∨ ~[(A • B) ∨ (X • Y)]

  21. [(~A ⊃ ~B) ∨ ~X] ≡ ~Y

  22. (A ∨ ~A) ⊃ (~B ⊃ ~X)

  23. ~[A ⊃ (B ∨ X)] ≡ (A ⊃ B)

 *24. ~(~X ⊃ Y)

  25. X ⊃ [(A • B) ∨ (X ⊃ Y)]

Chapter 14

PROPOSITIONAL LOGIC II

DETERMINING VALIDITY IN PROPOSITIONAL LOGIC

In this chapter, we turn to the examination of arguments which utilize truth functional propositions. Our quest for effective means for distinguishing valid from invalid arguments leads us to develop three proof techniques, which are **the truth table technique, the method of assigning truth values, and the method of formal proof.** The truth table technique, which we examine first, is a purely mechanical method for determining the validity of arguments. As we see in due course, it anticipates the method of assigning truth values in an important way. The technique of formal proof, unlike either of the other two techniques, utilizes two kinds of rules, which are known as *rules of replacement* and *rules of inference.* For valid arguments, these rules enable us to deduce the conclusion in one or more steps. (Some formal proofs can be quite long and challenging, but most of the ones in this chapter are not too lengthy. No sense in overdoing it.)

WHOA! HOLD ON!

The material in this chapter requires a different approach than the previous one. I recommend that you read it in short sections, making certain that you understand each section well before going on to the next. I also recommend that you tie your study of each section to the exercises at the end. (To make this easier to do, at appropriate points I've put in boxes, similar to this one, which point you to the right exercises.) It's particularly important to work the exercises for the sections on the rules of replacement and the rules of inference, for you can't construct formal proofs without understanding these rules, and understanding them is equivalent to being able to apply them, just as knowing how to ride a bicycle is equivalent to being able to guide one down the street without falling over.

Before doing anything else, we should establish our format for presenting arguments in symbolic form. **Our convention in presenting symbolized arguments is to enter each premiss on a separate line, with the conclusion on the same line as the last premiss. We introduce the conclusion by "∴", which means "therefore," and separate it from the last premiss by a slanted line.** This is an old and hallowed way of presenting arguments in propositional logic, and one which makes it easy to distinguish the premisses from the conclusion. In the following argument, for example, these conventions indicate that the first premiss is "F ⊃ (G • H)," the second premiss is "F," and the conclusion is "G • H:"

$$F \supset (G \bullet H)$$
$$F / \therefore (G \bullet H)$$

With this convention in place, we begin our examination of techniques for demonstrating validity and invalidity.

TRUTH TABLES
FOR ARGUMENTS

In constructing truth tables for arguments, we establish guide columns for the simple propositions in the argument and then enter columns for each of the argument's compound propositions. The truth table for the argument above looks like this:

	1	2	3	4	5
	F	G	H	G • H	F ⊃ (G • H)
A	T	T	T	T	T
B	T	T	F	F	F
C	T	F	T	F	F
D	T	F	F	F	F
E	F	T	T	T	T
F	F	T	F	F	T
G	F	F	T	F	T
H	F	F	F	F	T

> The numbers above each column are not a part of the truth table. Neither are the letters from top to bottom on the left. These are added only to make it easier for us to talk about the truth table. Columns 1, 2, and 3 are the guide columns. Since three simple propositions are used in the argument, eight rows are necessary to indicate every possible combination of truth tables.

The guide columns enable us to derive columns for each of the premisses and the conclusion. Column 4 is derived not only to serve as the column for the conclusion, but also to make it easier for us to establish a column for the first premiss. It is filled out by reference to columns 2 and 3. Since G • H is a conjunction, a "T" appears in and only in each row in which both G and H are true. Column 5, for the first premiss, is filled out by reference to 1 and 4. We read from left to right in this case, since "F" is the antecedent and "G • H" the consequent. "F," the second premiss, appears as the leftmost guide column, so we do not need to add another column for it.

In valid arguments, you recall, it is impossible for the conclusion to be false when each and every premiss is true. For this reason, **if the truth table** above **shows that the conclusion is false in any row in which each and every one of its premisses is true, the argument is invalid. If it does not show this, the argument is valid.** With this in mind, let's look at the truth table.

Columns 5 and 1 indicate the premisses of the argument, and column 4 indicates the conclusion. In B, C, D, F, G, and H, the conclusion is false, but in each of these rows one of the premisses is false as well. Since the conclusion is not false in any case in which both premisses are true, the argument is valid.

The truth table for this argument shows its invalidity:

$$I \supset (J \vee K)$$
$$\sim(J \bullet K) / \therefore \sim I$$

	1	2	3	4	5	6	7	8	
	I	**J**	**K**	**J ∨ K**	**I ⊃ (J ∨ K)**	**J • K**	**~(J • K)**	**~I**	
A	T	T	T	T	T	T	F	F	
B	T	T	F	T	**T**	F	**T**	**F**	Invalid by rows
C	T	F	T	T	**T**	F	**T**	**F**	B and C.
D	T	F	F	F	F	F	T	F	
E	F	T	T	T	T	T	F	T	
F	F	T	F	T	T	F	T	T	
G	F	F	T	T	T	F	T	T	
H	F	F	F	F	T	F	T	T	

The conclusion to this argument is in column 8, and the premisses are in columns 5 and 7. In B and C both premisses are true and the conclusion is false. Hence, the argument is invalid.

The truth table technique provides a purely mechanical means for determining the validity of arguments utilizing truth functional compound propositions. However, it becomes cumbersome. A truth table for an argument containing four simple propositions requires sixteen rows of T's and F's, and one for five requires thirty-two rows.[1] Although we limit ourselves to arguments with no more than four statement variables in this chapter, we can see the need for less cumbersome methods for determining validity. In proofs of invalidity by assigning truth values, which we examine next, we dispense with truth tables in our attempt to determine whether the conclusion of arguments can be false when their premisses are true.

You're now ready to try your hand at Exercise I.

---

[1] In general, where "n" indicates the number of statement variables, 2^n rows are required.

DEMONSTRATING INVALIDITY
BY ASSIGNING TRUTH VALUES

We demonstrate the invalidity of invalid truth functional arguments by assigning truth values to render their premises true and their conclusions false. These assignments constitute a proof of invalidity, since the conclusions in valid arguments cannot be false in any case in which each and every one of their premises is true.

To illustrate, let's construct a proof of invalidity for this argument with one premiss:

$$(A \bullet B) \supset C /\therefore B \supset C.$$

Our first step is to assign truth values to make the conclusion false. Since a conditional is false only when its antecedent is true and its consequent false, the only way we can do this is by assigning a truth value of true to B and a truth value of false to C.

Next, we determine whether the truth of the premiss $(A \bullet B) \supset C$ **can be sustained given this assignment of truth values** and a further assignment of either true or false to A. **In the premiss, we must retain the truth value assignments we made** to B and C **in the conclusion,** so the truth value assignment we give to A becomes crucial. What happens if A is given the truth value of true? In that case, $(A \bullet B) \supset C$ is false, since its antecedent is true and its consequent false. This assignment won't work, since our goal is to make the premiss true and the conclusion false. If A is false, however, the statement is true. Therefore, we must assign a truth value of false to A in order to make the premiss of the argument true while leaving the conclusion false.

We complete our demonstration by producing a table of truth value assignments, as follows:

$$(A \bullet B) \supset C /\therefore B \supset C$$

A	B	C
F	T	F

This argument presents a new wrinkle in demonstrating invalidity by assigning truth values:

$$D \supset E /\therefore (D \lor F) \bullet E$$

In the previous argument, we had no choice in assigning truth values to make the conclusion false. We had to make the antecedent of the conclusion true and the consequent false. In this argument, by contrast, the conclusion is a conjunction, so we can choose one of three ways to make the conclusion false. First, we can make $D \lor F$ true and E false. Second, we can make $D \lor F$ false and E true. Third, we can make both $D \lor F$ and E false. We begin by making E false and $D \lor F$ true.

There are three ways to make D ∨ F true. We can make both D and F true, or D true and F false, or D false and F true. Which combinations should we choose? With E false in the conclusion, we must make D false in order to make the premiss true. It doesn't matter what truth value we give to F, since the argument is invalid whether F is true or false. However, if F is given a truth value of F, then E can be given a truth value of either T or F. This shows that the invalidity of the argument can be demonstrated by more than one assignment of truth values. We complete our demonstration of invalidity by writing out all three truth value assignments, though only one is sufficient to demonstrate invalidity.

$$D \supset E /\therefore (D \vee F) \bullet E$$

D	E	F
F	F	T
F	F	F
F	T	F

In demonstrating invalidity by assigning truth values, we first assign truth values to render the conclusion false and then assign truth values to make the premisses true. Remember these points:

- For conjunctions to be false, one or both conjuncts must be false.
- For disjunctions to be false, both disjuncts must be false.
- For conditionals to be false, the antecedent must be true and the consequent false.
- For biconditionals to be false, the propositions on either side of the triple bar must have different truth values.

You're now ready to try your hand at Exercise II.

FORMAL PROOFS IN PROPOSITIONAL LOGIC

Our chief interest from this point on is formal proofs of validity, which require two kinds of rules, known as *rules of replacement* and *rules of inference*. We look first at the rules of replacement.

RULES OF REPLACEMENT

The **rules of replacement,** which are logical equivalences, are well named, since in each one of them **the statement on one side of the triple bar can replace the statement on the other side *anywhere* it occurs.** It's important for you to learn these rules well, for many formal proofs are impossible without them.

The ten rules we introduce in this section are given numbers, but that's only for ease of reference. You should learn the rules by name rather than by number. After the name of each rule, we provide its accepted abbreviation. You'll use the abbreviations in formal proofs, so it's a good idea to learn them along with the rule. So much for preliminaries. Let's get started.

Rule 1: Double Negation (D.N.): $p \equiv \sim\sim p$

Double negation indicates that the negation of the negation of a statement is equivalent to the statement. This perhaps seems obvious, but in ordinary discourse people sometimes get tangled up in double negations. I once heard someone say, "She used to be an ex-ballet dancer." The person *intended* to say, "She used to be a ballet dancer," but said "She's a ballet dancer" instead. After all, if she's no longer an ex-ballet dancer, she must be dancing ballet again! We symbolize

It is not the case that Jim did not attend the party

as

$$\sim\sim A,$$

which is equivalent by D. N. to

$$A.$$

Rule 2: DeMorgan's Theorems (DeM.): $\sim(p \bullet q) \equiv (\sim p \vee \sim q)$
$$\sim(p \vee q) \equiv (\sim p \bullet \sim q)$$

We use **DeMorgan's theorems** when we need to replace a conjunction with an equivalent disjunctive form, or vice versa. In applying the theorems, we shift a curl from outside parentheses to inside, or vice versa, and either exchange a "$\bullet$" for a "$\vee$" or a $\vee$ for a "$\bullet$." The theorems are stated above in their simplest form, but the following formulations suggest something of their scope:

$$\sim(\sim p \bullet q) \equiv (\sim\sim p \vee \sim q)$$
$$(p \bullet q) \equiv \sim(\sim p \vee \sim q)$$
$$\sim[(p \supset q) \bullet r] \equiv [\sim(p \supset q) \vee \sim r]$$

Rule 3: Distribution (Dist.): $[p \bullet (q \vee r)] \equiv [(p \bullet q) \vee (p \bullet r)]$
$$[p \vee (q \bullet r)] \equiv [(p \vee q) \bullet (p \vee r)]$$

Like DeMorgan's theorems, **distribution** indicates conditions in which a conjunction can be replaced by a disjunction or a disjunction by a conjunction. In distribution, however, one or both conjuncts of a conjunction are disjunctions and one or both disjuncts of a disjunction are conjunctions. The name *distribution* draws our attention to the way in which statements are relocated when the shift from one form to the other is made. For simplicity, let us move from left to right in the statement of the rule given above. In the first formulation of the rule, p occurs only once in the conjunction to the left of the triple bar, but is found in both disjuncts of the disjunction to the right. The position of q shifts as well, but neither it nor r occurs more than once in either formulation.

An appreciation of the claim made by distribution helps you remember the rule. The minimum condition for the truth of "p • (q ∨ r)" is the truth of p and the truth of either q or r. These, however, are the exact conditions under which "(p • q) ∨ (p • r)" is true. These possibilities are spelled out for the first form of the rule in the truth value assignments below:

Minimum Conditions for the Truth of [p • (q ∨ r)] and [(p • q) ∨ (p • r)] Are Exactly the Same

p	•	(q	∨	r)	(p	•	q)	∨	(p	•	r)
T	T	F	T	T	T	F
T	F	T	T	F	T	T

Notice, too, that either of the statements in either formulation of distribution is false if p is false or if both q and r are false. Both statement forms require and rule out the same truth value possibilities.

Rule 4: Commutation (Com.): $(p • q) \equiv (q • p)$
$(p \lor q) \equiv (q \lor p)$

Commutation makes it clear that the order in which statements occur in a conjunction or a disjunction is immaterial.

Rule 5: Association (Assoc.): $[p • (q • r)] \equiv [(p • q) • r]$
$[p \lor (q \lor r)] \equiv [(p \lor q) \lor r]$

According to the rule of **association,** in a conjunction (disjunction) with one simple conjunct (disjunct) and one conjunct (disjunct) which is itself a conjunction (disjunction), we can shift the punctuation from right to left, or left to right, without changing the truth value of the statement.

> Notice that in Rules 1 through 5, with double negation as the sole exception, the statements on either side of the triple bar are either conjunctions or disjunctions.

You're now ready to try your hand at Exercise III.

Rule 6: Material Implication (Impl.): $(p \supset q) \equiv (\sim p \lor q)$

Material implication sets forth the condition under which a conditional form can be exchanged for a disjunctive form, and vice versa.

Rule 7: Material Equivalence (Equiv.): $(p \equiv q) \equiv [(p \bullet q) \lor (\sim p \bullet \sim q)]$
$(p \equiv q) \equiv [(p \supset q) \bullet (q \supset p)]$

Material equivalence shows how an equivalence can be transformed into either a conjunction or a disjunction.

Rule 8: Exportation (Exp.): $[(p \bullet q) \supset r] \equiv [p \supset (q \supset r)]$

Exportation indicates that a conditional whose antecedent is itself a conjunction can be exchanged for a conditional whose consequent is a conditional, and vice versa.

Rule 9: Transposition (Trans.): $(p \supset q) \equiv (\sim q \supset \sim p)$

While commutation makes it clear that the order in which the statements occur in a conjunction or a disjunction is immaterial, **transposition** reminds us that order in a conditional is of critical importance. In cases in which p and q have different truth values, "$p \supset q$" is true when "$q \supset p$" is false, or vice versa. For this reason, statements in the antecedent and consequent of a conditional can be reversed, but only if each is negated.

Rule 10: Tautology (Taut.): $p \equiv (p \lor p)$
$p \equiv (p \bullet p)$

While the order of occurrence of statements in conjunctions and disjunctions is unimportant, the order of occurrence is significant in conditionals. In this respect, the conditional is unique among truth functional compound statements. The deep significance of this division among the forms is seen once more in connection with **tautology.** This rule states that a statement is equivalent to a conjunction or a disjunction in which each conjunct or disjunct is that same statement. This is because the conjunction or disjunction in question is true or false in exactly the same cases in which the statement is true or false.

You're now ready to try your hand at Exercise IV.

RULES OF INFERENCE

The rules of replacement are logical equivalences. The following rules of inference, which are indispensable for formal proofs, consist in one or two premises which entail a conclusion.

RULES OF INFERENCE

---

1. Modus Ponens (M.P.)

    p ⊃ q

    p

    ∴q

2. Modus Tollens (M.T.)

    p ⊃ q

    ~q

    ∴ ~p

3. Hypothetical Syllogism (H.S.)

    p ⊃ q

    q ⊃ r

    ∴ p ⊃ r

4. Disjunctive Syllogism (D.S.)

    p∨q

    ~p

    ∴ q

5. Constructive Dilemma (C.D.)

    (p ⊃ q) • (r ⊃ s)

    p ∨ r

    ∴ q ∨ s

6. Absorption (Abs.)

    p ⊃ q

    ∴ p ⊃ (p • q)

7. Simplification (Simp.)

    p • q

    ∴ p

8. Conjunction (Conj.)

    p

    q

    ∴ p • q

9. Addition (Add.)

    p

    ∴ p ∨ q

These rules are valid argument forms, as you can demonstrate for yourself by means of a truth table. **Unlike the rules of replacement, which indicate forms which can be substituted for other forms, the rules of inference indicate forms in which statements are added or eliminated.** For example, modus ponens and disjunctive syllogism show how p can be eliminated in favor of q, while addition shows how a statement can be added to another.

This difference between the two kinds of rules carries with it a difference in the way they are applied. **The rules of replacement can be applied to parts of lines, but the rules of inference can only be applied to whole lines.** These lines must be taken as independent or freestanding units. We cannot arbitrarily select a part of a line for application of a rule of inference. For example, the inference below is illegitimate:

	F	G	H
1. (F • G) ⊃ H	F	T	F
2. G ⊃ H 1, Simp. (Wrong!)			

This assignment of truth values to the right of the argument demonstrates the incorrectness of the inference. On this assignment, (F • G) ⊃ H is true, but G ⊃ H is false.

You're now ready to try your hand at Exercise V.

FORMAL PROOF

The technique of **formal proof consists in the deduction of the conclusion of an argument by means of one or more of the rules of replacement or rules of inference.** In many cases, one or more subconclusions are deduced, which make it possible to deduce the conclusion in stepwise fashion. Deduction of the conclusion is possible only for those argument forms and arguments which are valid, since the rules of inference automatically eliminate any subconclusions or conclusions which do not follow from the premises. In order to illustrate the technique, we present a simple argument and a proof of its validity. The rules used in the proof are indicated with standard abbreviations, and the line or lines to which the rule is applied are indicated by one or two numbers.

1. F ⊃ G
2. H ⊃ I
3. G ∨ H/∴ G ∨ I
4. ~G ⊃ H   3, Impl.
5. ~G ⊃ I   4, 2, H. S.
6. G ∨ I   5, Impl.

Line 4, which is the first step in the proof, follows from line 3 by Implication. It is a subconclusion deduced from line 3. We refer to it as **a *subconclusion,*** since it **is not the ultimate conclusion we seek. Each subconclusion we deduce is used as an additional premiss in reaching the ultimate conclusion of the argument.**

ONE LINE OR TWO?

Notice that the justifications for the inferences in lines 4 and 6 of the sample proof include a reference to one preceding line, while the justification for the inference in line 5 includes a reference to two preceding lines. Implication, which is cited in lines 4 and 6, is a rule of replacement. When it or any of the other rules of replacement are applied, only one statement is changed or transformed, so only one line number is required or relevant as a reference for the inference. Some of the rules of inference enable us to infer a conclusion from only one premiss, and these, too, since only one premiss is involved, require a reference to only one line. The rules in question are absorption, simplification, and addition. The remaining six rules of inference, however, make it possible to infer a conclusion from two premises and consequently require a reference to two lines. That explains why hypothetical syllogism, which is one of those six rules, has a two-line reference in line 5 of the proof above. In addition to hypothetical syllogism, the rules of inference which utilize two premises and hence require a reference to two lines, are these: modus ponens, modus tollens, disjunctive syllogism, constructive dilemma, and conjunction.

GETTING STARTED
ON A PROOF

Here's another sample proof:

1. (F ⊃ G) • (G ⊃ H)
2. F ∨ (I • J)/∴ H ∨ I
3. (G ⊃ H) • (F ⊃ G)   1, Com.
4. F ⊃ G   1, Simp.
5. G ⊃ H   3, Simp.
6. F ⊃ H   4, 5, H. S.
7. (F ∨ I) • (F ∨ J)   2, Dist.
8. F ∨ I   7, Simp.
9. ~ F ⊃ I   8, Impl.
10. ~ H ⊃ ~ F   6, Trans.
11. ~ H ⊃ I   10, 9, H. S.
12. H ∨ I   11, Impl.

Occasionally, you may be at a loss as to how to begin a proof. In such cases it sometimes helps to look at the conclusion. In the sample proof above, the conclusion is H ∨ I. H is found in the first premiss, and I in the second. How, then, can each be extracted from its respective premiss? Or how can the statements other than H and I be taken out of their respective premisses? These questions sometimes enable you to begin. In the proof, notice that G is eliminated from the first premiss in lines 3 through 6, while J is eliminated from the second premiss in lines 7 and 8.

In some cases, an idea for beginning a proof can be obtained by working back from the conclusion. In this approach, we ask what the last line before the conclusion might possibly be. In the case of H ∨ I, these three possibilities suggest themselves: H, I ∨ H, and ~H ⊃ I. If H is the last line before the conclusion, the conclusion follows by addition, while if I ∨ H is that line, the conclusion follows by commutation. Neither of these possibilities emerges in the sample proof, which shows that the technique of working backward from a conclusion is not an infallible guide to a proof strategy. However, it is worth noting that in the sample proof the conclusion did follow from ~H ⊃ I.

If the suggestions above do not solve the problem of getting started on a proof, take a sheet of scratch paper and begin combining different lines in pairs to determine whether anything begins to emerge. If you are working with an argument which you have symbolized, recheck your symbolization. An error in symbolizing can render a valid argument invalid, with the result that no proof is possible. If the argument is valid and symbolized correctly, you are sure to come up with a workable idea at some point! Finally, in developing proof strategies there is no substitute for practice. That's the reason for some of the exercises below.

You're now ready to try your hand at Exercises VI through XI.

Summary

In this chapter, we have examined arguments whose premisses and conclusions are truth-functional propositions. We began by establishing a convention for presenting these arguments. Next, we developed the truth table technique and the method of assigning truth values for demonstrating their validity or invalidity. Finally, we developed the method of formal proof, which enables us to demonstrate the validity of valid arguments. In the following paragraphs, we summarize the chief points concerning these conventions and methods which you should understand in order to work the exercises below. We begin with the conventions and proceed to the methods.

The premisses of symbolized arguments are written, each on a separate line, one after another. The conclusion is placed to the right of the last premiss and on the same line with it. To ensure that the conclusion is not confused with the last premiss, the two are separated by a slanted line and the conclusion is introduced by "∴". In the technique of formal proof, each of the premisses is numbered in consecutive order for ease of reference.

In the truth table technique, we establish guide columns for each simple proposition in the argument and use these to derive further columns for each of the premisses and the conclusion. In order to determine whether the argument is valid, we seek out the rows of the truth table in which each and every premiss is true. If the conclusion in any one of these rows is false, the argument is invalid. Otherwise, it is valid.

To demonstrate invalidity by assigning truth values, we assign truth values to the simple propositions in the argument, ensuring that each is assigned the same truth value in each of its occurrences. We begin the process of assigning truth values with the conclusion, giving its simple proposition or propositions truth values which make it false. Next, we proceed to the premisses, attempting to make each and every one of them true by assigning truth values to their component simple propositions. If we succeed in this process, we demonstrate that the argument is invalid, since in valid arguments it is impossible for the conclusion to be false when the premisses are true.

Formal proofs use rules of replacement and rules of inference. Rules of replacement are logical equivalencies which enable statements on one side of the triple bar to be replaced by statements on the other side wherever they occur. Rules of inference are valid argument forms consisting in either one or two premisses and a conclusion. Unlike rules of replacement, which can be applied to parts of lines, these rules must be applied to lines taken as a whole.

To construct a formal proof, symbolize the propositions of the argument and write them out as explained in the second paragraph of this summary. Next, apply the rules of replacement and inference until the conclusion is deduced. The last line of the proof is always the conclusion. Every other line of the proof is a subconclusion which serves as an additional premiss in deducing the conclusion of the argument.

RULES FOR FORMAL PROOFS OF VALIDITY

Rules of Replacement

1. **Double Negation (D.N.)**
   $p \equiv \sim\sim p$
2. **DeMorgan's Theorems (DeM.)**
   $\sim(p \bullet q) \equiv (\sim p \vee \sim q)$
   $\sim(p \vee q) \equiv (\sim p \bullet \sim q)$
3. **Distribution (Dist.)**
   $[p \bullet (q \vee r)] \equiv [(p \bullet q) \vee (p \bullet r)]$
   $[p \vee (q \bullet r)] \equiv [(p \vee q) \bullet (p \vee r)]$
4. **Commutation (Com.)**
   $(p \bullet q) \equiv (q \bullet p)$
   $(p \vee q) \equiv (q \vee p)$
5. **Association (Assoc.)**
   $[p \bullet (q \bullet r)] \equiv [(p \bullet q) \bullet r]$
   $[p \vee (q \vee r)] \equiv [(p \vee q) \vee r]$

6. **Material Implication (Impl.)**
   $(p \supset q) \equiv (\sim p \vee q)$
7. **Material Equivalence (Equiv.)**
   $(p \equiv q) \equiv [(p \bullet q) \vee (\sim p \bullet \sim q)]$
   $(p \equiv q) \equiv [(p \supset q) \bullet (q \supset p)]$
8. **Exportation (Exp.)**
   $[(p \bullet q) \supset r] \equiv [p \supset (q \supset r)]$
9. **Transposition (Trans.)**
   $(p \supset q) \equiv (\sim q \supset \sim p)$
10. **Tautology (Taut.)**
    $p \equiv (p \vee p)$
    $p \equiv (p \bullet p)$

Rules of Inference

1. **Modus Ponens (M.P.)**
   $p \supset q$
   p
   $\therefore q$
2. **Modus Tollens (M.T.)**
   $p \supset q$
   $\sim q$
   $\therefore \sim p$
3. **Hypothetical Syllogism (H.S.)**
   $p \supset q$
   $q \supset r$
   $\therefore p \supset r$
4. **Disjunctive Syllogism (D.S.)**
   $p \vee q$
   $\sim p$
   $\therefore q$
5. **Constructive Dilemma (C.D.)**
   $(p \supset q) \bullet (r \supset s)$
   $p \vee r$
   $\therefore q \vee s$

6. **Absorption (Abs.)**
   $p \supset q$
   $\therefore p \supset (p \bullet q)$
7. **Simplification (Simp.)**
   $p \bullet q$
   $\therefore p$
8. **Conjunction (Conj.)**
   p
   q
   $\therefore p \bullet q$
9. **Addition (Add.)**
   p
   $\therefore p \vee q$

Exercises

Answers to questions marked with an asterisk may be found in the back of the text.

I. Determine the validity or invalidity of the following by means of a truth table. For invalid arguments, indicate the row or rows which indicate invalidity.

1. F ⊃ G/∴ ~F ⊃ ~G

2. F/∴ F ⊃ G

3. F
   G/∴ F ∨ G

*4. F ⊃ G
   G ∨ ~G/∴ ~F

5. F ∨ G/∴ ~G

6. ~F ∨ ~G/∴ (F • G) ⊃ H

7. F ∨ G
   G/∴ F

8. F ⊃ G
   F ⊃ H
   G ∨ ~H/∴ ~F

*9. F ⊃ (G • H)/∴ F ⊃ G

10. (F • G) ⊃ H/∴ G ⊃ H

11. (F ⊃ G) • (F ⊃ H)/∴ F ⊃ (G • H)

12. (F ⊃ G) • (H ⊃ I)
   F ∨ H/∴ G ∨ I

II. Demonstrate the invalidity of the following arguments by assigning truth values.

1. ~(F • G) ⊃ H /∴ (F • G) ⊃ H

2. (I ⊃ J) • (K ⊃ L)
   J ∨ L/∴ I ∨ K

3. M ⊃ N
   O ⊃ N/∴ M ⊃ O

*4. P ⊃ (Q ⊃ R)/∴ Q ⊃ (R ⊃ P)

5. S ∨ (T • U)/∴ (S ∨ T) • U

6. V ⊃ W
   ~V/∴ W

7. (X ⊃ Y) ∨ (~Y ⊃ X)/∴ X ≡ Y

8. A ⊃ (B ∨ C)
A ⊃ ~(B ∨C)/∴ A ∨ C

*9. D ⊃ (E ∨ F)
(E ∨ F) ⊃ ~D/∴ D ∨ E

10. (G • H) ⊃ I
J ⊃ ~I/∴ G ⊃ J

III. For each of the following arguments, state the rule of replacement which allows the conclusion to be inferred from the premiss. Only the first five rules of replacement are used in this exercise. Use the suggested abbreviations for these rules.

> Examples: F • (G ∨ R)/∴ (G ∨ R) • F   Answer:Com.
> H ⊃ (C • K)/∴ H ⊃ ~(~C ∨ ~K)   Answer: DeM.

1. A ⊃ (B • C)/∴ A ⊃ (C • B)

2. ~~(D ∨ E) /∴ D ∨ E

3. (H • I) • (J • K)/∴ H • [I • (J • K)]

*4. ~R ⊃ ~(S • T)/∴ ~R ⊃ (~S ∨ ~T)

5. F • (G ∨ H)/∴ (F • G) ∨ (F • H)

6. ~(S ≡ T) ∨ ~ [~(U • V) ∨ (W ∨ X)]
∴ ~(S ≡ T) ∨ [~~(U • V) • ~(W ∨ X)]

7. Y • [Z ∨ (A ⊃ B)]/∴ (Y • Z) ∨ [Y • (A ⊃ B)]

8. Rv (~T ∨ ~S)/∴ (R ∨ ~T) ∨ ~S

*9. (L ∨ M) • (N • M)/∴ (M ∨ L) • (N • M)

10. O ∨ P/∴ O ∨ ~~P

IV. For each of the following arguments, state the rule of replacement which allows the concluson to be inferred from the premises. Only rules of replacement 6 through 10 are used in this exercise. Use the suggested abbreviations of these rules.

> Examples: (O ⊃ P) ∨ (O ⊃ P)/∴ (O ⊃ P)   Answer: Taut.
> R ⊃ (S • T)/∴ ~(S • T) ⊃ ~R   Answer: Trans.

1. S ∨ (T • T)/∴ S ∨ T

2. (R ∨ ~Q) ∨ ~T/∴ (~R ⊃ ~Q) ∨ ~T

3. (Q • R) ⊃ S/∴ ~S ⊃ ~(Q • R)

*4. L ⊃ (M ∨ M)/∴ L ⊃ M

5. N ⊃ [(O ⊃ P) ⊃ (Q ⊃ R)]
∴ N ⊃ [~(Q ⊃ R) ⊃ ~(O ⊃ P)]

6. A ⊃ (B ⊃ C)/∴ (A • B) ⊃ C

7. [B • (C ∨ D)] ∨ [~B • ~(C ∨ D)]/∴ B ≡ (C ∨ D)

8. ~V ⊃ (W ⊃ ~X)/∴ V ∨ (W ⊃ ~X)

*9. (D • E) ⊃ (F ∨ G)/∴ D ⊃ [E ⊃ (F ∨ G)]

10. [(M • N) ⊃ (O ⊃ P)] • [(O ⊃ P) ⊃ (M • N)]
∴ (O ⊃ P) ≡ (M • N)

V. For each of the following arguments, state the rule of inference which allows the conclusion to be inferred from the premiss or premisses. Use the suggested abbreviations for the rules.

Example: (P • Q) ⊃ (R ∨ S)
(R ∨ S) ⊃ (T ∨ ~U)/∴ (P • Q) ⊃ (T ∨ ~U)   Answer: H.S.

1. A ⊃ (B • C)
~(B • C)/∴ ~A

2. G • H/∴ (G • H) ∨ I

3. L ⊃ O
(J • K) ⊃ L/∴ (J • K) ⊃ O

*4. [(J • K) ⊃ O] • [P ⊃ (Q ∨ ~R)]
(J • K) ∨ P/∴ O ∨ (Q ∨ ~R)

5. T ⊃ (U ⊃ V)
T/∴ (U ⊃ V)

6. (D • E) ⊃ F/∴ (D • E) ⊃ [(D • E) • F]

7. (G • H) ∨ I
~I/∴ G • H

8. (M • N) • O/∴ (M • N)

*9. (M • N)
~S/∴ ~S • (M • N)

10. (U ⊃ V)/∴ (U ⊃ V) ∨ (W ⊃ X)

VI. Using the rules of inference and the rules of replacement, provide a justification for each line in the following proofs of validity. For examples of how to proceed, see the solutions to 4 and 9 in the Solutions to Selected Exercises section.

1. 1. A ⊃ (B • C)

2. A/∴ A • C

3. B • C

4. C • B

    5. C

    6. A • C

2. 1. (D ⊃ E) ⊃ F/∴ (F ∨ D) • (F ∨ ~E)

    2. ~(D ⊃ E) ∨ F

    3. ~(~D ∨ E) ∨ F

    4. (D • ~E) ∨ F

    5. F ∨ (D • ~E)

    6. (F ∨ D) • (F ∨ ~E)

3. 1. (F • G) ⊃ H

    2. H ⊃ ~G/∴ G ⊃ ~F

    3. (F • G) ⊃ ~G

    4. F ⊃ (G ⊃ ~G)

    5. F ⊃ (~G ∨ ~G)

    6. F ⊃ ~G

    7. G ⊃ ~F

*4. 1. [(A ⊃ B) • (B ⊃ A)] ⊃ (C • D)/∴ ~(A ≡ B) ∨ C

    2. (A ≡ B) ⊃ (C • D)

    3. ~(A ≡ B) ∨ (C • D)

    4. [~(A ≡ B) ∨ C] •[~(A ≡ B) ∨ D]

    5. ~(A ≡ B) ∨ C

5. 1. I ⊃ (J ⊃ K)

    2. I • ~K/ ∴ ~J

    3. I

    4. J ⊃ K

    5. ~K • I

    6. ~K

    7. ~J

6. 1. ~(L ⊃ M) ⊃ N

    2. ~M/∴ L ⊃ N

    3. ~N ⊃ (L ⊃ M)

    4. (~N • L) ⊃ M

    5. ~(~N • L)

    6. N ∨ ~L

    7. ~L ∨ N

    8. L ⊃ N

7. 1. H ⊃ I

    2. (H • I) ⊃ J/∴ H ⊃ J

    3. (I • H) ⊃ J

    4. I ⊃ (H ⊃ J)

    5. H ⊃ (H ⊃ J)

    6. (H • H) ⊃ J)

    7. H ⊃ J

8. 1. R ⊃ S

    2. ~~R

    3. [(S ∨ T) ∨ U] ⊃ V/∴ V

    4. R

    5. S

    6. S ∨ (T ∨ U)

    7. (S ∨ T) ∨ U

    8. V

*9. 1. ~F ∨ G

    2. ~F ⊃ H

    3. ~I ⊃ ~H/∴ ~I ⊃ G

    4. F ⊃ G

    5. H ⊃ I

    6. (F ⊃ G) • (H ⊃ I)

    7. F ∨ H

    8. G ∨ I

    9. I ∨ G

    10. ~I ⊃ G

10. **1.** C ∨ (D • E)

 2. ~(C ∨ D) ∨ E

 3. ~E • ~F/∴ C ⊃ G

 4. (C ∨ D) • (C ∨ E)

 5. C ∨ D

 6. (C ∨ D) ⊃ E

 7. ~E ⊃ ~(C ∨ D)

 8. ~E

 9. ~(C ∨ D)

 10. ~C • ~D

 11. ~C

 12. ~C ∨ G

 13. C ⊃ G

VII. Using the rules of inference and the rules of replacement, construct a formal proof of validity for each of the following:

 1. **1.** (N • O) ∨ (~N • ~O)

 2. ~O • ~P/∴ ~N

 2. **1.** (S • ~T) ⊃ U

 2. ~S ⊃ V/∴ ~(V ∨ T) ⊃ U

 3. **1.** ~W ∨ X

 2. ~(Y ∨ X) ∨ W

 3. ~ X/∴ ~Y

 *4. **1.** K ∨ L

 2. ~L • M/∴ K • M

 5. **1.** O ≡ P

 2. ~Q ∨ P

 3. R ⊃ O/∴ ~(R • ~P)

 6. **1.** Q

 2. ~R

  3. (Q ∨ R) ⊃ S

  4. ~S ∨ R/∴ ~Q

 7. 1. ~E ⊃ F

  2. (~E ∨ G) • [(~E • F) ⊃ ~I]

  3. ~G ⊃ J/∴ ~G ⊃ (~I • J)

 8. 1. (~Z ∨ A) • (B ⊃ C)

  2. ~A

  3. ~(Z • B) ⊃ (D ⊃ E)/∴ D ⊃ (D • E)

*9. 1. ~(K • L) ⊃ ~M

  2. M

  3. K ∨ N/∴ (~N ∨ ~O) ⊃ K

10. 1. Z

  2. W • X

  3. (Y • Z) ⊃ V/∴ W ∨ ~Y

VIII. Some of the following arguments are invalid. Construct a formal proof of validity for all valid arguments, and a proof of invalidity by the method of assigning truth values for the invalid arguments. Note: Your first step after symbolizing each argument should be to attempt a proof of invalidity. If you do not succeed in demonstrating invalidity, construct a proof of validity. Use the suggested symbols.

 1. If it is hot in the valley, then he will remain on the mountain. He will not remain on the mountain, so it is not hot in the valley. (H, R)

 2. He went to bed either because he was weary or because he found our company boring. He was obviously weary, so he must not have found our company boring. (W, B)

 3. If he was evasive, then the investment is risky or he lacks the money to invest. We know that the investment is risky, but he has the money to invest. Therefore, he was not evasive. (E, R, L)

 *4. If Marcy is right, our economic problems are due to our fiscal policy. If our economic problems are due to our fiscal policy, then it is time for a change at the top. It's time for a change at the top, so Marcy is right. (R, F, C)

 5. If Nick wins the bet, then he's happy, and if he's happy, he's insufferable. He's not insufferable, so he didn't win. (W, H, I)

 6. The party is either on Friday or Saturday. If the party is on Friday, then Thomas cannot attend and if it is on Saturday, then Alzada cannot attend. Therefore, either Thomas cannot attend or Alzada can't. (F, S, T, A)

 7. If the fence runs north and south, then if the gold is hidden twenty paces to the right of that oak tree, then Luke was lying about the old pirate's map. Luke was lying about the map, but the fence runs north and south, all right. I conclude that the gold is hidden twenty paces to the right of that oak tree. (F, G, L)

8. If Iris is the dancer who told Luke about the old pirate's map, then either Nick lied when he said she has fallen arches or he's never been in Rome on a Saturday night. Nick wasn't lying about those fallen arches, but he has been in Rome on a Saturday night. Therefore, Iris isn't the dancer who told Luke about the old pirate's map. (D, A, R)

*9. Either the party of the people will win a majority of seats or if basic freedoms are curtailed then the party of the right wins a majority of seats. The party of the right does not win a majority of seats. Therefore, if the party of the people does not win a majority of seats, then basic freedoms are curtailed. (P, F, R)

10. If Von Ragastein is a spy, then either his mistress is deceived or England is in danger. Either the czar is dedicated to peace or Von Ragastein is a spy. The czar is not dedicated to peace and Von Ragastein's mistress is not deceived. Therefore, England is in danger. (S, M, E, C)

IX. Construct a formal proof of validity or of invalidity, the latter by the method of assigning truth values, for each of the following arguments.

1. If you flirt with Felicia and hang out with Harry, then you don't pay attention to your poor old mother. Therefore, if you pay attention to your poor old mother, then if you flirt with Felicia then you don't hang out with Harry. (F, H, M)

2. If you flirt with Felicia and hang out with Harry, then you don't pay attention to your poor old mother. Therefore, if you don't hang out with Harry, then if you flirt with Felicia then you don't pay attention to your poor old mother. (F, H, M)

3. Either a nuclear threat is not imminent or it is urgent that we undo the damage to security which has already been done. If either the view of the current oversight committee is correct or it is urgent that we undo the damage to security which has already been done, then a nuclear threat is imminent. Therefore, the view of the current oversight committee is not correct. (T, U, V)

*4. Either the killer was careless or he did not leave his prints on the pistol. If he left no prints on the pistol we'll have to find some other clue as to his identity. This killer was not careless. If we have to find some other clue as to his identity, then in the interim we'll have to think of a convincing story for the press. You see what follows: either we think of a convincing story for the press or we look stupid. (K, P, C, T, S)

5. If her hand is forced and the stakes are high, then either she denies responsibility or she points the finger of blame at someone else. It is not the case that if the stakes are high, then she denies responsibility. Therefore, her hand is not forced. (F: Her hand is forced. S: The stakes are high. D: She denies responsibility. P: She points the finger of blame at someone else.)

6. If Allison accepts, then Bill has a date for the prom. It is not the case both that Carol is the first person on the dance floor and that Bill does not have a date for the prom. Therefore, either Allison does not accept or Carol is the first person on the dance floor.

7. If Crudmoeller leads with his left, then Meuller fakes to the left and Louie screams for blood. Ebenezer lays his money on Meuller only if Meuller fakes to the left. Sweat rolls down Meuller's face but he doesn't fake to the left. Therefore, either Crudmoeller doesn't lead with his left or Meuller doesn't fake to the left. (C, M, L, E, S)

8. If Crudmoeller feints to the left, then Jones counters with a right cross. If Carlotta places a bet on Jones, then Davis raises the odds against Crudmoeller. Either Jones counters with a right cross or Carlotta places a bet on Jones. Therefore, if Crudmoeller does not feint to the left, then Davis raises the odds against Crudmoeller. (F: Crudmoeller feints to the left. C: Jones counters with a right cross. P: Carlotta places a bet on Jones. R: Davis raises the odds against Crudmoeller.)

*9. If production increases but sales decrease, a surplus develops. The company will lower its prices if a surplus develops, but it will also lower its prices if it achieves new economies in production. The company does not achieve new economies in production although production increases. Therefore, the company either lowers its prices or develops new products. (P, S, D, L, E, N)

10. If Frank jumped the train outside of Syracuse and Ginger waited at the station until dawn, then Helvitia is Frank's girl. Only if the square root of two is a natural number is Helvitia Frank's girl. Helvitia is not Frank's girl and Ginger did not wait at the station until dawn. Therefore, if Frank jumped the train outside of Syracuse then Inez plans to have Frank arrested in Indianapolis. (F: Frank jumped the train outside of Syracuse. G: Ginger waited at the station until dawn. H: Helvitia is Frank's girl. S: The square root of two is a natural number. I: Inez plans to have Frank arrested in Indianapolis.)

X. Construct a formal proof of validity or of invalidity, the latter by the method of assigning truth values, for each of the following arguments.

1. It is either the case that Frank was in charge of intelligence or Grunfeld was the target and Hasan was not implicated in the plot, or that Irwin was not a double agent or Josephson was the assassin known as the "Jackal." It follows that if Irwin was a double agent and Josephson was not the assassin known as the "Jackal," then it is not the case both that Frank was not in charge of intelligence and that Hasan was not implicated in the plot and Grunfeld was the target. (F: Frank was in charge of intelligence. G: Grunfeld was the target. H: Hasan was implicated in the plot. I: Irwin was a double agent. J: Josephson was the assassin known as the "Jackal.")

2. If a wire is broken or the switch not thrown, then the light will not light and the chickens will freeze. Either the wire is broken or the switch not thrown or the insulation is broken. If the insulation is broken, then the chickens will be electrocuted. Therefore, either it is not the case that the wire is broken or the switch not thrown or the chickens are electrocuted. (W, S, L, F, I, E)

3. If Wilcox scores on an end run, then Christine cheers and Kloughless remains on the sidelines for the duration of the game. Christine doesn't cheer and Kloughless doesn't remain on the sidelines. Therefore, if Wilcox scores on an

end run only if Christine cheers, then Wilcox doesn't score on an end run. (W, C, K)

*4. If Frank fumbles on the forward pass and Audelia rolls her eyes in disdain, then Kloughless asks her to the dance on Saturday night. If Kloughless asks her to the dance on Saturday night and Wimpoutsky is off sides on the play then Audelia takes a pass on the dance. Wimpoutsky is off sides on the play, but Audelia (incredibly) does not take a pass on the dance. Therefore, either Frank does not fumble on the forward pass or Audelia does not roll her eyes in disdain. (F, A, K, W, P: Audelia takes a pass on the dance.)

5. If production increases but sales decrease a surplus develops. The company will lower its prices if a surplus develops, but it will also lower its prices if it achieves new economies in production. The company achieves new economies in production although production does not increase. Therefore, the company either lowers its prices or develops new products. (P, S, D, L, E, N)

6. Clovis's attending the lawn party is a sufficient condition of his having to drink Russian tea, and watching television is a necessary condition of his going to his club. If he drinks Russian tea or goes to his club, he becomes ill. But he does not become ill. Therefore, Clovis neither attends the lawn party nor goes to his club. (L, R, T, C, I)

7. If reinforcements do not arrive then lives are lost and the enemy prevails. If the supply lines are defended then the enemy does not prevail. Therefore, it is not the case that the supply lines are defended and reinforcements do not arrive. (R: Reinforcements arrive. L: Lives are lost. E: The enemy prevails. S: The supply lines are defended.)

8. If Reginald does not give up his suit and Mrs. Fitzhugh remains helpful, Laetitia may eventually give her consent and there will be a wedding. If Mrs. Fitzhugh remains helpful but Reginald does not give up his suit, then it may be possible to convince Laetitia anyway. If Laetitia can be convinced anyway, she may eventually give her consent. If Reginald does not give up, then Mrs. Fitzhugh will remain helpful. Therefore, Laetitia may eventually give her consent. (R, F, L, W, C)

*9. If Sally is wise and a crisis occurs, then her burden will not be unbearable and she will be true to her word. If a crisis occurs then she will not be true to her word. Therefore, either Sally is not wise or a crisis does not occur. (W, C, B, T)

10. If Barb files for divorce, then her family will either back her up or take the side of her husband. Barb's daughter will not be happy unless the court issues an order of protective custody. If either the court does not issue an order of protective custody or Barb's family takes the side of her husband then Barb's life is miserable. Barb files for divorce. Therefore, if Barb's daughter is happy then Barb's family does not back her up and her life is miserable. (F: Barb files for divorce. B: Barb's family backs her up. T: Barb's family takes the side of her husband. H: Barb's daughter will be happy. C: The court issues an order of protective custody. M: Barb's life is miserable.)

XI. Symbolize the following arguments and construct formal proofs of their validity. Use the suggested notation in your symbolizations.

1. If Marlowe is the author of some plays attributed to Shakespeare, then Berkowitz is incredulous and the novels of Mickey Spillane are timeless. If Marlowe is not the author of some plays attributed to Shakespeare, then literary criticism is not an exact science. If literary criticism is not an exact science then Berkowitz is incredulous. It follows that either Marlowe is not the author of some plays attributed to Shakespeare or Berkowitz is incredulous. (M, B, S, C)

2. Rachel reads Hume only if she is an independent thinker. Rachel reads Hume, or she is an independent thinker, or she does not find television advertising objectionable. She is not an independent thinker. Therefore, Rachel does not find television advertising objectionable. (H: Rachel reads Hume. T: Rachel is an independent thinker. A: She finds television advertising objectionable.)

3. If you understand the evil which lurks within the hearts of humans and if you comprehend the good of which they are capable, then you have the capacity to be a saint. Therefore, if you lack the capacity to be a saint, then if you understand the evil which lurks in the hearts of humans, then you do not comprehend the good of which they are capable. (E, G, S)

*4. Allison is angry and Betty is bemused if and only if Carlotta is incorruptible. Allison's anger is a sufficient condition of Betty's bemusement. Therefore, either it is not the case that Carlotta is corruptible and Allison is angry or it is the case that Betty is bemused. (A: Allison is angry. B: Betty is bemused. C: Carlotta is corruptible.)

5. If God is good then the claims of theologians are true. If either the claims of theologians are true or one follows Pascal's advice then attendance at church or synagogue is indicated. Therefore, if God is good then attendance at church or synagogue is indicated. (G, T, P, C, S)

6. If Roxmeier (the family dog) does not mark the furniture and his master pets him, then Roxmeier is either well trained or experiencing kidney failure. If Roxmeier does not mark the furniture, then if he is well trained, then his master may leave him in the house alone without fear. Either Roxmeier marks the furniture or if Roxmeier is experiencing kidney failure then a visit to the vet is indicated. Roxmeier does not mark the furniture and his master pets him. Therefore, either his master may leave him in the house alone without fear or a visit to the vet is indicated. (M: Roxmeier marks the furniture. P: His master pets him. T: Roxmeier is well trained. F: Roxmeier is experiencing kidney failure. H: His master may leave him in the house alone without fear. V: A visit to the vet is indicated.)

7. If Rocco shops in discount stores, then if he is a compulsive consumer his garage is filled with the discarded relics of a bygone modernity. If he is a compulsive consumer, then if his garage is filled with the discarded relics of a bygone modernity, then his house contains electrical appliances of every de-

scription. Therefore, if Rocco shops in discount stores, then if he is a compulsive consumer, then his house contains electrical appliances of every description. (S: Rocco shops in discount stores. C: He is a compulsive consumer. G: His garage is filled with the discarded relics of a bygone modernity. H: His house contains electrical appliances of every description.)

8. If the band is hired, then if Pauline plays lead, the management is pleased. If the band is hired, then if the singer doesn't yodel, the management is pleased. The tables are empty and the management isn't pleased. Therefore, either the band isn't hired or it is not the case that either Pauline plays lead or the singer doesn't yodel. (B, P, M, S, T)

*9. Either Wilfrid the Snatcher is not invited to the house party or Mrs. Peter Pigeoncote sends her regrets to the host. If Wilfrid is invited, then the host anticipates the loss of some part of his silver service. If Mrs. Peter Pigeoncote sends her regrets to the host, then if the host anticipates the loss of some part of his silver service then some member of his family must make a friendly inquisition through Wilfrid's baggage on the eve of his departure. Therefore, if Wilfrid the Snatcher is invited to the house party, then some member of the host's family must make said inquisition. (W, P, S, I)

10. If Wilfrid the Snatcher is invited to the house party, then both Mrs. Peter Pigeoncote and Mrs. Consuelo van Bullyon will send their regrets to the host. If either Mrs. Peter Pigeoncote or Mrs. Consuelo van Bullyon send their regrets to the host, then Wilfrid will have the scotch to himself. Therefore, if Wilfrid the Snatcher is invited to the house party he will have the scotch to himself. (W, P, B, S)

Appendix I

SPOTTING ARGUMENTS AND WRITING ARGUMENTATIVE ESSAYS

This appendix is divided into two sections. The first, which is intended to provide help in identifying arguments in writing, distinguishes reports and descriptions from writing containing arguments. The second considers the organization of argumentative essays and offers some practical suggestions for writing them. It is not necessary to read the first section in order to understand the second, so if you have no difficulty spotting arguments and your chief interest is in writing, you can skip over the first section.

DISTINGUISHING ARGUMENTS, REPORTS, AND DESCRIPTIONS

When its premises and conclusions have been identified and put in their proper place, an argument is seen to be an orderly arrangement of propositions whose essential and infallible mark is an assertion that some proposition, or some propositions, imply another proposition. The propositions which imply another proposition in an argument are the premises; the proposition implied is the conclusion. Premises provide the evidence for the conclusion. They are its proffered proof. If they do their proper work, the conclusion of the argument logically follows from them. The premises are the warrant, justification, and ground for the conclusion; and if the conclusion is thought of as the target of an argument, the premises are so many arrows aimed at it. This passage contains an argument:

There are two applicants for the position in sales. Justine Pearson, who was the first to apply, has a high school diploma and two years experience as a checker in a grocery store. Cheryl Brown, our other applicant, has a bachelor's degree in business and five years experience as a salesperson for one of our competitors. Since her education exceeds that of Ms. Pearson, and since her work experience is directly related to our needs, Ms. Brown is the more qualified applicant.

In this argument, "Ms. Brown is the more qualified applicant" is the conclusion, and her education and experience as compared with the education and experience of the other applicant are the evidence given for the conclusion.

While an argument is an ordered arrangement of propositions, not all ordered arrangements of propositions are arguments. The following is a case in point:

She arrived on Flight 230 at 7:29 A.M. Her driver, who was waiting for her by the limousine, tipped his hat to her and held the door. Following that, he placed her luggage in the trunk and got behind the wheel. Not a word was said. By the time they reached the freeway, the woman was asleep, the radio playing softly in her ear.

These sentences are a report of a series of events. The sentences exhibit an order, but the essential element of an argument, which is the assertion that one proposition follows from one or more others, is lacking. Inference, in fact, appears to be beside the point in this narrative. Here is another example of a report:

Those who objected to the proposal were concerned with the high cost of its implementation. They suggested that the additional staff which would be required would tax existing facilities in the short term and make it difficult to achieve previous objectives set by the board. In addition, the reallocation of personnel which the proposal would entail would make it difficult for the company to remain competitive in its traditional markets.

In support of the proposal, it was stated that additional staff could be added gradually, as space became available. The proposal, moreover, was said to be consistent with the board's objectives and a necessary step if the company was to introduce its established products in foreign markets.

In this passage, which is like those found in the minutes of staff meetings, arguments for and against a proposal are briefly summarized, but the writer does not assert any one of the arguments. The passage contains the arguments reported, of course, but no argument is adopted or defended in the passage. If the writer of the paragraphs had reported the arguments and then gone on to defend one of the reported arguments against the others, the passage would have contained both the arguments reported and the argument defended by the writer. In that case, the passage, or the portion of it in which the writer defended his or her own argument, would have been described as an argument. As it is, however, the writer sets forth no argument of his or her own, and the passage consequently cannot be described as an argument.

Arguments should be distinguished from reports, as the previous examples indicate. **They should also be distinguished from descriptions.** The following passage contains a description.

> A short fat man, with coarse black hair, widely spaced eyes, and a broad flat nose, stood before the fireplace. He wore a bulky green knit sweater, brown cotton pants, and battered brown loafers. In one hand he held a drink; in the other, a small paper plate piled high with hors d'oeuvres.

There is no argument in this passage. Statements describing a man are set forth, but nothing is inferred from the description.

Some passages are mixed in that they combine reasoning with a report or a description. Through slight alterations, the passage above may be made to combine reasoning with description.

> I saw a short fat man, with coarse black hair, widely spaced eyes, and a broad flat nose, standing alone before the fireplace. He wore a bulky green knit sweater, brown cotton pants, and battered brown loafers. In one hand he held a drink; in the other, a small paper plate piled high with hors d'oeuvres. It seemed to me that he'd come to the party to eat, not to mingle with the other guests.

In this passage, an inference about the man by the fireplace is reported, but no attempt is made to prove that the inference is correct. The narrator's inference would be described as an observation, not an argument.

Even though the passage contains no argument, the language of argument might be used to describe the narrator's inference. We might say that the narrator concluded from the facts, which were that the man stood off to himself and held a plate piled high with food, that he had come to eat, not to mingle. We could say as well that the facts were the supporting evidence for this conclusion. Nevertheless, the narrator did not argue that his conclusion was true or that it followed from the stated facts. Instead, his or her conclusion was reported as an observation based upon the facts.

Passages which contain reasoning are not always easy to distinguish from arguments, especially since the language of arguments lends itself so well to the description of such reasoning. Nevertheless, we must remember that **while persons infer conclusions from premises in arguments, not all inferences are made in the context of arguments.** This is illustrated by the passage just examined.

Arguments, as we have described them, always contain a claim that one proposition follows from one or more other propositions. If the narrator's purpose in the passage above had been different, the passage might have contained an argument. Let us rework the material in our example once more.

My car phone rang. It was Geraldine, my secretary. She'd been told that my contact at the party would be standing by himself and that he'd be holding food in his hand. That seemed crazy to me. The gathering was a cocktail party; everyone would be holding food. I needed something else to go on. "Geraldine," I said, but the signal was lost. I swore under my breath and tossed the phone to the floorboard. As soon as this case was over I was going to get a new car phone.

A man at the desk took my hat. His eyes widened when he saw the automatic under my sport coat, but he said nothing. Perhaps the look on my face discouraged conversation.

Inside the ballroom, my eyes fell upon a short fat man, with coarse black hair, widely spaced eyes, and a broad flat nose. The jerk wore a bulky green knit sweater, brown cotton pants, and battered brown loafers. In one hand he held a drink; in the other, a small paper plate piled three inches high with hors d'oeuvres; and on the top of all that, a bagel. He was standing alone by the fireplace. He was my contact, all right. I walked over.

In this passage, the line between observation and argument has been crossed. The narrator pieces the facts together and draws a conclusion, just as the narrator did in the previous example, but this time the narrator asserts that the conclusion follows from the facts. The argument is this: My contact is supposed to be standing by himself and holding food in his hand. That man is alone, and his plate is piled high with food. Therefore, he is my contact.

We have said that reports and descriptions are not arguments. They lack an assertion that one or more propositions imply another proposition. However, the accuracy or fairness of reports and descriptions may be called into question, and the individuals who prepared them may be called upon to defend them. A defense of a report or description should not be confused with the report or description itself. The defense will consist of one or more arguments whose conclusion is that the report or description is accurate or unbiased, but the report or description itself will nevertheless not be an argument. It will be the matter under discussion, and its contents will be the subject of the arguments in its defense, but it will not itself be an argument.

WRITING ARGUMENTATIVE ESSAYS

In writing to bring others around to your point of view, you can choose either the argumentative or the persuasive essay. If you choose the argumentative essay, you use argument to achieve your purpose, and if you choose the persuasive essay, you use methods which include appeals to the motives and interests of individuals, highly charged language calculated to elicit emotional responses, and, in some cases, distortions of fact. Because the persuasive essay can be very effective, it is worth serious study. In what follows, however, our chief interest is the argumentative essay.[1] We consider the organization of the argumentative essay and then offer some practical guidelines for writing.

ORGANIZATION OF THE ARGUMENTATIVE ESSAY

Argumentative essays can be logically divided into two parts. The first is the statement of the thesis of the essay, which is the proposition or point of view defended. (The thesis is expressed in the topic sentence of the paragraph in which it appears.) The second is the statement of evidence for and against the thesis. The evidence section can be further divided into the response to evidence against the thesis and the presentation of supporting evidence.

These logical divisions occur in several orders in actual essays. Some essays begin with the statement of the thesis, but others end with it. Still others both begin and end with the thesis statement.

In essays in which the thesis is stated at the beginning, one common practice is to follow the statement with a consideration of the evidence for and against and to conclude with a brief summary. When the thesis is stated at the end, one approach is to begin the essay with a statement of a problem to be solved or a question to be answered and to follow that up with considerations for and against. At the end of the essay, the thesis is stated as the solution to the problem or the answer to the question. When the

---

[1] The tactical maneuvers considered in Chapter 11 can be adapted to the persuasive essay, so if your interest is in persuasion, you should consult that chapter.

thesis is stated at both the beginning and end, the relevant evidence is naturally sandwiched in between.

There are several possibilities for arranging the material in the evidence section, and these apply to evidence for the thesis as well as evidence against. In cases in which the evidence is not all of the same weight, these two orders of presentation are possible:

- Begin with the weakest evidence and move to the strongest, or begin with the strongest evidence and move to the weakest.

When the available strands of evidence are of approximately equal weight, these orders are possible:

- Begin with the most widely known evidence and progress to the least widely known, or begin with the least widely known and progress to the most widely known.
- Begin with the evidence which can be presented in the briefest space and move to that which requires more space, or vice versa.

When the strands of evidence are chronologically or logically connected with one another, these orders are possible:

- Begin with the evidence discovered first, and proceed to the evidence discovered most recently.
- If some evidence provides a foundation or support for other evidence, begin with the foundational evidence.

The order you choose for presentation of your thesis and the evidence for and against is best determined after you have selected your thesis and gathered your evidence. If your essay is very long, you may find after reflection and experimentation that some parts lend themselves to one kind of organization while others lend themselves to another.

Thesis Stated at Beginning

The American economy should be stimulated by reducing taxes and allocating a portion of the current budget surplus for support of the Social Security system and Medicare. First, tax reduction would leave taxpayers with more money to invest or spend. The money would contribute to the growth of industry if invested, and create and sustain jobs if spent in the marketplace for consumer goods. Second, the money allocated to Social Security and Medicare would provide support to those sectors of the economy which provide crucial services for eligible Americans, many of whom have inadequate medical insurance.

Thesis Stated at End

It is widely reported that the United States government has a budget surplus, and some are calling for a tax cut. However, the future of Social Security is uncertain, and the programs of Medicare and Medicaid are inadequate to provide the level of medical assistance needed by older Americans and the medically indigent. Americans are entitled to these programs, and no alternatives to them are available. Therefore, **the budget surplus should be used to shore up these programs, and consideration of a tax cut should be taken up only when this has been done.**

Thesis Stated at Both Beginning and End

The tax burden on the American people should be lifted. At present, there is a budget surplus in the United States, which means that the government has taken in more money than it needs for defense and other vital programs. **Since that money belongs to American taxpayers, it should be returned to them in the form of a tax cut.**

GUIDELINES FOR WRITING ARGUMENTATIVE ESSAYS

In argumentative writing, as in other forms of writing, the best procedure is to critically evaluate your work before submitting it to others. Since this process can be difficult and time-consuming, we conclude this appendix with some markers to guide you safely along the shoreline of evaluation. If you read them before you do your writing, and then again afterward, they will likely help you.

- **Selection and statement of thesis.** Provide your readers with a clear statement of your thesis. Distinguish it from other theses which may be closely associated with it in the minds of your readers. Tell your readers why the subject is important and why they should be interested in it.
- **Clarity.** Work to eliminate ambiguous sentences from your arguments, since sentences which can be interpreted in more than one way are apt to be confusing. In addition, remember the audience for whom you are writing. Are you writing for experts on some subject or for people who know nothing about it? If for the latter, you'll have to "fill in the background." Suppose that you've read a novel by Toni Morrison in a literature class but that your little sister at home hasn't. In that case, you can't expect her to be interested in the novel, or understand your analysis of it, unless you tell her something about it.

  Passages which seem clear to you at the time you write them may not seem clear to you at a later time. To give yourself a little objectivity in looking at your work, put it aside for two or three days while you work on something else, and then read it through again. When you find an awkward sentence, or one which puzzles you, ask yourself what the problem is, and do the rewriting necessary to make it say just what you want it to say.
- **Accuracy.** Check and double-check your facts. Avoid hearsay evidence where possible, and when describing events or scientific experiments, draw as clear a distinction as possible between what can be known with certainty and what cannot. Also, give proper credit to your sources when you use information gained from someone else.
- **Completeness.** Provide adequate coverage of the topic you've selected. Don't omit anything of importance or anything which your readers might think is important. Do your best to anticipate questions or objections to your work, and respond to them even if they seem minor or trivial to you. Remember that you're not writing to convince yourself of the truth of what you're saying, but to convince others.
- **Consistency.** Don't make one claim in one part of your paper and a contradictory claim in another part. Leave it to others to disagree with you. Don't contradict yourself.
- **Relevance.** In Chapter 2, we define *relevant evidence* as "evidence which, if true, increases the likelihood that a proposition being defended is true." Our advice here is to rely upon relevant evidence in constructing your arguments. Relevance

in writing also includes sticking to the point. Once you know your thesis, resist the temptation to depart from it. Extraneous considerations distract your reader from the point you want to prove.

- **Fairness.** Avoid cheap tricks, including distortion of evidence and gratuitous emotional appeals, in arguing for your thesis. You might secure momentary acceptance of your position through such maneuvers, but in the long run, careful analyses of the facts coupled with patient attempts to eliminate confusions and draw attention to neglected or overlooked considerations are more likely to win the day.
- **Inventiveness.** Don't be content to repeat what others have said. Put the relevant material together in your own way and add your own unique insights. Your perspective may be just the one that's needed to advance the discussion!

Exercises

Answers to questions marked with an asterisk may be found in the back of the text.

I. For each of the following passages, select the classification which seems most appropriate.

  a. Contains a report of fact or opinion, but no inference or argument is evident.
  b. Contains a description, but does not include an inference or argument.
  c. Contains one or more inferences, but no argument.
  d. Contains an argument.

   Indicate your classification by the appropriate letter. State the conclusion in any of the passages which contain arguments.

   1. He was so ugly that people turned in the street to look at him. He could never efface himself in a crowd. He towered above most members of any crowd, and, rising above the square-set shoulders you saw the dark, ugly, striking face, and wondered who the man could be. It was a face you could never forget and never confuse with any other face, and according to your temperament it would repel or attract you. (From Cecily Ullman Sidgwick, "The Wife of Solomon.")

   2. Hakem's birthday present was larger than a bread box.

   3. Irate Citizen: I read in the paper where our high school laid off five teachers, and now I hear that we're going to accept over fifty students from the high school in Pleasant Mound to attend our school system at my tax expense. It just goes to show that the administration running our schools doesn't have the slightest idea what it's doing.

   *4. On the second of March, Lewis met with her attorney, who reportedly advised her to drop the matter. Afterward, she stepped into a diner on Black-welder Street and ordered a cup of black coffee. According to Phillips, who observed her from a booth in the rear, she seemed to know the cashier behind the counter but said nothing to him. As she sat lost in thought, her coffee grew cold before her. Around 11:30, when the diner began filling up with office workers, she laid a bill upon the counter and exited quickly. In the crowded street outside, Phillips lost her, and no one has seen her since.

5. Irate Citizen: After listening to the news about food stamp fraud, I thought about the sign in one of our local stores. It said, "We will accept food stamps for Easter candy and baskets." Then I suspect these people will go to that place over on Beecham Street to get free food to replace that spent on Easter candy and baskets.

6. It was perfectly still in the small gray house. Outside in the apple trees there were some blue-jays flitting about and calling noisily, like schoolboys fighting at their games. The kitchen was full of pale winter sunshine. It was more like late October than the first of January, and the plain little room seemed to smile back into the sun's face. The outer door was standing open into the green dooryard, and a fat small dog lay asleep on the step. A capacious cupboard stood behind Mrs. Dallett's chair and kept the wind away from her corner. Its doors and drawers were painted a clean lead-color, and there were places round the knobs and buttons where the touch of hands had worn deep into the wood. Every braided rug was straight on the floor. The square clock on its shelf between the front windows looked as if it had just had its face washed and been wound up for a whole year to come. (From Sarah Orne Jewett, "Aunt Cynthy Dallett.")

7. Letter to a Newspaper Editor: Prostitutes solicit customers along C_____ St. in broad daylight. To think that schoolchildren should be exposed to this as they walk to their neighborhood school a block away! It's outrageous! Something must be done! If the city council and the police won't bring an end to this, citizens must take action themselves.

8. Letter to a newspaper editor: Your story entitled "Widespread Drug Use in City Schools" left the impression that everyone in our high schools is a drug addict. That simply is not true. As a parent and leader of a local youth group, I have come to know many of our young people quite well, and I can tell you that they wouldn't even think of using drugs. You owe the young men and women of our city an apology. You should be printing articles which tell of the many fine achievements of our young people, rather than tearing them down with your so-called "investigative reporting."

*9. At precisely 7 o'clock in the morning, the major presented himself in full dress uniform at the office of the general and announced that his wife had left him for another man. His jaw was set and his voice firm as he spoke, but he avoided the general's eyes. How many Majors have the good fortune to marry their general's daughter as well as the misfortune of losing her?

10. The women turned onto the road which the van had taken. The road had fallen into disrepair. Its surface was marred by numerous holes. Around one curve, the surface was cracked in the middle, with one side slanting toward the valley far below. If the road had once had a center stripe, it was impossible to see it now.

11. Though he had been retired from the army for twenty years, Jim still thought of himself as a soldier. "And why not," he asked himself rhetorically. "Retired

musicians continue to think of themselves as musicians, so why can't I continue to think of myself as a soldier?"

12. "You'll notice that the desk in the photograph, and the body slumped across it, are entirely illuminated by sunlight from the windows," said Inspector Marvel.

"Yes," Sergeant Hathaway responded, "The lamp on the desk is obviously not lit."

"That means that Brewster is lying," Inspector Marvel went on.

"How is that?" asked an incredulous Hathaway. "Brewster states that he took the photograph immediately upon discovering the body."

"Yes, and he said he discovered the body in the late afternoon; but look at the shadow cast by the desk upon the bookcase."

"Yes, I see it, but I can't imagine what you're driving at."

"Think, man, think!" said Marvel. "Where does the sun rise?"

"Why, in the east."

"And on what side of the room are the windows located?"

"Hm, let's see." Hathaway's eyes rolled to the ceiling, and he looked first in one direction and then another. Finally, he said, "They're on the east side."

"That's right," said Marvel, "so . . . "

"So, I see what you mean," said Hathaway brightly. "If the sun were overhead, or in the west, the desk wouldn't cast a shadow upon the bookcase. Therefore, the photograph was taken in the morning."

"Precisely," said Marvel, reaching for his hat. "Come on."

"Where are we going?"

"We're going to pay a visit to Mr. Brewster," said Marvel over his shoulder. "I want to know why he lied about the time he discovered the body."

Hathaway threw on his coat, and followed Marvel down the hall. As he passed the soft drink machine, he fumbled in his pocket for change, but had none. Under his breath, he swore. It had been a long time since breakfast, and it would be a long time before he ate again.

13.

Laura: What is today's date?

John: Yolanda's party is next Friday, which is the twenty seventh, and this is Tuesday, so today must be the twenty fourth.

14. Dear Uncle D_____,

We had a break in the heat around here, so Ruth and I sat out in the backyard for awhile this morning. It was very pleasant. There were quite a few little squirrels chasing about in the trees and birds rustling about for food.

I particularly enjoy watching the squirrels. This morning, one leaped from one tree to another over a rather large space. The limb the squirrel landed on wasn't very large, and it bent into a half circle under the squirrel's weight. The squirrel hung on, and finally made it across the limb to the trunk of the tree.

Today, a local group is staging a reenactment of a Civil War battle which was fought near here. I learned not too long ago that U. S. Grant camped with his men just a little over five blocks from where our house now stands. The campground is in the backyard of a rather large brick house. (The house hadn't been built at the time Grant camped there.)

That's all the news. Not much has been happening.

Love,

Peter

15. Beautiful instances of experiment . . . are to be found . . . in the researches by which Dr. Wells discovered the cause of dew. If on a clear calm night a sheet or other covering be stretched a foot or two above the earth, so as to screen the ground below from the open sky, dew will be found on the grass around the screen but not beneath it. As the temperature and moistness of the air, and other circumstances, are exactly the same, the open sky must be an indispensable antecedent to dew. The same experiment is, indeed, tried for us by nature, for if we make observations of dew during two nights which differ in nothing but the absence of clouds in one and their presence in the other, we shall find that the clear open sky is requisite to the formation of dew. (From W. S. Jevons, *Elements of Logic.*)

II. Write narratives as described in each of the following.

1. Write a two-page description of one of the following: (a) The process of changing an automobile tire. Assume that your reader does not have mechanical ability and has never changed a tire. (b) The process of packing a suitcase. Explain why the process you describe is better than some others. (c) The ideal first date, including what the couple should do and how each should act toward the other.

2. Write a one- to two-page report of your chief activities last Monday. The report should be more than a list of what you did.

3. Write a one- to two-page paper in which you predict some event. Give reasons for your prediction. Do not choose something simple, such as "I predict that I won't eat breakfast tomorrow." Choose an event which involves other people and is essentially outside your control.

4. Read the following brief essay, then write a two-page paper in which you offer either a defense or a refutation of one of its theses. In your paper, explicitly state the thesis you are addressing, and follow one of the patterns of organization outlined above under the heading "Organization of the Argumentative Essay."

> In the nineteenth century, many serious and intelligent individuals believed that the human race was evolving to a state of perfection. In the early 1850s, Theodore Parker, a Transcendentalist minister, stated that by the end of the century the human race would have made sufficient moral progress to bring an end to war. By the end of the century, he said, the lion would lie down with the lamb. Others shared Parker's view.
>
> This exaggerated belief in the moral progress of humans was shattered by World War I, and the idea that the race is infinitely perfectible is slumbering for now. However, we humans love to think of ourselves as making progress, so there may come a time when intellectuals and others are again tempted to make strong claims regarding the perfectibility of the race. In anticipation of this, we should consider the criteria which it would be appropriate for us to use in determining whether moral progress has been made. We should ask ourselves what

would count as evidence that the race has progressed to a higher moral level. The question is difficult, but until we have answered it, we should avoid dogmatic pronouncements to the effect that humans today are superior to humans a decade or a century ago.

Table of Writing Exercises

The following table provides a guide to other writing exercises in this text.

CHAPTER	DESCRIPTION OF WRITING EXERCISES
3	Adding and subtracting emotive content from narratives. See "A Good Exercise," located in the box before the exercises for Chapter 3.
4	Outlining a hypothetical series of events. See Chapter 4, Exercise I, Number 1.
10	Writing an argumentative essay based on a dispute. See Chapter 10, Exercise I, Number 6.
10	Writing resolutions to disputes. See Chapter 10, Exercise III.
11	Critical analysis of a dispute of long duration. See Chapter 11, Exercise II, Number 2.

Appendix II

ACHIEVING CLARITY THROUGH DEFINITIONS

A *definition* is a statement of the meaning or meanings of a word. One meaning of the verb *define* is "to set the boundaries of." Speaking metaphorically, we can say that something defined has its borders indicated. Weight lifters speak of the definition of muscles. By this they mean the visible outline of muscles. In defining words, we attempt to state the boundaries, or discernible outlines, of their usage by some people at some particular time in some context. In this appendix, we identify several kinds of definition and consider the method of *definition by genus and difference,* which provides an excellent introduction to the examination of categorical propositions in Chapter 12.

KINDS OF DEFINITIONS

Some kinds of definition which we encounter in our attempt to achieve clarity in our thinking and writing are these:

- *Lexical definitions,* or dictionary definitions, are summary statements of the current meanings, or uses, of words. They can be accurate or inaccurate.
- An individual who introduces a new word or offers a new definition of an old word is said to provide a *stipulative definition.* Accurate lexical definitions are not arbitrary in that they report established usage, but stipulative definitions are arbitrary. By their nature, they cannot be inaccurate. In some cases, they come to be accepted by those who use the language. Examples of currently accepted words whose meaning was once stipulated are *telegraph, telephone,* and *television.* In an essay or speech, an individual may state that he or she is using a word with a particular meaning. If the meaning is new, the individual is offering a stipulative definition. If the meaning is one of several which the word already has, the individual is simply reporting his or her usage for the sake of clarity.
- The purpose of *precising definitions* is to reduce or eliminate the vagueness or ambiguity of words. Such definitions are particularly useful in cases in which words have two or more meanings which might be confused. In Chapter 5, we observe that *principle* and *rule* are often used interchangeably, but that in some cases it is useful to draw a distinction between them. When that distinction is drawn, the meaning of the terms is made more precise.

- The chief purpose of *persuasive definitions* is to influence the way in which a phenomenon is perceived. Through persuasive definitions, people attempt to create a favorable or unfavorable disposition toward something. "Religion is the opiate of the people" and "History is bunk" are examples of persuasive definitions.
- *Theoretical definitions* are constructed for some special purpose within particular areas of inquiry. In physics, *work* is defined as force times displacement in the line of force, while in logic, *valid* is defined as a deductive argument in which the premises, if true, provide conclusive evidence for the conclusion. These definitions are not always followed outside the areas of inquiry in which they are used. Outside of physics, work is often used to mean *employment* and outside of logic, valid may simply mean *legitimate,* as in "Henry had a valid claim to the throne." Theoretical definitions should not be classified as true or false but as adequate or inadequate for their intended purposes.
- Particular physical or mechanical actions are the stated meaning of terms in *operational definitions.* For Charles Sanders Peirce, who was a pioneer of this form of definition, the meaning of some terms can be indicated by pointing out the kind of response we can expect to get when we perform an action of a certain sort. In a widely reprinted article titled "How to Make Our Ideas Clear," he suggested that to say that something has *weight* is to say that it falls if no opposing force is present, and that to say that something is *hard* is to say that many other things do not scratch it. If necessary for some purpose, the hardness of an object can be specified by stating what material is being used in the scratching instrument, what surface is being scratched, and how much pressure is being applied. In this way one can be very clear about what it means to say that the surface is hard.

DEFINITION BY GENUS AND DIFFERENCE

For the practice it gives us in distinguishing good from bad definitions, we conclude this appendix with a consideration of the historically important method of *definition by genus and difference.* In this method, which was developed by the philosopher Aristotle, terms which indicate classes of things are defined by words which indicate (1) a wider class within which the defined class falls and (2) the manner in which the defined class differs from other classes which are also found within the wider class.

In definition by genus and difference the term being defined is taken to indicate a class known as a *species,* and boundaries to its use are set by placing the term within a wider class, which is known as the *genus,* and stating how it differs from other species within the same genus. The *difference* in *definition by genus and difference* refers to the distinguishing mark of the class being defined, or that which serves to differentiate it from other species within the genus. Aristotle's famous definition of *man,* by which he meant *human being,* is "the rational animal." In this case, *animal* is the genus while *rational* is the specific difference or distinguishing characteristic of the species. If *piety* is defined as "that form of justice in which one keeps one's agreements and never repays wrongs with wrongs," the genus is *justice* and the statements about keeping one's agreements and never repaying wrong with wrong are specific differences.

RULES FOR DEFINITIONS BY GENUS AND DIFFERENCE

By observing the following rules or guidelines for constructing definitions by genus and difference we can ensure, for the most part, that our definitions suit the purposes for which they are intended:

- **A definition should state the essential attributes or qualities of the species being defined.** Attributes of a bird are a spinal column, feathers, and wings. A football's qualities are its elliptical shape, length, and diameter.[1] *Essential attributes* of an object are those which cannot be removed from it without its becoming something else. These attributes are contrasted with *accidental* or *inessential qualities,* which are those whose presence or absence do not have an effect upon the nature or character of the object.

In some cases it is relatively easy to state the essential attributes of an object. Each of the qualities of birds mentioned in the last paragraph seems to be essential. Could a creature without wings be said to be a bird, or could a creature with wings but without feathers be so described? While creatures other than birds have spinal columns, could any creature without one be correctly described as a bird? It does not seem that it could.

On the other hand, it is not always easy to distinguish the essential from the accidental characteristics of an object. A football has an elliptical shape, surely, but is it essential that the object be a particular size, or inflatable, or made of some unique material such as leather? Some objects which are commonly called footballs are smaller than others. They are solid, and made of rubber. These, of course, are children's toys. Are they footballs in the strict sense of the term? This question can probably be answered with the observation that the child's toy is a football, but not one which would be accepted in serious play. The footballs which are used in high school, college, or professional games must meet certain requirements which are specified by the agencies which determine the rules of the game. Still, our question shows that on occasion we must ask ourselves what is essential to an object.

The walls of the room in which I am writing are lined with books. By *book* we mean "a collection of written or printed sheets which are bound together on one side and enclosed, as a rule, between protective covers." This seems to state the essential attributes of books. However, suppose that we expand our definition by saying that books are "things found in libraries." In saying this we have added an accidental characteristic to our definition, for while books are found in libraries, their presence there is not essential to their being books. Books are still books, after all, when they are checked out of the library. Many books, moreover, are never taken inside libraries. The problem with

---

[1] The football referred to here is the sort used for the game in the United States. In Great Britain and some other countries, the game of football, or "soccer" as it is called in the United States, is played with a round ball.

our addition to the definition is that it is a comment about books but not a statement of what they are. This same problem occurs in the definition of *attorney* as "a highly paid professional." In this definition, the part about the attorney being a professional is all right, though not specific enough to distinguish attorneys from other professionals. The part about attorneys being highly paid, however, says nothing about what attorneys are; it fails to state what is essential to being an attorney. Being highly paid is an accidental characteristic of attorneys. Some attorneys are not highly paid, some are unemployed, and some are retired, but that does not affect their status as attorneys. A better definition of *attorney* is "a person who has the legal power to act on behalf of another." This definition states the essential attribute of an attorney.

When faced with the need to define a term, it is sometimes helpful to ask whether the characteristics which spring to mind are ones which you associate with the objects denoted by the term but which other persons might not associate with them. This technique is not infallible, but in many cases it gets you started on a definition. Suppose, for example, that you are called upon to define *father*. In your case, it is to be hoped, your own father comes to mind and you think of him as a loving and helpful person. Still, you recognize that for individuals whose fathers mistreated them, the word *father* brings to mind a cruel and hateful person. Is either a loving character or hatefulness a part of the definition of father? No; while children associate these opposite characteristics with actual fathers who have them, these associations are psychological only and have no part in the definition of the term. A father by definition is simply a "male parent." The words in quotation marks indicate the essential defining characteristics.

- **A definition should not be needlessly evaluative.** Definitions can contain unnecessary judgments or opinions. The famous definition of *religion* as "the opiate of the people" is an example.[2] This is a special case of stating accidental or inessential attributes, but our rule underscores the importance of keeping evaluations out of definitions.
- **A definition should not use the term being defined.** Definitions containing the term being defined are *circular*. To say "A *woman* is a woman" is obviously circular, but "A *cause* is what produces an effect and an *effect* is what produces a cause" is circular as well. The justification for this rule is the observation that a term cannot explain its own meaning.
- **The term being defined and the definition should be equivalent.** It should be possible to replace the term being defined by the definition, and vice versa. If Aristotle's famous definition, given above, is correct we should be able to say either "Human beings are rational animals" or "Rational animals are human beings" with no gain or loss of meaning.

Definitions which break the equivalence rule are either too broad or too narrow. **A definition is *too broad* if it omits the specific difference or utilizes a genus which is too wide.** For example, the definition of *horse* as "an animal" is too broad in that it leaves off the specific difference, or attribute(s) which distinguish horses from other animals such as human beings and goats. The definition of *ewe* as "a female

---

[2] This definition is used above as an example of a persuasive definition.

animal" contains the specific difference (female), but is too broad because its genus (animal) is too wide. Genus errors like this are possible since several classes can be placed in relation to one another in an order of increasing breadth. Ewes are in the class of sheep, but sheep in turn are in the class of animals, and animals fall within the still wider class of living things. Animals is the proper genus for defining sheep, but the proper genus for defining ewes is sheep, not animals.

Definitions which exclude members of the class being defined break the equivalence rule by being *too narrow.* "Individuals between the ages of eighteen and twenty-one" is too narrow to use in a definition of *college students,* since some college students are outside those age groups. Similarly, "an individual who was born in the United States" is too narrow a definition of *United States citizen,* since naturalized citizens are excluded by the definition.

- **A definition should not be stated in obscure or figurative language.** Don't attempt to define a term whose meaning is unknown with other terms whose meanings are equally unknown. Samuel Johnson defined *net* as "a reticulated texture with small interstices" and *network* as "anything reticulated or decussated, at equal distances, with interstices between the intersections." These examples would seem to be sufficient to illustrate obscurity, though it must be remembered that a definition which is obscure to one person might not be obscure to another. One of the author's professors in undergraduate school defined a *rut* as a "grave with both ends knocked out." The statement was provocative, and some students were awestruck, but statements like the professor's should not be taken as substitutes for definitions. Metaphors are not definitions.
- **A definition should not be negative when it could be positive.** In a definition an attempt should be made to state what something is rather than what it is not. The statement that a dentist is neither a veterinarian nor a chiropractor is true, but it is not a definition of *dentist.* One might begin a definition by saying what something is not, but one should end with a positive statement if at all possible.

A definition can break more than one of the six rules. Suppose we were to define *dog* as "a short-haired pet with four legs and paws rather than hoofs." Being a pet has nothing to do with being a dog, so the definition mentions an inessential characteristic of the class of dogs. By replacing *pet* with *animal* this problem is eliminated, but the definition is still too narrow since it excludes dogs with long hair.

SAMPLE EVALUATIONS
OF DEFINITIONS

For further practice in applying the rules, we consider some other definitions.

Wife: A married female who is often found in the vicinity of the kitchen.

The words "married female" are properly the definition of *wife.* The remainder of the definition is a comment about wives which does not state attributes essential to an individual's being a wife. A wife is a wife even if she never enters a kitchen. The comment, too, may suggest a particular view of the status of women and thus be needlessly evaluative.

Human being: A biped capable of exercising reason.

Four observations regarding this definition are in order. First, *biped* means "animal with two feet," but does the person reading the definition know that? If not, then *for that person* the definition is obscure. Second, human beings ordinarily have two legs, but is the possession of two legs essential to being human? Some humans have one leg; some have none at all. Third, is the ability to exercise reason unique to humans? Are gorillas, for example, incapable of reasoning? If they are, then reasoning ability is not a differentiating characteristic of humans. Fourth, is the ability to exercise reason essential to being human? Newborn babies and comatose individuals are not capable of exercising reason, but are they not human beings? The definition is too narrow in that it eliminates these individuals.

The following definitions of *paternalism* are taken from student exams:

1. Paternalism is when government steps in to provide warning labels, or represents the consequences of doing a certain action, in regards to advertising.
2. Paternalism deals with advertising. It is concerned with government intervention in advertising. For example, cigarettes are not allowed to advertise on TV, and the cigarettes are required to have warning labels on them to warn the public.
3. Paternalism is the role government takes in protecting our interests and keeping us safe like a "parent" would.
4. Paternalism—relationship of an individual, institution, or such that acts in a guiding or authority figure to another to protect and, in other words, act like a parent.

Definitions 1 and 2 are too narrow in that they state that paternalism is limited to advertising. In that it does not limit paternalism to advertising, definition 3 is broader than 1 and 2, and better than 1 and 2 for that reason.

Definitions 1, 2, and 3 are too narrow in that they limit paternalistic acts to the government. While governments do act in a paternalistic manner on occasion, other institutions and individuals do as well. Definition 4 is superior to the others in that it does not limit paternalistic acts to the government.

The use of *parent* in 3 and 4 is arguably appropriate, though not consistent with the original meaning of *paternalism*. In Latin, *pater* means "father." The word *paternalism* originally indicated a system of governance in which citizens, employees, students, or some other group are treated in a manner in which a father would treat his children. In Latin, *mater* means "mother," but English-speaking people never adopted *maternalism* to indicate a system of governance in which individuals were treated in the manner in which a mother would treat her children. In recent years, however, many individuals have come to use the word *paternalism* to indicate parent-like actions, as opposed to actions like those of a father only. This is an example of the growth of language by generalization.

Summary

Definitions state the meaning of terms. In definition by genus and difference, the term being defined, which is taken as the species, is placed within a wider class, which is the genus, and its difference, or distinguishing characteristic, is stated. In constructing definitions by genus and difference, the following guidelines are helpful:

- State the essential attributes.
- Don't offer evaluations.
- Keep the term you're defining out of the definition.
- Strive for a definition which can be substituted for the word you're defining.
- Avoid figurative language as well as words as obscure as the one you're defining.
- State what the word means, rather than what it doesn't mean.

HELPFUL HINT

In practice, of all the rules for definition by genus and difference, the toughest to apply is probably the essential attributes rule. It's not always easy to distinguish essential from accidental qualities. It's some help (though not as much as you'd like to have) to remember that the distinction must be made in connection with the term being defined and the audience for whom the definition is intended.

The distinction between the essential and the accidental is important not just in definitions, but in other critical thinking areas as well. For example, in Chapter 5, we consider a fallacy called *accident*. In this fallacy, a generalization is applied to a case with features which render it inapplicable. In definitions, accidental characteristics are those which can be, but need not be, exhibited by the objects denoted by the term being defined. Because they may or may not be exhibited by the objects, they don't serve to distinguish those objects from others to which the term being defined does *not* refer.

Exercises

Answers to questions marked with an asterisk may be found in the back of the text.

I. Construct definitions by matching the most appropriate terms. Terms in the "Genus" and "Difference" columns may be used more than once.

Term Being Defined	Definition	
	GENUS	**DIFFERENCE**
1. Automobile	1. Boat	1. Backless
2. Beverage	2. Dog	2. Brass
3. Bicycle	3. Humor	3. Cloven hoofed
*4. Canoe	4. Instrument	4. Coarse
5. Coed	5. Mammal	5. Cutting
6. Father	6. Meal	6. Hoofed
7. Fox terrier	7. Odor	7. Light
8. Fragrance	8. Parent	8. Liquid
*9. Girl	9. Refreshment	9. Male
10. Guitar	10. Seat	10. Married
11. Hamlet	11. Vehicle	11. Pleasant
12. Horse	12. Village	12. Self-propelled
13. Knife	13. Woman	13. Small
*14. Pig		14. Stringed
15. Ribald		15. Student
16. Sire		16. Two-wheeled
17. Snack		17. Young
18. Stool		
*19. Trumpet		
20. Wife		

II. Evaluate the following definitions with reference to the rules for definitions by genus and difference. Definitions can be criticized for stating "accidental characteristics" or in other words for failing to state essential attributes. The "needlessly evaluative" definition is one form which such definitions take. Definitions may fail by being "circular," "too wide" or "too narrow," or by being stated in "obscure" or "figurative" language. They may also be "negative" rather than positive, or affirmative. The terms in quotation marks can be used as brief indications of the problems with the definitions. Remember that a particular definition can have more than one problem. Some of the definitions below may be free from difficulty. If you find one, write "No problem" as your answer.

   1. *Human beings* are featherless bipeds.
   2. *Man* is the salt of the earth.
   3. *Ethics* is that obscure discipline discussed by philosophers and other pedants.
 *4. *Furniture* is any one of several material objects used for sitting or sleeping.
   5. *Thunder* is the roar of a motorcycle.
   6. A *dinosaur* is a terrible carnivorous creature.
   7. A *planet* is a heavenly body.

8. A *locomotive* is an iron horse.

***9.** An *airplane* is a self-propelled vehicle.

10. A *unicorn* is a mythical creature.

11. A *tricycle* is a cycle with three wheels.

12. A *star* is a pinpoint of light in the firmament of human destiny.

III. For this exercise, follow the instructions for Exercise II.

1. *Evolution* is "an integration of matter and a concomitant dissipation of motion; during which the matter passes from an indefinite incoherent homogeneity to a definite coherent heterogeneity; and during which the retained motion undergoes a parallel transformation."[3]

2. *Movies* are the stuff of which dreams are made.

3. *First water* are diamonds or pearls of the highest quality.

***4.** *Minerals* are substances which can be classed neither as animal nor as vegetable.

5. *Hedonism* is the view that pleasure is the greatest good.

6. *Hair* is a woman's crowning glory.

7. A *planet* is a celestial body.

8. A *Moslem* is a person who believes in one God.

***9.** A *polytheist* is one who believes that there is more than one God.

10. A *sick individual* is one who is not well.

11. *Ethics* is the generalized meaning thought of the individual comparing the thought to specific areas and relating to other individuals.

12. *Politics* is trying to get others to do what you don't want to do yourself.

13. *Logic* has to do with questions of what people believe about thinking.

***14.** A *frog* is a vertebrate organism of the class Amphibia.

15. A *tricycle* is a velocipede.

IV. For this exercise, follow the instructions for Exercise II.[4]

1. A *phonograph* is a mechanism for recording and reproducing sounds.

2. A *sea* is a body of water, next in size to the oceans, which is entirely, or almost entirely, surrounded by land.

3. A *library* is a collection of books generally for personal use and not meant for sale.

***4.** A *wagon* is a conveyance mounted on wheels and drawn by some animal, usually a horse.

5. *Oxygen* is the most important gaseous element known, without which combustion and animal life would be impossible.

6. A *sensation* is a modification of consciousness produced by the excitation of a cortical center through the agency of an afferent nerve current.

---

[3] This definition by Herbert Spencer is quoted in Adam Leroy Jones, *Logic: Inductive and Deductive: An Introduction to Scientific Method* (New York: Henry Holt and Company, 1909), 61.

[4] The definitions are taken, with alterations, from A. L. Jones, *Logic: Inductive and Deductive: An Introduction to Scientific Method* (New York: Henry Holt and Company, 1909), 62–63.

7. A *book* is a combination of leaves and cover.

8. A *sundial* is a device for telling time by means of the sun.

*9. *Public opinion* is the opinion of people generally.

10. A *student* is one whose principal business is study.

11. A *just judge* is one who never shows partiality in his decisions.

12. *Wood* is the ligneous part of trees.

13. *Football* is a game which is usually played in America with a large ball in the shape of an oblate spheroid, whereas in England a spherical ball is used.

*14. A *medical work* is one which treats of some diseases.

Appendix III

INFORMAL FALLACIES AND TACTICAL MANEUVERS: FIFTY ARGUMENTS FOR ANALYSIS AND DISCUSSION

Identify the fallacies and tactical maneuvers in the following passages. Possible answers are given in the Table of Fallacies and Tactical Maneuvers below. (For review purposes, the table also indicates the chapters in which each fallacy or tactical maneuver is discussed.) Some of the following passages do not contain fallacies or tactical maneuvers. For those passages, answer "No Problem."

Table of Informal Fallacies and Tactical Maneuvers

FALLACIES AND TACTICAL MANEUVERS	CHAPTER
Accent	4, 11
Accident	5
Ad Hominem Argument	4, 11
Amphiboly	3
Argument from Authority	4
Argument from Force	4, 11
Argument from Ignorance	11
Argument to the People	4
Argument from Pity	4
Complex Question	4
Composition	3
Division	3
Equivocation	3
False Cause	7
Hasty Generalization	5
Irrelevant Conclusion	11
Poisoning the Well	11
Slippery Slope	11
Straw Man	11

Answers to questions marked with an asterisk may be found in the back of the text.

1. Some people say that it's wrong to be judgmental, but for my part I don't see how we can avoid making judgments. When we cross a city street we judge the speed of oncoming cars, and when we marry we judge whether someone will be a good partner for us. So it's preposterous to say that we ought not to be judgmental.

2. What made you think that a woman like Lois would ever fall in love with you?

3.

Nick [Holding up a newspaper]: Say, Jaime, listen to this ad. It reads, "For Sale: German Shepherd belonging to elderly lady who loves children."

Jaime: That's a strange ad, isn't it? The advertiser tells us that she loves children, but what does that have to do with the dog?

Nick: My thought exactly.

*4.

Ami [Pointing down the street]: Look at that car! It's sliding on the ice!

Scott: Yeah; and it's headed straight for that fire hydrant.

Ami: Oh, no! It's broken the fire hydrant and water is spraying everywhere!

Scott: That's terrible! I don't think cars should be allowed to drive on city streets, do you?

Ami: No, I don't!

5. Henrietta the maid to the police inspector: You haven't been able to come up with any evidence to show that I stole the necklace from the bedroom of the Countess. Therefore, I did not steal the necklace.

6.

Joe: You used to smoke cigarettes, didn't you?

Scott: Yes.

Joe: Well, then, I don't think that your opinion that I ought to stop smoking is worth very much. You smoked yourself, for goodness sake.

7. Student: One of my friends has a cassette by Jewel, a pop artist. It's titled *Pieces of You*. On the cassette cover, Jewel says, "what we call human nature in actuality is human habit." If Jewel says it, it must be true. Perhaps I ought to tell my psychology professor.

8.

Professor Gray: The argument against allowing students to speak in class is both lucid and compelling.

Professor Black: I doubt that, but let me hear the argument.

Professor Gray: All right; it goes like this: If you allow students to speak in class, they'll offer opinions, won't they?

Professor Black: It seems likely.

Professor Gray: Of course it does; and if you allow them to offer opinions, the first thing you know, they'll want to lead the class discussion. If you let them lead the class discussion, it won't be long before they'll want to write the exams for the class; and if you let them write the exams, they'll want to grade them. After that, they'll want to be the professor in the class.

Professor Black: So what you're saying is that if we let students talk in class it won't be long before we're out of a job.

Professor Gray: That's it exactly.

Professor Black: Well, Gray, I must say that you've opened my eyes to the dangers of class discussion! I'm in your debt.

Professor Gray: Think nothing of it. You'd have done the same for me.

*9.

Assistant Manager: Carlton, our new stock clerk, doesn't seem to have a care in the world. He hums a happy tune while he works.

Manager: Then you'd better watch out for him.

Assistant Manager: Why?

Manager: Most accident-related injuries in the workplace are caused by careless persons.

10. Fast food restaurants are found all over the United States. There's a fast food restaurant in the next block. Therefore, it's found all over the United States.

11. In general, there is nothing wrong with a person drinking a beer or two on Saturday night. Therefore, it's all right for airplane pilots to drink a couple of beers before their scheduled flights.

12.

Horace: [Standing at the mailbox, with a large envelope in his hand] Look at this! Our problems are over! We're millionaires!

Cora (Horace's wife): Let me see that.

Horace passes the envelope to Cora, who reads this in the lower left-hand corner:

Some day we hope to be able to tell you that

YOU HAVE WON A MILLION DOLLARS!

13.

Beverly: I've been taking an antihistamine, and it's dried me out. I can feel it in my sinuses.

Jody: It must have affected your humor.

Beverly: Why do you say that?

Jody: Your humor's pretty dry.

*14. Professor Jacobs must know everything there is to know about the subject she teaches. This entire semester, no one in the class has asked her a question which she hasn't been able to answer.

15.

Polly: Listen to this headline: "Man shot by police charged with burglary."

Marina: Good grief! If a policeman has been charged with burglary, I think he ought to be removed from active duty, don't you?

Polly: Indeed I do.

16. Mr. Sewell has been charged with high crimes and misdemeanors. He is, therefore, guilty of the charge.

17.

Erika: We were at the gaming tables that night. Kowalczyk entered the game at a quarter after nine.

Danielle: Oh, I see. You were playing with U.S. currency.

Erika: What? I don't understand you.

Danielle: Well, you said "a quarter after nine;" in gambling vocabulary, that must mean "nine dollars and twenty five cents."

Erika: Where did you get that idea?

Danielle: Would you believe that it just came to me out of nowhere?

Erika (with a sigh): Yes.

18. In the following passage, Mr. Hawk errs in his reasoning. What fallacy does he commit?

Mr. Hawk: The prints of Hudiakovski's shoes were found in the dust of the hardwood floor, and his fingerprints were found on the murder weapon. We must conclude that he is the murderer.

Inspector Marvel: Not so. The evidence you cite shows that Hudiakovski was probably in the room, and that he touched the murder weapon, but it does not show that he is the murderer.

*19.

Carson: What made you decide to go to medical school?

Stratton: I found at an early age that I had a talent for healing people.

Carson: Really?

Stratton: Yes. When I was only five years old, my mother slipped a disk in her back. For two weeks she was bedridden and in excruciating pain.

Carson: And you healed her?

Stratton: Yes.

Carson: How?

Stratton: I cut a pair of wings from a dead bat and buried them forty paces to the south of the oak tree in our back yard. Two days later, my mother's pain was gone.

Carson: That's amazing.

Stratton: Yes, I thought so, too. Of course I'll be able to do even more than that once I've finished medical school.

Carson: No doubt.

20. Years ago, at a place called Round Springs Park in Oklahoma, I attended a blue-grass music festival. The sky was a beautiful, cloudless blue, but the grass was bleached to the color of hay by a blazing sun, which heated the air to 98 degrees. Clouds of dust followed my car as I rolled into the parking lot. Susan, my date for the day, looked dubiously out the window. "Will those hurt you?" she asked, referring to the grasshoppers leaping around the windows of the car.

"No," I said. "They're just grasshoppers."

"But there must be thousands of them," she said, "and they're hopping every-where. They'll get in my hair and on my clothes."

"Come on," I said encouragingly. "There won't be any grasshoppers around the stage."

"All right."

Susan and I left the parking lot and followed a sign which pointed toward the stage. We passed row upon row of camping trailers. Amateur musicians stood by many of the trailers, playing old time bluegrass favorites. In a few minutes we came upon a guitar and banjo duo who were very good. We stopped to listen, and I, at least, forgot about the professionals on stage.

After a couple of tunes, the two musicians took a break and lit cigarettes. One said, "You remember last Thursday when you took Mildred to the city?" (By "the city" he meant Oklahoma City.)

"No, I took her on Friday," said the Other.

"It was Thursday," said the One.

"No, Friday," said the Other.

"Thursday."

"Friday."

"Thursday."

"Friday, dammit."

"Look, I don't care what you say. It was Thursday!"

"Why, you . . . ," said the Other and hit the One in the jaw.

There ensued one of the worst fist fights I have ever seen. Susan and I looked at one another in wonder, then back at the fighters. Why we didn't move on, I don't know. I suppose that we didn't know what to think. How could a disagreement so trivial lead to a fight so fierce?

The men stirred up clouds of dust, crushed grasshoppers with their boots, and tore down a canvas awning attached to the trailer. Finally, the One threw the Other to the ground, straddled his chest, and pinned his shoulders to the ground with his knees. Thus positioned, he hit the Other in the face and drew his arm back to hit him again. Before he could do so, the Other croaked "Wait!" through parched lips.

"Well?" said the One, his fist poised for another blow.

"You know what?" the Other said weakly. "I think I did take Mildred to the city on Thursday."

"That's more like it," said the One, getting to his feet. The Other continued to lay where he was.

Susan and I moved on. "That's an interesting way to decide a question of fact, isn't it?" she said. I shook my head in assent.

Late that evening, Susan and I walked back to my car with the sounds of banjos ringing in our ears. We made a wide circle around the camping trailers, in case we might get into a dispute with someone.

21.

Stacy: Have you seen that new movie called *Deception?*

Beverly: No

Stacy: It's based upon a novel by Nick Coste. His novels are excellent, so the movie's bound to be excellent, too.

22. Mr. Hudd, who grew up in the cold of Siberia, is a healthy and vigorous man. I suspect that the cold Siberian winters made him strong. I'm going to force my son to go without a coat in the winter. I want him to be strong like Mr. Hudd.

23.

> **Drew:** I'll bet you're pretty good at math, aren't you?
>
> **Stacy:** Why do you say that?
>
> **Drew:** My Mother's name is Stacy, and she's a mathematical wizard.

*24.

> **Amy:** The doorman in my office building is a cheerful person and very helpful, too. He usually hails a cab for me when I leave the building.
>
> **Peter:** That's very nice of him.
>
> **Amy:** Yes, it is. You know, he's so nice I think I'll give him a gift this Christmas, some money perhaps.
>
> **Peter:** I wouldn't do that.
>
> **Amy:** Why not?
>
> **Peter:** If you give him a gift at Christmas, he'll expect one at the next holiday— St. Patrick's Day, Easter, Passover, you name it.
>
> **Amy:** I hadn't thought of that.
>
> **Peter:** No? Well, take it from me: Give him a gift at Christmas and before you know it you'll be giving him gifts on Halloween and Groundhog Day. There won't be any end to it.
>
> **Amy:** Could I smile at him on Christmas?
>
> **Peter:** Maybe, but I'd be careful. You never know what a smile could lead to.
>
> **Amy:** Oh, that's ridiculous. Smiles aren't dangerous.
>
> **Peter:** Well, don't say I didn't warn you.

25.

> **Darrell:** [Sitting at the breakfast table with the fingers of one hand coiled through the handle of a coffee cup] I love your home-baked bread.
>
> **Micki:** So do I. That bread machine you gave me for my birthday was a wonderful idea.
>
> **Darrell:** What kind of bread did you bake this time?
>
> **Micki:** Panatone.
>
> **Darrell:** Oh, great. The loaf of panatone which you baked last week was wonderful.
>
> **Micki:** [Carrying two plates, each holding a thick slice of bread, to the table] Here we are.
>
> **Darrell:** It smells wonderful.
>
> **Micki:** [After sitting at the table, buttering her bread, and taking a big bite] Hm, that's funny.
>
> **Darrell:** What's funny?
>
> **Micki:** This bread tastes all doughy.
>
> **Darrell:** I didn't want to say anything, but you're right. What makes it doughy?
>
> **Micki:** I don't know.
>
> **Darrell:** Did you cook this loaf as long as you cooked the last one?
>
> **Micki:** Yes.

Darrell: Did you use the same flour?

Micki: Yes.

Darrell: What about the yeast?

Micki: No difference there.

Darrell: Did you add more fruit this time?

Micki: No, the ingredients are all the same.

Darrell: Then it's a mystery.

Micki: Oh, I know why it's different.

Darrell: Why?

Micki: I added the ingredients in a different order this time.

Darrell: That's the only difference between this loaf and the last one?

Micki: Yes.

Darrell: That has to be it, then.

Micki: I'll bake another loaf and add the ingredients in the same order as before.

Darrell: Good idea. By the way, this bread may be doughy, but it still tastes good.

Micki: Why, thank you.

Darrell: Don't mention it. [Pauses momentarily.] By the way, did I tell you I lost my job yesterday?

Micki: No, you didn't.

Darrell: Oh, sorry. It musta slipped my mind.

Micki: That's all right.

26.

Professor Carey: Old Professor Leam died of a heart attack last night.

Professor Pope: Yes, it's tragic, isn't it?

Professor Carey: Yes, and it proves the point I've been making for years.

Professor Pope: What point is that?

Professor Carey: That we professors are seriously overworked. I hope that Leam's death serves to drive that point home to the administration of the college.

27.

Dolores: Harry stole my biology text.

Bill: Can you prove that he stole it?

Dolores: No, I cannot.

Bill: In that case, I have to conclude that he didn't steal it. If you can't prove that he did it, then he must not have done it.

28.

Manager: I approve of the current guidelines for granting promotions.

Disgruntled Employee: Of course you approve of the guidelines; you've already been promoted to manager.

Manager: It seems to me that you object to the guidelines simply because you're afraid you won't be promoted.

*29. No one has been able to prove the existence of the Lochness Monster. Therefore, the Lochness Monster does not exist.

30. Mr. Smith speaks to the editor of the local small town newspaper: "Hello,   Jim. This is Ed Smith. Say, I was just thinking about that series of full-page ads I've been running in your newspaper, and it occurred to me that my boy needs a summer job. Do you think you could find some work for him at the paper? I'd appreciate it."

31.

Larry: Dr. Calhoun, the veterinarian, says that my dog has worms.

Samantha: I don't know why you'd trust him. He told me there was nothing wrong with my dog, but she died the next day.

32. One of my teachers in elementary school, a Mrs. Brumbeau, told my class that we should read the newspaper every day in order to be well informed. But her husband was the editor of the local newspaper. All Mrs. Brumbeau was trying to do was increase the circulation of the paper.

33. Actual statement of a frustrated young man to his girl friend: I love you with all my heart, and I want you to know that I'm going to kill your dog if you don't believe me.

*34.

Student: I attended class, so you shouldn't have penalized me for being absent.

Professor: I have no record that you attended class, so I had to penalize you in accordance with my stated policy.

Student: You have no record, eh? Well, then, since you can't show that I wasn't in class you should give me credit for being there.

35.

Assistant Manager: I told our employees that they could take their breaks whenever they wanted to.

Manager: Are you crazy?

Assistant Manager: Why? What's wrong?

Manager: What's wrong! We can't let employees decide when they're going to take their breaks. If we let them decide that, they'll want to choose their own working hours; and next they'll want to decide what days of the week they work. After that, they'll want to set their own vacation times. When that happens, we might as well close our doors, for we'll be in a condition of anarchy.

36. Those who believe that God exists are able to approach the future with confidence. The belief, then, is most beneficial. It follows, doesn't it, that God exists.

37. Professor: Students whose course average is less than 60 at the end of the semester receive a grade of F for the course. Ms. Spring's average is "47." Therefore, she receives an F for the course.

38. Professor: In general, students who do not attend class regularly are not interested in doing well. Therefore, Geraldine, who has missed class on seven occasions due to epileptic seizures she had shortly before class, is not interested in doing well.

*39.

Jim: I've asked Bonnie to go out with me on several occasions, and she's always turned me down.

Elojio: How many times have you asked her to go out?

Jim: Oh, six at least.

Elojio: Then I'd say she doesn't want to go out with you.

Jim: Do you really think so?

Elojio: Yes.

40. If you offer him a ride to school on your motorcycle, he'll ask you if he can take it for a drive some time. If you let him take it for a drive, he'll ask you if he can keep it for a day. If you let him do that, he'll ask you if he can take it on a trip. If he takes it on a trip, you'll never see it again. Therefore, if you offer him a ride to school on your motorcycle, you'll never see it again.

41.

Mrs. Shepherd: Louis, why did you steal money from Amanda's purse?

Louis: The Devil made me do it.

42. They say that those who live by the sword shall die by the sword, but my great grandfather made and sold swords for a living, and he didn't die by the sword.

43. B. F. Skinner, the behaviorist psychologist, conducted numerous learning experiments with pigeons. He favored the method of positive conditioning, which consists in rewarding the subject when he or she performs an action which the experimenter wishes to reinforce.

It is said that in one series of experiments Skinner placed some pigeons in cages which had electrically activated food pellet dispensers mounted in their sides. When a pigeon performed the expected action, Skinner pressed a switch and a pellet was shot from a dispenser. After some time, the pigeons realized that if they performed the action they would receive a reward. They learned, for instance, that if they hopped upon a little stool mounted in the cage, then hopped off again and flapped their wings, they would receive a pellet.

One day, when he returned to his lab after lunch, a curious scene greeted Skinner's eyes. The pigeons in the cage were maintaining a variety of awkward positions. One stood with one wing extended, another with both wings extended. Still another was standing on one leg, while the one next to it was holding its beak in the water trough. At first, Skinner was bewildered by this. He soon discovered, however, that the food pellet dispensers had malfunctioned in his absence, shooting pellets into the cage. The pigeons, who wanted more food, had assumed the position they were in when the food pellet dispensers shot food into the cage!

*44.

Defense Counsel: Your honor, I have called six witnesses, none of whom have been able to place my client at the casino at the time of the burglary.

Judge: [Interrupting] And what conclusion does counsel draw from that remarkable circumstance?

Defense Counsel: I was coming to that, your honor. My colleague for the prosecution has argued that the robbery took place at 1 A.M., just as the evening receipts were being counted. Defense concurs in this but observes that while one witness testifies that she saw my client at the casino at 11 on the evening of the burglary, none of the witnesses—not one—is able to testify that he was there at 1 A.M., when the robbery took place. I conclude from this that my client is not guilty.

Judge: Does counsel have anything further to add?

Defense Counsel: No, your honor, since it is an unassailable fact that my client must have been at the scene of the robbery in order to have done it.

45. I am certain in my own heart that if each of us practiced justice, and did not encroach upon his or her neighbors' rights that our nation would practice justice and not encroach upon other nations' rights.

46. In the following passage from Lewis Carroll's *Alice's Adventures in Wonderland,* Alice is speaking with the Gryphon and the Mock Turtle.

"When we were little," the Mock Turtle went on at last, ... "we went to school in the sea. The master was an old Turtle—we used to call him Tortoise—"

"Why did you call him Tortoise, if he wasn't one?" Alice asked.

"We called him Tortoise because he taught us," said the Mock Turtle angrily. "Really you are very dull!"

47. In the following passage from Lewis Carroll's *Alice's Adventures in Wonderland,* Alice has met up with the Duchess for a second time.

"You can't think how glad I am to see you again, you dear old thing!" said the Duchess, as she tucked her arm affectionately into Alice's and they walked off together.

Alice was very glad to find her in such a pleasant temper, and thought to herself that perhaps it was only the pepper that had made her so savage when they met in the kitchen.

"When *I'm* a Duchess," she said to herself (not in a very hopeful tone, though), "I won't have any pepper in my kitchen *at all.* Soup does very well without—Maybe it's always pepper that makes people hot-tempered," she went on, very much pleased at having found out a new kind of rule, "and vinegar that makes them sour—and camomile that makes them bitter—and—and barley-sugar and such things that make children sweet-tempered. I only wish people knew *that*: then they wouldn't be so stingy about it, you know—"

48. Unidentified student: Last month, the renovation of the campus student center was completed. Some of us smokers sought out the smokers' lounge, where we'd spent many happy hours before the renovation was begun. Imagine our surprise when we discovered that the lounge had been designated a nonsmoking area! Smoking is no longer allowed in any part of the student center.

My story gets worse. This month the administration announced that henceforth no smoking will be allowed in any of the classroom buildings. Next month they'll probably say that students can't smoke in their own dorm rooms. And after that, they'll say that they can only smoke outside. But don't think the puritans in the administration will stop there. No way. Next, they'll lay down a rule that says that students can only smoke outside when it's 20 degrees and snowing. After that, of course, they'll bring out the wooden stakes and burn everyone who doesn't go to church on Sunday! We smokers must unite and not allow our rights to be trampled underfoot! Let our bonds be those which unite us, rather than those which bind us in smokeless servitude. Let us rise up together! This can be our finest hour if, like the gladiators of old, we march together upon the administration and demand restoration of the freedom so cruelly and thoughtlessly denied us!

*49. When I was in elementary school, which was before the days of VCRs, the local theatre in the little southern town where I lived showed a double feature with a serial every Saturday. The double features were always cowboy movies, while the serials featured heroes like Batman and Superman.

I loved to go to the theatre on Saturday, especially in the summer when it was hot. Armed with a tall bag of popcorn, I'd find a seat in the center aisle near the front and watch the action on the silver screen for three, four, or five hours. When I left the theatre, my tired eyes would fill with tears as they struggled to adjust to the merciless sun, and sometimes I'd have a headache for the rest of the day. At the time, the headaches seemed a small price to pay for the spine-tingling action I'd witnessed.

One of my favorite cowboy stars was The Durango Kid. When he wasn't wearing his disguise, The Durango Kid was known as "Steve." He'd have a different last name in every movie, but his first name would always be Steve. In disguise, The Durango Kid wore a black suit and a black kerchief mask which covered his nose and the bottom part of his face. His mask was always ironed to perfection. The Durango Kid would be in a fist fight with three other men, leap on a horse to overtake a crook, and topple him from his horse in a wild and dangerous leap, but when he arose from the dust his mask would always be wrinkle-free. I thought that was amazing.

One Saturday, some of my friends and I played baseball in a vacant lot down the street from my house, and I forgot all about the movies. Next morning, as I checked the movie ads in the newspaper over a bowl of cereal, I discovered that I'd missed the latest Durango Kid movie! "Oh, no," I thought; but then I noticed that the movie would be shown again on Monday evening. There was still hope.

I approached my mother with a series of carefully crafted arguments. "Say, Mom, guess what; I missed The Durango Kid movie on Saturday."

"That's too bad." Mom twirled the drive wheel on her Singer sewing machine and it sprang to life. Carefully, she pushed a piece of cloth under the bobbing needle and nudged it forward in a curving line as the needle did its work.

"But there's still hope," I said.

"Hope for what? Rain? It has been dry."

"No, hope for me seeing The Durango Kid movie."

"Is it shown next Saturday?"

"No, but it's shown again on Monday night. I could go then."

"No, you couldn't. Monday is a school night. Besides, I don't want you going downtown at night. It's dangerous after dark; you might be kidnapped." Mom held the garment up before her. She was making a dress.

"That's going to be a pretty dress," I said. "And don't worry about it being a school night. I always get my schoolwork done in study hall."

"Even so, it will still be dangerous downtown," Mom rejoined.

"Either you or Dad could drive me down and pick me up," I said brightly. "It's not far, and after the show I'd wait inside until I saw the car. The movie's over at 9, and I'd be in bed by 10."

"No, I told you; I don't want you going downtown at night. Something could happen to you in the theatre."

Mom was feeding her dress into the Singer again, and things didn't look good for me. I pulled another arrow from my quiver of arguments. "I can understand your concern about the danger, but do you realize how much time and effort goes into making a good cowboy movie like The Durango Kid?"

"Huh?"

"Time and money. I'll bet Steve—The Durango Kid, I mean—has worked for months and months to get this movie ready for his fans."

"Well, I don't see how that . . . "

"And moreover, " I broke in, "just think how you'd feel if you'd gone to all that trouble to make the movie and your fans didn't show up to see it. You'd be crestfallen, I'll bet."

"Crestfallen?" Mom was surprised that I knew this word.

"Yes, crestfallen. And moreover, you should think not only of Steve's feelings, but of mine as well. I'm your son, and I'll be simply miserable if I don't get to see the movie. I'll always wonder what I missed if I don't go. And, I'll also feel like a traitor; well, not like a traitor, maybe, but like I, uh, like I let Steve down. Oh, Mom, can't I go, please?"

"All right, I guess so; but just this once."

"I promise, if you let me go, I'll . . . What did you say?" Mom's words had been slow in sinking in.

"I said that you can go, but just this once. I'll drive you down myself."

"Oh, Mom, thanks. You won't regret this, I promise you." Saying this, I hugged Mom around the neck.

So, I got to see The Durango Kid on Monday night, and it was great. I enjoyed watching the movie with all the grownups who went at night. When I left the theatre, I walked with a slight swagger.

Several weeks later I missed the Saturday afternoon movies again. I wasn't worried, however, for I remembered how easily I'd been able to persuade Mom to let me go to the movies on Monday night. Confident in the power of my arguments, I nonchalantly strolled into the kitchen, where Mom was washing dishes. I leaned against the counter next to the sink where Mom stood, and said, "Say, Mom, guess what? I missed the cowboy movies on Saturday."

"That's too bad." Mom held a plate under the hot water tap as she spoke, and rinsed it.

"But there's still hope," I said.

"You mean the movies will be shown again next Saturday?"

"No, I mean they'll be shown again on Monday night. I could go then."

"No, you couldn't."

"Surely you don't mean that."

"Yes, I do. Monday is a school night, and it's dangerous for someone your age to go downtown alone at night." Mom put several glasses in her wash pan and added a little soap to the mix.

"Let me dry a few of those dishes for you," I said, grabbing a towel, "And don't worry about it being a school night. I finish all my assignments before I get home."

"Even so, it's dangerous downtown."

"Either you or Dad could drive me, like last time."

"No."

"I know it's dangerous, but last time I got home safely. Where does this pot go?"

"In the lower cabinet on the left."

"These movies are some of the best of their kind. One of them's in Technicolor."

"No."

"And think of how much it would mean to the stars to have the theatre filled. And think of how much it would mean to me to be there."

"No."

"I have enough money saved from my allowance to pay for my ticket."

"You always pay for your ticket that way. The answer is no."

"Don't you realize how much this means to me?"

"Yes, I do. You'll be crestfallen."

"And still you say no?"

"Yes, I do. The answer is no. Be careful with those glasses." Mom wrung out her dishcloth and hung it over the faucet to dry. "I'll be in the living room with your father. Thanks for your help."

"You're welcome." I dried the rest of the dishes in stunned disbelief. Where did I go wrong? Did I use the wrong arguments? Surely not; they worked the last time. Was Mom in a bad mood? She didn't seem to be. It just didn't make sense.

All through Monday I told myself that Mom would have pity on me at the last minute and tell me I could go to the movies. She'd say, "Oh, I know how much those movies mean to you. I'll drive you over and pick you up afterward." But it was apparent at supper on Monday that my movies were the farthest thing from her thoughts. And so I missed the movies that night and vowed that I'd be the first kid in line at the ticket window next Saturday afternoon. And the Saturday afternoon after that, too.

50.

A Dance of Fallacies[1]

BY MEREDITH CARGILL

Ray 1: I'm getting really annoyed by all the pornography around these days.

Sue 1: I know what you mean. I think it's disgusting.

Ray 2: I really think something ought to be done about it, you know? The government needs to put a stop to it.

Sue 2: You mean censorship?

---

[1] Unpublished manuscript reprinted by permission of the author.

Ray 3:   I guess you could call it that. I call it public decency. It's the same as not being allowed to go naked in public or not littering. It's a nuisance and should be controlled.

Sue 3:   But wouldn't that violate the constitution or something? Don't they have the right to free speech?

Ray 4:   I believe in free speech as much as the next guy. I believe they have the right to say whatever they want to say. But I also believe some people have gone too far and need to be stopped. They've proved they don't deserve the freedom, so it should be taken away.

Sue 4:   But what harm does it do? Some of it is not so bad, and it sometimes has some good literature and other articles.

Ray 5:   It's all perverted. And it does all kinds of harm. You remember that rape and murder case in town last year?

Sue 5:   Of course. It was all over the papers.

Ray 6:   Well, it came out in the trial that the defendant owned tons of porn. He had shelves and shelves full of dirty magazines and videotapes. And he even admitted on the stand that he raped and killed that woman just to experience for himself what he had seen so often in his smut. So you see, if we just control the pornography, we could eliminate most of the crimes against women.

Sue 6:   Didn't that guy have other problems, too? Like, wasn't he on medication of some kind?

Ray 7:   Where did you get that idea?

Sue 7:   I read about it on the Internet.

Ray 8:   Well, you can't believe what you find on the Internet. The Internet is just anybody's crazy ideas.

Sue 8:   Even if this guy was motivated by reading and watching pornography, is the solution censorship?

Ray 9:   That's how to get at the root cause. Look at the statistics. Liberalization of pornography was the result of a few court decisions in the mid-1960s. Then the rate of sex crimes and violent crimes against women jumped up in the late sixties. Also, the late sixties saw the rise of all sorts of other social problems, such as teenage pregnancies and widespread drug use. Obviously, the freedoms granted to pornographers have caused a great deal of harm, so returning to censorship is the solution.

Sue 9:   You trace it all to court decisions.

Ray 10:   Yes, if only the Supreme Court had decided the *Milton v. Arizona* case differently in 1965, we wouldn't be in this mess now.

Sue 10:   But don't you think there is also harm in restricting speech too much? A harm to people's rights?

Ray 11:   You want to talk about harms? Think of what happened last year. That guy didn't just rape and kill that woman, he mutilated her, and beat her, and knifed her repeatedly. She suffered. She *suffered*. And she left a three-year-old daughter without any parents. That kid will not be able to grow up normal now. She's scarred for life. Where's your humanity, woman? Do you have ice water in your veins? What would you say if that happened to you?

Sue 11: Well, I . . .

Ray 12: Geez, you are more of an imbecile than I thought. With airheads like you running around, it's no wonder this country is going to the dogs.

Sue 12: Maybe we should just drop it.

Ray 13: You'd like that, wouldn't you? You just don't like to have your liberal views challenged. I know what you liberals want—you want pornographers to be free so they can move in next door and do what they want with our children. That's what you want.

Sue 13: Look, there's really no cause to get so upset at me. I said I didn't like pornography.

Ray 14: But you don't yet see why some censorship is justified. Maybe if I yanked out this handful of your hair you would change your mind.

Sue 14: Hey! Let go!

Ray 15: Okay, but be warned.

Appendix IV

EXTENDED EXERCISES IN THE EXAMINATION OF REASONING

1. MICHELLE SHAW, "SHOW SIGNS OF REFORM"[1]

The debate over how to effectively punish criminals is as old as crime itself. From execution to reform, conservatives and liberals alike have sought to make society safer for law-abiding citizens. While they may agree on the ultimate goal, they often disagree with the means, and a new practice is quickly becoming controversial. The Illinois State Supreme Court recently overturned a ruling made by a lower court involving Glenn Meyer, a farmer in Southern Illinois who was convicted of assault. It seems that he has the tendency to fly into fits of unprovoked rage and lash out at whoever happens to be near. On several occasions, this has caused serious injuries to unsuspecting guests who were paying him a visit. Generally, he is a mild-tempered and well-mannered individual, but his outbursts are said to be caused by a psychological disorder and therefore unpredictable. The original judge did not feel that the circumstances of this case warranted jail time (he is an elderly man and has dependents) and chose instead to order him to post a 4 × 8 sign on his property reading "Warning. A Violent Felon Lives Here. Travel At Your Own Risk." Meyer appealed, and the Supreme Court agreed that this was an unconstitutional decision.

---

[1] *The Rambler, 121,* no. 14 (April 25, 1997), 3.

So far, the states have been fairly inconsistent in deciding this issue of cruel and unusual punishment. In the last few years, judges have ordered people to publish apologies in local newspapers, wear T-shirts advertising their crime, and put bumper stickers on their cars, among other strategies. These so-called "shame" punishments have been overturned by some higher courts and upheld by others. In a similar case in Tennessee, a higher court ruled that a convicted child molester did not have to post a sign on his property.

While the eighth amendment protects people from cruel and unusual punishments, I fail to see the "cruelty" of protecting society from dangerous criminals. After all, that is the idea behind the jail system; we keep felons away from others until they are deemed capable of living in society without causing further harm. As we all know, this is often an idealistic dream, and the rate of repeat offenders continues to grow. For certain types of criminals, such as sex offenders, it is not even known if they can ever be "cured."

Unfortunately, the justice system is often resigned to turning people loose and simply waiting for them to commit another crime. Once they have served their time, people cannot be kept in jail based on the suspicion that they will break the law again. And with the current parole policies and prison overcrowding, very few criminals actually serve their entire sentence.

While there is no point in needlessly humiliating someone, it seems very appropriate that a community has the right to know if a dangerous criminal is in their midst. If child molesters were required to post a sign stating their conviction, parents in the neighborhood might think twice about letting their child associate with that person. If a violent felon posted a sign similar to the one on Glenn Meyer's property, people would know they were putting themselves at risk and be able to make a well-informed decision. It would certainly not deter everyone, but that's not the point. The point is that people are given the information they need to assess the risk. The government requires tobacco companies to print warnings on packs of cigarettes, not so that everyone will stop smoking, but so that people know what they are putting themselves at risk for.

Some may argue that this policy would be unfair to the criminals who do reform. I think it would be practical to place a time limit on this type of warning: statistics show that the majority of reoffenders commit new crimes within their first few years back into society. After a certain length of time, the chance of a new offense would be lessened, and the need to warn others would not be as great. And for those who argue that it is labeling someone guilty until proved innocent, I say that it is merely stating the facts. The only people required to post warnings would be those who had been convicted of a crime, and the sign would only state the offenses for which they were found guilty.

Yes, the Constitution grants certain rights to individuals, but when your rights begin to interfere with my rights, I have a right to protection. We need to stop worrying so much about the rights of criminals and start worrying more about the rights of law-abiding citizens to be protected from dangerous offenders.

---

2. TONY DELGIORNO, "SHAME'S NOT THE GAME"[2]

Every criminal should be made to serve the time for the offense he or she has committed against society. I am a strong believer in making the punishment fit the crime, but the latest punishment for criminal offenders has been overturned in the courts as an extreme

---

[2] *The Rambler, 121,* no. 14 (April 25, 1997), 3.

and unconstitutional act. The punishment would resurrect the days of the *Scarlet Letter* by making convicted felons display a sign in their front yard stating that they have been convicted of a crime. The tactic is one of embarrassment, and if a person has already served time in prison or paid their dues to society in any way, this is an extreme measure.

This is against any person's civil liberties in the United States, especially in a country that prides itself on protection of human rights. It is wrong to make a person endure the public shame and humiliation for a crime for which they may be truly remorseful or at the least served time for. Allowing this sort of treatment to continue would not allow a person to proceed with his or her life in a meaningful way since they would publicly have to acknowledge once again what they have done wrong in their lives. How is someone to get on with their lives if everyone knows their dark past? We know that there is discrimination against anyone that has been found guilty in a court of law, making this knowledge open in such a public manner would keep people from finding employment, let alone finding a decent neighborhood in which to live.

Once a person has done the time, that person has the right to go on with his life. To make him wear a symbol of his disgrace is indeed cruel and unusual punishment.

---

3. ANGELA BENEDICT, "SEND IN THE CLONES"[3]

In the course of human history, many scientific milestones have been reached. Many of these milestones have greatly improved people's health and lives and allowed people to do new things and go places that were mere fantasies in bygone eras. Three years before the dawn of a new millennium, perhaps the greatest achievement has been made—the successful cloning of a living, animate being.

Some shudder at this scientific marvel and fear even the remotest negative consequences will become a reality. A majority of these fears are drawn straight from the pages of contemporary science fiction. Many fear that cloning could be used to make an army of "superhuman" beings bent on world domination. I will address this fear later, but first I would like to look at the more realistic possibilities of cloning.

I see many wonderful and life saving benefits that could be had with this new knowledge. First, no one can easily forget the heart-wrenching images of dead and dying people from famine-plagued countries so prevalent in the media, especially during the middle 1980s. With cloning, famine could be eradicated if it is utilized properly. Livestock and vegetation could be produced in quantities sufficient to feed these starving countries. No more would the blight of hunger hold the people of the world in its deadly grip. Since cloning is no more than the making of a genetically identical twin to the cell donor, there would be no fear of unhealthy contaminants tainting this food source, at least not from the cloning process itself.

As food prices rise, both from inclement weather for particular vegetation and from years when there are low birth rates in livestock, one can see how cloning would be useful in lowering the prices of food. Cloning will not necessarily end with merely making an identical twin. Cloning technology could advance so that genetic manipulation along with cloning could yield better vegetation that is more resilient against negative growing

---

[3] *The Rambler, 121,* no. 11 (March 7, 1997), 3.

conditions. Livestock could be developed that would produce leaner and better meat. As more and better food sources become a reality, the price of food would more than likely go down as supply would be able to meet demand. This would help the problem of starvation not only in famine-plagued countries but also in industrialized nations such as the U.S. Impoverished families would be capable of buying more food for their money. Many elderly people, who often go without their much-needed medication because they have only enough money for either food or medicine, could afford to purchase both and not put their health in jeopardy.

Some may fear that the lowering of prices would put farmers and other food producers in danger of losing profit. However, if only a sufficient amount of food is produced to meet demand, and that amount is lowered or raised in response to the need that year, farmers would probably not lose profit. In fact, if a farmer grows a type of food that is more resilient to circumstances that would normally reduce his crop, he would actually make more of a profit, benefitting from increased yields. Cloning a type of animal or vegetation that yields more would put farmers in a very good financial situation.

Another benefit, perhaps further down the road, would be more availability of donor organs. It is possible that in the future cloning could be used to clone a new organ for a person in need of one. Another benefit would be that the cloned organ could be cloned from the cell of the patient and thus, the new organ would be an exact duplicate of the organ the person now has, minus the disease or injury. This would eliminate the need of organ donor recipients from having to take medication for the rest of their lives to prevent rejection and also reduce the risk to almost zero of initial rejection after the operation. When one looks at the statistics of how high a demand for donor organs there is compared with the very limited supply, one can see how very precious this benefit would be.

Many scientists have also raised the possibility that cloning could be utilized to rid the world of genetic diseases such as Cystic Fibrosis. Healthy tissue could be cloned in place of diseased tissue in persons with genetic diseases, thus ridding them of the disease. Even better would be the possibility that cloning could lead to ways to prevent the disease from even occurring in the developing fetus. People with a history of genetic defects who now have decided not to have children for fear of passing on the disease could experience the joys of parenthood.

Many are afraid that the technology of cloning will fall into the hands of a madman or some other negative influence, as I stated earlier. They fear a race of superhumans that would be made into an army would be formed and dominate the earth. I understand such concerns but at the same time, the scientific facts must be entertained.

First, the cloning process in many ways resembles the procedure infertile couples go through to become pregnant. In this process, sperm is injected straight into the egg, increasing the chances of fertilization. In the cloning process, the original DNA of the fertilized egg is removed and replaced with the DNA taken from the cell of the being that is to be cloned. The egg is then implanted into the uterus of a being of the same species. The egg grows and develops just as a normal embryo does and is born. It is an exact duplicate of the being the cell was taken from. Actually, nature performs this feat fairly often when fraternal twins are formed.

As one can see, cloning is not an instant process where a full-grown adult human steps out of a "cloning booth" as in an episode of a science fiction program. Any cloned species must grow at the same rate its species normally grow. Also, it is not born with a blank mentality open and ready to be fed instructions and beliefs to be carried out without question like a robot to do the biddings of a madman. It will develop a personality and think independently just as any other person. If raised in a different environment than the being it was cloned from, it will more than likely develop a different personality and repertoire of behaviors from its "twin." Even naturally occurring fraternal twins often grow to have separate personalities when brought up together. We have little to fear that a negative influence would clone people to be used as his unquestioning slaves.

Many people fear that which is unfamiliar or new to them. This includes technology. All of the fears expressed about cloning are normal reactions to a new scientific breakthrough. For every new technology, doubt and fears have been expressed. Many of these technologies that have been feared in the past turned out to be very beneficial and even life saving. Cloning can be a wonderful benefit to humankind. As with any scientific advance, it must be handled responsibly and intelligently. Anything in the wrong hands can be a danger, from a car to cloning. Strict and clear rules and regulations in regard to cloning should be immediately worked out now that cloning has been made possible. With these rules and the proper administration of them, cloning could be the answer to many world problems that have so far been unsolvable. I look forward to seeing how cloning will affect our world and am optimistic that it will lead to a brighter tomorrow.

4. MICHELLE SHAW, "NO CLONES HERE"[4]

If you've turned on a television or picked up a newspaper in the last week, you've probably seen a picture of Dolly, the first sheep to be cloned from a "donor" sheep. A mammary cell was extracted and grown in a test tube before being fused with the nucleus from another sheep. The embryo is then implanted in a "surrogate mother" sheep, where it grows normally.

Scientists have been experimenting with this practice since the 1970s, but it remained mostly theory until the lamb was cloned. While the technique has never been tried on humans, scientists now admit that it appears to be possible. Most are quick to condemn this idea, saying that it will never happen because of the ethical principles involved.

However, these same scientists extol the virtues of cloning sheep and other mammals, claiming that it could lead to healthier livestock and possible breakthroughs in the medical field. Personally, I feel that this is another example of science going too far; our technology has surpassed our morality. There are many unsettling ethical possibilities that must be examined in light of this cloned sheep.

While the idea of healthier animals and being able to feed more of the world's population sounds great, it has several drawbacks. First of all, there is a need for diversity in genetic makeup. If an entire herd had the same genetic material, one sick animal could easily kill all of the others. Also, reproduction is no longer practical because of the problems of breeding animals that are too similar. Mother nature intended animals (and people) to have a diverse genetic makeup to ensure survival and continuation of the species. Scientists are on dangerous territory when they try to "improve" the natural process of life.

President Clinton has already called for a national bioethics advisory panel to review the legal and ethical implications of cloning humans. Earlier, he acted to deny funding for human embryo research. The Scottish scientists who developed the cloning technique say

---

[4] *The Rambler, 121,* no. 11 (March 7, 1997), 3.

that it is not meant to be tried on humans. Somehow, that does not sound reassuring. There are plenty of irrational and insane people in the world, and you can almost bet that somewhere, someone is contemplating this very possibility. Congress is already considering a government wide ban of federal funding for research on human cloning, but it has not been decided if the government would have the power to stop private companies from doing their own experiments. And of course, it is up to each country to set its own laws for this situation. Basically, there is no way to ensure that there will be a worldwide, enforceable ban on human cloning. If you can, imagine for a moment what could happen if this information fell into the wrong hands. Hitler would have been thrilled to have this type of resource available. But we are not talking about robots or computers, we are talking about trying to artificially create human beings. We must have more respect for life than to begin thinking of it as something that can be broken down into a scientific experiment and replicated in the laboratory. The love between a man and a woman that leads to the creation of a precious new life cannot be duplicated with all the experiments and trials in the world. Nothing should try to replace this basic act of humanity.

5. MICHELLE SHAW, "CHARACTER COUNTS"[5]

It has only been recently that the media has begun to scrutinize every detail of politicians' personal lives. The public is now privy to information about extramarital affairs, drug and alcohol use, financial dealings, and much more. While some may find the information shocking, many people seem to be so accustomed to scandal that they disregard it as irrelevant. To many, it no longer matters if a politician cheats on his wife or swindles money. It's to be expected, and as long as he gets his job done, who cares?

Yet a politician's private life and public life are entwined. Having an affair may not directly affect someone's job performance, but what does it say about that person's character? If someone is willing to lie to the person they have committed their life to, what makes you think they are going to be truthful with Joe Public? If someone is willing to alter the records of their campaign contributions, are you willing to trust them with your personal money? And if someone will trade political influence for personal profit, can they be trusted to use that political influence for the good of the American people?

6. TONY DELGIORNO, "QUALIFICATIONS COME FIRST"[6]

Constantly, we are bombarded with news stories that talk about the unethical nature of our elected officials. However, how much does a charge of sexual misconduct or accusations of possible financial impropriety have to do with getting the job done? The answer is: not much.

---

[5] *The Rambler, 121,* no. 9 (February 7, 1997), 3.

[6] *The Rambler, 121,* no. 9 (February 7, 1997), 3.

Let us take the accusations that are leveled against President Clinton. First of all, President Clinton is constantly charged with the age-old tale of "he is a womanizer, a cheat, and a sexual harasser." All of a sudden, opponents of the President charge that because of all these things and the immorality of it all he cannot be trusted with the highest office in the land. Let us look back in history for a moment. Thomas Jefferson was rumored to have a mistress that was a slave, but he is revered to this day for his actions during the revolution and his two-term presidency. Franklin Roosevelt had mistresses before his presidency and was rumored to have them during his four terms in office. Eleanor swore that she would never sleep in the same bed with him again, but she remained the loyal political wife. FDR brought the country out of the Great Depression and led the allies to victory in World War II. After the fact, we now all know about what John Kennedy did, but he was on his way to being one of the greater presidents after the Bay of Pigs and the Cuban Missile Crisis. However, he did not live to fulfill his duties. The point is, these great leaders of our nation did not have their personal conduct thrown in their face, and they proved to be very effective presidents.

Today, then, why do we have to know everything about Bill Clinton's life? His personal life is of no concern as long as it does not interfere with his duties as President. However, having his enemies constantly throw it in his face does impede on his ability to put his full attention towards the problems of the nation. It is not important; leave him alone.

When it comes to Clinton's dodging the draft—who cares? We all have respect for what our veterans have done for us, but there are many other leaders who have never served as well, but we have trusted them with very important positions. For example: Newt Gingrich, Dan Quayle, Dick Cheney (former defense secretary), and many others throughout history. Serving in the military is not a prerequisite for serving as a political leader. Just read the Constitution if you don't believe me.

Throughout our nation's short history, our leaders have lied, cheated, and acted immorally in their personal lives, but we regard most of them to be great men. As long as their misdeeds do not interfere with their governance or do not break the law, then there is no problem. Character is not an issue. Their ability to do the will of the people in an efficient manner that benefits us all is the issue.

---

7. TONY DELGIORNO, "FORGET FIRE"[7]

On July 4, 1991, people across this great land participated in one of the most patriotic events since World War II. This event was the Independence Day celebration marking the victory of the United States over Saddam Hussein in the Gulf War. Flags waved for the hundreds of thousands of men and women that had been a part of the most decisive military victory in history. This day also honored the people who had given their lives in this conflict and many others so that we may live free and in a stable world.

These people died for their countries, yet in the name of freedom of speech, the flag that they defended, the flag that draped their caskets, is desecrated in many different ways—most notably by being burned in protest. Yes, one of the ideals that these brave people died for was freedom of speech, but can we not show them respect by keeping sacred their symbol of freedom?

---

[7] *The Rambler, 121,* no. 10 (February 21, 1997), 3.

Burning the flag is the most disrespectful act of hatred towards the veterans of the United States. Most Americans (78%) feel this same way and would support government action to protect the U.S. flag. The flag is one of the most sacred symbols we have; if there is a need to protest, there are other means by which to do so. The Bill of Rights does guarantee the right to peaceful assembly. If this form of protest is not good enough, do not desecrate a symbol of honor. If you hate the United States so much that you would destroy its one true symbol of freedom, then you can live elsewhere.

---

8. MICHELLE SHAW, "BURN, BABY, BURN . . . "[8]

As difficult as it is to get people to agree on anything these days, recent polls show that 78% of registered voters favor a constitutional amendment that would protect the American flag from such derogatory activities as burning it. At the risk of being called a communist, fascist, anti-American, or worse, I will tell you that I am part of the other 22% of the population. Before you jump to the conclusion that I am unpatriotic, let me explain my reasoning.

Do I believe in democracy? I think it works better than any other system we've found. Am I proud to be an American? Most of the time, although we are guilty of our share of atrocities. Would I want to live in any other country? No, not for any length of time. To tell you the truth, I don't even like the idea of burning the flag. It's not something that I would ever do, and certainly not something that I would recommend to others. I can think of many other ways of protesting or expressing dissatisfaction with the government which I consider more effective. I understand that many would consider abuse of the flag to be an insult to the millions of brave men and women who have fought to protect our liberties. I would not blame someone for thinking that this was offensive. But while we are guaranteed the right to life, liberty, and the pursuit of happiness, I don't remember anything in the Constitution that promised we would never have to be offended or confronted by ideas that we don't particularly like or agree with.

This is where free speech comes in. I may not agree with you but in the name of democracy, I must allow you freedom of expression, even if I totally disagree with your beliefs. As long as your right to freedom of speech isn't interfering with my right to life, liberty, and the pursuit of happiness . . . I have no right to interfere. Yes, there is a definite irony here. The people who fought to preserve someone else's first amendment rights must stand by and watch that symbol of freedom being abused. Do they have to like it? No. Do they have to allow it? Yes, if they truly believe in a democratic society.

It is not necessarily anti-democratic to believe in burning the flag. Rather, I would argue that it is anti-democratic to say that you can't; if free speech is only protected as long as the majority approves of it, what kind of free speech is that? Not very free, if you ask me. And as the great patriotic song says, "I'm proud to be an American, where at least I know I'm free. . . . "

---

[8] *The Rambler, 121,* no. 10 (February 21, 1997), 3.

Solutions to Selected Exercises

CHAPTER 1 EXERCISES

I.

    4. Thus.

II.

    4. Command or expression of a wish or desire.

    9. Question.

III.

    4. Most people act in their own self-interest. In some cases, the self-interest of one is the disadvantage of another. It is to the advantage of one group to pollute streams and rivers in manufacturing goods to make money, and to the disadvantage of those who are affected by the pollution. Those who are affected by the pollution, however, are unwilling to spend their money to clean up the pollution caused by others. Therefore, <u>it is necessary for the federal government to set environmental regulations to ensure that environmental pollution is cleaned up.</u>

IV.

    4. The separation of these boards must be due to some other cause than the application of force.

    9. It is not true that philosophy is a waste of time because it bakes no bread.

CHAPTER 2 EXERCISES

I. The goals of inductive arguments are to (1) begin with true premisses and (2) assert the conclusion with a degree of probability which neither exceeds nor falls short of that which is justified by the premisses.

II.

    4. Invalid. A refutation by alternate conclusion: The premisses do not rule out the possibility that Shelby might be admitted to the theater by a ticket purchased for him by a friend.

    9. Valid. Hypothetical syllogism.

III.

    1. Evaluation of "Brandon Sweeney Hears a Complaint." The case for Arthur's being moved may be stronger than the case for his leaving the dorm. As a dorm counselor, Brandon may not have the authority to refund Arthur's money. On the other hand, the university has not given Arthur what a tenant might reasonably expect in the circumstances.

CHAPTER 3 EXERCISES

I.

    4. Division.

II.

    4. The statement is ambiguous. Does *bank* mean *shore* or a place where money is kept? No equivocation, but two meanings of bank are possible.

CHAPTER 4 EXERCISES

II.

    4. Argument to the people.
    9. Argument from pity.

III.

    4. Ad hominem fallacy in that the response to the senator bypasses his claim. The citizen's point might be a good one to take up later in the discussion after the senator's claim has been addressed, but as a refutation of the senator's claim the response is fallacious.
    9. Argument from authority.

IV.

    4. William's conclusion is a cautious one based upon evidence. First, the conclusion is cautious; all that it claims is that it is possible, rather than likely or necessarily the case, for humans to face death without fear. Second, the statement is based upon evidence. Only one instance of an actual death faced without fear is sufficient to establish possibility in a case like this.

CHAPTER 5 EXERCISES

I.

    4. The distinction is between the truth of a generalization and the claim that it is well grounded. A generalization can be true even though it is not well grounded. If a generalization is not well grounded, there is little reason to believe that it is true even though in fact it may be true.

II.

    4. No fallacy. A claim that may or may not be true. No argument in support of the claim is provided.
    9. Hasty generalization.

CHAPTER 6 EXERCISES

I.

3. (The rhubarb pie.) Darrell is saying that there is no reason to repeat an experience which is known to be painful, but Micki could build a reply based upon the fact that relevant dissimilarities weaken an analogy. She could say that breaking a leg is not like eating a piece of pie. Thinking of the fact that she did not make the rhubarb pie which Darrell detested, she could also observe that Darrell should consider that he has liked other kinds of pies which she has made. In addition, Micki might say this: "But I'm sure the rhubarb pie you had wasn't at all like mine. My family has a special recipe for rhubarb pie. I've never tried another rhubarb pie that tasted anything like it."

8. (The conductor and the political leader.) Weak analogy. Relevant dissimilarities weaken the inference. A musical performance presumably rules out the possibility of consultation, though it might be unwise of a conductor not to work with his or her orchestra members in a consultative manner in practice.

II.

4. (Employees taking breaks.) There is no argument to be evaluated in this passage. The writer simply points to a similarity in the drugstore employee case and a famous argument for the existence of God.

7. (Origin of the moral faculty.) Strong analogy. The question of the origin of the relevant cognitive ability is excluded from ethics just as it is from geometry. Sidgwick emphasizes relevant similarities in the practices of two areas of intellectual inquiry.

CHAPTER 7 EXERCISES

I.

4. Sufficient condition: it fails to rain. Necessary condition: the crop will be lost.

9. Sufficient condition: Darrell says "I'm sick and tired of doing all the work around the house." Necessary condition: Micki screams.

II.

4. (Medical students.) Accident.

9. (Texts.) Hasty generalization.

III.

4. (Officer Singh.) Accident.

9. (Beth and the purse snatcher.) Hasty generalization.

IV.

4. (Murders on Montmartre.) There is insufficient evidence to state that the tall man dressed in black is the murderer. His being seen at the sites of the murder may simply be an accidental circumstance. If the murders were by gunshot and the man was seen running from the scene with a smoking gun in his hand after

every murder, the link between the man and the murders would be much stronger. Detectives seek to establish motive, means, and opportunity. The presence of the man possibly relates to the latter, but mere presence establishes neither motive nor means.

CHAPTER 8 EXERCISES

II.

    4. The statement as made may simply be intended to state that Stephanie is a poor student. However, a ranking may be intended. The scale in that case is first rate, second rate, and so forth.

CHAPTER 9 EXERCISES

II.

    4. Verbal.
    9. Criteriological.

III.

    4. Factual, though what is meant by a barrier to trade will of course have to be specified.
    9. Factual. The question as to whether there is a relation between increases in interest rates and increases in the deficit is factual.

CHAPTER 10 EXERCISES

II.

    4. Negotiable in principle, though perhaps not in practice.
    9. Negotiable in principle, though perhaps not in practice.

III.

    4. There is more than one dispute in this conversation, but the disputes are independent of one another. The first dispute is over the honesty of Carlotta's great grandfather. Let us classify this dispute as criteriological. Is Carlotta's great grandfather basically an honest man as Carlotta claims? Will our criterion for answering this question be a single moral error or a few moral errors or will it be a pattern of behavior? All individuals err on occasion, but when behavior of a certain sort is repeated by an individual one may say that it is indicative of that individual's character. Carlotta's great grandfather is an interesting case, since he cheated his customers for a considerable period (repeated behavior) but told them the truth in the end.

        It might also be pointed out that characters are developed over time and that the character of Carlotta's great grandfather might have been better in the end when he told his customers the truth than at the beginning when he deceived them. One might argue that there was moral progress in the case of Carlotta's great grandfather.

The second dispute centers on this question: Is alcoholism inherited? In the end this dispute will be factual, but as it is developed by Sam and Teri our attention is drawn to the ambiguity of the issue. Criteria will need to be established to determine whether a condition is inherited. It is not clear from the discussion what it would mean to say that alcoholism is inherited. It makes a difference whether one speaks of inheriting a disease, a tendency to engage in behavior which will lead to a disease or a chemical intolerance. Babies whose mothers take drugs are addicts when born. Is this an inherited disease? Does one inherit a tendency to drink or is one led to drink by one's environment (group relations, advertising)? Would PKU be an example of an inherited intolerance analogous in some way to the intolerance for alcohol which Sam and Teri mention? Through an attempt to answer some of these questions the disputants might determine the nature and extent of their disagreement.

9. Factual. The dispute might be resolved in this way:

Peutrell: All right, I'll humor you. Why do you say the carburetor won't work?

Carlotta: It just stands to reason. That tiny ball was in the box of your rebuilding kit and the people who put those kits together don't put in unnecessary parts. Oh, I know that if you buy a disassembled shelving unit you'll probably have an extra bolt or nut or two when you've put it together, but these carburetor kits aren't like that. They give you what you need and nothing extra. Besides, even with the shelving unit you're not given parts you don't need for nothing.

Peutrell: Hm.

Carlotta: If you don't believe me there's an easy way to find out whether I'm right, you know.

Peutrell: What's that?

Carlotta: Try to start your engine. If I'm right it won't run.

This proposed resolution requires no knowledge of carburetors, but those with specialized knowledge might have written this resolution:

Carlotta picks up the sheet of instructions which came with the accelerator pump rebuilding kit. The first few steps bear the greasy imprint of Peutrell's boot heel, but the rest are readable. Peutrell is fishing for his ignition key as Carlotta, a thin smile on her face, breaks the stubborn silence into which Peutrell has led them.

Carlotta: Hey, Peutrell, that little ball is the pump inlet ball check. Without it all the gas from the accelerating pump is just going to flow back into the fuel bowl every time you press the accelerator. You're not going to do any accelerating without that little ball.

Peutrell: Let me see those instructions!

Carlotta: You know, the logical thing would have been to read the instructions first.

CHAPTER 12 EXERCISES

I.

    4. O. Negative. Subject term: press releases. Predicate term: trustworthy documents (Distributed).

    9. E. Negative. Subject term: moot questions (Distributed). Predicate term: questions which require an answer (Distributed).

II.

    4. All individuals who can receive advanced degrees are graduate students.

    9. All those who jest at scars are those who never felt a wound.

III. Syllogisms in standard form.

    4. (Restaurants) Fallacies: Undistributed middle, existential fallacy.

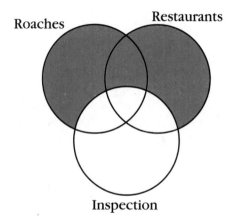

    9. (Art forms) Fallacy: Undistributed middle.

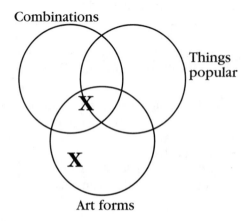

IV.

    4. (Gas mileage) Illicit distribution.

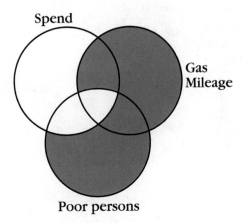

    9. All unhappy persons are persons to be pitied.
        All sacrificers of honor are **unhappy** persons.
        Therefore, all **sacrificers** of honor are persons to be **pitied.**
        Valid.

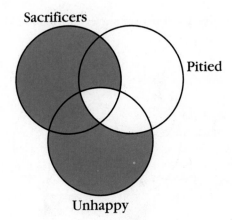

V.

4. No **hobos** are persons with elaborate **plans.** Some hobos are persons who can spin elaborate **yarns.** Therefore, some persons who can spin elaborate yarns are not persons with elaborate plans. Valid.

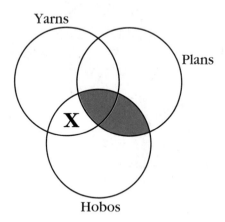

9. All individuals who believe that it is bad luck to have a woman on board ship are superstitious individuals.

Some retired sailors are individuals who believe that it is **bad luck** to have a woman on board ship.

Therefore, some **retired sailors** are **superstitious** individuals.
Valid.

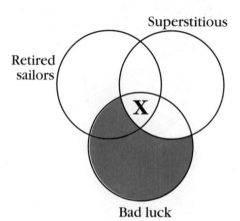

VI.

4. All things which should be avoided are harmful stimulants.
All coffees are harmful **stimulants.**
Therefore, all **coffees** are things which should be **avoided.**
Fallacy: Undistributed middle.

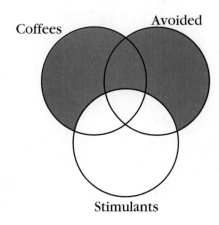

9. All rapists are inhuman individuals.
All those who pollute the environment are **rapists.**
Therefore, all those who **pollute** the environment are **inhuman** individuals.
Fallacy: Equivocation on "rapist." (On a Venn diagram, the argument appears to be valid.)

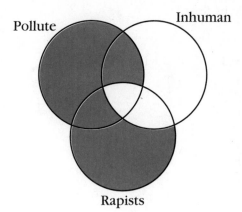

CHAPTER 13 EXERCISES

I.

    4. B ∨ Y   True

    9. A ⊃ ~Y   True

  14. (A ∨ B) • (~X • Y)   False

  19. [(A • B) ∨ X] ∨ Y   True

  24. (~A ≡ ~B) ∨ (X ⊃ Y)   True

II.

    4. A • (~X • Y)   False

    9. (A ⊃ X) ≡ (A ⊃ Y)   True

  14. (A ≡ B) ⊃ (X • Y)   False

  19. X • [(A • B) ∨ (X • Y)]   False

  24. ~(~X ⊃ Y)   True

CHAPTER 14 EXERCISES

I.

  4. F ⊃ G
     G ∨ ~G/∴ ~F

F	G	F ⊃ G	~G	G ∨ ~G	~F
T	T	T	F	T	F
T	F	F	T	T	F
F	T	T	F	T	T
F	F	T	T	T	T

            Invalid by Row 1

  9. F ⊃ (G • H)/∴ F ⊃ G

F	G	H	G • H	F ⊃ (G • H)	F ⊃ G
T	T	T	T	T	T
T	T	F	F	F	T
T	F	T	F	F	F
T	F	F	F	F	F
F	T	T	T	T	T
F	T	F	F	T	T
F	F	T	F	T	T
F	F	F	F	T	T

             Valid.

II.

    4. P ⊃ (Q ⊃ R)/∴ Q ⊃ (R ⊃ P)
       <u>P Q R</u>
       F T T

    9. D ⊃ (E ∨ F)
       (E ∨ F) ⊃ ~D /∴ D ∨ E
       <u>D E F</u>
       F F T
       F F F

III.

    4. ~R ⊃ ~(S • T)/∴ ~R ⊃ (~S ∨ ~T)
           DeM.

    9. (L ∨ M) • (N • M)/∴ (M ∨ L) • (N • M)
           Com.

IV.

    4. L ⊃ (M ∨ M)/∴L ⊃ M
           Taut.

    9. (D • E) ⊃ (F ∨ G)/∴ D ⊃ [E ⊃ (F∨G)]
           Exp.

V.

    4. [(J • K) ⊃ O] • [P ⊃ (Q ∨ ~R)]
       (J • K) ∨ P/∴ O ∨ (Q ∨ ~R)
           C.D.

    9. (M • N)
       ~S/∴ ~S • (M • N)
           Conj

VI.

    4.

       1. [(A ⊃ B) • (B ⊃ A)] ⊃ (C • D)/∴ ~(A ≡ B) ∨ C

       2. (A ≡ B) ⊃ (C • D)   1, Equiv.

       3. ~(A ≡ B) ∨ (C • D)   2, Impl.

       4. [~(A ≡ B) ∨ C] • [~(A ≡ B) ∨ D]   3, Dist.

       5. ~(A ≡ B) ∨ C   4, Simp.

9.

  1. ~F ∨ G

  2. ~F ⊃ H

  3. ~I ⊃ ~H/∴ ~I ⊃ G

  4. F ⊃ G   1, Impl.

  5. H ⊃ I   3, Trans.

  6. (F ⊃ G) • (H ⊃ I)   4, 5, Conj.

  7. F ∨ H   2, Impl.

  8. G ∨ I   6, 7, C. D.

  9. I ∨ G   8, Com.

  10. ~I ⊃ G   9, Impl.

VII.

  4.

    1. K∨L

    2. ~L • M/∴ K • M

    3. M • ~L   2, Com.

    4. M   3, Simp.

    5. L ∨ K   1, Com.

    6. ~L   2, Simp.

    7. K   5, 6, D. S.

    8. K • M   7, 4, Conj.

  9.

    1. ~(K • L) ⊃ ~M

    2. M

    3. K ∨ N/∴ (~N ∨ ~O) ⊃ K

    4. M ⊃ (K • L)   1, Trans.

    5. K • L   4, 2, M. P.

    6. K   5, Simp.

    7. K ∨ O   6, Add.

    8. (K ∨ N) • (K ∨ O)   3, 7, Conj.

9. K ∨ (N • O)   8, Dist.

10. ~K ⊃ (N • O)   9, Impl.

11. ~(N • O) ⊃ K   10, Trans.

12. (~N ∨ ~O) ⊃ K   11, De M.

VIII.

4. (Marcy is right.)

R ⊃ F   R F C

F ⊃ C   F T T

C/∴ R   F F T

9. (The party of the people.)

P ∨ (F ⊃ R)   P F R ~R ~P

~R/∴ ~P ⊃ F   F F F   T   T

IX.

4. (The killer was careless.)

1. K ∨ ~P

2. ~P ⊃ C

3. ~K

4. C ⊃ T/∴ T ∨ S

5. ~P   1, 3, D. S.

6. C   2, 5, M. P.

7. T   4, 6, M. P.

8. T ∨ S   7, Add.

9. (Production increases.)

1. (P • S) ⊃ D   P S D L E N

2. (D ⊃ L) • (E ⊃ L)   T F F F F F

3. ~E • P/∴ L ∨ N   Invalid.

X.

4. (Frank fumbles.)

1. (F • A) ⊃ K

2. (K • W) ⊃ P

3. W • ~P/∴ ~F ∨ ~A

4. ~P • W   3, Com.

5. ~P		4, Simp.
6. ~(K • W)		2, 5, M. T.
7. ~K ∨ ~W		6, De M.
8. W		3, Simp.
9. ~K		7, 8, D. S.
10. ~(F • A)		1, 9, M. T.
11. ~F ∨ ~A		10, De M.

9. (Sally is wise.)

1. (W • C) ⊃ (~B • T)		
2. C ⊃ ~T/∴ ~W ∨ ~C		
3. ~(W • C) ∨ (~B • T)		1, Impl.
4. [~(W • C) ∨ ~B] • [~(W • C) ∨ T]		3, Dist.
5. [~(W • C) ∨ T] • [~(W • C) ∨ ~B]		4, Com.
6. ~(W • C) ∨ T		5, Simp.
7. (W • C) ⊃ T		6, Impl.
8. T ⊃ ~C		2, Trans.
9. (W • C) ⊃ ~C		7, 8, H. S.
10. W ⊃ (C ⊃ ~C)		9, Exp.
11. W ⊃ (~C ∨ ~C)		10, Impl.
12. W ⊃ ~C		11, Taut.
13. ~W ∨ ~C		12, Impl.

XI.

4. (Allison is angry.)

1. (A • B) ≡ ~C		
2. A ⊃ B/∴~(C • A) ∨ B		
3. ~A ∨ B		2, Impl.
4. (~A ∨ B) ∨ ~C		2, Add.
5. ~C ∨ (~A ∨ B)		4, Com.
6. (~C ∨ ~A) ∨ B		5, Assoc.
7. ~(C • A) ∨ B		6, DeM.

9. (Either Wilfrid the Snatcher is not invited to the house party or Mrs. Peter Pigeoncote sends her regrets to the host.)

1. ~W ⊃ P

2. W ⊃ S

3. P ⊃ (S ⊃ I)/∴ W ⊃ I

4. W ⊃ P   1, Impl.

5. W ⊃ (S ⊃ I)   4, 3, H.S.

6. (W • S) ⊃ I   5, Exp.

7. (S • W) ⊃ I   6, Com.

8. S ⊃ (W ⊃ I)   7, Exp.

9. W ⊃ (W ⊃ I)   2, 8, H. S.

10. (W • W) ⊃ I   9, Exp.

11. W ⊃ I   10, Taut.

APPENDIX I EXERCISES

4. A.

9. B.

APPENDIX II EXERCISES

I.

	Genus	Difference
4. Canoe	1	7
9. Girl	13	17
14. Pig	5	3
19. Trumpet	4	2

II.

4. Furniture ANSWER: Too narrow. Tables and chests are not used for sitting or sleeping.

9. Airplane ANSWER: Too broad. Automobiles and motorcycles are also self-propelled vehicles.

III.

    4. Minerals ANSWER: Negative.

    9. Polytheist ANSWER: No problem.

    14. Frog ANSWER: Too broad. The definition is broad enough to include toads and salamanders.

IV.

    4. Wagon ANSWER: Too narrow: not all wagons are drawn by horses.

    9. Is there circularity here? If so, is it vicious?

    14. Too narrow.

APPENDIX III EXERCISES

4. Hasty generalization.

9. Equivocation.

14. Argument from ignorance.

19. False cause.

24. Slippery slope.

29. Argument from ignorance.

34. Argument from ignorance.

39. No fallacy.

44. Argument from ignorance.

49. The little boy uses the argument from pity.

Select Glossary

(Numbered references are to chapters)

Absorption (Abbr.: Abs.) The rule of inference, which states "p ⊃ q, therefore p ⊃ (p • q)." 14.

Accent A fallacy in which one attempts to secure agreement to a proposition by emphasizing certain points and not mentioning or not emphasizing others which are relevant. Quoting out of context is one version of the fallacy of accent. 4.

Accident (1) An inessential quality of an object; one whose elimination has no effect upon other qualities of the object. (2) A quality of an object which does not serve to define it. Appendix II.

Accident, fallacy of An informal error of reasoning in which a generalization is applied to a case with features which render the rule inapplicable. A paradigm example is this: "Exercise is good for the heart. Therefore, cardiac patients should be made to jog in the halls of the hospital." The generalization is found in the premiss of the argument. The case to which the rule is applied is found in the conclusion. Accident is the reverse of hasty generalization. 5.

Addition (Abbr.: Add.) The rule of inference which states "p, therefore p v q." 14.

Ad hominem A fallacy in which attention is directed to the individual who has made a statement rather than to the statement itself. 4, 11.

Adequacy, problem of The difficulty of determining what evidence is sufficient to establish the truth of a conclusion. In general, evidence is adequate if it is (1) true and (2) relevant, and if (3) no more is claimed in the conclusion than is warranted by the premisses. 2.

Affirmative proposition A categorical proposition which asserts either that all or a part of the subject class is included in the predicate class. A and I propositions are affirmative. 12.

Ambiguous (1) An equivocal term whose meaning cannot be determined from the context in which it is used. (2) A statement which has more than one possible meaning and whose intended meaning cannot be determined from its use. Compare with Vague term. 3.

Amphiboly A sentence whose grammatical structure renders it ambiguous. "I have lived here twice two and four years" is an example. It is impossible to state whether the meaning of the sentence is intended to be "I have lived here eight years" or "I have lived here twelve years," since it is impossible to know whether *twice* refers to "two and four" or only to "two." The **fallacy of amphiboly** consists in choosing the wrong interpretation of an amphibolous statement. 3.

Analogy A similarity between two or more things which are otherwise dissimilar. 6.

Antecedent That part of a conditional proposition which states a sufficient condition; often, but not necessarily, introduced by *if.* 7.

Argument (1) An ordered arrangement of propositions whose essential and infallible mark is an assertion that some proposition, or some propositions, known as *premisses,* imply another proposition, known as the *conclusion.* (2) A series of two or more propositions so arranged that one or more are claimed to provide evidence for another. (3) A series of propositions in which

335

one proposition is inferred from one or more other propositions. 1.

Argument, deductive An argument in which it is asserted that the premises provide conclusive evidence for the conclusion. 2

Argument, inductive An argument in which it is asserted that the premises provide evidence for the probable truth of the conclusion. 2

Argument, sound See Sound.

Argument, valid See Valid Argument.

Argument form The structure of an argument, as distinguished from its content. 2.

Association (Abbr.: Assoc.) The rule of replacement which states
"$[p \bullet (q \bullet r)] \equiv [(p \bullet q) \bullet r]$"
or "$[p \vee (p \vee r)] \equiv [(p \vee q) \vee r]$." 14.

Authority, argument from An informal fallacy in which an appeal is made to an authority outside his or her area of expertise. 4.

Background conditions The assumptions which may be made in any particular situation regarding the conduct to be expected from others. 8.

Categorical proposition One in which it is asserted that all or a portion of one class is included in, or excluded from, another. 12.

Cause The sufficient condition for the occurrence of an event; the conditions which must have preceded an event for it to have happened. 7.

Clear term A term whose meaning is understood. 3.

Coercion An attempt to influence an individual through the use of force, either physical or psychological. 4.

Collective The use of a general term to denote a group of objects taken together as a whole. *Committee* and *mob* are collective terms. Compare with Distributive. Also, see Composition, fallacy of. 3

Commutation (Abbr.: Com.) The rule of replacement, which states
"$(p \bullet q) \equiv (q \bullet p)$" or
"$(p \vee q) \equiv (q \vee p)$." 14.

Comparison A statement of the similarities and differences of two or more objects. A statement of the form "This is _____ than that" indicates a comparison. 8.

Complex question An informal fallacy in which a simple yes or no response is demanded to an issue or question which involves a variety of dissimilar factors or considerations or which must be answered piecemeal or in stages. 4.

Composition, fallacy of A *collective* term is one which indicates a number of things which, taken together, make a whole. Thus, *regiment, gang, church, jury,* and *government* are not the individuals which form these units but the individuals as they stand together. John Smith is not the regiment, but a member of it, and so forth. On the other hand, there are general terms which serve to indicate individuals taken one by one, or in a **distributive** sense. John Smith is a *soldier,* for example, and Spike is a *criminal.* A fallacy of composition occurs when a term is used distributively in a premiss but collectively in the conclusion which is supposed to follow from it. It is fallacious to argue that because Spike and Lefty are criminals, the church of which they are members is criminal. 3.

Conclusion (1) That proposition which is asserted to be proved by the premiss or premisses in an argument. (2) That proposition in an argument which is inferred from one or more other propositions known as *premisses.* 1.

Condition, necessary That in the absence of which a phenomenon will not occur or cannot exist. Fuel, for example, is a necessary condition for the running of an automobile engine. 7.

Condition, sufficient That in whose presence a phenomenon will occur, but whose absence does not in every case ensure that the phenomenon will not occur. My being invited to your house is a sufficient condition for my knocking on your door at 7 P.M., but my not being invited but wanting to borrow a cup of sugar from you might also be a sufficient condition for the same action. 7.

Conditional proposition A compound proposition in which it is asserted that one component proposition, known as the *con-*

sequent, will never be false when another component proposition, known as the *antecedent,* is true. 7.

Conjunction (Abbr.: Conj.)   The rule of inference which states "p, q, therefore p • q." 14.

Consequent   That part of a conditional proposition which states a necessary condition; often, but not necessarily, introduced by "only if." 7.

Constructive dilemma (Abbr.: C.D.) The rule of inference which states "(p ⊃ q) • (r ⊃ s), p ∨ r, therefore q ∨ s." 14.

Contradiction   A proposition whose truth is logically impossible. Any proposition which has the form p • ~p, or which can be reduced to that form.

Criterion   A means by which a judgment is reached. Some criteria are properties whose presence indicates or implies the presence of some other property or properties. Thus, the position of the fluid in a thermometer is a criterion for stating whether someone has a fever. 8.

Critical thinking   The activity in which an individual attempts to form or evaluate judgments with the aid of relevant and reliable considerations. Introduction.

Deduction   A form of inference in which it is claimed that the conclusion, which is the proposition inferred, is conclusively established by the premises. Compare with Induction. 2.

Definition   A statement of the meaning, or meanings, of a word. Appendix II.

DeMorgan's Theorems (Abbr.: DeM)   The rule of replacement which states "~(p • q) ≡ (~p ∨ ~q)" or "~(p ∨ q) ≡ (~p • ~q)." 14.

Disjunction   A compound proposition made up of two or more simpler propositions known as *disjuncts.* "Either p or q" and "either p or q or r" are forms of disjunctions. Such propositions are false if none of their disjuncts are true. 13.

Disjunctive syllogism (Abbr.: D.S.)   The rule of inference which states "p ∨ q, ~p, therefore q." 14.

Dispute   A relationship of opposition between two or more parties in which there is

(1) a difference of opinion, (2) an argument by one party to the effect that its opinion is true and the opinion of the other party false, and (3) a response by the other party, or by someone interested in the issue, to this argument. 9.

Distribution (Abbr.: Dist.)   The rule of replacement which states "[p • (q ∨ r)] ≡ [(p • q) ∨ (p • r)]" or "[p ∨ (q • r)] ≡ [(p ∨ q) • (p ∨ r)]." 14.

Distributive   The use of a general term to denote individuals taken singly, or one by one. In "That desk in the corner is cluttered," *desk* is used distributively. Compare with Collective. 3.

Division, fallacy of   This fallacy occurs when a term is used collectively in a premiss but distributively in the conclusion which is supposed to follow from it. Opposite of the fallacy of composition. 3.

Double negation (Abbr.: D.N.)   The rule of replacement which states "p ≡ ~~p." 14.

Equivalent   Said of two propositions which have the same truth value. Two propositions are equivalent to one another either when they are both false or when they are both true. Where "F" and "G" are any two propositions taken at random, they are said to be **materially** equivalent if they happen as a matter of fact to share the same truth value. However, if F and G share the same truth value, but must do so given their logical form, they are said to be **logically** equivalent to one another. 13.

Equivocation   A shift from one meaning of an equivocal term to another. The **fallacy of equivocation** occurs when a conclusion is secured by slipping from one meaning of a term to another in the course of an argument. 3.

Evidence, adequate   Evidence which is sufficient to establish the truth of a conclusion. In general, evidence is adequate if it is (1) true and (2) relevant, and if (3) no more is claimed in the conclusion than is warranted by the premises. 2.

Evidence, relevant   Evidence which, if true, increases the likelihood that a proposition being defended is true. 2.

Exclusive premises, fallacy of A formal error of the categorical syllogism which occurs when each premiss is negative. 12.

Existential condition for disputes The requirement, necessary for the existence of a dispute, that parties who differ from one another set themselves in opposition to one another. 9.

Existential fallacy A formal error of the categorical syllogism which occurs when the conclusion is either an I or an O proposition, but neither of the two premises is an I or O proposition. 12.

Explanation (1) A clarification of some obscure meaning or a description of how some puzzling occurrence fits in with or follows from some preceding events. (2) A verified hypothesis. 1.

Exportation (Abbr.: Exp.) The rule of replacement which states "[(p • q) ⊃ r] ≡ [p ⊃ (q ⊃ r)]." 14.

Fact A circumstance or state of affairs which is not in doubt or which has been verified in some way. 4, 9.

Fallacy (1) An error of reasoning. (2) A mistake, or defect, in an argument. (3a) Fallacies are classified as informal or formal. In informal fallacies, the error can be traced to the content of the argument or to an ambiguity either in a term (equivocation) or in the structure of a proposition (amphiboly) within the argument. When the problem is in the content of the argument, the premisses are irrelevant to the conclusion (ad hominem argument, for example). In formal fallacies, the error can be traced to the form of the argument, with the form making it possible for the premisses of the argument to be true and the conclusion false. (3b) Fallacies can also be classified as inductive or deductive. Some informal fallacies are inductive (hasty generalization), while others are deductive (accident). Formal fallacies are deductive. The undistributed middle is an example of a formal fallacy.

Force, argument from A fallacy in which the truth or falsehood of a statement is decided upon the basis of an appeal to force. 4, 11.

Four terms, fallacy of An error of the categorical syllogism in which there is a shift in meaning in the use of a term. 12.

General term A term which does not name an individual and which may be applied equally to any of an indefinite number of objects. 3.

Generalization A statement which applies to more than one case. 5.

Hasty generalization An inductive fallacy in which a conclusion is drawn from an insufficient sample or from a sample which is unrepresentative. In the hasty generalization, the generalization is found in the conclusion. 5.

Hypothetical syllogism (Abbr.: H.S.) The rule of inference which states "p ⊃ q, q ⊃ r, therefore p ⊃ r." 14.

Ignorance, argument from A fallacy in which it is claimed either that a proposition is false because it has not been proved to be true or true because it has not been proved to be false. 11.

Illicit distribution, fallacy of A formal error of the categorical syllogism in which a term, other than the middle term, is undistributed in a premiss and distributed in the conclusion. 12.

Induction A form of reasoning in which a conclusion is derived from observed instances of a selected kind and in which, it is claimed, the truth of the generalization is established with a relative degree of probability. 2.

Invalid A deductive argument in which it is logically possible for the conclusion to be false when the premises are true. 2.

Judgment (1) An act of mind, as when one makes an inference, compares two objects, ranks something on a scale, applies a principle to a particular case, or makes a generalization based upon specific instances. (2) The specific content of a proposition, statement, ruling, decision, or assertion. 8.

Justification A consideration, fact, or reason which is sufficient to establish the correctness of a judgment, decision, or action. 1.

Logic The science which consists in the description and evaluation of arguments. 1.

Major term In a categorical syllogism, the predicate term of the conclusion. 12.

Manipulation An attempt to influence an individual through the use of techniques of suggestion of which the individual is unaware. 4.

Material equivalence (Abbr.: Equiv.) The rule of replacement which states "$(p \equiv q) \equiv [(p \bullet q) \lor (\sim p \bullet \sim q)]$" or "$(p \equiv q) \equiv [(p \supset q) \bullet (q \supset p)]$." 14.

Material implication (Abbr.: Impl.) The rule of replacement which states "$(p \supset q) \equiv (\sim p \lor q)$." 14.

Middle term In a categorical syllogism, the term which occurs in each of the premisses. 12.

Minor term In a categorical syllogism, the subject term of the conclusion. 12.

Modus ponens (Abbr.: M.P.) The rule of inference which states "$p \supset q$, p, therefore q." 14.

Modus tollens (Abbr.: M.T.) The rule of inference which states "$p \supset q$, $\sim q$, therefore, $\sim p$." 14.

Negative fallacy A formal error of the categorical syllogism which occurs when the conclusion is either an A or an I proposition and one of the premisses is either an E or an O. 12.

Negative proposition A categorical proposition which denies either that all or a part of the subject class is included in the predicate class. E and O propositions are negative. 12.

People, argument to the A fallacy which takes two forms. In one form, one uses highly charged words or phrases in an attempt to secure agreement to a proposition or cause without citing relevant evidence which would serve to prove that the proposition is true or the cause worthy. In the other, one appeals to public or popular opinion in an attempt to secure assent. 4.

Piling fact upon fact Strengthening an argument by citing a number of relevant facts rather than only one or two. This approach recognizes that a number of facts taken together with one another can sometimes make a case which no one of them could have done by itself. 2.

Pity, argument from A fallacy in which it is argued that an individual's statement is true or cause justified because that individual (for some reason or other) deserves sympathy or pity. An irrelevant appeal to sympathy or pity. 4.

Poisoning the well The attempt to undermine the credibility of an individual so that the statements of that individual will not be believed; discrediting the testimony of a witness. 11.

Post hoc ergo propter hoc A particular form of the fallacy of false cause in which it is mistakenly assumed that one condition or cluster of conditions is the cause of another simply because it preceded the other. The Latin phrase may be translated as "after this, therefore because of this." 7.

Premiss A proposition whose truth is taken for granted, or assumed, in the course of an argument; a proposition which is claimed to provide evidence for the truth of another proposition, known as the *conclusion*. 1.

Principle A beginning, foundational, or fundamental affirmation or belief. A statement which is taken as the foundation for a judgment. 5.

Proposition A statement which, as opposed to nonsense utterances, questions, commands, requests, and exclamations, is either true or false. 1.

Relative term A term whose meaning must be determined from the context in which it is used. *Inexpensive* and *rich* are examples. Standards are sometimes necessary to determine the meaning of such terms. 8.

Sample A part which is assumed to be representative of a whole; a specimen. 5.

Simplification (Abbr.: Simp.) The rule of inference which states "$p \bullet q$, therefore, p." 14.

Slippery slope An argument to the effect that while a particular resolution or demand may appear to be innocent or unproblematic in itself, it will nevertheless, if adopted or granted, lead to further resolutions or demands which will be less innocent or unproblematic but which will have to be adopted or granted since the original resolution or demand was adopted or granted. Adoption of the original resolution is like taking a first step on a slippery slope. When that step is taken, your foot slips and you're forced to take another step in which your foot slips again. The process continues until you've reached the bottom of the summit from which you began. 11.

Sound A valid (deductive) argument in which each and every premiss is true. 2.

Standard This word is often used as a synonym for *criterion*, but a distinction between the two terms is drawn in the text in order to clarify rank orderings. Terms used in rankings are relative. Their meaning is tied to the objects to which they happen to refer on a particular occasion. *Small, medium,* and *large* are ranking terms. Suppose we are referring to Japanese men. A large Japanese man will be one whose weight and height fall within a certain range. That range of weight and height is the standard for application of the word *large* to Japanese men. For American men there would probably be a different standard for application of the same term. 8.

Straw man An issue-related diversionary tactic in which a disputant states another disputant's position in an easily refutable form. 11.

Syllogism An argument in which a conclusion is derived from two premisses. 12.

Tactics. The method or technique for securing a goal. 11.

Tautology (1) A proposition whose falsehood is logically impossible. (2) (Abbr.: Taut.) The rule of replacement which states "p ≡ (p ∨ p)" or "p ≡ (p • p)." 14.

Term (1) A word whose function is to refer to objects or classes of objects, as well as actions, circumstances, qualities, and thoughts. A term can be a single word or several words taken together. (2) In categorical logic, nouns or noun phrases which denote classes of things. 3, 12.

Thesis of an argumentative essay The proposition or point of view defended. The thesis is in the topic sentence of the paragraph in which it appears. Appendix I.

Transposition (Abbr.: Trans.) The rule of replacement which states "(p ⊃ q) ≡ (~q ⊃ ~p)." 14.

Truth value Statements or propositions are either true or false. The truth value of a true proposition is "true," and the truth value of a false proposition is "false." 1.

Undistributed middle, fallacy of A formal error of the categorical syllogism in which the middle term is distributed in neither of its occurrences. 12.

Vague term A term with a range of applications, some of which are problematic or indefinite. A classic example is the word *beard*. Clearly, fully bewhiskered men have beards, while clean-shaven men do not. In between fully bewhiskered and clean-shaven, however, it is not always clear whether beard correctly applies. If a man goes without shaving for a day or two, does he have a beard? No; he has stubble and is accurately described as "unshaven," but he has no beard. Suppose he goes for a week without shaving. In all likelihood, he still does not have a beard, though by this time some of his friends may have begun to ask him if he is growing a beard. Does the man have a beard after not having shaved for a month? For two months? We can't say without seeing him, but we know that if he continues not to shave, at some point we will say that he has a beard. Other examples of vague words are *costly, thick,* and *scientific*. As in the case of *beard,* these words are clearly applicable at one extreme and clearly inapplicable at the other, but, unless standards for their application are set, somewhere between the two extremes their application is problematic. 3, 9.

Valid argument An argument in which it is impossible for the conclusion to be false when the premisses are true. Only deductive arguments are valid. 2.

Venn diagrams A system of overlapping circles invented by British logician John Venn (1834–1923) for the purposes of representing categorical propositions in graphic form and determining the validity of categorical syllogisms. 12.

Index

Credits and Acknowledgments

The author records his thanks for the use of the selections reprinted in this book by permission of the following publishers and copyright holders:

Kluwer Academic Publishers for excerpt from *Theoretical Medicine,* Volume 4, 1983, p. 31, "Disease and Value: A Rejection of the Value-Neutrality Thesis," by George J. Agich. Reprinted with kind permission from Kluwer Academic Publishers.

Newsweek for excerpts from Kenneth L. Woodward and Mary Lord, "Making It in America." From *Newsweek,* January 5, 1976, p. 67. Copyright 1976, Newsweek, Inc. All rights reserved. Reprinted by permission.

The New Yorker Magazine, Inc. for "Notes and Comment," in "The Talk of the Town," *The New Yorker,* May 2, 1983, p. 29. Reprinted by permission; copyright 1983, The New Yorker Magazine, Inc. All rights reserved.

Sage Publications, Inc. for excerpt from Richard Wendell Fogg, *The Journal of Conflict Resolution* (Vol. 29, No. 2) pp. 330–358, copyright 1985 by Sage Publications. Reprinted by permission of Sage Publications, Inc.